R₀ .99

D1554880

Bible Student's Commentary

Exodus

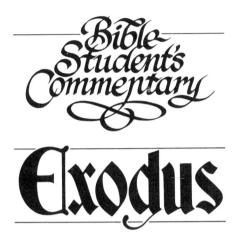

Exodus

Translated by Ed van der Maas

W.H. Gispen

Regency
Reference Library
Zondervan Publishing House
Grand Rapids, Michigan

THE BIBLE STUDENT'S COMMENTARY — EXODUS
Originally published in Dutch under the title:
Korte Verklaring der Heilige Schrift,
by J. H. Kok, B. V. Kampen, The Netherlands.

Regency Reference Library is an imprint of Zondervan
Publishing House, 1415 Lake Drive, S.E.,
Grand Rapids, Michigan 49506

Library of Congress Cataloging in Publication Data

Gispen, Willem Hendrik, 1900–
   Exodus.
   (Bible student's commentary)
   1. Bible. O.T. Exodus—Commentaries. I. Title. II. Series:
Korte verklaring der Heilige Schrift, met nieuwe vertaling. English.
BS1245.3.G5713   222'.12077   82-1866
                        AACR2
Zondervan: ISBN 0-310-43970-1

Designed and edited by Edward Viening

Printed in the United States of America

85 86 87 88 89 90 91 92 / 12 11 10 9 8 7 6 5 4 3 2

CONTENTS

Publisher's Foreword

Foreword

The leading evangelical commentary on the whole Bible among the Dutch-speaking people is a set of 62 volumes entitled *Korte Verklaring Der Heilige Schrift*. Unfortunately, the *Korte Verklaring* has not been widely known in the English-speaking world, although a number of the contributors and editors have made contributions to biblical and theological studies that have been acknowledged outside the Netherlands.

Publication of this highly regarded commentary began in the 1930s and 40s, with occasional additions and updating, and continued into the 60s. It was designed as a commentary for the lay reader who does not have a knowledge of Hebrew and Greek or a detailed knowledge of critical questions. It has admirably served this purpose and yet at the same time has been highly regarded and frequently used by scholars because of its exegetical insights.

The Bible Student's Commentary at last will make the *Korte Verklaring* available to the English-speaking world. It is adapted for English use by incorporating the text of the New International Version into the commentary discussion. Where appropriate, the original contributor's discussion has been edited to reflect the wording of the NIV and translation issues among the other English versions. *The Bible Student's Commentary* is a work of enduring value in terms of the exegetical material that it makes available to the serious student of Scripture.

The Publishers

Introduction

I. *Name*

The book that we know as Exodus is a continuation of the narrative that began in Genesis as we see from 1:1. It never existed separately, but always as the second book of the five books of Moses. It is part of the first division of the Hebrew canon called the Torah (teaching or law), which since the second century A.D. has also been called the Pentateuch or "the five books." Exodus thus brings us in contact with the entire Pentateuch problem. But since the general introduction to the Pentateuch has been included in the volume on Genesis in this series, only that which is necessary for a correct understanding of Exodus is discussed here.

The name "Exodus" used in the English versions is derived from the Septuagint (the Greek "translation of the seventy," abbreviated LXX), which calls our book "Exodos Aiguptou" or "Exodos," i.e. "(the) going out of Egypt" or "(the) going out." This name is used also by the Vulgate (the Latin version accepted by the Roman Catholic Church as authentic, which calls it "Exodus"), by Philo (Jewish author and contemporary of Christ) who calls it "Exodus" and also "Exagoge" or "(the) leading out," and the Peshitta (the standard Syriac version). In the Hebrew Masoretic text the book is named after its first words: "Names" or "And these are the names." (See commentary on 1:1.)

Strictly speaking the name "Exodus" fits only the first part of the book (1:1–15:21), which tells us of the Exodus from Egypt. In these chapters frequent mention is made of a "leading out" of Egypt, either by the Lord, or by Moses, or by Moses and Aaron (cf. 3:10–12; 6:6, 13, 26, 27; 7:4; 12:17, 42, 51; 13:3, 9, 14, 16). In 6:6; 7:4, 5; 12:17, 42, 51; 13:3, 9, 14, 16 it is the Lord who leads His people out. Also mentioned is the "bringing up" out of Egypt by the Lord (cf. e.g. 3:8, 17). Sometimes the word

1

"deliver" is used, again by the hand of the Lord (cf. 3:8; 6:6; 15:13). Repeatedly Pharaoh is commanded to "let the people go" (4:21, 23; 5:1, 2, 3, 24; 6:11; 7:2, 14; etc.). The Israelites "go out" or "journey out" of Egypt (cf. 11:8; 12:31, 37, 41; 13:3, 4, 8). The name "Exodus" is thus appropriate for 1:1–15:21 and virtually suggests itself in these chapters. Indeed, elsewhere in the Scriptures the Lord Himself calls the deliverance of Israel from Egypt a "being led out" by Him. Suffice it to mention Exodus 20:2.

The name "Exodus" does not, however, fit the second part of the book (15:22–40:38), which describes the making of the covenant between the Lord and Israel at Sinai. But the name goes back many centuries and the Exodus is in fact the indispensable prerequisite for the making of the covenant (29:46), and a fundamental fact in Israel's history.

II. *Authorship*

The question as to who must be considered the author of Exodus is of course related to the problem of the Pentateuch as a whole. Exodus itself is an important factor in this problem, since it contains sections that (at least in part) clearly indicate Mosaic authorship. I refer to 17:14; 24:4; 34:27. In 17:14 Moses appears to have recorded the battle with the Amalekites "on a scroll" (KJV: "in a book"). This, when compared with Numbers 33:2, indicates the existence of a travelogue written by Moses. Moses must also be considered the author of the "Book of the Covenant," which included at least 20:22–23:33 (cf. 24:4). In 34:27 Moses is instructed to write down what is found in 34:11–26. Thus, according to the information in Exodus itself, Moses was the author of the historical and legal sections. He also may have been a poet, although it is not stated that he wrote the song in 15:1–21. Perhaps 15:19 indicates that this song existed separately or that it was taken from an older collection of songs. Otherwise no one is mentioned as author of parts of the book or of the book as a whole.

Moses may be considered the author of the sections just mentioned. But 1:1–15:21 also shows that we must assume the hand of a later author or redactor (cf. 1:11; 11:3b; 12:37; and 16:35 in the second part of the book; and perhaps also 3:1; 4:27). But Moses, the great prophet, educated at the court of Pharaoh (ch. 2), deserves primary consideration for having also provided the material for the remainder of the book. A later author then has put this Mosaic material in the form in which we now know it, having inserted the genealogies, legal provisions, etc. in the existing historical narrative.

Data outside the Pentateuch point in the same direction, especially the Psalms. On the basis of the Psalms we may assume that the Pentateuch was already known in David's youth, largely in its present form. The unknown author, or rather redactor, thus must have lived in the period between Moses' death and David's youth.

The question of the sources used by Moses in Exodus can be dealt with briefly. If we assume that Moses was the primary author of the contents of the Pentateuch and thus also of Exodus (contrary to the opinion of some the art of writing was known centuries before Moses, cf. Hammurabi), then he must have been dependent on information from others only for the genealogies and for the contents of 1:1–2:10. He may have heard from his mother and from Miriam (cf. 2:1–10) about his youth, and may have been instructed by his parents in the material he records in chapter 1. The source hypothesis (theory) sees the authorship of Exodus in an entirely different light, but has been unable to maintain its position, especially in the light of archaeological discoveries. And the facts are also underestimated by those who (like Gunkel and Gressmann) feel that Exodus is a collection of "sagas" that have their parallels in world literature, so that Exodus is then the result of centuries of oral tradition that embellished and aggrandized the original events, including the plagues, the person of Moses, and the crossing of the sea. Should we attribute such importance to oral tradition as a formative factor in the Scriptures? Cf. commentary on 10:1–2; 12:24–27; 13:8–9, 14–16.

III. *Contents and Purpose of Exodus*

⋇ As we saw in the preceding section, Exodus consists of two parts: the description of Israel's miraculous departure from Egypt (1:1–15:21), and the making of the covenant (15:22–40:38).

The book as a whole gives us the revelation of the adoption of Israel as the Lord's people (6:7; 19:5–6). Of this adoption the Exodus is the "negative," and the making of the covenant the "positive" aspect. Together they form the establishment of the theocracy (rule of God) in Israel. The Exodus liberates Israel from Egypt through miracles, the making of the covenant binds Israel to the Lord through commandments.

The purpose of the book is to describe Israel's redemption and adoption by the Lord, and thus to show His faithfulness to the covenant He made with Abraham, Isaac, and Jacob (3:6, 15–16; 6:3–8; 32:13), and to describe the fulfillment of His promises, especially those concerning the seed of the woman (Gen. 3:15), while Pharaoh in his opposition typifies the seed of the serpent. It is striking that the 300 years between the death of Joseph and Israel's oppression are passed over in silence, while chapters 3–40 cover a much shorter period in great detail. This shows that the historiography of the Bible has its own theocentric character.

The fact that Moses plays a prominent role in the deliverance and covenant does not in any way contradict the God-glorifying purpose of the book, since Moses is only an instrument and ambassador of God. It actually makes the church aware of the relevance of this book as part of one Scripture, since it shows that its redemption and adoption as God's people always involves a Mediator (cf. 1 Cor. 10:1–11; Heb. 3:1–6; Rev. 15:3), Comments throughout this commentary deal with the importance of Moses. For his importance and place as lawgiver, see Introduction, VIII (pp. 24–28).

Thus Exodus has a theo-Christocentric character, i.e. both God and Christ stand at its center, even to the extent that we must turn to extrabiblical sources for many interesting details, such as the names of the Pharaohs. But this does not exhaust the meaning of the book. Exodus proclaims Christ as the Suffering One in the life of Moses, in his birth and persecution; his being taunted, not least of all by his own people. It encourages God's people in oppression and deprivation; it warns them against a sinful lack of trust in His guidance; it points to their calling to be a royal priesthood, a holy and purchased nation, and it points out what is theirs: God Himself has made His dwelling with His people in the pillar of cloud and fire, in the tabernacle of the Sinaitic covenant.

To us the book speaks especially of the deliverance from the slavery of sin. The blood of the Passover lamb speaks to the Christian of the Lamb slain for us (cf. ch. 12). In Pharaoh we see the progressive hardening of the heart and the power of the enemy, Satan, behind him, as well as a prediction of the ultimate destruction of Antichrist. Add to all of this the Ten Commandments, which as a ''law of gratitude'' is still of great importance to the church, and we cannot but see that Exodus, with its truly human characters and its literary beauty, must be considered a book of inestimable value and significance.

Finally a word about the historical character of the book. Some scholars deny the existence of Moses. Others consider Moses to have been a historical figure, while Aaron on the other hand is a product of priestly imagination. Attention is also drawn to the fact that Israel seems to show little Egyptian influence, which would be amazing after such a long stay in Egypt.

To begin with the latter: there are numerous traits in Exodus, especially in 1:1–15:21, which hint at an accurate knowledge of Egyptian conditions and customs and, it is thought, also of the Egyptian language. I have mentioned these instances throughout the commentary.[1]

---

[1]See A. S. Yahuda, *Language of the Pentateuch,* (1933). While we don't agree with him in every respect, his observations should be taken into consideration to the extent that they can be verified. But see also Gleason L. Archer, *A Survey of Old Testament Introduction,* p. 104n.

If Aaron is a product of priestly imagination, then the problem still remains as to why Aaron does not always show himself in a favorable light in Exodus, e.g. in the story of the golden calf. And without Moses the beginnings of Israel's history are incomprehensible. As Abram Sachar points out: "It has been suggested that even if this whole picturesque account were purely mythical, even if there were no Moses, it would be necessary to create one to account for the developments which transformed the early history of the Hebrews. . . . Upon his existence depends an understanding of the major problems of early Hebrew history."[2] He is the key figure in the Exodus and in the giving of the law, and is attested to by the entire Old Testament. Moses is the prophet whose calling is described in chapters 3–4, but who was not fully accepted as a servant of the Lord by the people of Israel to whom he was sent until after the drowning of the Egyptians in the Red Sea (14:31).

IV. *Contents of 1:1–15:21*

Analysis of 1:1–15:21 shows the following main divisions. After a backward glance at the arrival of Jacob and his sons and their households (1:1–5), the next section (1:6–22) describes what happened after the death of Joseph and his brothers. The Israelites, due to an exceptional increase in their numbers, cause Pharaoh and the Egyptians to become envious and fearful, and they try by various unsuccessful means to oppress the Israelites. Chapter 2 mentions the birth, rescue, and youth of Moses, the future deliverer of Israel, whose premature action necessitates his flight to Midian. After forty years the Lord appears to Moses in a burning bush (3:1–4:17). In spite of his objections Moses is sent to Egypt to deliver the Lord's people and on the way from Midian to Egypt he meets his brother Aaron; together they approach the elders of the oppressed Israelites (4:18–31). But Pharaoh categorically refuses to release Israel, even temporarily, and the only result of Moses' and Aaron's action is more severe oppression for Israel (5:1–18). Events frequently take a different turn than we would expect in this story: Moses' killing of the Egyptian is the beginning of forty years of oppression without relief for Israel (ch. 2). Moses' journey to Egypt is interrupted by an attempt on God's part to kill him (ch. 4). God leads the Israelites in such a way that Pharaoh pursues them and drives them into a corner in order that He may reveal His power all the more clearly (ch. 14). And the author heightens the suspense inherent in the historical events: when the situation becomes critical and the deliverance,

---

[2]Abram Leon Sachar, *A History of the Jews* (New York: Alfred A. Knopf 1958), pp. 17–18.

the final plague, is near, the narrative is interrupted by detailed legal provisions (chs. 12-13).

When the oppression increases because of Moses' and Aaron's action the Israelites blame them. But the Lord encourages Moses (5:19-6:8), and Moses in turn must encourage Israel by proclaiming that the Lord will adopt Israel as His people. The narrative is somewhat curiously interrupted by the genealogies of Reuben, Simeon, and Levi, and such interpolations involuntarily raise the question as to whether the author has made use of various sources. The answer must undoubtedly be in the affirmative, but this does not argue against single authorship. And it does not support the well-known source hypothesis of Wellhausen, which uses the term "sources" in an entirely different sense of independent literary products that originally existed side by side, and were compiled and interwoven into our Pentateuch by an unknown redactor. The original documents each represented a different viewpoint and can presumably be reconstructed on the basis of the names they used for God, as well as of other characteristics. Four main sources are distinguished in Wellhausen's theory: the Jahwist (J), which uses the name Jahweh or Lord; the Elohist (E), which uses Elohim or God; the Deuteronomist (D), and the Priestly Codex (P). This theory is discussed in more detail in the introduction to the volume on Genesis in this commentary series.[3]

The facts do not support this hypothesis. Nevertheless, an analysis of 1:1-15:21 shows that Exodus is based on sources in the sense of existing traditions, genealogies, etc. (cf. also Introduction, III, pp. 3).

After the genealogies the narrative continues with the first miracle performed before Pharaoh (6:28-7:13). This is ostensibly not followed by another miracle, but the ten plagues are actually ten miracles. Only this first one (Aaron's staff turned into a snake) does not have the nature of a plague. The ten plagues follow (7:14-11:10). For an analysis of this section see Introduction, VI, pp. 16-21.

I shall touch briefly here on one point that has been brought up in connection with the plagues, especially by Wellhausen's followers, viz. the relationship between Moses and Aaron. The Wellhausen school sees in the fact that Aaron is mentioned along with Moses in the carrying out of God's commands, or when they act on their own initiative, the influence of the Priestly Codex. This "source" is supposed to date from a time when the temple and priests were the dominant influence in Israel. And since the development of Israel's religion and history is viewed from an evolutionary

---

[3]See also Gleason L. Archer, *A Survey of Old Testament Introduction* (Chicago: Moody Press, 1964), pp. 73-95.

perspective, it is assumed to have developed from the primitive to the advanced, prophetism being its highest expression. The Priestly Codex is therefore placed in or after the Babylonian captivity.

I must admit since Aaron is sometimes mentioned along with Moses, and sometimes Moses alone is mentioned, this presents problems in 1:1–15:21. But it is crucial for the exegete to deal with the text of the sacred narrative in what we might call "good faith." In other words, when in the revelation of the burning bush (4:10–17) Aaron is given by the Lord to Moses as his prophet (7:1), then we must accept this as true. But when Moses is the one who speaks when they stand before Pharaoh (and this happens repeatedly, cf. 8:1; 9:1; 10:1; etc.), then we must assume either that it was Aaron who actually spoke, or that Moses himself had found the boldness to address Pharaoh, even when accompanied by Aaron. If these solutions are considered unsatisfactory then we must look for another solution. But the essential point is that in the text there is no trace of rivalry between Moses and Aaron, let alone of "rivalry" between various sources, the one favoring Moses, the other Aaron. And neither is there thus any question of a revision of the original story that is supposed to form the basis of Exodus.

After the tenth plague is announced (11:1–10) the Passover is instituted (12:1–28). Verse 1 gives the impression that this section originally existed independently. This is generally to be expected of those sections of the Pentateuch that contain legal provisions (cf. 24:4; 34:24; Deut. 17:18, which presuppose the separate existence of the so-called Book of the Covenant, containing at least Exod. 20:22–23:33; 34:11–26; and the so-called Royal Law, Deut. 17:14–20). It is therefore certainly possible that 12:1–28 also existed separately and was appropriately incorporated here by the author or the final redactor.

The tenth plague, the death of the firstborn, and Israel's departure from Egypt are described in 12:29–42. But the narrative is once again interrupted in 12:43–51 and 13:1–16, this time by regulations concerning the celebration of the Passover by strangers, and the consecration of the firstborn. Even if we accept the fact that the Lord revealed these things to Moses at the time and that Moses passed them on to Israel on that occasion, they need not have been part of the narrative originally. In my opinion the historical narrative is, as it were, the framework, the skeleton, of the Pentateuch. The legal and poetic sections may have been incorporated after first having existed separately.

The crossing of the Red Sea is described in 13:7–14:31, a feat that the Egyptians tried to imitate unsuccessfuly. And this first part of Exodus concludes with Israel at the Red Sea and the song of Moses (15:1–21).

V. *Contents of 15:22–40:38*

The first part of Exodus (1:1–15:21) describes the Lord's leading Israel out of Egypt. This section deals with the making of the covenant at Sinai and ends with the Lord's coming down to live visibly among His people, which was the purpose of the Exodus (cf. 29:46). It consists of legal sections embedded in an historical framework. In order to facilitate the overview I will deal with these separately.

A. *The Historical Framework*

The historical sections, which continue the narrative of the Pentateuch, are 15:22–20:21; 24:1–18; 31:18; 32:1–40:38. Of the latter, 34:10–26 contains regulations and is dealt with under B, while 35:1–39:43 is closely connected with 25:1–31:17. Before taking a closer look at the historical sections we must first state that the author who inserted the legal sections intended to write history. The text does not give us any indication that later contradictory schools or viewpoints are reflected in different parts of this book, or that a generous redactor allowed these sections to stand side by side and the various traditions concerning the giving of the Mosaic law to have their say. Vriezen, for example, writes that "ch. 34 is an independent tradition concerning the Sinai-revelation. . . . The Israelite canonical historiography did not hesitate to preserve an old divergent tradition side by side with the virtually catholic tradition given in Exod. 19–24 and Deuteronomy."[4] According to him these two traditions represent two theological schools in ancient Israel, one emphasizing the religious and moral, the other the cultic and religious aspects. The Sinai tradition in Exodus 32–34 then originated with the latter. Others could be quoted with different examples. But we are convinced that, even if the legal sections of Exodus once existed separately, their historical setting is correct.

The author immediately presents us with the grumbling of the Israelites and the blessing of the Lord (15:22–27); and so it continues: manna and quail (16:1–36), Massah and Meribah (17:1–7). No wonder that Israel's wilderness journey still provides us, the Israel of the New Testament, with a mirror to get to know ourselves (cf. 1 Cor. 10:1–11). But Moses and Aaron, and especially Moses, did not have an easy task dealing with such a nation. Already in 17:4 Moses complained to the Lord: "What am I to do with these people? They are almost ready to stone me." It is especially because of these grumblings that he becomes a type of the suffering Christ (cf. also Luke 24:27). Yet Israel had in Moses an incomparable gift from

---

[4]Vriezen, "Litterair-historische vragen aangaande de Dekaloog, I," *Nieuwe Theologische Studiën* (Jan. 1939), p. 16.

its God (see pp. 24–28), as shown by the way in which Amalek was defeated at Rephidim (17:8–16). It is all the more striking that in chapter 18 Jethro gave wise counsel and that this same Moses accepted his advice concerning the regulation of the administration of justice, a story that definitely speaks in favor of the reliability of Israel's tradition. Here, as throughout the Scriptures, even the greatest in the kingdom of God are shown to be men of like passions as we are. There is no trace of an attempt on the part of any of the authors of the Bible to postulate at any cost the originality of Israel's customs and institutions, which is all the more reason to accept those sections that introduce the Lord speaking as the Giver of the law.

In the third month after the Exodus Israel arrived at Sinai, the same mountain where the Lord appeared to Moses in the burning bush (19:1; 3:1–4:17). There Moses received from the Lord the words he was to speak to Israel, the words that also constituted the two parts of the covenant that was to be made (19:5–6). There the unforgettable appearance of the Lord took place, and the Ten Commandments were given (20:1–17). There Israel also realized its need for a mediator such as Moses (20:18–21). Around and on that mountain the making of the covenant took place with various ceremonies and above all an impressive theophany (24:1–18), and there the people accepted the Book of the Covenant. Concerning the Book of the Covenant (20:22–23:33), and the regulations pertaining to the tabernacle that follow (25:1–31:17), see commentary on these sections.

For forty days and forty nights Moses received instructions for the house of the Lord in the midst of Israel; he was shown its various parts, and finally received the two tablets with the Ten Commandments (31:18). But at the same time the people of Israel were already violating the covenant made so recently by making and worshiping the golden calf, a sin that was severely punished. The people were humbled and upon Moses' intercession the Lord finally renewed the covenant. As the sign of this new covenant the Lord gave Moses two new stone tablets inscribed by His finger. Moses asked for, and was granted, the privilege of seeing the Lord's back and hearing the Lord proclaim His name. When Moses came down from Mount Sinai after forty days and forty nights his face was radiant (32:1–34:35). Concerning the instructions he received (34:10–26), see pp. 314–16.

After this incident we move toward the realization of the Lord's stated purpose behind the Exodus (cf. 29:46): the establishment of His tabernacle, the visible sign of His presence among His people. Israel, thanks to the Lord's grace, now showed itself from its best side in the implementation of the regulations concerning the tabernacle: they worked hard and gave generously (35:1–39:43). After Moses erected the tabernacle on the Lord's orders (40:1–38) the glory of the Lord filled the tabernacle (40:34–35).

Thus ends the book. Israel could continue its journey to the Promised Land, but for the time being it remained at Sinai (cf. Num. 10:11ff.).

B. *The Legal Sections*

The legal sections are:
a) the Ten Commandments (20:1–17)
b) the Book of the Covenant (20:22–23:33)
c) instructions concerning the tabernacle (25:1–31:17)
d) 34:10–26 (the so-called cultic decalogue)

Strictly speaking 35:1–19 should be mentioned here as well, but it contains no instructions that are not given in 25:1–31:17.

Before looking at these sections individually we must first consider their relationship to each other. And the first important consideration is that we must allow ourselves to be guided by the historical character of the sections mentioned under A, i.e. we must consider them as factual. First, Israel heard the proclamation of the Ten Commandments (19:1–20:17). The Ten Commandments (or Decalogue) was the constitution for Israel's national existence, and contained the still valid principles by which peoples' lives are to be ordered. But the people were afraid and said to Moses: "Speak to us yourself and we will listen. But do not have God speak to us or we will die" (20:19). When Moses approached the billowing smoke the Lord gave the so-called Book of the Covenant, which probably consists of 20:22–23:33. The ceremony of the making of the covenant between the Lord and Israel at Sinai (24:1–18) is based on this book. Much has been written about the Book of the Covenant. It has been suggested that many of the provisions it contains were made when Israel was in Canaan, since they presumably presupposed that the people had settled in the Promised Land. But it is entirely possible that Israel received warnings and instructions regulating their relationship with the inhabitants of Canaan while they were still at Sinai or in the desert. It is striking that legal provisions and regulations concerning the ceremonial worship stand side by side. Thus instructions concerning worship (20:22–26), rights of Hebrew slaves (21:1–11), social concerns (21:12–36), and also instructions concerning their relationship to the Lord (23:13–33) follow one another. The latter deal with the Sabbath, the warning not to invoke the names of other gods, the requirement to appear three times per year before the Lord at the three great festivals, etc. On the basis of this "Book of the Covenant" the covenant between the Lord and Israel was made (24:7). But Eissfeldt,[5] Vriezen,[6] and

---

[5]Eissfeldt, *Einleitung in das Alte Testament,* Tübingen, 1934, pp. 241ff.
[6]Vriezen, *Nieuwe Theologische Studiën*

others are of the opinion that the "Book of the Covenant" refers to the decalogue (20:1-17) and thus maintain that there has been a change in the order of the text; the original sequence was 20:18-21; 20:1-17; 24:1-18. But in my opinion neither the text itself nor the critical data support this. According to the text as it stands the Lord proclaimed Israel's constitution (20:1-17). Then He gave a specific application of those general principles to Israel, which by its fear and its request that Moses be intermediary amply showed that it was not yet ready for its prophetic task: to hear what the Lord had to say directly, without an intermediary. This specific application is what we find in the "Book of the Covenant," which deals with Israelite situations and relationships (slavery, cattle, vineyards, etc.), both those that already existed in the wilderness and those that would develop in Canaan (cf. Deut. 4:14). And it was precisely to arm His people beforehand against the threat of "Canaanization" that the Lord impressed on them the regulations concerning their worship, His great festivals, and warned them against Canaanite customs. The headings of the various sections of the Book of the Covenant indicate that it further defined the relationship with both God and neighbor. The Book of the Covenant touched on every one of the Ten Commandments. It was an elaboration and application of the decalogue for Israel as a nation, whose King is the Lord. And these regulations and statements were recorded separately as the Book of the Covenant, and the covenant was made on the basis of this book, since it contained the application of the decalogue to the need of the moment.

This approach to the Book of the Covenant, suggested by the text itself, clarifies much, such as e.g. the agreement between the Book of the Covenant and Exodus 34:10-26. The latter has been interpreted as a so-called cultic decalogue, an independent counterpart to the decalogue of 20:1-17. This decalogue, which has a ceremonial character, then is attributed to a different "source" and is supposed to contain a different tradition than that found in Exodus 20. But as we shall see in the commentary on 34:10-26, the context must be the determining factor and leads to a different conclusion. Israel had sinned with the golden calf, but the Lord relented after Moses' intercession. But now that the Book of the Covenant had been violated, a new book of the covenant was needed, which mainly restated and inculcated the ceremonial regulations of 23:13-33. Why? Because with the golden calf Israel had sinned precisely in the area of worship. Israel was on its way to Canaan and would hopelessly succumb by adopting Canaanite worship. Thus it would be unable to fulfill its calling: to give the world the Messiah (Gen. 12:1ff.), unless the ceremonies that the Lord instituted were seen as the only true ones. Therefore they were being impressed again on Israel.

So there is an element of truth in calling 34:10–26 the "cultic decalogue." At that point in Israel's history the decalogue had to be interpreted for Israel primarily in terms of their worship. The Ten Commandments had to be presented in a cultic form, which was also the case in the instructions concerning the tabernacle (25:1–31:17). Negatively those ceremonial regulations constituted a boundary, a protection against the inhabitants of Canaan. Positively they served to point Israel to the coming Messiah. Thus also the second part of Exodus has a Christocentric character and speaks to us as Christians even in its legal sections.

a) *The Ten Commandments (20:1–17)*
    See above and commentary on 20:1–17
b) *The Book of the Covenant (20:22–23:33)*
    See above and commentary, especially on 21:1

When, as we shall see in the commentary, many parallels appear to exist between the Book of the Covenant and the laws of other ancient near-Eastern nations, especially the well-known Code of Hammurabi (cf. commentary on 20:1–17), we must not forget that besides these parallels there are many significant differences. The Book of the Covenant exhibits an entirely different spirit than the Code of Hammurabi. In the Book of the Covenant the God of Israel speaks; in the Code of Hammurabi the king, a human being, is glorified, beginning with the lengthy introduction that precedes the actual legal provisions. The fact that the style of the legal provisions shows parallels with other ancient laws can be explained by the fact that Moses was educated at the Egyptian court and was familiar with such laws. The Lord's revelation utilizes Moses' background.[7] The laws in the Book of the Covenant vary as to the way they are worded, a fact that receives much attention today. Yet the Lord revealed this Book of the Covenant to Moses on one single occasion. Concerning the forms of the various laws, see commentary on 22:18–20.

The Book of the Covenant thus raises several questions, but the content is the most important one. Can we find a theme, a thread that runs through this section that at one time existed independently? I already answered this question in part when I called the Book of the Covenant the elaboration of the decalogue for Israel as a nation, whose King is the Lord. On the basis of 24:3 I divide the Book of the Covenant at 21:1 into "words" and "laws." I then take 20:22–26 and 23:13–33 to contain the "words," while the "laws" make up the section in between (21:1–23:12). The regulations concerning Israel's worship and its relationship to the Lord thus

---

[7] Cf. my articles, "De Semietische achtergrond van het Oude Testament," *De Heraut*, no. 3111-3118 (1937).

constitute the framework of the Book of the Covenant. The "laws" further elucidate the sixth, eighth, seventh, sixth, fifth and ninth commandments, although I must emphasize that these are not absolutely separated (cf. especially 22:18–20 and 22:28–31, although 22:18–20 could very well be interpreted as instructions for those in authority). Thus all the commandments of the so-called second tablet of the Ten Commandments are dealt with, except for the tenth commandment, while the first tablet encompasses the whole and is mentioned indirectly. The decalogue then forms the basis for the Book of the Covenant. The first and second commandments are elucidated in 20:22–26, the first, second, third (cf. 23:20–21), and fourth (23:14–19) commandments in 23:13–33. Furthermore, the purpose of the warning against intermingling with the inhabitants of Canaan determines to a large extent the selection of the various sins used as warning examples and deterrents. It has been said that the decalogue is mentioned very infrequently in the Old Testament. But the Book of the Covenant proves the decisive significance attributed to the Ten Commandments.

c) *Instructions concerning the tabernacle (25:1–31:17)*

The instructions concerning the Tabernacle require a separate discussion. The implementation of these instructions is described in 35:1–39:43. The details and the typical meaning of the various parts are discussed in the commentary, but here I want to deal with more general matters.

The historicity of these chapters, which adherents of the source hypothesis ascribe to P, does not need a separate defense. Apart from the fact that in recent years more historical value has been attached to this section, little would be gained by presenting a counterargument for every argument brought against its historicity. Suffice it to mention only the most important one. It is assumed that 33:6–11 contains an older tradition concerning a simple tent of the congregation, attributed to E. P then would later have developed the ideal design found in these chapters, based on this tradition and influenced by the (already destroyed) temple of Solomon and Ezekiel's vision (Ezek. 40–48). See commentary on 33:6–11.

There can be no doubt that the text presents these instructions and their implementation as historical. And we must not underestimate the skill of the Israelites with the materials that they either brought from Egypt or bought from the caravans that traveled through the Sinai peninsula. Also, Bezalel and Aholiab and their helpers were skilled for their task by the Spirit of the Lord (cf. 31:1–11; 35:30–36:7).

But the most important question deals with what significance we must assign to the tabernacle on the basis of the Scriptures. Some have seen a representation of the universe in the tabernacle: the court depicting the earth, the tabernacle itself heaven. The table of the bread of the Presence then stands for the twelve months, the lampstand for the seven planets, etc. Whatever the merit of this view, it is found in Josephus, Philo, among many of the church fathers, and among many Jewish scholars. Another view (especially by Cocceius, etc.) is that the tabernacle represents the church, the court depicting the external visible church, the tent the true invisible church, while the Holy Place stands for the militant church, and the Most Holy Place for the church triumphant. Bähr, who lists various views in his *Symbolik des Mosaischen Cultus,* holds that the tabernacle represents the creation of heaven and earth. Keil believes that the tabernacle embodies the kingdom that God has established in Israel, primarily on the basis of the forms, measurements, and numbers involved. This kingdom will one day encompass the entire world. The shape of the Most Holy Place, a cube, points to the purpose of its completion (cf. Rev. 21–22).

There are of course excesses in the typological interpretation of the tabernacle and its furnishings. To give one example, Witsius, a moderate follower of Cocceius, interpreted the fact that the ark was made in part of wood and in part of gold as pointing to the two natures of Christ. But excess does not detract from the validity of seeking a symbolic meaning. The question is only: Which method is correct? How can we avoid being arbitrary?

We are dealing here with only a small portion of the ceremonial law, the law concerning the tabernacle, while consecrated persons (29:1–37), acts (e.g. 29:38–46), and times (31:12–17) are dealt with in passing and are discussed in more detail in Leviticus. Our primary rule in interpreting the ceremonial sections must be to let the Scriptures speak for themselves. We are on safe ground if the Bible suggests a symbolic interpretation or if we can derive such an interpretation from the Bible itself.[8] Applied to these sections of Exodus this means that we can arrive at a correct view of the symbolical meaning of the tabernacle only if we examine what the Bible says here and elsewhere.

The tabernacle was the house of the Lord, the sanctuary where God dwelled in the midst of His people (25:8–9). Moses built it according to a plan the Lord had shown him. In 38:21 it was called "the tabernacle, the tabernacle of the Testimony." This "Testimony" refers to the Ten Commandments (25:16, 21–22) that were placed in the ark that was the throne of the Lord among Israel (25:22). Exodus itself gives us the idea of the tabernacle as the dwelling place of God among Israel (supported else-

---

[8]Cf. my "De Ceremoniële Wet" (Lecture, Twenty-first Scholarly Congress of the Free University, Amsterdam, July 1, 1936) and "Zinnebeelden der Wet," *De Heraut,* March-April 1939.

where, e.g. Num. 16:9); in this tabernacle the Lord met with representatives from His people, hence the name "Tent of Meeting," which is given to both the tent mentioned in 33:7–11 and the tabernacle (cf. 27:21; 28:43; 29:4, 10–11, 30, 32, 42, 44; 30:20, 26, 36; 31:7; 35:21; Num. 4:3ff.; 11:16ff.).

The word "tabernacle" (from the Latin *tabernaculum*) means "tent" or "dwelling." We must make this "dwelling" our starting point (cf. commentary on 25:8–9; 26:1; cf. 29:45–46). Even though this tent consists in part of wood covered with curtains and even though the various numbers and dimensions as well as several of the colors[9] have undoubtedly a symbolical significance, "dwelling place" is its primary aspect (cf. Rev. 21:3). But this dwelling of the Lord among His people, represented by the descent in the cloud of His glory (40:34–35) was possible only because there were a priesthood and sacrifices (ch. 28—29). As King of the people with whom He made His covenant He had this portable sanctuary made in accordance with Israel's circumstances on their journey. And in this imperfect form (the Lord dwells in, yet is separated from, Israel in the Most Holy Place) this tabernacle points toward the end: God will dwell among men (Rev. 21:3) and have a more intimate fellowship with them than He had with Adam and Eve in paradise (Gen. 3:8). The priesthood and the sacrifices point to the manner in which Christ will achieve this goal. The Epistle to the Hebrews alone would be sufficient proof that this view is scriptural.

Although the tabernacle was the dwelling place of the Lord among Israel, can we determine if its shape represents something else? I believe that the Scriptures indicate that heaven is the dwelling place of God. In my opinion the tabernacle is the earthly representation of that heavenly reality (see commentary on 25:8–9). The Epistle to the Hebrews is especially decisive here (cf. Heb. 8:2). Hebrews 10:20 does not contradict, but rather amplifies this view: the function of the curtain that closed off the Most Holy Place refers to the body of Christ. The expression "lived among us" (John 1:14) does not require us to see the tabernacle as a representation of Christ.

We should not be surprised that the construction of the tabernacle takes up so much of Exodus. It has been of supreme importance for the history of God's kingdom on earth. Although the fortunes of this sanctuary after Israel's arrival in Canaan were discouraging, what it represents is still encouraging to us as it points to heaven, where Christ our High Priest lives forever to pray for us (Heb. 9:24–28; cf. Rev. 1:4–6).

d) *34:10–26 (the so-called cultic decalogue)*
See above and commentary on 34:10–26.

---

[9]Cf. "De Ceremoniële Wet"

VI. *The Plagues*

We must devote a separate section to the so-called plagues (7:14–11:10; 12:12, 29–30)⸱ These are: water changed to blood (7:14–25); frogs (8:1–15); gnats (8:16–19); flies (8:20–32); plague on livestock (9:1–7); boils (9:8–12); hail (9:13–35); locusts (10:1–20); darkness (10:21–29); death of the firstborn (11:1–10; 12:12, 29–30). They are preceded (7:8–13) by the story of Aaron's staff turning into a large snake before Pharaoh.

I used the term "so-called plagues." The Scriptures, and especially Exodus, use various words, viz.

wonders (3:20; 4:21; 7:3; 11:9, 10; Deut. 4:34; 6:22; 7:19; 26:8; 29:3; 34:11; Neh. 9:10; Pss. 78:43; 105:27; 106:22; Jer. 32:20–21; Acts 7:36)

signs (4:17, 28; 7:3; 8:23; 10:1–2; Num. 14:11, 22; Deut. 4:34; 6:22; 7:19; 26:8; 29:3; 34:11; Neh. 9:10; Pss. 78:43; 105:27; Jer. 32:20–21; Acts 7:36)

plagues (9:14)

diseases (15:26; cf. Deut. 7:15)

stroke (11:1; NIV: "plague")

blow (12:13; NIV: "destructive plague")

When we take a closer look at these terms, we see what the Scriptures consider their essence. The word used in 3:20 for "wonders" indicates something extraordinary, or wonderful. The same word is found in Psalm 106:22. In 4:21 the word for "wonder" indicates "something that draws attention" even as in the other references listed above (except 3:20 and Ps. 106:22). "Signs" point to something, in this case the power of the Lord. The word used in 9:14 actually means "blows," from the verb "to strike or smite," which occurs in 8:2. In 11:1 "stroke" is from the verb "to touch, strike," while the word used in 12:13 is related to the word for "blows" used in 9:14.

The names for the plagues thus point in the direction of exceptional, unusual phenomena, used by the Lord to get Pharaoh's attention, and invested by Him with a destructive character, as a cursory glance at the list of plagues shows. The wonders and signs are directed against the Pharaoh and Egypt; they are means employed by the Lord in His struggle with the stubborn king of Egypt. Even the story of the staff that devours the staffs of the Egyptian "magicians" (7:8–13) is threatening in nature.

Sometimes a distinction is made between wonders and plagues, and the assumption is then made that the story in Exodus is a combination of three "sources," each with its own version of the events. One of these "sources" presented a number of plagues that were nothing more than clever feats on the part of Moses and Aaron against the Egyptian magicians. Thus it is something like a contest between the Lord, the God of Israel, and the gods of the Egyptians who lose the contest ignominiously. But these plagues were harmless, merely "wonders." Another source then supposedly presented the real plagues, while the third source mentioned both "plagues" and "wonders." Our story in Exodus then would be the product of a redactor who here, as throughout the Pentateuch, wove these sources into one narrative.

Apart from the objection that can be raised against the source hypothesis in general, we can also point out that to the extent that we can speak of a "contest," it was initiated by Pharaoh and the Egyptian "wise men." This theory, furthermore, can be arrived at only on the basis of arbitrary text-critical operations.

If we take the text as it stands as our starting point, we can divide it as follows:

1. Plagues that can be imitated by the Egyptian magicians (first and second plagues)
2. Plagues that can be brought on only by Israel's God (third through tenth plagues) through
   a. His restrained power (third through sixth plagues)
   b. His unbridled power (seventh through tenth plagues)

There is thus a climax. And this progression is seen in other respects as well. Not only does 9:14 announce the last four plagues as a group of plagues of a very serious nature, but the reaction of the Egyptians shows increasing fear, and Pharaoh's attitude an increasingly stubborn hardening. The tension reaches its climax in chapter 11, where the open break between Pharaoh and Moses takes place.

In the first plague the wise men support Pharaoh in his opposition and refusal to let Israel go (7:22). The second plague is more serious than the first, since Pharaoh is not safe from the frogs in his own palace. He requests Moses' intercession, but continues to refuse when Moses' prayer is answered (8:15). This is probably the reason why Pharaoh is not warned before the third plague. This plague (gnats) is, like the preceding two, a nuisance, but not lethal, and cannot be imitated by the Egyptian magicians. Pharaoh is warned before the fourth plague and requests Moses' and Aaron's intercession, but again hardens his heart when the plague ends. While during the second plague he promises to let the people go, this time he is willing to allow Israel to bring sacrifices in Egypt itself if they pray for the plague to cease (8:25). Moses refuses to accept this and Pharaoh gives in to his objections (8:26–30). By the fourth plague (flies) mention is made for the first time of the Lord's making a separation between Egypt and

17

Goshen, where His people lived (8:22). The same is true in the case of the fifth plague (plague on livestock). Pharaoh again is warned in advance, and the result is that he hardens his heart. By the sixth plague (boils, 9:8–12) the magicians are for the first time mentioned as victims (9:11). The seventh plague (hail) is the first of the final group of a very serious nature. Before this plague strikes, the Lord advises man and beast to take shelter (9:19–20). Goshen is spared, and Pharaoh admits to limited guilt after the plague begins (9:27) and promises to release Israel (9:28). Moses does not refuse the request for intercession, but says that he knows that Pharaoh and his servants do not yet fear the Lord (9:30). This is quite a different tone than Moses' very courteous consent to the first request for intercession (cf. 8:8–11). But the relationship deteriorates further. When, after the announcement of the eighth plague (locusts, 10:1–20), Pharaoh, under pressure from his fearful officials, calls Moses and Aaron back, he appears to be willing to let the men go into the desert to worship the Lord, but not the women, children, and livestock (10:8–11). When the plague comes after Pharaoh "drives them out of his presence" he confesses his sin and requests intercession. Once again the plague ceases. When the ninth plague comes (darkness, 10:21–29) Pharaoh is prepared to let the women and children go as well, as long as the livestock remains behind as security. But Moses' patience is exhausted and he demands that, in addition to their own livestock, Pharaoh give the Israelites sacrifices and burnt offerings for the Lord (10:24–26). This is the breaking point, and Pharaoh threatens Moses with death if he comes before him again (10:28). Moses then announces the tenth plague, the death of the firstborn sons, and leaves Pharaoh "hot with anger" (11:1–10), after which the tenth plague indeed results in the release of Israel (ch. 12).

A progression is also seen in the fact that after the first five plagues Pharaoh "hardened his heart" (7:22; 8:15, 19, 32; 9:7), while after the plagues that follow "the LORD hardened Pharaoh's heart" (9:12; 10:20, 27; 11:10).

This brief summary shows that Gressmann's contention that the text has been virtually obliterated by the redactors is unfounded, to say nothing of the assertion that the narrative lacks any historical basis. If Amenhotep II is indeed the Pharaoh of the Exodus, then traces of the plagues are not entirely absent, although attempts will have been made to erase them since they were not exactly flattering for Egypt. No monuments of this king are found after the fifth year of his reign, which indicates a period of decline. He was not succeeded by his oldest son (see commentary on ch. 11 and Manetho's story related by Josephus, Introduction, VII, p. 23). Only the tenth plague is mentioned in 4:22–23, but this does not prove that only the tenth plague belongs to the oldest tradition.

Are the plagues magnified or intensified natural phenomena? And are they directed against the gods of Egypt? Knight especially has tried to show that this is the case, and some of the plagues are indeed directed against the gods of the Egyptians (cf. 12:12; Num. 33:4), viz. the first, second, fifth, and ninth (see commentary on these plagues). There are also plagues that represent a "normal" phenomenon on an exceptionally large scale, but it is still necessary to explain how the Lord commands and announces their arrival, how He increases them to such an enormous scale, and how He gives Moses such power, while sparing Israel. These are the second, fourth, fifth, seventh, eighth, and ninth plagues. But the first, third, and sixth plagues are wonders that do not fall into the second category, since water turning into blood, dust into gnats, and ashes into boils are not "natural" phenomena, like the arrival of frogs, flies, the plague on livestock, hail, locust, and darkness. As for the tenth plague, I am of the opinion that the Lord used pestilence (see ch. 11), in which case we have here a "natural" phenomenon, extraordinarily magnified and selective.

Indications concerning the time of the plagues are found in 9:31–32; 10:3–6; 13:4; 23:15. The following section deals with the year of the Exodus. The month is mentioned in 13:4 and 23:15: Abib, or late March-early April. The seventh plague (hail) appears to have taken place at the end of January or early February (cf. 9:31–32); the swarms of locusts also visit Egypt in the spring (10:3–6), while the "chamsin," the hot south wind (cf. 10:21–29), blows in Egypt in March and April. (See also commentary on the individual plagues.)

The duration of the plagues is mentioned in the case of the first and ninth plagues (7:25; 11:22–23), while the tenth, and perhaps also the fifth and sixth plagues took place instantaneously. Thus I take the total number of plagues to be ten; I do not consider 7:9–13 one of the plagues, but rather a warning wonder. The expression "ten plagues" is not found in the Scriptures. In Psalm 78:42–51 six plagues are mentioned, in Psalm 105:28–36 eight, both representing a selection from the ten plagues in Exodus. If the text is divided into three "sources" (Jahwist, Elohist, and Priestly Codex) the first one usually contains seven, the other two five plagues each. These plagues are then carried out by the Lord (Jahwist), or Moses (Elohist), or Moses and Aaron (Priestly Codex). It is true that the Lord announces the fourth, fifth, and tenth plagues; Moses the seventh, eighth, and ninth; and Moses and Aaron the first, second, third, and sixth. But this does not constitute an adequate basis for splitting up the text into "sources;" rather, it is a reflection of what actually happened. The author of the plagues is in all ten cases the Lord who accomplished His purpose either Himself or through Moses and Aaron and the staff. The Lord's adversary is the

Pharaoh of Egypt. By means of the plagues He wants to move Pharaoh to grant the request to let Israel go into the desert to worship the Lord (cf. 3:18–20). This surly adversary becomes through his stubbornness a victim of the Lord and drags his people with him into the punishment. On the other hand Israel, the Lord's people, is protected from and liberated through this punishment, and is, as is expressly stated in some cases, spared in the land of Goshen. We may assume that Israel did not suffer from any of the plagues.

The belief that the value of the story of the ten plagues is strictly moral (i.e. that it merely seeks to express the impotence of man's strongest efforts of will when he wants to oppose God, and the insufficiency of all efforts to thwart God's purpose) and not historical is incorrect. But this view is at least on a higher level than that which sees in this narrative only a means to add to the beauty of the story, or to increase the suspense.

Viewed in the context of the Bible as a whole Pharaoh and his officials represent the seed of the serpent. Behind his opposition is the raging of Satan against the woman and her seed, and his defeat and the ease with which the Lord gains the victory have a typical meaning, especially when we look at the purpose of the plagues. The Lord explicitly states this purpose in 3:20; 4:21–23; 6:1, 5, 6, 13; 7:1–5, 17; 8:1–2, 10, 20–22; 9:1–2, 13–18; 10:1–3; 11:1. The immediate purpose is the liberation of Israel. Apparently in conflict with this is the fact that the Lord Himself hardens the heart of Pharaoh and his officials; yet this is in keeping with the Lord's ultimate purpose: to glorify Himself. This (from Pharaoh's standpoint) sinful hardening of the heart justifies the sending of the plagues, which are for both Egypt and Israel the means that lead to an understanding that the Lord is both Lord and God. Egypt never came to this understanding, although there is an occasional glimmer (cf. 8:19; 10:7). Pharaoh's professions always turn out to be hypocritical. Therefore the plagues are punishment for Egypt: a prelude to the catastrophe at the Red Sea, and a prophecy of the plagues that will precede the final judgment of Satan, the world, and Antichrist (cf. Joel and Rev.). The Lord accomplished His purpose with the nucleus of Israel, while the carnal Israelites only participated in the external redemption from the house of slavery in Egypt. All of Israel is commanded (10:2) to tell its children and grandchildren about the plagues, so that the plagues became part of Israel's memory and find an echo in the Psalms and other books of the Bible (cf. Pss. 44:2–4; 74:13–15; 78:42–51; 105:28–36; 106:21–22; 2 Tim. 3:8 where traces of an oral tradition may be discerned; Josh. 2:10 and 9:9 which indicate that the report of the plagues had reached other nations; Josh. 24:5–7; Judg. 6:8–9; 1 Sam. 12:8; 1 Kings 8:51; Neh. 9:9–11;

Ps. 135:8–9; Jer. 2:6; 11:4; 32:21; Hos. 11:1; 12:13; Amos 2:10; 9:7; Mic. 6:4). Since the plagues serve to liberate Israel they also are proof that God keeps His covenant (cf. 2:24; 3:15–17; 6:4–8); they are a stage on the road toward the inheritance of the Promised Land. The plagues are weapons in the Lord's hand against Egypt, the means used to redeem Israel. They are mentioned in the Scriptures to comfort God's people with the strength of His hand, especially in days of oppression and persecution, and thus will gain in relevance toward the end times, even if there no longer is a literal Goshen. Egypt was used to refine Israel; the plagues struck Egypt because it oppressed Israel.

Finally, I believe that we can see a threefold scheme in the narrative only to the extent that in each case similar facts are described. Involuntarily the same expressions are then used. This points precisely to one author and thus we can explain the parallel descriptions of the first, second, fourth, fifth, sixth, and seventh, and of the third, eighth, and ninth plagues.

VII. *The Date of the Exodus*

The Book of Exodus does not mention the name of the Pharaoh during whose reign Israel left Egypt, nor of any of the other Pharaohs who played a role in the oppression and deliverance of Israel. The result has been much conjecture on the part of Old Testament scholars. Many of them consider the question of the date of the Exodus and of the entry into Canaan one of the most difficult problems of the Old Testament, and an abundance of literature has been devoted to this problem. This is not the place to deal with the question in detail, but I want to touch on the salient points. Two views are predominant; the one holds that the Exodus took place under the Pharaohs of the eighteenth dynasty (1580–1321 B.C.), while the other places the Exodus in the nineteenth dynasty (1321–1205 B.C.).

Exodus itself allows for the possibility of either viewpoint since it mentions more than one Pharaoh. First it speaks of "a new king, who did not know about Joseph" (1:8) who began the oppression of Israel. Moses was born during his reign (2:2). But this does not help us much, since neither the Pharaohs of the eighteenth nor those of the nineteenth dynasty knew Joseph. But proponents of the late date for the Exodus (nineteenth dynasty) claim that this new king must have been Rameses II, since the store cities he had built are called Pithom and Rameses in 1:1. The latter was built by the famous Rameses II (1300–1234 B.C.). It follows from 2:23 that this Pharaoh had a long reign, and we know that Rameses II reigned for more than 65 years. Thus, according to this view, he must have been the Pharaoh of the oppression, while the Exodus took place under his son Merneptah (1234–1225 B.C.).

On the other hand, an inscription has been found in which Merneptah boasts that he plundered Israel in Canaan. It seems impossible that during Merneptah's brief reign Israel left Egypt, entered Canaan, and was defeated, all by the same Pharaoh. The assumption has therefore been made that part of Israel was oppressed in Egypt, while another group never left Canaan and was defeated by Merneptah as stated in the inscription.

If we accept the nineteenth dynasty as the dynasty of the Exodus we find ourselves in conflict with Genesis 46:7ff. and Exodus 1:2ff., as well as with other scriptural data, which state that *all* Jacob's sons went with him to Egypt. Attractive as it may be to consider Rameses II, the proud builder, as the Pharaoh of the oppression, it leads to insoluble difficulties. It is true that Egyptian sources mention the Habiru as "haulers of brick" under Rameses II, but the question is whether the Hebrews have any connection with these Habiru. Besides, "Hebrews" is a term that includes not only the Israelites; Ammonites, Moabites, and others can also be considered Hebrews.

The name "Rameses" for one of the store cities seems to point unquestionably to Rameses II. But it is probable that this city, which already existed under the Hyksos (the foreigners who ruled Egypt several centuries before the nineteenth dynasty), was rebuilt by Rameses II and that 1:11 refers to the city by its later name (see also commentary on 1:11).

I have already noted that Exodus also allows for an early (eighteenth dynasty) date. The eighteenth dynasty also had a ruler who was involved in extensive building projects, who had a long reign, who was antagonistic toward foreigners, and who was even more cruel than Rameses II. This was Thutmose III (1501–1447 B.C.). The Exodus then could have taken place under his successor, Amenhotep II (1447–1421 B.C.). Much can be said in favor of this date. We have paintings, dating from the reign of Thutmose III, depicting Semites working as slave laborers on building projects (cf. commentary on 5:8). The princess who took pity on the baby found in the Nile and who named him Moses (Exod. 2) may have been the later queen Hatshepsut (1501–1479 B.C.). She was a woman who would have had the courage to defy an order of Pharaoh. We then can also better understand the plagues under Amenhotep II and the general situation under this Pharaoh of whom we have very little information. It is also striking that during the final years of the reign of Amenhotep III (1421–1376 B.C.) Egypt's hold over Syria and Palestine weakened, and that under Amenhotep IV (1380–1362 B.C.), the well-known worshiper of the sungod, the Habiru invaded Canaan. The vassals of Pharaoh complained time and again, and sent many letters requesting help, but Akhenaten (as Amenhotep IV was also called, because he worshiped the sun) ignored them. This provides a parallel with the invasion of Canaan by the Israelites, described in Joshua and Judges, which is too marked not to link them with the Habiru (although their invasion must perhaps be dated somewhat later).[10] This is possible also from a linguistic standpoint, since "Habiru" and "Hebrews" may be derived from the same root.

Furthermore, Josephus (*Against Apion* I, 227–277) relates a story of the Egyptian historian Manetho who wrote during the third century B.C., and whose work has been preserved only in citations by later authors. An Egyptian king, Amenhotep, defeated and expelled a large number of Egyptian lepers who rebelled against him and had made an alliance with Jerusalem. According to Josephus, Manetho describes the leader of these lepers as follows: "They say that the priest who gave them their polity and laws came from Heliopolis and was called Osarsif after the god of Heliopolis, Osiris, and that, when he joined these people he changed his name to Moses." This story may contain an inaccurate recollection of the event described in Exodus 4:6–7.

But all of this, important as it may be, is not the most essential. As evangelical Christians our first question must be: "What does the Bible itself say?" And then we find that the biblical data make the nineteenth-dynasty date untenable.

According to 1 Kings 6:1 the 480th year after the Exodus coincides with the fourth year of Solomon's reign. We know from Assyrian inscriptions that the fourth year of Solomon's reign was 969 B.C. Thus, according to 1 Kings 6:1 the Exodus took place in 1449 B.C. But since at that time Thutmose III was still Pharaoh in Egypt, and since he died before the Exodus (2:23), the date of the Exodus must be set at 1447 or ca. 1445 B.C. (See also commentary on 1:8; 12:40; etc.).

The fact that the total number of years in the Book of Judges comes to more than 480 does not argue against this date, since some of the judges served at the same time in different parts of the land (cf. also Judg. 11:26). I used to think that Joseph and Jacob and his sons came to Egypt during the period of the Hyksos Pharaohs who, since they themselves were invaders, were kindly disposed toward other Asiatic tribes, and I felt that the Bible agreed with this. But this view is untenable. The Hyksos ruled Egypt approximately 1652–1542 B.C., while Jacob arrived much earlier.

Abraham's calling must have taken place around 2090 B.C. Israel was in Egypt for 430 years (12:40), so that Jacob arrived there ca. 1875 B.C. (1445 + 430) when he was 130 years old (Gen. 47:9). He was thus born ca. 2005

---

[10] Yadin's excavations at Hazor seem to argue against a fourteenth-century date for the conquest of Canaan, however, since Hazor appears to have been destroyed around 1200 B.C.

B.C. Isaac was 60 years old when Jacob was born (Gen. 25:26); therefore Isaac was born around 2065 B.C. Abraham was 100 years old when Isaac was born (Gen. 21:5) and thus was born ca. 2165 B.C. And since Abraham was called when he was 75 years old (Gen. 12:4) this must have taken place ca. 2090 B.C. (See also the volume on Genesis in this series, the discussion on chap. 39.)

VIII. *Moses*

Moses was one of the greatest figures of the Old Testament (see p. 4). He was also of paramount significance for the history of revelation, and his historicity is generally acknowledged today. Yet the famous historian Eduard Meyer considered the question of Moses' historicity of no importance for historiography. And he criticized those who acknowledged Moses' importance for their failure to provide him with any content or to show what he had accomplished. Meyer considered it an "empty phrase" to say that Moses declared Jahweh to be Israel's God.[11] Hölscher considered the stories about the patriarchs and Moses' time pure sagas. And under the influence of Meyer, who believed Moses to be the legendary patriarch of the priests of the sanctuary of Kadesh, Hölscher classified the history of Moses among the savior legends. Moses then was a legendary hero, who was thought to have founded the Levite cult at Kadesh, the old center of the tribe of Levi; we cannot know anything about the factual basis of the Moses-legends beyond speculation. The historical core is beyond recovery.[12] Meyer considered Deuteronomy 33:8–11, Moses' blessing of Levi, to be an independent "source" containing an old Levite tradition concerning Moses.

We would be inclined to ignore such a view. Yet it teaches us something. Although Wellhausen's view has passed its zenith, the worldview in which it prospered is still with us. We are faced here with a viewpoint that cannot be justified even from a strictly scientific standpoint. And many scholars have presented valid arguments (especially against Meyer) such as Edelkoort, who disputes Meyer's elimination of Egypt from the history of Israel.[13] Meyer's and Hölscher's arguments raise numerous questions. Why did Israel give Moses an Egyptian name? Why are the priests of Kadesh otherwise unknown to us? Why did Israel invent a period of Egyptian oppression? Would this not be a tradition that would be likely to be suppressed at all costs? A denial of the historicity of Moses presents us with

---

[11]Eduard Meyer, *Die Israeliten und ihre Nachbarstämme* (1906), p. 451 n.1.

[12]Hölscher, *Geschichte der israelitischen und judäischen Religion* (1922), pp. 1, 43, 64–65, 68.

[13]Edelkoort, *Uittocht en Intocht*, p. 45ff.

serious problems, and requires a playing fast and loose with the Scriptures, since they do not in any way support this idea. And it is hardly fair when Gunkel blames the variety of viewpoints concerning Moses on the condition in which the traditions have come down to us. It is rather a case of arbitrarily accepting those parts of the Scriptures that support a given hypothesis while rejecting the rest as untrustworthy. Meyer himself is forced to make one exception to his criticism that no one has succeeded in making Moses a figure with historical content, viz. those who accept the tradition as historical truth. If we read ''Scriptures'' instead of ''tradition'' then Moses was a concrete figure from the Bible-believing perspective, according to Meyer.

There is also no basis for considering Moses to be a mythical figure. Volz correctly calls the historicity of Moses a postulate. And Kittell says: ''If tradition were silent about the figure of Moses we would have to presuppose its existence. Since tradition has preserved it we must accept it as historical.''[14]

I already mentioned the significance of the excavations and the work of Yahuda (p. 4). I still hold the date of the Exodus presented there to be the most probable one. But if the Pharaoh of the Exodus is Amenhotep II then the suggestion made by Kittel and others that Moses' religion was influenced by the sun worship of Akhenaten or Amenhotep IV (cf. pp. 22–23) is invalidated.

Most contemporary Old Testament scholars of various schools accept the historicity of Moses, and generally have respect for his character; they consider him one of the great men of the Old Testament whose religious personality, however much a mystery, has left its imprint on Israel's religion. But not all use the same method to come to definite conclusions concerning his acts and significance. There is an a priori scepticism that questions whether it will ever be possible to arrive at more than a hazy, indistinct picture of Moses. The most striking recent viewpoint is the so-called ''sagen-geschichtliche'' view of Gressmann (*Moses und seine Zeit,* 1931) and Gunkel. According to them the story of Moses' birth, which reflects a frequently found motif, must immediately be considered historically untrustworthy. And Gressmann treats all stories concerning Moses in the same way, retaining only the specifically Israelite ''core'' of the ''Moses sagas.'' He is thus left with a great leader, but not with a complete personality such as the Scriptures give us.

We could mention the views of others as well, such as König, Kittel, Sellin, Volz, Beer, Wilhelm Caspari. Let me mention only the latter.

---

[14]Kittel-Obbink, *Het Oude Testament in het licht der nieuwere onderzoekingen,* p. 164.

Caspari posed three questions: Did Moses exist? Who was Moses? What did Moses do and how did he do it? Caspari does not expect that the debate about these questions will ever be fully settled. He points to the mystery inherent in every personality, and deems it best to determine what things looked like before and after the appearance of a major figure on the historical scene. Thus we deal with *facts,* with the "program" of the individual, rather than with the mystery of the soul. When dealing with the events in the life of the hero contained in the tradition, agreement of these events with the "program" would indicate that we are dealing with a later addition that is an expression of this "program." Thus disagreement with the "program" is a hallmark of the historical reliability of certain distinct traits in the image of the hero. Yet both the "programmatic" and the *programmwidrig* (nonprogrammatic") must be taken into consideration. Thus Moses performing miracles and Moses the teacher are both programmatic and therefore less reliable expressions of how later generations saw him. But nonprogrammatic, and therefore very probably historical, is the fact that Moses died mysteriously, and was possibly even murdered.

None of this leads to a satisfactory picture of the person of Moses. And the main reason is that the value of the Pentateuch as an historical document is underestimated, and that the various "sources" represent interpretations of Moses rather than reliable factual statements. The journey through the wilderness especially takes a beating; many assume a direct route to Kadesh, and not everyone accepts the fact that *all* of Israel went to Egypt, but rather that part of Israel remained in Canaan, another part in Kadesh. None of these views are free of subjectivism. And when Gressmann at the end of his book exclaims that every historian who has touched the seam of Moses' robe must consider himself fortunate we witness unnecessary poverty. Those who accept the Bible as God's Word have more than that seam, also where the person of Moses is concerned. They know of his birth, his miraculous rescue, his youth, and his being raised at Pharaoh's court, where he came in contact with the form and content of ancient near-Eastern laws. They also are aware of his temper and the refining-process he experienced, his testing in Egypt and Midian, which brought him in contact with the Arabic world. When we see him as leader of Israel we encounter his impatience and his gentleness, his virtues and his shortcomings, his faithfulness and his faith (cf. Heb. 11:23–29), as well as his disappointment with his own people, his relationship with the Lord, his marriage, and his death on Mount Nebo. He saw the Promised land but was not able to enter it. For those who accept the Scriptures as the Word of God Moses is not a nebulous figure, but a man of flesh and bone, a mighty and purified man.

Some contemporary writers see Moses primarily as a national hero, others as a prophet, or as the founder of a religion, or a priest. But all of these are partial perspectives; all aspects of his person fall in their proper place when we read the Bible as God's Word.

Sometimes we get the impression that the early critics took Moses' image and smashed it to pieces, while the more recent critic is happy to retrieve as large a piece as possible. There is no trace of any synthesis, unless the end result is the traditional image of Moses of the Christian church. This is the most satisfactory and the most pure since it is taken directly from the Scriptures. We must of course attempt to come as close as possible to the Moses of the Bible. It is therefore possible to make changes or corrections in the traditional image. It is possible that Knight's assumption is correct, that during his first forty years Moses was a general in the Egyptian army that defeated the Nubians. Acts 7:22 favors this. Knight points out that Nubia was conquered in 1485 B.C. when Moses was about forty years old, and that Stephen's statement in Acts 7:22 must refer to events in Moses' life before his flight. And Josephus mentions the tradition that Moses married an Ethiopian princess, which Knight relates to the Cushite wife of Numbers 12:1. This would clarify Pharaoh's fear when he heard of the killing of the Egyptian, that the successful general would liberate his people. Knight's assumption is appealing although we do not have to agree with him. Gressmann's contribution is that he focused on Moses as a national hero. Sellin presents interesting discussions of Moses as a prophet. He believes to have discovered a Moses-tradition in the prophets, and especially in Hosea; Moses, the founder of a religious community in the wilderness who preached a moral faith in God, became a martyr and was murdered as a sacrifice for his prophetic office in Shittim, when his people reached a civilized country and broke with their religion. Sellin bases Moses' bloody end on a few texts in Hosea (5:1; 9:10; 12:1; 13:1) and maintains that Hosea knew this tradition of Moses the martyr. According to Sellin Numbers 25:3, 5 was originally (E) a continuation of verses 6–15 (since reworked by P) which described how Moses, who had a Midianite wife, was killed by the priests after his order against those who joined in worshiping the Baal of Peor. Besides this prophetic tradition, Sellin distinguished also the ancient Judaic (Jahwistic), Levitic (Deut. 33:8–11), and Ephraimite Moses traditions. He considered only one fact in Moses' life prior to his public appearance historic, viz. his flight to Midian. He listed certain points that were part of the content of Moses' beliefs concerning God.

Budde has pointed out that Sellin was not the first one to assume Moses' violent death. Goethe accused Joshua and Caleb of assassinating Moses. They got rid of Moses, whom they considered a cruel and incompetent ruler, because he had removed Miriam and Aaron.

Fortunately Sellin's hypothesis has not been widely accepted. Its foundation is considered to be too shaky, which is indeed true since it consists of arbitrary changes especially in the Hosea texts mentioned above. Caspari had to agree that Moses' meeting a violent death would be a "non-programmatic" element of the first order, but preferred to think of illness or obscurity.

But a concept such as Sellin's shows that one's view of Moses ultimately depends on one's view of the Scriptures, since (in Sellin's case) it involves several arbitrary conjectures concerning the text of Hosea, while allowing Deuteronomy 34 to stand as belonging to a different tradition, and considering Numbers 25 to have been revised. However, considering all this gives us more appreciation for Moses as the suffering prophet.

Frequently the error is made of underestimating the pre-Mosaic period. Köhler correctly pointed out that the Old Testament never speaks of Moses as the founder of the Jahweh religion.[15] De Groot writes: "According to the Bible not Moses but God Himself is the founder of this religion."[16] The emphasis is on Moses' religion, Moses' personality (Volz!), Moses' concept of God, rather than on the actual revelation of Moses' God Himself. Yet the trend today is toward a rehabilitation of Moses, including Moses the law giver (cf. commentary on 20:1–17, where reference is made to the Code of Hammurabi).

But when we take the Bible as a whole as our starting point, we come to see that the greatest honor accorded Moses is that he is a mediator. It is especially in his role as mediator that he stands out in the second part of Exodus (cf. 19; 20:21; 24; 25:22; 32:7ff.; cf. Gal. 3:19). As mediator between the Lord and Israel Moses is a type of Christ, the Mediator of the covenant of grace. Christ is the better Mediator, although Moses was willing to have himself blotted out of the book of life for the sake of his people (32:31–32[17]; cf. Heb. 3:5–6a). Jesus Christ is the Servant of the Lord par excellence. Moses' work organized Israel into a nation that had the privilege of foreshadowing the coming of that Christ in its laws and institutions, and of expecting that all that Moses as mediator was allowed to do in God's house would at one time be surpassed by the Son Himself, who took the servant's place once and for all.

---

[15]Theologie des Alten Testaments (Tübingen, 1936), p. 21.

[16]*Mozes, de middelaar zijns volks* (1936), p. 3; cf. Noordtzij, *God's Woord en der eeuwen getuigenis* (2nd ed.), p. 341.

[17]Cf. K. Schilder, *Christus in Zijn lijden*, Vol. III, pp. 211ff.

Exodus Commentary

Part One

The Lord Leads Israel Out of Egypt
(1:1–15:21)

1. *Names* (1:1–5)

1:1 *These are the names of the sons of Israel who entered Egypt with Jacob, each with his family.*

In Hebrew the first word of Exodus is "and." It actually says "and these," which the KJV translated as "these now," while most later versions simply say "these." The "and" indicates that Exodus is a continuation of the account of the history of mankind that began in Genesis, the history of Abraham and his descendants, and of the seed of the woman (Gen. 3:15). Many of the historical books of the Old Testament begin with "and": Exodus, Leviticus, Numbers, Joshua, Judges, Ruth, 1 and 2 Samuel, 1 and 2 Kings, Ezra, and Esther. Our book thus forms part of one majestic whole. The Jews derived the name of the book from the first words of the verse: "Names" (see Introduction, I, pp. 1).

The following verses indicate that the expression "the sons of Israel" must be understood in a literal sense here and not as meaning "Israelites" (children of Israel). The use of "Israel" in the first part of the verse and of "Jacob" in the second part may be for the sake of variety, but it also serves to make clear that "the sons of Israel" here means Jacob and his sons. The arrival in Egypt of these sons and their father is described in Genesis 46:1–7. Our verse is strongly reminiscent of Genesis 46:8. The theme of the narrative is now resumed, but first there is a brief summary and review.

1:2–5 *Reuben, Simeon, Levi and Judah; Issachar, Zebulun and Benjamin; Dan and Naphtali; Gad and Asher. The descendants of Jacob numbered seventy in all; Joseph was already in Egypt.*

Reuben, Simeon, Levi, Judah, Issachar, and Zebulun are mentioned first, as they were in Genesis 46:8–12. These were all sons of Jacob's wife Leah (cf. Gen. 29:32–35; 30:17–20). Jacob's daughter Dinah is not mentioned but is counted as one of the seventy persons. Jacob's sons are referred to as heads of their own families (v. 1). From these families the nation of Israel was formed. After Leah's sons comes Benjamin, the son of Jacob's second wife, Rachel (Gen. 35:16–18). In a listing of Jacob's sons Joseph should also be mentioned here, but he did not come with Jacob since he was already in Egypt (v. 5). Then follow the sons of Jacob's other wives: the sons of Rachel's maid Bilhah (Dan and Naphtali; Gen. 30:4–8), and the sons of Leah's maid, Zilpah (Gad and Asher; Gen. 30:9–13).

Genesis 46:8–17 mentions the sons of Jacob and Leah first, followed immediately by those of Zilpah (Gad and Asher). Joseph and Benjamin, Rachel's sons, come next, and finally the sons of Bilhah (Dan and Naphtali). Our verses thus come somewhat closer to listing Jacob's sons according to age than does Genesis 46, since Dan and Naphtali were born before Gad and Asher. According to verse 5, 70 persons came with Jacob to Egypt. The Septuagint gives the total as 75. Genesis 46 mentions 66 people (not counting the wives of Jacob's sons), but if we include Jacob himself and Joseph and his two sons who were already in Egypt, the total comes to 70, which agrees with the number in our text. The total can be broken down as follows: Jacob, Reuben and his sons, Simeon and his sons, Levi and his sons, Judah and his three sons and two grandsons, Issachar and his sons, Zebulun and his sons, and Dinah, who is not mentioned (33 persons; cf. Gen. 46:8–15); Gad and his sons, Asher and his four sons, one daughter and two grandsons (16 persons); Joseph and Benjamin and their sons (14 persons); and finally Dan and Naphtali and their sons (7 persons; cf. Gen. 46:16–25). It appears that Exodus 1:1–5 is based on Genesis 46:8–27 or that both are based on an older document.

The question remains: Where did the LXX get the figure 75? The solution lies in its translation of Genesis 46:8–27. The LXX has an addition after verse 20 that states that Manasseh had a son Machir, who in turn had a son Gilead, and that Ephraim's sons were Sutalaam (who had a son Edem) and Taam. Thus the total of Rachel's offspring increases in the LXX to 19 as compared to 14 in the Hebrew text. Stephen in Acts 7:14 follows the LXX.

2. *Exceptional Growth and Unavailing Oppression of Israel in Egypt* (1:6–22)

Verses 6–22 describe what happened to the Israelites after Joseph and his brothers and their entire generation had died. Israel grew phenomenally in accordance with God's promise to Abraham, Isaac, and Jacob (Gen. 12:2; 13:16; 15:5; 17:6; 18:18; 22:17; 26:4; 28:14; 35:11; 48:4). But Israel's growth created envy and fear on the part of the Egyptians, who, on orders of their king, began to oppress Israel ruthlessly by means of forced labor. When this did not have the desired effect, Pharaoh instructed the two midwives of the Hebrew women to kill all newborn males. When they ignored this order because they feared God, the command was given to throw all newborn Hebrew males into the Nile.

This is an important episode in the struggle between the seed of the woman and the seed of the serpent (Gen. 3:15). Note that we must see not only the miraculous growth of Israel (cf. Acts 7:7) as a fulfillment of God's promise to Abraham, but also the oppression (cf. Gen. 15:13). What the Lord told Abraham came to pass: both the promise and the announcement of adversity. It has already become clear in this chapter that the battle was between God and the king of Egypt (cf. v. 20 and v. 22). But what impresses us in the light of Genesis 15:13 is that in the oppression Pharaoh and his people carried out God's will without being aware of it. God's principle is: through suffering to glory. The oppression was to be to the glory of the Lord, so Egypt was a house of slavery from which His people, Israel, were led out with wonders. We can call this a messianic principle (cf. also Acts 4:27–28). Ultimately this was an attack of Satan on the Messiah who was to come out of Israel.

1:6 *Now Joseph and all his brothers and all that generation died.*

Joseph's death (the Hebrew uses the singular: "then Joseph died") was the last event mentioned in Genesis (Gen. 50:24–26). According to this verse Joseph's brothers also died in Egypt (which incidentally proves that the Scriptures know nothing of a separation of the tribes, some of whom never went to Egypt), as well as the entire generation that had known Joseph and his brothers.

1:7 *But the Israelites were fruitful and multiplied greatly and became exceedingly numerous, so that the land was filled with them.*

Verse 7 speaks of a miraculous growth. The Israelites were fruitful and the land filled with a strong, young nation, powerful through sheer numbers.

The Jews are still a fertile people, as they were in Egypt, a land which, according to tradition, was favorable to human fertility. They "multiplied greatly" (the same word is used in e.g. Gen. 1:20–21; 9:7). It was thus not normal growth, but bordered on the miraculous, so that it was expressed by several terms: "they became exceedingly numerous." The different terms may also indicate that this process took some time. The result was that the land (Goshen, cf. Gen. 47:4, 11) and the surrounding area (since Exod. 3:22 and 12:23 indicate that they also lived among the Egyptians) "was filled with them." The phenomenon already evident during Joseph's lifetime continued vigorously (Gen. 47:27). Land and promise worked together, the supernatural factor (the promise) used the natural (the land, Egypt).

1:8 *Then a new king, who did not know about Joseph, came to power in Egypt.*

The new king who came to power in Egypt did not remember the great services Joseph had rendered to Egypt. His relationship with Israel was not based on gratitude and Joseph was no longer of any significance to him. He belonged in all probability to a different dynasty than did the Pharaoh who had honored Joseph and extended hospitality to Joseph's family (note the word "new"). Who was this new king?

In the Introduction (p. 22) I argued that the Exodus took place around 1445 B.C. under Amenhotep II (1447–1421 B.C.). The new king, who had not known Joseph and who initiated the oppression, was then Thutmose I (1539–1514 B.C.). His grandfather Amosis (1580–1559 B.C.) was the founder of the eighteenth dynasty and the man who successfully fought for freedom against the Hyksos. These Hyksos were Asiatics who had invaded Egypt and who, although they later adopted the Egyptian culture, were friendly toward fellow Asiatics and thus probably continued the policy of their Egyptian predecessors of Joseph's time. The oppression of Israel thus coincided with a resurgence of a nationalistic spirit in Egypt after the expulsion of the Hyksos dynasty. The Hebrews were allowed to remain in Egypt even after the Hyksos leaders were gone, as were probably many of the noncombatants, those who did not belong to the Hyksos army. After the expulsion of the Hyksos, those who remained were used for the building of temples, etc., an enterprise that now flourished.

Thutmose I invaded Palestine and Syria and even reached the Euphrates. The description of the treatment of the Israelites in the following chapters is in harmony with his cruelty. In a war with Nubia he personally killed the king of Nubia with his javelin and on the journey back hung his body upside down from the bow of his ship. During his invasion of Canaan he was a cruel conqueror. He erected many buildings in Egypt, which also agrees with the description of Israel's oppression by means of forced labor.

1:9, 10 *"Look," he said to his people, "the Israelites have become much too numerous for us. Come, we must deal shrewdly with them or they will become even more numerous and, if war breaks out, will join our enemies, fight against us and leave the country."*

The new king directed the attention of his people ("look"), first of all the members of his court and officials, to the fact that the Israelites surpassed the Egyptians in numbers and power. This was probably an exaggeration, but in any case he deemed it necessary to take steps against Israel to check its growth. He expressed the fear that in case of an invasion (Asiatics frequently invaded the Nile delta) Israel, which lived on the border, would turn against Egypt and attack it, and leave the country. This last statement seems strange: on the one hand the king was displeased with Israel's growth; on the other hand he did not want to lose their slave labor in his building projects, as shown by the fact that subsequently Egypt did not want to let Israel go. Hence the statement: "we must deal shrewdly with them."

The oppression was thus motivated by envy and jealously. That in which the godly rejoice (cf. Ps. 105:24) provokes the envy of unbelievers. Although Pharoah was somewhat fearful, he still thought enough of his own power to believe that with wisdom (or shrewdness; the word here is less negative than in Ps. 105:25 where the Israelite poet calls "subtle" what Pharaoh called "wisdom") he could keep Israel under his thumb and exploit her.

Thus we have here the first historical example of an anti-Jewish mentality comparable with modern antisemitism. But in our verses the underlying causes was the envy of the seed of the serpent toward the seed of the woman.

1:11 *So they put slave masters over them to oppress them with forced labor, and they built Pithom and Rameses as store cities for Pharaoh.*[1]

The means chosen to keep Israel small and subservient was forced labor. Israel had to build the store cities of Pithom and Rameses under the direction of "slave masters" (lit.: "captains or overseers of forced labor").

---

[1]The LXX adds here "and On, which is Heliopolis" (city of the sun). There is no reason to add this to the text, since the LXX probably added "Heroopolis" after Pithom. A scribe probably read this as "Heliopolis," while the other name, On, was then inserted later.

This was indeed a wise measure from the Egyptian standpoint since it served a dual purpose. The Egyptians hoped to stem the miraculous increase of Israel, since hard labor always resulted in the death of many laborers. And at the same time two cities were built close to Goshen to protect the Eastern border of the Nile delta. At the time of Thutmose I a writing was known, called "The instruction of King Merikare," in which King Khety III (ca. 2000 B.C.) instructed his son Merikare. One of the instructions was: "Build cities in the delta; a man's name is not lessened by what he has done and an inhabited city is not harmed."

As stated in the Introduction (p. 22), many are of the opinion that the name Rameses clearly indicates that the Pharaoh who issued the order was Rameses II. But this is not necessarily the case. In the first place it was a peculiarity of Rameses that he named older cities after himself—a cheap way of insuring that his name "would not be lessened." It is therefore not at all impossible that we have here a situation similar to that in Genesis 47:11 where the land of Goshen was also called the land of Rameses, perhaps due to a later redaction of the biblical narrative (cf. Introduction, II, p. 2).

It is also worth noting that in the foundations of Rameses (Tell el-Retabeh, see below) a child's skeleton has been found, which would point to the Semitic custom of bringing sacrifices at the time foundations were laid, and this supports the assumption that Rameses was founded during the Hyksos period. Pithom ("house or temple of Atum," the creator) is believed to have been discovered at Tell el-Maskhutah or Heroopolis, where Naville uncovered large grain warehouses, although others disagree with this identification and believe Tell el-Maskhutah to be Succoth, which then must be distinguished from Pithom. (See also commentary on 12:37.)

Rameses is thought to have been found at Tell el-Retabeh, although others lean toward Zoan or Tanis, and it is not impossible that more than one city was named after Rameses. Both cities lie outside the land of Goshen, to the East, assuming that Goshen was northeast of modern Cairo, west of the Wadi Tumilat, and bounded by Tell el-Kebur, Belbes, and Saft el-Henna. Some also consider the store cities to be located in Goshen in a wider sense.

1:12 *But the more they were oppressed, the more they multiplied and spread; so the Egyptians came to dread the Israelites.*

The oppression resulted in increased growth, which made an uncanny impression on the Egyptians who did not yet know which God they were dealing with. The author captures this well; the verb translated "dread"

(NIV) means "to feel a loathing, abhorrence, sickening dread." The same word is used in e.g. Numbers 21:5; 22:3.

1:13, 14 *And worked them ruthlessly. They made their lives bitter with hard labor in brick and mortar and with all kinds of work in the fields; in all their hard labor the Egyptians used them ruthlessly.*

The reaction of the Egyptians shows that sin, as it were, generates its own momentum: the feeling of dread did not cause them to leave this strange people alone. Rather, they now became ruthless in their oppression and made the Israelites' lives bitter by increasing the demands placed on them, both in building and in the fields. And along with all of this they mistreated and badgered them, of course on the assumption that an embittered life saps and undermines a man's strength. At the end of verse 14 we read that the hard labor the Egyptians forced on the Israelites was accompanied by cruelty: "they used them ruthlessly."

"Hard labor in brick and mortar" involved both the making of bricks from Nile clay, that were dried in the sun, and the actual building with these bricks. "All kinds of work in the fields" consisted especially of heavy labor in the irrigation system. The Israelites had to bring up the water from the Nile to the fields above by means of an irrigation device, a paddle wheel that was driven by foot, and was hard to operate (cf. Deut. 11:10–12).

1:15–21 *The king of Egypt said to the Hebrew midwives, whose names were Shiphrah and Puah, "When you help the Hebrew women in childbirth and observe them on the delivery stool, if it is a boy, kill him; but if it is a girl, let her live." The midwives, however, feared God and did not do what the king of Egypt had told them to do; they let the boys live. Then the king of Egypt summoned the midwives and asked, "Why have you done this? Why have you let the boys live?"*

The midwives answered Pharaoh, "Hebrew women are not like Egyptian women; they are vigorous and give birth before the midwives arrive."

So God was kind to the midwives and the people increased and became even more numerous. And because the midwives feared God, he gave them families of their own.

The king of Egypt, in my opinion Thutmose I, had yet another, more radical plan. Notice that he was the instigator. The conflict rapidly became a duel between God and the Pharaoh. It has been said that the plan to kill the newborn males of the Israelites was in conflict with the desire to use them as laborers, and that these verses therefore belong to a different "source" than the preceding verses. But we must not forget that the primary purpose of the building plan was to prevent the multiplication of Israel (see v. 10) and that now, because of their miraculous growth in spite of oppression, it struck the Egyptians as something repulsive and loathsome that had to be trampled to death.

The king summoned the two Egyptian midwives of the Hebrews (perhaps the two most important ones; there may have been more than two). It does not make sense to assume that Hebrew midwives are meant, since the king's plan would then have been doomed to failure from the start. The speech in verse 16 also indicates that the king was not dealing with women who themselves were Hebrews. The names Shiphrah and Puah are of uncertain origin. "The authenticity of these names has often been denied by modern scholars, but both names have turned up as names of women among the Northwestern Semites of the second millennium B.C., one attested in the eighteenth century, the other in the fourteenth."[2]

"Hebrews" is a name that included more than only the Israelites. The Israelites were frequently called Hebrews by foreigners, and when dealing with foreigners they called themselves Hebrews. The king instructed the midwives to kill the newborn males; the girls could be spared, perhaps to serve later as harem girls.

The expression "when you . . . observe them on the delivery stool" presents somewhat of a problem. The Hebrew literally reads: "when you see on both discs." Several explanations have been proposed: (1) change one vowel and read "stones" instead of "discs"; the stones then were the chair in which the woman sat while giving birth, or stones on which she leaned, or the private parts; (2) the word is found also in Jeremiah 18:3, where it refers to the two discs of the potter's wheel; the comparison is then between the discs of the potter's wheel and the vessel on the one hand, and the womb and the child on the other; (3) some think of a bed of bricks on which the child was placed immediately after birth to check whether it was capable of living or perhaps should be put to death. Perhaps excavations will shed more light on this question. The verb "observe" could be translated as an imperative: "observe the birth; pay attention to it."

The midwives perceived the situation more clearly than Pharaoh and the Egyptians, probably because they were more aware of the religious ideas of the Israelites due to their intimate association with them. They feared and respected the (invisible) God of the Israelites more than the (visible) Pharaoh; they dared to defy the king's orders (Heb. 11:23) and allowed the newborn males to live. We may not be able to approve of the fact that,

---

[2]W. F. Albright, *The Biblical Period from Abraham to Ezra* (New York: Harper and Row, 1963), pp. 22–23.

when called to account, they pointed to the superior strength of the Hebrew women as compared to the Egyptian women. Even if this were true (and this has indeed been observed also among Arabic and Syrian women), it is unlikely that as a rule the birth had taken place before the midwife arrived. Their answer was thus a "white lie," resorted to in order to extricate themselves from a conflict of duties: to fear God or Pharaoh. God was kind to the midwives, not because of that lie, but because the principle of the fear of God was implanted in the hearts of these pagan women. The fact that Pharaoh did not punish them indicates that the lie was in any case close to what he knew to be true, and may in part also have been a result of the impression made by the word they used, which in the NIV is translated "vigorous." It is not impossible that the word means "small livestock, sheep, goats." The midwives then said that the Hebrew women were like sheep and goats when the gave birth. They used a contemptuous expression, thus escaping Pharaoh's wrath.

Verse 21 indicates how God blessed the midwives: "He gave them families of their own" (lit.: "He made them houses"). The benefaction fits the action, since they refused to cooperate in the destruction of the families of Israelites. The struggle was between God and Pharaoh: the latter called to account but could not punish; God protected and blessed these same people. Pharaoh was the enemy, God the friend of Israel.

1:22 *Then Pharaoh gave this order to all his people: "Every boy that is born you must throw into the river, but let every girl live."*

Finally Pharaoh decided to order the Egyptians to throw all newborn Israelite males into the Nile. The Israelites themselves had to obey this order concerning their own children (Acts 7:19; Heb. 11:23), and must thus be considered part of "all his people."

It is striking that the order did not even specify the boys "of the Israelites": the author was interested only in one people. Pharaoh began to concentrate on the Israelite danger: it was rapidly becoming a matter of honor with him. He did not know that he was being used by Satan to make an attack on the promised Savior of the world, later typified by Moses who emerged as God's chosen one in the next chapter (see Matt. 2: the murder of the children in Bethlehem, designed to remove Jesus). A Jewish midrash (explanation, commentary) says that the Pharaoh of the oppression tried to heal his own leprosy by bathing in the blood of the Hebrew children.

Thus far we have seen four measures designed to enslave and oppress the Israelites:

a. forced labor
b. forced labor combined with cruelty ("ruthlessness")
c. the order to the midwives to kill the newborn males
d. the order to the Egyptian people to throw the newborn males into the Nile.

After the first and third measures we read, almost like a refrain: the Israelites increased, the miraculous growth continued. That was God's countermove. After the fourth measure God's countermeasures also became stronger: Moses was born.

3. *Birth, Rescue, and Youth of Moses* (2:1–10)

The birth, rescue, and youth of Moses must be considered a work of God's providence to keep His people Israel alive. In the previous chapter we saw Satan in action against the seed of the woman. God, on the other hand, seemed to work slowly: He did not take an adult hero, but started at the beginning. God did not build cheaply; He wanted to prepare Himself a chosen vessel. In the case of Joseph it was different: there the man was in place before the famine (cf. Ps. 105:17). Here the oppression came first, then the decisive rescue measure. God's providence used natural factors: motherly love, sisterly love, a woman's pity, Israelite acumen, Egyptian culture. It also used faith. It was precisely the commandment to throw the boys into the Nile that brought Moses to the Egyptian court!

Moses is here a type of Christ, come into the world as a child and saved by a miracle. The difference is that the Christ's circumstances were humbler, the means God used simpler (no Egyptian court). God uses means but is not bound by them. Today we find the concept that this story is legendary. Pharaoh supposedly had a dream that a Hebrew woman would give birth to a boy who would deprive him of his throne and his life. That is why Pharaoh ordered all boys to be drowned. Later the persecution of Moses in this saga was expanded to include all Hebrews. Reference is then made to the birth sagas of other heroes. Thus the story of the birth and "abandonment" of Moses belongs to a large body of similar legends. These elements, together with the fact of Israel's oppression, are then woven into one narrative. Such a view is contrary to the Scriptures, which state that not Pharaoh, but rather Moses' parents saw something special in their child (2:2; cf. Heb. 11:23, and even more strongly Acts 7:20).

2:1 *Now a man of the house of Levi married a Levite woman.*

We know that this "man of the house of Levi" was called Amram, the "Levite woman" (who was also Amram's aunt) Jochebed (Exod. 6:20;

Num. 26:59). See commentary on 6:20 concerning the problems connected with these texts.

Israel would not have looked in the first place to the house of Levi for help (cf. Gen. 34:25–31; 49:5–7; 1 Cor. 1:27–29), although their patriarch, Levi, did have courage. Cf. also Moses' anger in verse 12 of this chapter.

Some translate verse 1: "Now a man of the house of Levi *had* married a Levite woman." There is indeed a period of at least fifteen years between the first and second verses, since Miriam was much older than Moses (cf. v. 4).

2:2 *And she became pregnant and gave birth to a son. When she saw that he was a fine child, she hid him for three months.*

This son was born while the order of 1:22 was in force. The mother (which does not necessarily exclude the father; the LXX reads "they saw") saw that he was "a fine child" (KJV: "goodly"), that is, attractive, well-formed, but here perhaps also: robust, promising. The mother saw something special in the child (a future savior?). See Acts 7:20–21 and Hebrews 11:23, which indicate that the beauty of the child was taken by the parents to be a sign that God intended something special for him. By faith Moses' mother ignored the visible reality of the oppression, was prompted to set herself against Pharaoh's power, and ignored the order of the tyrant. The Jewish historian Josephus mentions a separate revelation of God to Amram concerning Moses' future greatness, but it is not necessary to accept this.

2:3 *But when she could hide him no longer, she got a papyrus basket for him and coated it with tar and pitch. Then she placed the child in it and put it among the reeds along the bank of the Nile.*

The child appears to have grown well, so that after only three months it became impossible to hide him. And now we see the confidence of his mother's faith. She waterproofed a basket, made of the sticky papyrus found along the Nile, with tar (a bitumen imported in Egypt from Palestine) and pitch. Several words in this verse are derived from the Egyptian language, which supports the historicity of this account.

Papyrus was also used to make small boats that navigated the Nile, as well as other things, including paper. Papyrus is no longer found in Egypt.

The word for "basket" is the same word used for Noah's ark. It may have been a ruse to make a basket that looked like those used by the Egyptians to transport their idols on ships from one city to another in processions. The Egyptian princess, who entered the picture later, must have thought that it was one of those baskets, and that it had fallen from a ship. The boy in his basket was placed among the high reeds of the Nile, possibly there where the mother knew that Pharaoh's daughter usually bathed, but in any case so that the basket could not be dragged downstream by the current.

2:4 *His sister stood at a distance to see what would happen to him.*

As a precaution Moses' sister Miriam (15:20; Num. 26:59) stayed close to the basket, to be able to step in should some unexpected minor danger arise, and to be able to tell the family, who did not want to lose sight of the child, what happened. Faith, does not lead to a disregard of the means. Everything had been arranged down to the details.

2:5 *Then Pharaoh's daughter went down to the Nile to bathe, and her attendants were walking along the river bank. She saw the basket among the reeds and sent her slave girl to get it.*

The vivid description now shifts to a different scene. Pharaoh's daughter and her entourage came down to the Nile. According to the dating suggested in the Introduction (p. 22) this may have been Hatshepsut, one of the most remarkable women in the history of Egypt, and indeed of the world. She was the daughter of Thutmose I (1539–1514 B.C.) whom I believe to be the king who issued the order that all boys be drowned (see also commentary on 1:8). Since Moses was 80 years old when the Exodus took place he was born around 1525 B.C. Hatshepsut was her father's favorite and after his death became very influential under her weak husband Thutmose II (1514–1501 B.C.), even to the extent that her brother (or stepson?) Thutmose III (1501–1447 B.C.) had no say at all during her lifetime, no matter how famous he later became (see Introduction, p. 22). She ruled Egypt from 1501–1479 B.C. Monuments of Hatshepsut still exist, although Thutmose III later tried to eradicate her name. She ruled in peace, built temples, and sponsored expeditions; her grave has been found. When Moses was born she was still only "Pharaoh's daughter," yet she had sufficient influence to be able to keep Moses alive. It was natural that her attendants would walk up and down the bank to keep undesired persons at a distance while she bathed. She saw the basket and thought perhaps of a lost procession basket (see commentary on v. 3) and sent her slave girl to get it.

2:6 *She opened it and saw the baby. He was crying, and she felt sorry for him. "This is one of the Hebrew babies," she said.*

The author described her surprise superbly. Whatever she expected, it was certainly not this. And when she saw the baby his (not accidental!) crying aroused her womanly pity; she concluded from the fact that he was abandoned that he was a child of the Hebrews (circumcision was also an Egyptian custom).

2:7 *Then his sister asked Pharaoh's daughter, "Shall I go and get one of the Hebrew women to nurse the baby for you?"*

The child's sister had waited anxiously and made quick and clever use of the pity she saw in Pharaoh's daughter. The offer to find a woman to nurse the baby was exactly the right thing to do, now that the child would not drown.

2:8 *"Yes, go," she answered. And the girl went and got the baby's mother.*

This was indicated by the princess' answer. And soon Miriam returned with the child's mother. What miraculous divine guidance!

2:9–10 *Pharaoh's daughter said to her, "Take this baby and nurse him for me, and I will pay you." So the woman took the baby and nursed him. When the child grew older, she took him to Pharaoh's daughter and he became her son. She named him Moses, saying, "I drew him out of the water."*

The mother was even (and there is a touch of humor in this) rewarded by the princess for nursing her child, which she no longer had to keep hidden since it had been adopted by Pharaoh's daughter. Yet God's plan went beyond the mere rescue. When the child no longer needed nursing and was thus about three years old, the official adoption took place and Moses got a place at the (separate) court of the daughter of the oppressor. It has been said correctly that "the enemies of the Hebrews raise the fine child, the tyrants of God's people provide him with the weapons of knowledge with which he will soon wrest away their prey from them" (B. Wielenga, *De Bijbel als Boek van Schoonheid*, p. 137). In this connection see Acts 7:21–22. Egypt was to help mold the deliverer of Israel. God did not need Israel; He could use someone trained in the school of Egypt, but who was intended for Israel. Moses probably was educated along with the children of the Egyptian noble houses by the priests who were entrusted with education in Egypt. He was instructed in theology, astronomy, medicine, mathematics, and other subjects, in virtually everything that was part of the intellectual domain of the civilized world of that time.

The princess called the boy Moses (Hebrew: *Mošeh*), since she "drew him out of the water" (Hebrew *Mašah* = "to draw"). But since she did not speak Hebrew, what did *Mošeh* mean in Egyptian?

The common view is that Mošeh was an Egyptian word, meaning "child" or "son." The name then would mean something like "child of an unknown father." Others see the name as an Egyptian abbreviation of "ra (=Re)-mes-su," i.e. "Re (the sun god) begot him." Moses' real name then would have been Rameses. But in that case the author of Exodus would have misinterpreted the Egyptian name as a Hebrew name.

One of the more recent explanations seems to be the most plausible one: the name Mošeh was an Egyptian name, consisting of *mw* (water) and *seh* (lake). *Mw* here stands figuratively for "child, son," and *seh* was one of the names for the Nile. Mošeh then means "child of the Nile." The boy's name was to keep alive the memory of the fact that he was found in the Nile, which is precisely what the Hebrew name Mošeh emphasizes. Our author therefore knew of the Egyptian meaning of Mošeh. He knew that *seh* referred to the Nile, and he accurately represents this as Mošeh, meaning literally "from the water," since the Egyptians also called their rivers "water." The Hebrew explanation of the name ("I drew him out of the water") retains two elements. The connection of the Egyptian name Mw-seh with "water" (the Nile) contains the king's daughter's explanation of the boy's name. In the connection between Mošeh and the Hebrew word *mašah* ("draw out") lies the author's additional explanation. This is the opinion of Yahuda, who has done much comparative research in the languages of Egypt and of the Pentateuch.

4. *Moses Killed an Egyptian; Flight to and Stay in Midian; His Marriage* (2:11–22)

These verses show that Moses, besides being interested in his own people, also possessed the quality of standing up for the oppressed (vv. 11–14, 17). God had given him the innate aptitude to serve as Israel's deliverer in order to thwart Satan's plan. But his killing of the Egyptian shows that the rough material of his natural ability had not yet been refined: he ran ahead, and had not yet learned to wait. God used the flight to Midian and his stay there to refine Moses. In spite of his marriage Moses continued to consider Midian a foreign country (vv. 18–22). Yet we must see in Moses' standing up for the Hebrews and the resulting flight the principle of faith and the choice of faith (see Heb. 11:24–27). He wanted to act as *redeemer* too soon, but God's time had not yet come and Israel was not yet ready (see Acts 7:25). But as a *man of faith* he made a right decision in spite of the sinful consequences. The refining process was to unite the redeemer and the man of faith: the principle of faith was to pervade the fulfillment of his calling. His stay in Midian made Moses humble (Num. 12:3) and taught him to wait, so that when the call came, he even shrank from it (3:11). The oppressed seed of the woman was God's business; God, not Moses was to take the initiative in the redemption of Israel, which is more than a standing up for human rights.

2:11 *One day, after Moses had grown up, he went out to where his own people were and watched them at their hard labor. He saw an Egyptian beating a Hebrew, one of his own people.*

"One day" takes us some forty years beyond the events described in verses 1–10 (see Acts 7:23). In contrast to verse 10 "had grown up" refers to Moses' reaching middle age (see Gen. 21:20; 1 Sam. 3:19). He left the palace to watch as an interested observer the oppression of his own people (KJV: "brethren"). Note that what drew Moses was the tie with his own people. The Hebrew means: "to watch something with emotion." And thus he witnessed an Egyptian slave driver beating a Hebrew—it does not say that he killed him. The word order at the end of this verse especially shows that Moses felt the tie with his people: it was one of his own people. For "hard labor" see commentary on 1:11.

2:12 *Glancing this way and that and seeing no one, he killed the Egyptian and hid him in the sand.*

It is natural that Moses would look around ("glanced this way and that"), but it also shows that he did not think of giving the sign to an open rebellion; yet he offered himself as redeemer, liberator and expected Israel to realize this (Acts 7:25). He did not see anyone. Yet someone may have been around, or the rescued Hebrew may have told what happened. We get an impression of Moses' impetuous character and strength in the killing of the Egyptian. His hiding the body in the sand did not indicate a careful burial, but shows that he wanted to keep the matter a secret. It does not speak of a systematic plan.

Moses' act must be condemned, and it was punished by God by his flight to and stay in Midian. But it is striking that a direct punishment by the Lord was not mentioned in so many words. Moses' sin was a quick temper (although his looking around indicates that there was also some hasty deliberation) and "jumping the gun." He had no right to act as judge. Moses did not yet have a divine appointment; he had not yet been called. And he lacked the patience to wait for that call. Yet we must not forget that Moses acted for the rights of his people and in his position risked everything for the sake of his people. Augustine was of the opinion that, even

43

though the Egyptian was harmful and evil, he should not have been killed by one who had not as yet been "ordained." But he also believed that people who are capable of virtue frequently outwardly show vices that precisely point to what virtues they are capable of if those virtues are systematically exercised. He compared Moses' act with that of Peter who wanted to defend the Lord Jesus with the sword, and said that "such a great heart must be cultivated, even as the soil must be cultivated to produce fruit."

Moses' misdeed thus clearly shows what he would ultimately be suited for: redeemer or deliverer of Israel. We have here the "shortcomings of his virtues."

2:13, 14 *The next day he went out and saw two Hebrews fighting. He asked the one in the wrong, "Why are you hitting your fellow Hebrew?"*

The man said, "Who made you ruler and judge over us? Are you thinking of killing me as you killed the Egyptian?" Then Moses was afraid and thought, "What I did must have become known."

The following day Moses saw something that grieved and astonished him (expressed by "behold," KJV, not translated in NIV). He was deeply concerned about the situation of the Hebrews and once again went out to be with them. But now he saw two Hebrews fighting. How remarkable, because the Egyptians were their common enemy. Israel was still sinful and unrefined! Moses broke up the fight and asked for the reason. One of the two appeared to be in the wrong. The Hebrew word here can also mean "wicked, guilty of sin." Here it means "guilty in this particular matter." Moses asked the one why he hit his fellow Israelite, who in their common distress was his "neighbor." Note that Moses entered into his role of protector and set himself up as judge—he, the Egyptian prince who was here to find his own people. The answer of the guilty man was like a cold shower. The question in itself was to the point, but it showed an obtuseness and a narrowmindedness, a failure to see Israel's case in its entirety (Acts 7:25): "Who made you ruler and judge over us?" This twofold description appears to contain an allusion to two Egyptian offices. "Ruler" (KJV: "prince") was a justice, a member of the supreme court; "judge" was an ordinary judge. Moses could not claim the latter title; he was not even a judge, let alone a "ruler." The literal Hebrew translation is "a man who is a ruler"; this is not an unusual construction in Hebrew. In Leviticus 21:9 "a man who is a priest" is the same as "a priest," and "a man, who is a prophet" (Judg. 6:8) is a prophet. To take "man" as the third and highest title in the sense of "grand vizier" is contrary to Hebrew usage, although it would provide a neat sequence: "Man" higher than "ruler," which in turn is higher than "judge." Moses was none of these. The remark per se was correct. But the Hebrew was in fear of his life. He asked whether Moses made this inquiry in order to kill him like he killed the Egyptian the day before. Thus the man saw in Moses only a meddler. Moses now became afraid since his sin had become known; but he did not flee.

2:15 *When Pharaoh heard of this, he tried to kill Moses, but Moses fled from Pharaoh and went to live in Midian, where he sat down by a well.*

Moses fled only when Pharaoh heard about what had happened and wanted to execute him. This flight can be viewed as an act of faith (cf. Heb. 11:27), when we take into consideration that Moses made no effort to straighten out the matter and to reconcile himself with the king. The Pharaoh who wanted to kill Moses was Thutmose III (1501–1447 B.C.). If the princess in 2:5 was Hatshepsut (which is not certain), she must already have died, since Moses at this point was more than forty years old. Nothing argues against the possibility that some time passed between Moses' rash act and his flight, and that the former took place while Hatshepsut was still alive. But all of this is hypothesis. If it is true what tradition says and Acts 7:22 seems to support, viz. that Moses had already been a successful general in the Egyptian army, especially in campaigns against Nubia, then Pharaoh's attempt was due not so much to the seriousness of that one incident as to his fear that Moses would become the leader of a Hebrew insurrection.

Moses fled to Midian, to the south and southeast of Canaan. The northwestern portion of the Sinai peninsula was also considered part of Midian, as well as Mount Sinai itself (see 3:1; Hab. 3:7). The Midianites were nomads who lived on the steppe, descendants of Abraham and Keturah (Gen. 25:2) who, along with Abraham's other concubines, were sent to the land east of Canaan (Gen. 25:6). Moses settled on the steppe inhabited by the Midianites between Egypt and Canaan and one day came to a well.

2:16, 17 *Now a priest of Midian had seven daughters, and they came to draw water and fill the troughs to water their father's flock. Some shepherds came along and drove them away, but Moses got up and came to their rescue and watered their flock.*

The religion of the priest of Midian (or rather, of that part of Midian) may not have been very corrupted. It is possible that Moses encountered many stories about the patriarchs in the traditions of Midian. But I do not therefore accept the so-called Kenite hypothesis (see below). The seven daughters of this priest first had to draw the water to fill the trough from which the sheep and goats (the region was not fertile enough for cattle) could drink. Moses then witnessed how the shepherds came and chased them away. The priest thus did not have much secular power. Once again Moses stood up for the oppressed, although his action was now more moderate, and helped the women. It seems to have been, and still is, the custom that the unmarried women of the Sinai peninsula worked as shepherdesses and enjoyed more freedom among the Bedouins than married women. We have here a truly oriental afternoon scene, reminiscent of Genesis 29.

2:18, 19 *When the girls returned to Reuel their father, he asked them, "Why have you returned so early today?"*

They answered, "An Egyptian rescued us from the shepherds. He even drew water for us and watered the flock."

The priest's name was Reuel, i.e., "friend of God," although this does not indicate which god. The same person is called Jethro in 3:1 (see commentary there). His daughters took Moses for an Egyptian, probably because of his dress. When they reported the incident to their father he reproached them for their lack of hospitality, something in which the people from the East excel. It is striking that the priest had acquiesced in the daily slighting of his daughters, and was grateful for Moses' help.

2:20–22 *"And where is he?" he asked his daughters. "Why did you leave him? Invite him to have something to eat."*

Moses agreed to stay with the man, who gave his daughter Zipporah to Moses in marriage. Zipporah gave birth to a son, and Moses named him Gershom, saying, "I have become an alien in a foreign land."

Moses allowed himself to be persuaded (the Hebrew verb implies this) to stay with Reuel, who gave him his daughter Zipporah as wife, in keeping with a father's authority in those days. The name Moses gave their child shows that Moses in Midian was homesick for Egypt, where his people lived and were oppressed. "Ger" means "alien, stranger," "shom" is related to "there." Moses expressed the fact that he was a stranger under protection in the country of an alien, non-Israelite people. In spite of the kindness he received, and the blessing of a child that God gave him in his marriage, he felt himself an exile, in the process of being refined.

A brief word about the Kenite hypothesis. Moses' father-in-law belonged to the Kenites (see Judg. 1:16). Yet he is called a Midianite in Numbers 10:29. Most likely "Midianite" was the broader and "Kenite" the narrower term, or the Kenites may have been a Midianite tribe. The Kenite hypothesis claims that these Kenites were the original worshipers of Jahweh, and that Moses gained his religious knowledge concerning Jahweh in Midian from his father-in-law. Israel then chose this god of the Kenites as its own at Sinai.

The Bible is silent about this, and thus it is only a hypothesis, which does not gain in credibility when we consider the statement that Moses tended the flock of his father-in-law (3:1) and that he was not called his disciple or student. Also, the appearance in chapter 3 does not give the impression that Moses here encountered the God of the Kenites. Furthermore, the name Reuel means "friend of God" and not "friend of Jahweh." Only later do we find names that are composites of the name Jahweh in the case of Kenites who became part of Israel, e.g., Jehonadab ("Jahweh has given"?, 2 Kings 10:15; also Jer. 35:6, 8, 10, 14, 16, 19). And in 3:7 Jahweh speaks of *"My* people," referring to Israel.

A rather curious interpretation of this section results when the Kenites are promoted, or rather demoted, to traveling blacksmiths on the basis of Judges 4, where Heber and Jael had a hammer and a pin. The slighting of Reuel's daughters then could be explained on the basis of the contempt the shepherds felt for the indispensable itinerant families of blacksmiths. And the god of these Kenites or blacksmiths was then the blacksmith's fire, which was the god who appeared to Moses in the burning bush.

5. *Death of Pharaoh; God Remembered His Covenant When Israel Cried for Help* (2:23–25)

Israel as a nation also was as yet unrefined (v. 14). God refined both the man Moses and the people of Israel (vv. 15–22, 23–25) until they turned to God (vv. 23–25) and God turned to them (v. 25 and ch. 3ff.) because of His covenant (v. 24).

2:23 *During that long period, the king of Egypt died. The Israelites groaned in their slavery and cried out, and their cry for help because of their slavery went up to God.*

"During that long period" (lit.: "and it happened during those many days") seems to have been a standard formula, derived from the Egyptian, indicating the continuation of the narrative. The "long period" refers to Moses' stay in Midian, which lasted forty years (cf. 7:7; Acts 7:23, 30).

The king of Egypt who died was Thutmose III (1501–1447 B.C.). His successor and the Pharaoh of the Exodus was Amenhotep II (1447–1421 B.C.), a cruel ruler, who continued the forced labor of the Israelites (perhaps contrary to what the Israelites expected when he became king). Amen-hotep's mummy has been found and shows him to have been a man of powerful physique. One of the inscriptions also praises him for his physical strength. He proved his cruelty when, after a victory over Syria, he carried seven Syrian leaders upside-down from the bow of his ship on the trip up the Nile, after which he personally sacrificed them. The author of Psalm 136 states that this Pharaoh drowned in the Red Sea, but this is probably not based on an independent oral tradition. Pharaoh's drowning is not mentioned in 14:27; 15:4; Deuteronomy 11:4. Psalm 135:15 may be a poetic description of Egypt's defeat.

As for this verse, note the climax: they groaned, cried out, cried for help! It seems that the author wanted to express that only now did they turn of one accord to God. We should not forget that Israel, while in Egypt, also served the gods of Egypt (see Josh. 24:14; Ezek. 20:5–10; 23:2–3, 8, 19, 21, 27; cf. also Deut. 26:7). God, we are told, heard and paid heed. Concerning the "cry for help" going "up to God," contrast "up to heaven" in 1 Samuel 5:12. Israel was far richer!

2:24 *God heard their groaning and he remembered his covenant with Abraham, with Isaac and with Jacob.*

Next it is said (in human terms) that God remembered His covenant with Abraham, Isaac, and Jacob. The promise of this covenant is expressed in Genesis 12:7; 13:15, 17; 15:7, 18; 17:7–8, 19; 22:15–18; 24:7; 26:3–4; 28:13–15; 35:9–13; Exodus 32:13; Deuteronomy 34:4; etc. It is also found in Psalm 105:11: "To you I will give the land of Canaan as the portion you will inherit." (See also Acts 7:5.) God had to honor His promise. The Exodus had to take place to make the promise of the covenant a reality (see Gen. 15:14; 46:4; Exod. 6:5).

2:25 *So God looked on the Israelites and was concerned about them.*

God now directed His attention to the Israelites "and was concerned about them" (lit.: "and God knew"; the LXX reads: "and God was known to them" or "revealed Himself to them"). Thus God knew them in the sense of being concerned about them, a concern He showed by acting on their behalf. And His first action was the appearance to Moses.

6. *The Lord Appeared to Moses in a Burning Bush* (3:1–4:17)

The Lord's appearance to Moses in the burning bush can be analyzed as follows:

3:1–6—the appearance described
3:7–10—Moses sent to Egypt
3:11–22—Moses' objections and the Lord's rebuttal
4:1–17—further resistance by Moses; signs and the Lord's anger.

This appearance is very important. The last time the Lord appeared was in a vision to Jacob at night, before Jacob came to Egypt (cf. Gen. 46:2–4; see commentary on 3:4–5, 6). At that time the Lord repeated the promise that Jacob would become a great nation (see commentary on 1:6–22). But that was four centuries ago. We saw in chapters 1 and 2 that the growth and oppression were a fulfillment of God's plan and word; that in the blessing of the midwives, and in the birth, rescue, and youth of Moses He showed His providence. But He did not appear in a direct, personal revelation until now, when (according to 2:23–25) the situation was critical.

The significance of this section is manifold, but primarily this, that the link between the oppressed nation of Israel and Moses was established while at the same time the Lord gave Himself an eminent name (3:14). We also get to know Moses better. Note that the final restatement of his assignment was spoken by the Lord in anger (4:14–17), because Moses maintained his opposition for so long. The road to deliverance for Israel was full of obstacles, even within Jacob's descendants themselves.

3:1 *Now Moses was tending the flock of Jethro his father-in-law, the priest of Midian, and he led the flock to the far side of the desert and came to Horeb, the mountain of God.*

What follows took place many years after Moses' arrival in Midian; according to Acts 7:30 it was forty years later. Moses had become the shepherd of his father-in-law's flock (cf. commentary on 2:16–17); Reuel is here called Jethro. The name is probably a title and may mean "highness, eminence" (see commentary on 2:16 concerning "priest of Midian"; commentary on 2:15 concerning the location of Midian). "The far side of the desert" means that on this occasion Moses had taken his flock beyond the steppe and had even left the arid desert north of the mountains behind. This region, like the Sinai plateau itself, provided sufficient food for camels, goats, and sheep. Moses now reached the mountains with his flock. "The far side of the desert" may mean that Moses came out of the er-Raha and saw Mt. Horeb before him, if we can identify the latter with Râs es-Sufsafeh (see below). An abundance of water and enough food for large herds can be found in the valleys of the mountain range, which is probably referred to here. That is thus where Moses went. Mt. Horeb was called the "Mountain of God." This must have been written after the giving of the law on that mountain or otherwise added by a redactor. Since the LXX reads "to Mt. Horeb" the latter is more likely.

Horeb and Sinai are two names for the same mountain, just as Hermon is also called Sirion (Deut. 3:9; Ps. 29:6). According to tradition this mountain was one of the peaks of the Gebel Musa in the northern part of the Sinai peninsula. The highest peak of the Gebel Musa range is the southernmost (7362 ft.), called Gebel Musa (Mountain of Moses) in the narrower sense. The northernmost peak, Râs es-Sufsafeh (Willow Peak), is slightly lower (6541 ft.), but has nevertheless been considered to be the mountain of God, i.e., the mountain of the giving of the law, by most scholars since the middle of the last century. At the base of this mountain (which had to be fenced off, and thus rose directly out of the plain, 19:12, 23) lies the er-Râha or Sinai Desert (19:2). This desert, together with the surrounding valleys, is large enough to accommodate even a people as numerous as Israel; from this desert the Gebel Musa is not visible, while the entire plain is visible from the Râs es-Sufsafeh, but not from the Gebel Musa.

Palmer, an Englishman, who in 1868–1870 traveled in the region of Israel's wandering in the wilderness, calculated that the er-Râha is large enough to accommodate all of Israel's estimated two million people if each person were allotted 11 square feet. The area of the Gebel Musa range has more water than any other part of the peninsula; water runs through no less than four nearby valleys. East of the Gebel Musa range, and thus southeast of the Râs es-Sufsafeh, lies the well-known convent of St. Katherine in the Wadi ed-Deir, the Valley of Jethro or Hobab. In this valley Moses, according to legend, tended the flock of his father-in-law. The Gebel Musa range can be climbed from the convent, which is still in use.

Although I believe the Râs es-Sufsafeh to be Sinai or Horeb[3] (insofar as I can make a judgment on the basis of the literature and photographs), some scholars do not place Sinai in the Gebel Musa range at all. Some even reject Israel's stay in the Sinai peninsula altogether and seek the mountain of God across the Gulf of Aqaba in northwestern Arabia, since they are looking for a volcano. This idea is based on a misinterpretation of the biblical data, especially of Exodus 19. Others (among them Ebers, who traveled through Goshen to Sinai in 1871) identify the mountain of God with the Gebel Serbal northwest of the Gebel Musa range. The Gebel Serbal is 6732 feet high, but appears to be much higher when viewed from

---

[3]According to Georg Ebers the monks of the Convent of St. Katherine call the entire range Horeb and the individual peaks Sinai. Ebers considers Sinai and Horeb to the be same, based on 1 Kings 8:9; 19:8; Psalms 68:9, 18; 106:19; 2 Chronicles 5:10; Malachi 3:22; Nehemiah 9:13; Sirach 48:9.

the Wadi Feiran than the Râs es-Sufsafeh seen from the er-Râha.[4]

The Wadi Feiran is an oasis that can hardly be called a desert or steppe, and furthermore does not seem to be large enough to accommodate as many people as the Israel of the Exodus. Ebers admits that the view from Râs es-Sufsafeh presents a much broader, more majestic, and better defined foreground than the view from Gebel Musa, and that it is large enough to hold the camp of Israel. The elevation is less important than the vantage point from which it is viewed. The objections raised against the Gebel Musa range, namely the lack of food for the people in that desert and the cold during the winter months, are not insurmountable. God provided manna daily, there were springs and, as we saw, food for the animals: although the er-Râha is a sandy desert covered with rocks it is sparsely covered with vegetation suitable for animals. And Israel could prepare itself against the cold, which can be fierce only in December and January. Furthermore, Palmer points out that there are indications that the Sinai peninsula was much more fertile at the time of Israel's journey than it is now. He notes that due to the present barrenness of the land climatic changes are much more keenly felt than in other parts of Arabia. The temperature can fluctuate as much as fifty degrees centigrade between day and night, while not much material can be found to provide protection against the cold, or shade to protect from the heat.[5]

3:2–3 *There the angel of the* Lord *appeared to him in flames of fire from within a bush. Moses saw that though the bush was on fire it did not burn up. So Moses thought, "I will go over and see this strange sight—why the bush does not burn up."*

The "angel of the Lord" was a revelation of the Lord Himself (cf. vv. 4ff., where the Lord is the subject). This angel of the Lord appeared to Abraham (Gen. 16:7; 22:11); He appeared in human form in Judges 6 and 13, and perhaps in Genesis 16. Here He appeared as "flames of fire" that had settled on a bush on the ground near Horeb. We do not know what kind of bush it was; according to Jewish tradition it was a bramble bush. We can read "*in* flames of fire," as do most English versions, but "as flames of fire" is better. The fire, which the angel of the Lord chose as the form in which to appear, did not consume the bush. This was to get Moses' atten-

---

[4]Wadi Feiran lies at approximately 2001 feet. The Gebel Serbal thus rises about 4724 feet above the wadi. The er-Râha has an elevation of about 5300 feet and the Râs es-Sufsafeh is 1542 feet higher. Ebers says that of all the mountains he knows in the East this one most deserves the name "throne of God."

[5]E. H. Palmer, *"Desert of the Exodus."*

tion: Moses called the fact that the bush did not burn up a "strange sight." He did not know yet that he faced an appearance of the Lord (see v. 6b), but decided to take a look at this strange phenomenon. The fire thus constituted both the peculiarity and the essence of the appearance. The bush that did not burn up drew attention to the special nature of this fire that was not of earthly origin. The earthly bush could come in contact with the heavenly fire without being destroyed. The form the Lord chose for His appearance attested the peaceable purpose: the Lord could descend on an insignificant plant, symbol of that which is most humble and even despised, tempering His all-consuming blaze. What follows (e.g., vv. 6–9) seems to indicate that the Lord would deal with Israel as the fire with the bush: sanctify it and recognize it as His people without destroying it, taking into consideration the weakness of His people.

3:4–5 *When the L*ORD *saw that he had gone over to look, God called to him from within the bush, "Moses, Moses!"*

And Moses said, "Here I am."

"Do not come any closer," God said. "Take off your sandals, for the place where you are standing is holy ground."

Yet this did not diminish His holiness, and the Lord called to Moses when he approached and commanded him to take off his sandals out of reverence for the ground that carried His appearance. Those sandals carried the dirt from his journey, and man must be pure when he approaches God. Hence the custom in many oriental religions of entering temples or shrines barefoot, as e.g., the Muslims when they enter their mosques. An address and response similar to that in verse 4 is found in Genesis 46:2. The Lord Himself was in the bush. The fact that "God" is used as a name here indicates that for Israel He was simply God without qualifications.

3:6 *Then he said, "I am the God of your father, the God of Abraham, the God of Isaac and the God of Jacob." At this, Moses hid his face, because he was afraid to look at God.*

It is striking that the Lord here called Himself first the God of Moses' father (cf. 2:1; Gen. 46:3). This argues against the idea that Moses derived the name of God, Jahweh (see below), and the concept of God from the Kenites or especially from Jethro (see commentary on 2:21–22 and 15:2). Then He also called Himself the God of Abraham, Isaac, and Jacob. No wonder that Moses became afraid and hid his face in his robe, since no one could see God and live (33:20; Judg. 6:22; 13:22; 1 Kings 19:13; Isa. 6:2).

Jesus later used the name "God of Abraham, Isaac, and Jacob" as proof for the resurrection of the dead (cf. Matt. 22:32; Mark 12:26; Luke 20:37).

3:7–10 *The* Lord *said, "I have indeed seen the misery of my people in Egypt. I have heard them crying out because of their slave drivers, and I am concerned about their suffering. So I have come down to rescue them from the hand of the Egyptians and to bring them up out of that land into a good and spacious land, a land flowing with milk and honey—the home of the Canaanites, Hittites, Amorites, Perizzites, Hivites and Jebusites. And now the cry of the Israelites has reached me, and I have seen the way the Egyptians are oppressing them. So now, go. I am sending you to Pharaoh to bring my people the Israelites out of Egypt."*

Now follows the Lord's message for Moses. The reason for the message was His awareness of the misery of His people, of their cries for help because of their slave drivers and their suffering. The Lord presented Himself here as a careful observer who, because of what He had seen and heard, was aware of the situation in which His people found themselves. He called the Israelites "my people." And He had come down to deliver them and to lead them to the land promised to their fathers, the land that was good and spacious, and that flowed with milk and honey (signs of prosperity and fertility). Perhaps the honey was honey from grapes or dates, in which case the products mentioned here represented agriculture and cattle raising; but we should think in the first place of honey from bees (see *Zondervan Pictorial Encyclopedia of the Bible* [ZPEB] "Honey," 3:196). The land now belonged to several groups of people. The Canaanites were the descendants of Canaan, the son of Ham (Gen. 10:6); they lived primarily along the sea coast and the Jordan River (Num. 13:29). According to Genesis 10:15–17 the Hittites, Amorites, Perizzites, Hivites, and Jebusites also descended from Canaan, and thus must be considered Canaanites in the broader sense of the word. The same is true in Genesis 10:19; 12:6. The land Canaan probably derived its name from its inhabitants. Opinions differ as to when the Canaanites entered the land.

The Hittites were a well-known people, who were powerful in Moses' time. A group of them lived in the mountains of Canaan (Num. 13:29) and probably arrived there after the Hittites from Asia Minor had put an end to the Amorite dynasty of Hammurabi (ca. 1800–ca. 1600 B.C.; Hammurabi 1704–1662 B.C.). They subsequently fought the Egyptians for supremacy during the time of Rameses II (1300–1234 B.C.). The Hittites probably invaded Asia Minor from Russia around 2000 B.C. They had an unusually large number of gods. Uriah, Bathsheba's husband, was a Hittite (2 Sam. 11:3). Their capital was near the present-day village of Boghazkoy in Asia Minor where excavations have been carried out; it was destroyed in 1200 B.C., after which their empire disintegrated into small states. The rulers of the Hittites once sent gifts to Thutmose III. The Hittite laws show similarities to the Mosaic laws (see ZPEB, "Hittites," 3:165). Some scholars feel that the Hittites in Palestine must be distinguished from those in Asia Minor and that they actually were a different people.

The Amorites lived in the mountains (Num. 13:29), as well as east of the Jordan, where they conquered the land of the Moabites under their King Sihon during Israel's invasion; their capital was Heshbon (Num. 21:21–32). Og of Bashan was also a king of the Amorites (Num. 21:33–35; Deut. 3:10; etc.). The Babylonians called the Syrian mountains and the Western land Amurra. All the inhabitants of the land are called Amorites in Genesis 15:16. It is not known from which country they came, perhaps from Arabia (see ZPEB, "Amorites," 1:140).

We do not know who the Perizzites were. Some translate the name "inhabitants of the villages" (see ZPEB, "Perizzites," 4:704).

The Hivites lived in Shechem (Gen. 34:2), and in Gibeon, Kephira, Beeroth, and Kiriath Jearim (Josh. 9:17), and below Hermon (Josh. 11:3). Not much more is known about them.

The Jebusites were the inhabitants of Jerusalem. They also lived in the mountains (Num. 13:29). They were conquered by David (see ZPEB, "Jebusites," 3:412).

In verse 9 the Lord repeated the fact that Israel's cry had reached Him, but now He said that He knew of the sinful oppression by the Egyptians and the hardships to which they subjected the Israelites. Then followed the announcement that He was sending Moses to Pharaoh to bring the Lord's people out of Egypt (v. 10). "So now" draws the conclusion: the Lord had selected Moses for the work of redemption.

3:11–12 *But Moses said to God, "Who am I, that I should go to Pharaoh and bring the Israelites out of Egypt?"*

And God said, "I will be with you. And this will be the sign to you that it is I who have sent you: When you have brought the people out of Egypt, you will worship God on this mountain."

But Moses considered himself unworthy of the honor to bring either the Lord's revenge or His help. But he expressed his reservations only in the form of a question. The Lord told Moses, however, that the sign that *He* (the "I" is emphatic) had sent him would be the fact that the Israelites would worship God on this very mountain. In other words, the purpose of his mission would.be accomplished. Note that the Lord gave Moses a guarantee that *He* was truly the One who sent him. Any possible doubt as to whether he was really dealing with the Lord in this phenomenon, and whether the Lord really considered him worthy of the honor of being Israel's liberator had thus been answered.

3:13–14 *Moses said to God, "Suppose I go to the Israelites and say to them, 'The God of your fathers has sent me to you,' and they ask me, 'What is his name?' Then what shall I tell them?"*

God said to Moses, "I am who I am. This is what you are to say to the Israelites: "I AM has sent me to you."'"

Moses asked what he had to tell the Israelites when they asked him what God's name was. The Israelites served other gods in Egypt besides the true God (cf. commentary on 2:23). And Moses himself also wanted the support of God telling him His name. God's answer, intended to take away Moses' fear that he would not be able to answer the question, is the well-known "I am who I am." The Lord's essence is being. In itself this did not provide Israel with an answer as to *who* God is. But in the context the name is very comforting: the Lord is the God of the covenant (see v. 15). As such He remains the same, is consistent. What He is in general comforts His people through its application to the specific situation (Israel's oppression) and the special relationship (covenant) that already existed between Him and Israel's ancestors, and now ("I am") will also exist between Him and the descendants "from generation to generation." The Lord is above "moods." The name could also be translated "I shall be who I shall be." But the "I am who I am" even more clearly expresses the impossibility to express His nature in a name. He is who He is, and Moses could only say "I am" has sent me.

3:15 *God also said to Moses, "Say to the Israelites, 'The Lord, the God of your fathers—the God of Abraham, the God of Isaac and the God of Jacob—has sent me to you.' This is my name forever, the name by which I am to be remembered from generation to generation."*

Or, as the Lord continued after a brief pause, Jahweh, which we translate "Lord." This name is here linked with the Hebrew verb *hayah*, "to be." We can take "Jahweh" as the third person masculine singular, "He is," "The One who is." Sometimes the name is also represented by Jehovah, but this is based on a misunderstanding. Hebrew consists of consonants only; the vowels were never written. God's name was Jhwh. In a literal application of the third commandment this name was never pronounced, but in reading was replaced by "Adonai" or "Lord," another name for God. Most English versions translate both Jahweh and Adonai as

"Lord," but indicate the difference by using small capitals for Jahweh ("LORD"). When the vowel system that expressed vowels by means of dots and lines placed under and next to the consonants was developed, the vowels of Adonai (a, o, a; i = j and is thus a consonant) were placed under and next to the consonants of Jhwh. The purpose was to say: read here "Adonai." But sometimes the vowels of Adonai are read together with the consonants of Jhwh, and thus we get Jehovah, which is actually nonsense. The correct vowels of Jahweh are not known, however, since the Jews did not pronounce the name. Most probable is Jahweh since the Samaritans appear to have pronounced the name of God that way. With this name Moses was to approach the Israelites. The proclamation Moses was to make to them ended with "has sent me to you." The following statement was initially intended for Moses only: it was the Lord's everlasting glory that He was the God of Israel's forefathers, of Abraham, Isaac, and Jacob. We should not forget that each of these three names evoked memories of many instances of God's guiding providence and expressions of His faithfulness to the covenant made with Abraham. They also brought to mind the promises made to the patriarchs. He was who He was, both for those forefathers and for Israel; He was "from generation to generation," never changing.

3:16 *"Go, assemble the elders of Israel and say to them, 'The LORD, the God of your fathers, the God of Abraham, Isaac and Jacob, appeared to me and said: I have watched over you and have seen what has been done to you in Egypt.'"*

In verses 16–22 Moses was instructed to go from Midian to Egypt and to assemble the elders, which indicates that in Israel authority lay with the elders, i.e., the heads of the families, clans, and tribes. The narrative does not inform us when this development took place. Moses had to turn to the official representatives of the people. It was no longer a revolution on his own initiative! And he could now speak on behalf of Jahweh, the God of the fathers, and announce that He had appeared to him and had told him that He was fully aware of what had been done to them in Egypt ("I have watched over you," lit.: "I have certainly visited you" in the sense of "taking a practical interest in." The same word is used in 4:31, the same expression in 13:19; Gen. 50:24).

3:17 *'"And I have promised to bring you up out of your misery in Egypt into the land of the Canaanites, Hittites, Amorites, Perizzites, Hivites and Jebusites—a land flowing with milk and honey.'"*

But the Lord was not merely concerned; Moses was to continue to say that the Lord had decided (lit.: "and I said") to lead them up (the word indicates "from low to high") out of their misery in Egypt to the land of the nations mentioned in verse 8, here again called "a land flowing with milk and honey." When the Lord appeared first to Abraham, and later also to Isaac and Jacob, He promised in each instance that He would give them the land of Canaan (cf. commentary on 2:24). Now He appeared to Moses with the same promise. This proved that Moses was a true prophet, whose message was in agreement with the earlier revelation (cf. Deut. 13:1–5).

3:18 *"The elders of Israel will listen to you. Then you and the elders are to go to the king of Egypt and say to him, 'The Lord, the God of the Hebrews, has met with us. Let us take a three-day journey into the desert to offer sacrifices to the Lord our God.'"*

This verse was also initially intended for Moses alone. Moses himself was encouraged with the prediction that the elders would listen to him. He then had to go to the king of Egypt, together with the elders. The name "Hebrews" was used again since they were dealing with a non-Israelite (cf. commentary on 1:15). Through Moses as intermediary the Lord also encountered the elders. The request to be allowed to make a three-day journey into the desert to offer sacrifices to God was sincere. Why not? Could not the Lord test the king of Egypt first in the lesser thing before He presented him with the demand to release His people? The expression "three-day journey into the desert" does not give us any information about the location of Horeb since it was not specifically mentioned in this request.

3:19–20 *"But I know that the king of Egypt will not let you go unless a mighty hand compels him. So I will stretch out my hand and strike the Egyptians with all the wonders that I will perform among them. After that, he will let you go."*

The Lord told Moses before he even went to Egypt that Pharaoh would not grant the request "unless a mighty hand compels him" (KJV: "no, not by a mighty hand"). But even if it took a mighty hand to accomplish the purpose, the Lord would stretch out His hand and show the Egyptians the full extent of His power and strike them with His wonders and mighty acts. After this the king, whose refusal would bring such disasters on his land and his people (concept of solidarity, cf. 7:5) would let them go. These verses provide a strong proof of God's omniscience and of the fact that all things are predetermined in His counsel.

3:21–22 *"And I will make the Egyptians favorably disposed toward this people, so that when you leave you will not go empty-handed. Every woman is to ask her* *neighbor and any woman living in her house for articles of silver and gold and for clothing, which you will put on your sons and daughters. And so you will plunder the Egyptians.''*

The Lord even predicted that Israel would not depart empty-handed, as He had told Abraham (cf. Gen. 15:14). Note that the women are mentioned here: the weak would plunder (cf. Ps. 68:12 KJV) and the children would carry away the treasures from Egypt. The plundering of Egypt accentuates the fact that the king would declare war on the God of the Hebrews by his refusal; and the hand of the Lord would triumph so brilliantly that women and children would carry away the spoils. And it is also the Lord who would make the Egyptians favorably disposed toward Israel, so that the Egyptian women willingly acceded to the request of the women of Israel. This verse incidentally shows that the Israelites lived among the Egyptians and even under the same roof. Some give ''ask'' the meaning of ''ask to borrow,'' referring to the three-day celebration in the wilderness; it is then assumed that the Israelites gave the impression that they would return everything afterward. But this refers to the Exodus, to what happened after the refusal to let the people go for three days (v. 19). The Lord never ordered His people to be deceitful.

4:1 *Moses answered, "What if they do not believe me or listen to me and say, 'The LORD did not appear to you'?"*

But Moses continued his opposition. First, he brought up his own unworthiness (3:11), then that he would not be able to answer when asked for the name of the God of the fathers who appeared to him (3:13). God had defused these two arguments by reassuring Moses that His help would offset Moses' unworthiness, by promising Moses a future sign (3:12), and by giving Moses His name and its explanation, as well as by telling Moses what would happen until He triumphed over Egypt (3:14–22). Now Moses came up with something else. So he came to Israel with the name ''Jahweh''; they would not believe him or listen to him and think him a liar (the LXX adds ''What will I say to them?'' at the end of this verse, thus making it a request for information rather than an objection). Moses thus did not really feel like going to Egypt. The reason may be his experience of many years ago, but certainly also the fact that he had come to think more modestly about his own suitability.

4:2–5 *Then the LORD said to him, "What is that in your hand?"*
"A staff," he replied.
The LORD said, "Throw it on the ground."

Moses threw it on the ground and it became a snake, and he ran from it. Then the Lord said to him, "Reach out your hand and take it by the tail." So Moses reached out and took hold of the snake and it turned back into a staff in his hand. "This," said the Lord. "is so that they may believe that the Lord, the God of their fathers— the God of Abraham, the God of Isaac and the God of Jacob—has appeared to you."

The Lord now took a different approach. The promise of a future sign was ineffective, the revelation of His plan for the future was not capable of bringing Moses to obedience, and thus the Lord now gave him signs then and there, proofs of His power. The first sign was that Moses' staff (which according to an Arabian saga was taken from paradise by Adam, but according to Moses' own words was nothing more than an ordinary staff) was changed into a snake. Moses ran away from the snake, but when he picked it up after the Lord told him to do so it once again became a staff. This miracle served to convince Israel that the God of their fathers had indeed appeared to Moses. The Lord (flame of fire that does not consume the bush!) responded to Moses' objection and provided him with the means to remove the doubt of the Israelites that existed only in Moses' imagination. But it was not only this sign.

4:6–8 *Then the Lord said, "Put your hand inside your cloak." So Moses put his hand into his cloak, and when he took it out, it was leprous, like snow.*

"Now put it back into your cloak," he said. So Moses put his hand back into his cloak, and when he took it out, it was restored, like the rest of his flesh.

Then the Lord said, "If they do not believe you or pay attention to the first miraculous sign, they may believe the second."

The Lord instructed Moses to put his hand inside his cloak (KJV: "bosom"; the folds of the cloak above the waistband, which, since the cloak was drawn up, were ample to hide or carry objects), and (KJV: "and behold," indicating surprise) when he withdrew his hand it was leprous, with the snow-white eruption characteristic of the disease. But on the Lord's orders Moses put it once again inside his cloak and (KJV: "behold") it had been "restored, like the rest of his flesh." This was a still more impressive sign, and even more suited to bring any unbelievers among the Israelites to belief in Moses' claims.

4:9 *"But if they do not believe these two signs or listen to you, take some water from the Nile and pour it on the dry ground. The water you take from the river will become blood on the ground."*

But the Lord went even further. He said that, if these two signs had not led them to believe Moses, he should take water from the Nile and pour it on the dry ground, and the water would become blood. Moses performed these three signs before the Israelites in verses 30–31.

4:10 *Moses said to the LORD, "O Lord, I have never been eloquent, neither in the past nor since you have spoken to your servant. I am slow of speech and tongue."*

Moses realized that he was rather bold in continuing to resist God's assignment. That is why he began with an expression that means something like "with your permission," "pardon me." Moses addressed God here as Adonai ("Lord"), the master or owner, the powerful. It is interesting that during this appearance Moses addressed God twice (4:10, 13), but in neither case did he use the name God had revealed to him. Now that Moses could no longer use the argument of Israel's possible unbelief, he pointed to his own lack of eloquence. He was not a man of words, not a speaker; he never was and God's words to him had not changed this. He was "slow of speech and tongue," and did not find it easy to make speeches.

4:11–12 *The LORD said to him, "Who gave man his mouth? Who makes him deaf or dumb? Who gives him sight or makes him blind? Is it not I, the LORD? Now go; I will help you speak and will teach you what to say."*

This objection was really a reproach, but the Lord informed Moses that He was responsible for his lack of eloquence, since He gave Moses his mouth, but that He was also the one who had the power to make a person mute or deaf, seeing or blind. And after this reprimand He once again commanded Moses to go to Egypt with the promise that He would help Moses speak and would teach him what to say (cf. Matt. 10:19; Mark 13:11; Luke 21:14–15).

4:13 *But Moses said, "O Lord, please send someone else to do it."*

All of Moses' arguments to back up his refusal had been refuted. And now it turned out that Moses did not *want* to go. Reverently (as in v. 10, "with your permission") but firmly he said that the Lord had better send someone else, anyone else.

4:14 *Then the LORD's anger burned against Moses and he said, "What about your brother, Aaron the Levite? I know he can speak well. He is already on his way to meet you, and his heart will be glad when he sees you."*

No wonder that the Lord finally became angry, now that Moses refused without any reason at all. He made provision for Moses' last objection (even though He had already answered it) by promising Moses His direct help and instruction. The Lord had already provided: Aaron the Levite could speak well; he was already on his way to meet Moses and would be happy to see his brother. It is not clear why Aaron is called here "the Levite"; perhaps there were other Aarons.

4:15 *"You shall speak to him and put words in his mouth; I will help both of you speak and will teach you what to do."*

Moses could share the words of the Lord with him and the Lord would help both of them to speak and would teach them what to do.

4:16 *"He will speak to the people for you, and it will be as if he were your mouth and as if you were God to him."*

Aaron would stand before the people of Israel and speak the words of Moses to them. The relationship between Moses and Aaron would be that of deity and mouthpiece; Aaron would be Moses' prophet, his spokesman (cf. 7:1).

4:17 *"But take this staff in your hand so you can perform miraculous signs with it."*

This is the end of the dialogue. Moses was not to forget to take his staff with which he would perform the signs. And thus the appearance ended. The Lord had appointed Moses as redeemer of His people Israel.

7. Moses Leaves Midian for Egypt (4:18–23)

4:18 *Then Moses went back to Jethro his father-in-law and said to him, "Let me go back to my own people in Egypt to see if any of them are still alive."*
Jethro said, "Go, and I wish you well."

Moses immediately returned with his flock to his father-in-law, who here is called Jether, his third name beside Reuel (2:18) and Jethro (3:1); but it is apparently synonymous with Jethro, which is used in verse 18bff. Most versions do not make a distinction and translate "Jethro." Moses informed Jethro of his plan to visit his people in Egypt. The term "my own people" (KJV: "my brethren") may mean his family (Amram was probably still alive, see commentary on 6:18, 20), but it is logical to assume that Moses went to see "his people" in the sense of "Israel." Jethro appears to have been accommodating by nature (cf. also commentary on 2:18–19), since his only response to give Moses his best wishes for the planned journey, even though Moses was in Jethro's service (cf. 3:1).

4:19 *Now the LORD had said to Moses in Midian, "Go back to Egypt, for all the men who wanted to kill you are dead."*

The Lord once again appeared to Moses in Midian with a new word of encouragement. Moses no longer had to fear any consequences of the incident with the Egyptian; all those who wanted to kill him were dead (cf. 2:23; Matt. 2:20). The rest of the narrative also indicates that Moses' murder was forgotten in Egypt.

4:20 *So Moses took his wife and sons, put them on a donkey and started back to Egypt. And he took the staff of God in his hand.*

Moses' sons are mentioned here, although thus far only the birth of Gershom has been referred to (2:22). But Eliezer had also been born by this time (18:4). On the other hand, only one son is mentioned in verse 25. Moses walked, his wife and children rode on a donkey. His staff is also mentioned; the "staff of God," since God had made that staff an instrument for the performance of miracles (cf. vv. 2–15, 17) and consecrated it.

4:21–23 *The LORD said to Moses, "When you return to Egypt, see that you perform before Pharaoh all the wonders I have given you the power to do. But I will harden his heart so that he will not let the people go. Then say to Pharaoh, 'This is what the LORD says: Israel is my firstborn son, and I told you, "Let my son go, so he may worship me." But you refused to let him go; so I will kill your firstborn son.'"*

Before his departure Moses received a second revelation, which is more than merely a restatement of what the Lord had already said to him at Horeb (3:19–20). There Moses was told to perform the miracles only before Israel (cf. v. 5, 8–9), but now this is expanded: he also had to perform them before Pharaoh. The word for "wonders" is not the same as that used in 3:20; the word here is "something that draws attention." Again Pharaoh's refusal was predicted, this time not as something that God knew beforehand, but as something that He Himself brought about (cf. v. 21 with 3:19). This hardening (lit.: "I will make strong") of Pharaoh's heart is proof of God's absolute omnipotence (cf. Rom. 9:18). Moses was told this to keep him from becoming discouraged. If Pharaoh refused to let the people go, and thus showed his hardness of heart, it was ultimately caused by God Himself. But after Pharaoh's refusal Moses had to remind him (and this again focuses on Pharaoh's responsibility) that Israel was God's firstborn son (cf. Hos. 11:1; "firstborn son" indicates a special love: Israel was formed from Abraham and Sarah by a miracle, and God loves Israel as *His* people, cf. 3:7). The Lord had given Pharaoh the option to let that son worship Him (cf. 3:18), but he would have freely chosen to refuse when Moses said this to him. The Lord would therefore kill *his* firstborn son! The Lord already knew the outcome of the battle and predicted in Midian what later would be the tenth and final plague. He led everything toward that outcome by hardening Pharaoh's heart. Moses thus received a revelation of God's greatness before he left on his difficult mission to redeem Israel, a mission he did not mention to Jethro.

8. *The Lord Seeks to Kill Moses and Is Satisfied by the Circumcision of His Son* (4:24–26)

4:24–26 *At a lodging place on the way, the LORD met Moses and was about to kill him. But Zipporah took a flint knife, cut off her son's foreskin and touched Moses' feet with it. "Surely you are a bridegroom of blood to me," she said. So the LORD let him alone. (At that time she said "bridegroom of blood," referring to circumcision.)*

This is a curious story, characterized by the same mysterious element as Genesis 32:24–32. In a caravansery or lodging place between Midian and Egypt the Lord met Moses with the intention of killing him. How this happened, whether we have to think of a man who struggled with him and whom Moses and Zipporah recognized as the Lord (some translations read: "the angel of the Lord," and one manuscript of the LXX reads "an angel," indicating a visible appearance, cf. 3:2–3), or an acute illness, we do not know. It is possible that this is a remnant of a more extensive narrative. In any case, the reason for the Lord's attack on Moses, who was doing what God had told him to do, was immediately clear to Zipporah. Without anyone telling her to do so she took a sharp rock and used it as a knife to circumcise her son (cf. Josh. 5:2–3; stone knives were used in antiquity and increased the solemnity of the rite of circumcision). Usually the son is understood to be Gershom, but since verse 20 speaks of sons, and the word circumcision is used in the plural in verse 26, I believe that we must think here of the younger son, Eliezer (18:4). Gershom then had already been circumcised, but Moses, under pressure from Zipporah, had neglected to circumcise his second son. That this happened at Zipporah's instigation follows in my opinion from her action and from her words later. The touching of Moses' feet with the foreskin of her son was symbolic of the sacrifice that her marriage to Moses had required of her. And the fact that she called Moses "bridegroom of blood" shows that she felt that circumcision was cruel to her child, and yet this was the only way for her to keep Moses as her husband. The fact that the Lord "let him alone" (v. 26) shows that His anger was caused by the fact that Moses' son had not been circumcised. Zipporah then repeated that Moses was her bridegroom through the circumcision of her sons and had become her bridegroom once again since his life was spared, but not without the shedding of blood. Some tribes, especially in Arabia, had the custom of circumcising their young men prior to marriage. Moses, who was circumcised as a child, had now, according to Zipporah, become her bridegroom after and because of circumcision, but the circumcision was that of her son. The word used here for "bridegroom" is related to an Arabic word meaning "to circumcise." Although I do not believe that Moses' marriage was originally matriarchal in nature (i.e., the woman considered the children to belong to her tribe since she continued living with her relatives and her husband moved in with her) and underwent a change here, it is true that during his journey to Egypt Moses emerged fully as the head of his household.

This view gives the story the purpose of showing that Moses, before he could act as a leader and redeemer of Israel, was himself called to uphold the demands of the Lord as the God of the covenant. There had to be nothing that could be said against Moses' family: he had to obediently fulfill God's requirement of circumcision. He who brought the message of the covenant had to be obedient himself to that covenant in his own household. It also shows that the Lord ruled over Moses and his children, and that Zipporah's negative influence was counteracted. Later Paul said that the unbelieving woman is sanctified through her believing husband, which finds expression in the fact that the children are sanctified (cf. Gen. 17:9–14; 1 Cor. 7:14). The fact that one of Moses' sons (and thus probably the younger one) was uncircumcised was a sign of decline and apostasy and a transgression in the eyes of God (cf. also Gen. 17:14).[6]

9. *Moses and Aaron Meet; They Appear before the Elders of Israel With Positive Results* (4:27–31)

These verses describe the fulfillment of the Lord's promise in verses 14–16: the meeting between Moses and Aaron and their departure for

---

[6]The LXX differs from the Hebrew text in verses 25–26. Verse 26 is omitted entirely in the Vatican Codex, while Zipporah's statement reads as follows: "He ordained the blood of the circumcision of my son." This reading may be based on a free rendering of "Surely you are a bridegroom of blood to me" (v. 25) and "bridegroom of blood" (v. 26).

Egypt, where Aaron became Moses' spokesman before the Israelites, who responded positively.

Some exegetes assume that Moses sent Zipporah and the children back to Jethro after the circumcision of Eliezer, in order to establish agreement with 18:1ff.; this is probably correct.

4:27, 28 *The LORD said to Aaron, "Go into the desert to meet Moses." So he met Moses at the mountain of God and kissed him. Then Moses told Aaron everything the LORD had sent him to say, and also about all the miraculous signs he had commanded him to perform.*

The Lord told Aaron, who was probably in Egypt, to go and meet Moses in the desert. He must thus have left the country secretly. Note that Aaron, who immediately obeyed God's command, met Moses at the mountain of God (see commentary on 3:1), that is, exactly where the Lord had promised they would meet. Aaron greeted Moses with a kiss, which is still an oriental custom. Moses thoroughly informed Aaron (see v. 15a) and in the following verses Aaron took the lead.

4:29–31 *Moses and Aaron brought together all the elders of the Israelites, and Aaron told them everything the LORD had said to Moses. He also performed the signs before the people, and they believed. And when they heard that the LORD was concerned about them and had seen their misery, they bowed down and worshiped.*

Moses and Aaron took the lawful course of action and on their arrival in Egypt first called together the elders of Israel (see 3:16). Aaron, in accordance with verse 16, was the spokesman and told the elders everything the Lord had said to Moses; he also performed the signs before the elders and the people (vv. 1–9). It is extremely encouraging, especially for Moses, that the Lord's prediction (vv. 8–9) came true and that the people believed Moses' and Aaron's claims. They received the message with great reverence: the Lord had taken notice (3:16) and had seen their misery (3:17). They fell on their knees and bowed to the ground.

10. *Pharaoh Refuses Moses' and Aaron's Request to Let the People Go and Increases the Oppression* (5:1–18)

In the preceding section the Lord's prediction concerning their favorable reception by Israel was fulfilled. Now it appears that Pharaoh's attitude was also in agreement with what the Lord had said (see 3:18–19; 4:21–23). For the first time since the kings of Egypt had carried out God's plan without realizing it, and had experienced His opposition (ch. 1–4), the struggle came out into the open and the Lord came directly to Pharaoh with a message. But Pharaoh showed himself unwilling to grant even the least request, and made the situation even more difficult for the Israelites.

5:1 *Afterward Moses and Aaron went to Pharaoh and said, "This is what the* LORD, *the God of Israel, says: 'Let my people go, so that they may hold a festival to me in the desert.'"*

The elders were to go with Moses to Pharaoh (3:18), but this is not mentioned here. Aaron took their place (4:14–16) and was probably again the spokesman (4:16, 29–31). The Pharaoh is Amenhotep II (see commentary on 2:23). Concerning the request to let the people go so that they could hold a festival in the desert, see commentary on 3:18. Note that the Lord here is referred to as "the God of Israel" and not "the God of the Hebrews," even though the request was to Pharaoh (see commentary on 1:15 and 3:18; cf. also 4:22).

5:2 *Pharaoh said, "Who is the* LORD, *that I should obey him and let Israel go? I do not know the* LORD *and I will not let Israel go."*

Pharaoh's answer was very arrogant. Since he had never heard of the Lord, the god Jahweh of Israel, he refused the (in the context of that time) reasonable request to let Israel go. It is unmistakable that after many years of oppression the arrogance had to cover up the still existing fear of Israel (see 1:9–10, 12), while at the same time the Egyptians had found it useful to have a slave people, so that they did not want to lose them.

5:3 *Then they said, "The God of the Hebrews has met with us. Now let us take a three-day journey into the desert to offer sacrifices to the* LORD *our God, or he may strike us with plagues or with the sword."*

See 3:18. In order to persuade Pharaoh Moses and Aaron added that the Lord might "strike us with plagues or with the sword" if they did not make this journey to bring sacrifices. They tried to make Pharaoh see the request from the standpoint of "the Hebrews" (see 1:15; 3:18).

5:4, 5 *But the king of Egypt said, "Moses and Aaron, why are you taking the people away from their labor? Get back to your work!" Then Pharaoh said, "Look, the people of the land are now numerous, and you are stopping them from working."*

But Pharaoh asked Moses and Aaron why they tempted the people to neglect their work and told them to go back to work themselves (see 1:11; 2:11). Pharaoh was poorly informed; he did not know that Moses and

Aaron were not subject to forced labor. He remarked that the "people of the land" were already numerous. The "people of the land" were either the class of idlers between the higher and lower classes of Egypt, or the rabble, the riff-raff, that lived in the countryside. The latter is probably the intended meaning in this context, especially since verse 4 does not equate them with idlers. Pharaoh said: there is already much riff-raff that causes me concern. And now you want to take them away from their work, turn them into idlers, by letting them interrupt their forced labor and giving them rest, either by causing them to slack off in their work while they are waiting for the outcome of your request, or by giving them three days' vacation, which could turn out to be a dangerous experiment.

For Pharaoh's line of thought in verse 5, cf. 1:9–10. The old fear reasserted itself. Pharaoh said that he was surprised that Moses and Aaron wanted to make the rabble a still more serious danger for him and Egypt. "The people . . . are now numerous": therein lay an indirect admission of the failure of the plan of the Pharaoh of chapter 1, which was implemented by him and his successors.

5:6–9 *That same day Pharaoh gave this order to the slave drivers and foremen in charge of the people: "You are no longer to supply the people with straw for making bricks; let them go and gather their own straw. But require them to make the same number of bricks as before; don't reduce the quota. They are lazy; that is why they are crying out, "Let us go and sacrifice to our God.' Make the work harder for the men so that they keep working and pay no attention to lies."*

The old fear and distrust, rekindled by the action and message on behalf of Israel's God, finds expression in what Pharaoh did next. He summoned two groups of people: first the slave drivers of the Israelites (cf. 3:7), who were Egyptians. The slave drivers were probably the same officials as the slave masters in 1:11. An example of their behavior follows in verse 13 (see also 2:11). The second group were the foremen. The term literally means "writer," which may indicate that their main function was to keep records of the work performed. The "slave drivers" then probably dealt with these foremen, rather than directly with the slaves. They were officials, selected from among the Israelites themselves and appointed by the slave drivers to keep a record of the work performed by their fellow Israelites. According to verse 14 the foremen were responsible to the slave drivers for the work done by the laborers.

When these Egyptians and Israelites stood before Pharaoh (according to v. 10 they went out from Pharaoh) he issued an order that would not have been unworthy of the Pharaoh who ordered all newborn males to be drowned (1:22). Until now the Egyptians provided the chopped straw used in the making of bricks (cf. 1:14; the straw made the bricks made of Nile clay firmer). But no more! The Israelites now had to somehow find a way to gather the straw themselves, which was a time-consuming job. But— and this is the difficult part—the daily quota of bricks would remain the same, it "will not be reduced at all," since the Israelites were lazy and apparently had too much time on their hands, so that they could think about holding a festival for their god (cf. also v. 17). Murals have been found from the time of Thutmose III, the father of Amenhotep II, depicting the building of the temple of Amon at Thebes, which show laborers at work. The inscription reads: "The overseer says: the staff is in my hand, do not be lazy" (cf. v. 14; Isa. 10:24). The best remedy was to increase the work load (cf. 1:14), so that they would be too busy to pay attention to lies, which was what Pharaoh called the words of Moses and Aaron, whose reliability he questioned: the words of the Lord to His people, His special revelation!

5:10–14 *Then the slave drivers and the foremen went out and said to the people, "This is what Pharaoh says: 'I will not give you any more straw. Go and get your own straw wherever you can find it, but your work will not be reduced at all.'" So the people scattered all over Egypt to gather stubble to use for straw. The slave drivers kept pressing them, saying, "Complete the work required of you for each day, just as when you had straw." The Israelite foremen appointed by Pharaoh's slave drivers were beaten and were asked, "Why haven't you met your quota of bricks yesterday or today, as before?"*

The foremen apparently did not have the courage to point out how unreasonable this measure was. They left the palace and relayed Pharaoh's message to the people of Israel (v. 10–11). They had to gather their own straw wherever they could find it and as a result the people swarmed all over Egypt to gather the threshed-out stalks to chop them up for use as straw. An involved process! And it now appeared that the slave drivers welcomed Pharaoh's order. They pressed the people, they drove and hurried them and reminded them of the regulation that each day's quota had to be filled, the same as before. "When you had straw" (KJV: "when there was straw") can only mean here "As when straw was provided" as the LXX and the Samaritan Pentateuch read (v. 13). The foremen took the brunt of it and were beaten by the slave drivers when they did not meet their quota; not that the foremen had to make bricks themselves, but they were responsible for the production.

5:15–18 *Then the Israelite foremen went and appealed to Pharaoh: "Why have you treated your servants this way? Your servants are given no straw, yet we are*

told, 'Make bricks!' Your servants are being beaten, but the fault is with your own
people.''

Pharaoh said, "Lazy, that's what you are–lazy! That is why you keep saying,
'Let us go and sacrifice to the Lord,' Now get to work. You will not be given any
straw, yet you must produce your full quota of bricks.''

It must have been very bad indeed, for the Israelite foremen dared to
request an audience with Pharaoh to complain about the treatment of those
who were his slaves. They listed their grievances. The end of verse 16
presents a problem. Some manuscripts (e.g., the LXX) read with a small
change in the text "and you have done wrong against your people" or
"will you do wrong against your people?" The Hebrew text as we have it
is best translated "and *your* people are at fault," in this case the Egyptian
slave drivers. Pharaoh was not blamed, but was called upon as arbiter,
which made more sense. But Pharaoh had not changed his mind and again
reproached the foremen (and thus the Israelites) for their laziness (see also
v. 8), which led to their request to be allowed to go and sacrifice to the
Lord. He sent the foremen away with the order to go to work, and to meet
their full quota without being given any straw.

11. *The Lord Encourages Moses; Israel Is Told of the Future Theocracy* (5:19–6:9)

This section contains another revelation from the Lord to encourage
Moses. Although Pharaoh's refusal had been foretold by the Lord (see
introductory note on previous section), Moses seems not to have been
prepared for the intensification of the oppression that accompanied the
refusal. Important in this new revelation was God's statement that He was
not known to the patriarchs by the name Jahweh or Lord (6:1–2). It was
disappointing that, although this message contained such a rich revelation
for the Israelites (6:6–8), they no longer listened to Moses (6:9). The battle
between the Lord and Pharaoh seemed hopeless for the Lord.

5:19–21 *The Israelite foremen realized they were in trouble when they were told,
"You are not to reduce the number of bricks required of you for each day." When
they left Pharaoh, they found Moses and Aaron waiting to meet them, and they
said, "May the Lord look upon you and judge you! You have made us a stench to
Pharaoh and his servants and have put a sword in their hand to kill us."*

The perplexed foremen (see commentary on 5:6–9) now realized that
they were in a bad position. Some versions read "since they had to say"
(RSV: "when they said"), rather than "when they were told" (KJV: "after it
was said"), probably on the basis of the LXX, indicating that their plight

consisted in the fact that they had to relay Pharaoh's message to the Israelites; "when they were told" is probably to be preferred. Concerning the "number of bricks required each day" see commentary on 5:8, 13, 18; concerning "reduce" see commentary on 5:8, 11.

When they left the palace they encountered Moses and Aaron (the word for "found" is the same as "strike" in 5:3b), who were waiting for them with understandable curiosity to see what the outcome of the audience would be; the foremen probably went to Pharaoh after consulting with Moses and Aaron and the elders. The foremen were not very friendly toward Moses and Aaron (understandably so, yet reflecting a lack of faith in God's promise, 4:30) whom they suddenly saw as responsible for this new misery. They called on the Lord to be judge and avenger, since Moses and Aaron had made the Israelites "a stench" (cf. Gen. 34:30), i.e., had given them a bad name before Pharaoh and his officials and slave drivers, so that their putative laziness could now be turned into an excuse to annihilate Israel.

5:22–23 *Moses returned to the Lord and said, "O Lord, why have you brought trouble upon this people? Is this why you sent me? Ever since I went to Pharaoh to speak in your name, he has brought trouble upon this people, and you have not rescued your people at all."*

Moses and Aaron seem to have fled from the angry group in consternation. Note that Aaron is not mentioned. Moses now sought the Lord (see also commentary on 6:28–29) with a complaint that began with a two-part question. In the first place, why had the Lord ("Adonai," i.e., "lord, master, owner," cf. commentary on 3:15) brought trouble on His people? The unreasonable aspect here is that Pharaoh's personal responsibility was totally excluded, the reasonable aspect that Moses saw the Lord as the first cause of the increased oppression.

The second question was why the Lord had sent him. The facts (v. 23a) had justified Moses' refusal after all (3:11; 4:10, 13), and even the fear he expressed in 4:1 (cf. 5:19–21). Furthermore, Moses reproached the Lord that He had not "rescued" His people at all (cf. 3:8). Moses was disheartened by the first disappointment and ignored what the Lord had already told him in 3:19–20 and 4:21, and would now tell him again.

6:1 *Then the Lord said to Moses, "Now you will see what I will do to Pharaoh: Because of my mighty hand he will let them go; because of my mighty hand he will drive them out of his country."*

The Lord was not angry. His answer contained a new element: not only would Pharaoh let the people go (cf. 3:20; 4:21, 23; 5:1–2) because of the

Lord's mighty hand (cf. 3:19), but he would even drive them out of his country (cf. 11:1; 12:33, 39).

6:2-3 *God also said to Moses, "I am the LORD. I appeared to Abraham, to Isaac and to Jacob as God Almighty, but by my name the LORD I did not make myself known to them."*

After a brief pause the Lord continued His revelation to Moses in answer to his complaint (5:22-23). At least this is the impression we get from the text which appears to be a unit since Moses, after fleeing from the foremen, received a message for them and the Israelites at the end of this revelation (vv. 6-8). Many contemporary exegetes see in 6:2ff. a section from a different source, which parallels 3:1ff., and thus gives a different account of Moses' calling. But apart from the fact that this splitting up of the text into different sources makes it impossible to determine the truth, it also contradicts the logical unity of the text as it stands.

God ("Elohim") said to Moses: "I am the LORD" (Jahweh, cf. 3:14; "He is," "the One who is"). Moses and his fellow Israelites and contemporaries should appreciate the fact that they had heard that name and could use it. They were privileged in this above Abraham, Isaac, and Jacob, to whom the Lord appeared as God Almighty (El Shaddai), but who did not know His name Jahweh. El Shaddai consists of "El" (God), which seems to be derived from a root meaning "to be strong," and "Shaddai," of which many interpretations are given, but which seems to correspond most closely to our "Almighty."

Note that the Lord here said that Abraham, Isaac, and Jacob did not know the name Jahweh. But in the history of these patriarchs the name Jahweh occurs both in the narrative and in God's words to them and vice versa, although God does reveal Himself as El Shaddai to Abraham (Gen. 17:1) and to Jacob (Gen. 35:11).[7]

---

[7]Examples of the use of the name "Jahweh" in the history of the patriarchs are:

(a) in the narrative text: Genesis 12:1, 4, 7, 17; 13:10, 13, 14;15:1, 4, 6, 18; 16:7, 9, 10, 11, 13; 17:1; 18:1, 13, 17, 20, 22, 26, 33; 19:16, 24, 27; 20:18; 21:1; 22:1, 15; 24:1, 21, 26, 52; 25:21, 22, 23; 26:2, 12, 24; 28:13; 29:31; 21:3; 38:7, 10; 39:2, 3, 5, 21, 23. In 12:8 and 13:4 Abram calls on the name of the Lord; in 26:25 Isaac calls on the name of the Lord.

(b) in the words of the patriarchs and others to God and vice versa, and in conversations: Genesis 15:2 (Abram to God), 15:7 (God to Abram; but the LXX, among others, has "God" rather than "Jahweh"); 15:8 (Abram to God); 16:2 (Sarai to Abram); 16:5 (Sarai to Abram); 18:14 (God to Abraham); 18:19 (God Himself); 19:13 (angels to Lot); 19:14 (Lot to his sons-in-law); 22:14 (Abraham); 22:16 (the Angel of the Lord to Abraham); 24:3, 7 (Abraham to his servant, see also 24:40); 24:12 (Abraham's servant to God); 24:27 (Abraham's servant to Rebekah); 24:31 (Laban to Abraham's servant); 24:35, 40, 42, 44, 48 (Abraham's servant to Laban and Bethuel); 24:50-51 (Laban and Bethuel to Abraham's servant); 24:56 (Abra-

The end of 6:3 reads literally: "but by my name Jahweh I was not known to them" (KJV) or "I did not make myself known to them" (NIV).

How can we reconcile this statement with the facts in Genesis, especially since the people in Genesis frequently used the name Jahweh? Some have taken refuge in the assumption that the occurrence of the name Jahweh before Exodus 6 must be attributed to the various authors and thus does not reflect actual use of the name. But that is contrary to the belief in the reliability of the Bible, and also lacks proof.

We must therefore accept both the statement in verse 3 and the facts mentioned above, and we can only see verse 3 in the light of those facts. The Lord says that Abraham, Isaac, and Jacob did not know Him by the name "Jahweh." What did they know about that name? They no more realized the rich meaning of that name than did Laban, or Bethuel, or a Mesopotamian. He was known to them as God Almighty, not as Jahweh, the One who is. Until this time the name Jahweh was "dead capital," since the patriarchs experienced more of God's omnipotence than of His constancy throughout the centuries with regard to Israel (cf. commentary on 3:13–15). Note that in Isaac's blessing of Jacob the name God (Elohim) is used (Gen. 27:28). In this connection see Genesis 28:3, "May God Almighty bless you"; 32:29, where God evades Jacob's question as to His name and does not yet give the rich explanation of the name Jahweh that he gives in Exodus 3; 33:20, where Jacob confines himself to the expression "the God of Israel"; 43:14, where Jacob in a tense situation says: "and may God Almighty grant you mercy before the man"; chapter 45, where Joseph makes himself known to his brothers, and uses the name God (Elohim) according to the author; 46:2–4, where God calls Himself God (El and Elohim) in His last appearance to Jacob. The possibility exists that a redactor was at work here, but nevertheless, the name Jahweh in its full meaning was not used. In Genesis 48:3 Jacob reminded Joseph of the appearance of God Almighty (see Gen. 35:11); cf. also the blessing of Manasseh and Ephraim (Gen. 48:14–22).

Our explanation agrees essentially with the translation of the LXX "and my name LORD I did not make known to them," which is also the translation adopted in the NIV and RSV. The word for "make known" can also mean "explain, clarify." See Ezekiel 20:4 and 22:2 where "make known" means "confront," viz. the known sins of the fathers.

---

ham's servant to Laban and Bethuel); 26:22 (Isaac); 26:28–29 (Philistines to Isaac); 27:7 (Isaac to Esau, Rebekah to Jacob); 27:20 (Jacob to Isaac); 27:27 (Isaac to Jacob); 28:13 (God to Jacob, although the reading "Jahweh" here is uncertain); (28:16 (Jacob); 28:21 (Jacob); 29:32, 33, 35 (Leah); 30:24 (Rachel); 30:37 (Laban to Jacob); 32:9 (Jacob to God).

The name Jahweh is also repeatedly used in Genesis 1–11.

Another explanation stresses the fact that God said here to Moses "I am the LORD" (v. 2), after the fathers had used that name without the Lord having revealed Himself to them as such. The Lord then confirmed here this use of the fathers and made Himself known for the first time as Lord or Jahweh. Genesis 15:7 and 28:13 are then explained as prolepsis (i.e., a word is used that should not be used until later) and/or the textual uncertainty of those verses is pointed out.

Although Genesis 18:14 does not present a definite declaration beginning with "I am . . . ," it still stands in the way of the idea that the fathers used the name Jahweh on their own responsibility.

6:4–5 *"I also established my covenant with them to give them the land of Canaan, where they lived as aliens. Moreover, I have heard the groaning of the Israelites, whom the Egyptians are enslaving, and I have remembered my covenant."*

After the Lord had pointed out to Moses the advantage the Israelites had over the patriarchs, He reminded him again of the covenant with the patriarchs and of the fact that He had remembered the covenant (cf. Ps. 105:12; Ps. 105:8–13 is based on Exod. 6:4–5). Concerning "alien" (gēr), see commentary on 2:21–22. Concerning verse 4 see also commentary on 2:24 and 3:17. Concerning verse 6: "groaning" also occurs in 2:24; "enslaving," cf. 1:13; "have remembered my covenant," cf. 2:24; "I" in verse 5 is emphatic: *"I"*, who have established the covenant (v. 4).

6:6–8 *"Therefore, say to the Israelites: 'I am the LORD and I will bring you out from under the yoke of the Egyptians. I will free you from being slaves to them and will redeem you with an outstretched arm and with mighty acts of judgment. I will take you as my own people, and I will be your God. Then you will know that I am the LORD your God, who brought you out from under the yoke of the Egyptians. And I will bring you to the land I swore with uplifted hand to give to Abraham, to Isaac and to Jacob. I will give it to you as a possession. I am the LORD.'"*

After the initial disappointment of the increased oppression Moses again had to address Israel on the Lord's behalf, because God established and remembered His covenant with the patriarchs. First, he had to remind Israel of the fact that God was the Lord (Jahweh), and then that He would redeem them (cf. 3:15–17). That this redemption would be accomplished only "with an outstretched arm" (cf. the synonymous expression "by a mighty hand," 3:19; 5:24) and mighty acts of judgment indicates that Pharaoh and the Egyptians would continue to deserve the Lord's punishment by their oppression of Israel; but Israel would be redeemed from the yoke of the Egyptians.

The third announcement Moses had to make on the Lord's behalf was the most important one. He would adopt Israel to be His own people and He would be their God; this would be preceded by the blessing of experiencing what it meant to have the Lord as their God: they would be brought out from under the yoke of the Egyptians (see v. 6; for the entire verse, see 19:6). Here we come to the essential meaning of the entire Book of Exodus, which gives us both the Exodus and the making of the covenant at Sinai: the Lord adopted the descendants of the patriarchs as His people and promised them that He would be their God; in other words, the establishment of the theocracy on earth (cf. Introduction, p. 4). Added to the explanation of the name Jahweh (ch. 3) is this: from now on the Lord would not only look on the Israelites as individuals, but would establish a relationship with Israel as a people; the Almighty, the Lord became *king* and the proclamation of that kingship took place at Sinai after the Exodus (ch. 19ff.).

After the adoption the Lord would bring them to the land that He "swore with uplifted hand" (cf. Gen. 22:16; 24:7; 26:3; 60:24; Ps. 105:8–9) to give to Abraham, Isaac, and Jacob, and (the fourth thing Moses had to tell them) He would give it to them as an inheritance and possession: "I am the Lord!" The name and what it expressed were thus again emphatically brought to mind. Concerning the giving of the land, see commentary on verse 4.

6:9 *Moses reported this to the Israelites, but they did not listen to him because of their discouragement and cruel bondage.*

Moses relayed this message to Israel. We might expect that this tremendous message would encourage Israel, but instead they refused to listen to Moses "because of their discouragement" (KJV: "anguish of spirit"; RSV: "broken spirit"; lit.: "shortness of spirit"). I prefer to translate "because of their impatience" (cf. Prov. 14:29 where "short of spirit" is contrasted with "patient"; Eccl. 7:8, where "long of spirit" means "patient"; Job 21:4; Mic. 2:7, KJV: "is the spirit of the Lord straitened," RSV: "is the Spirit of the Lord impatient."). The people had become impatient, first with all those promises that did not help, and also because of their heavy labor (cf. 1:14).

12. *Moses and Aaron Are Sent Again to the Israelites and Pharaoh* (6:10–13)

6:10–11 *Then the Lord said to Moses, "Go, tell Pharaoh king of Egypt to let the Israelites go out of his country."*

Once again the Lord intervened to keep Moses from becoming discouraged. He sent him back to Pharaoh, called here the "king of Egypt," to underline the contrast with the "God of Israel" in whose name Moses went.

6:12 *But Moses said to the LORD, "If the Israelites will not listen to me, why would Pharaoh listen to me, since I speak with faltering lips?"*

Moses had two objections (cf. 4:10–12, which is not a doublet of 6:12, however). The first one is very understandable: since the Israelites would not listen to him (v. 8), why would Pharaoh? The second objection is the same as in 4:10 (cf. commentary on 4:10 and 6:30): "I speak with faltering lips" (lit.: "I am of uncircumcised lips"). His lips were closed, they opened with difficulty (cf. the expression "uncircumcised—i.e, closed —of heart," Lev. 26:41; Jer. 9:26; Ezek. 44:7, 9; and "uncircumcised of ear," Jer. 6:10).

6:13 *Now the LORD spoke to Moses and Aaron about the Israelites and Pharaoh king of Egypt, and he commanded them to bring the Israelites out of Egypt.*

The Lord seemed to have answered Moses' objections. Aaron was mentioned again and was sent together with Moses, since Moses once again had claimed his own inadequacy (4:13–16; cf. also commentary on 7:1–5).[8]

13. *Genealogy of Reuben, Simeon, and Levi* (6:14–27)

The author inserts the genealogy of Reuben, Simeon, and Levi because Moses and Aaron were from the tribe of Levi; and for that reason Reuben and Simeon are mentioned only briefly.

6:14 *These were the heads of their families:*
The sons of Reuben the firstborn son of Israel were Hanoch and Pallu, Hezron and Carmi. These were the clans of Reuben.

See Genesis 46:9; Numbers 26:5–6; 1 Chronicles 5:3. "Families" means literally "houses of their fathers." "Their" may refer to Moses and Aaron, in which case it was written by the author of this chapter, but may also have been copied from a list that originally had a different context.

---

[8]The Hebrew reads: "And the LORD spoke to Moses and Aaron and gave them a charge to the people of Israel and to Pharaoh . . ." (cf. KJV); the words "to the people of Israel" are omitted in the LXX but must be considered authentic. They summarize again Moses' and Aaron's mission, which was both to their own people and to Pharaoh. See verses 26–27.

The tribes consisted of clans and these in turn of families with a common ancestor, and these again of households or "men" (with their households). See Joshua 7:14, 16–18.

6:15 *The sons of Simeon were Jemuel, Jamin, Ohad, Jakin, Zohar and Shaul the son of a Canaanite woman. These were the clans of Simeon.*

See Genesis 46:10; Numbers 26:12–13; 1 Chronicles 4:24. The LXX calls Saul the "son of the Phoenician woman." Concerning the Canaanites see commentary on 3:7–10.[9]

6:16 *These were the names of the sons of Levi according to their records: Gershon, Kohath and Merari. Levi lived 137 years.*

See Genesis 46:11; Numbers 3:17; 26:57; 1 Chronicles 6:11, 16; 23:6.

6:17 *The sons of Gershon, by clans, were Libni and Shimei.*

See Numbers 3:18; 1 Chronicles 6:17; 23:7.

6:18 *The sons of Kohath were Amram, Izhar, Hebron and Uzziel. Kohath lived 133 years.*

See Numbers 3:19; 1 Chronicles 6:18; 23:12. According to the LXX Kohath lived 130 years. According to verse 20 Amram was the father of Aaron and Moses, and according to verse 16 and this verse the son of Kohath, and therefore the grandson of Levi. But the Levites were in Egypt for 430 years (12:40). This list indicates that there were four generations during that period: Levi, Kohath, Amram, and Aaron and Moses. Moses was 80 and Aaron 83 years old when they appeared before Pharaoh (7:7), which means that they were born to Amram 80 and 83 years respectively before the Exodus. If we assume that Amram was about 40 at the time, then he was born 123 years before the Exodus. If we further assume that Amram was born when Kohath was 30 years old, then Kohath was born approximately 153 years before the Exodus, which is impossible since Kohath, the son of Levi, was born in Canaan (Gen. 46:11), before Jacob

---

[9]The names in this verse correspond to those in Genesis 46:10. Numbers 26:12–13 and 1 Chronicles 4:24 read "Nemuel" instead of "Jemuel" and "Zerah" instead of "Zohar." These discrepancies are possibly the result of different ways of writing the same name (see van Gelderen on 1 Kings 1:3 in this commentary series on the pronunciation "l" instead of "n"). Zohar and Zerah may also be different forms of the same name. Ohad is mentioned only in Genesis 46:10 and here; it is likely that his name does not belong in the text.

and his sons came to Egypt. Amram, the father of Aaron and Moses was thus a descendant, but not the son of Kohath. Kohath did have a son named Amram (Num. 3:27-28), so that the Amram of verse 18 and the Amram of verse 20 were two different people.[10]

It occurs often that the genealogies skip a few generations (cf. Ruth 4:18-22; Matt. 1). In Matthew 1 the author's purpose was to present three times fourteen generations, and thus, e.g., in verse 8 Ahaziah, Joash, and Amaziah are omitted. And in the same way we have here: Levi, Kohath, Amram (v. 18), Amram (v. 20), Aaron and Moses. In all probability clarity was sacrificed for the sake of arriving at four generations on the basis of Genesis 15:16. This view is supported by what we know about Aaron's wife Elisheba (see commentary on vv. 23-25).

6:19 *The sons of Merari were Mahli and Mushi. These were the clans of Levi according to their records.*

See Numbers 3:20; 1 Chronicles 6:19; 23:21.

6:20 *Amram married his father's sister Jochebed, who bore him Aaron and Moses. Amram lived 137 years.*

See Exodus 2:1ff.; Numbers 26:59 (the addition "and Miriam his sister" after Moses in some manuscripts and versions probably stems from this verse). "His father's sister," i.e., his aunt. If his father was Kohath, Jochebed would have been the daughter of Levi, which is impossible and is not meant in Numbers 26:59 (KJV; cf. NIV margin), which mentions Levi as the patriarch rather than the father. The NIV thus correctly paraphrases "born to the Levites." In Leviticus 18:12 and 20:19 the marriage between a man and his father's sister was forbidden, but this regulation did not yet exist when Amram married Jochebed. The LXX reads "a daughter of the brother of his father," probably in view of the references in Leviticus.

---

[10]Lange cites Thiele, who follows a different line of reasoning to arrive at the same conclusion: "According to Num. 3:27f., the Kohathites were divided (at the time of Moses) into the four branches: Amramites, Izharites, Hebronites, and Uzzielites; these together constituted 8,600 men and boys (women and girls not being reckoned). Of these the Amramites would include about one fourth, or 2,150. Moses himself, according to Exod. 18:3-4, had only two sons. If, therefore, Amram, the son of Kohath, the ancestor of the Amramites, were identical with Amram, the father of Moses, then Moses must have had 2,147 brothers and brothers' sons (the brothers' daughters, the sisters and sisters' children not being reckoned). But this being quite an impossible supposition, it must be conceded that it is demonstrated that Amram the son of Kohath is not Moses' father, but that between the former and his descendant of the same name an indefinitely long list of generations has fallen out" (J. P. Lange, *Exodus*, Zondervan, 1960, p. 18). (tr.)

6:23–25 *Aaron married Elisheba, daughter of Amminadab and sister of Hahshon, and she bore him Nadab and Abihu, Eleasar and Ithamar.*

The sons of Korah were Assir, Alkanah and Abiasaph. These were the Korahite clans.

Eleasar son of Aaron married one of the daughters of Putiel, and she bore him Phinehas.

These were the heads of the Levite families, clan by clan.

See Numbers 3:2; 26:60; 1 Chronicles 6:3, 24:1. Note that the names of Moses' wife and children are omitted. This indicates that the author who wrote this also wrote 2:21–22 where these names were already given. Aaron's family had not yet been mentioned. Furthermore, this genealogy gives the names of the heads of priestly clans and families, and Moses was not a priest. Aaron's wife was from the tribe of Judah (cf. Num. 1:7; 2:3; 7:12, 17; 10:14). Elisheba belonged to the sixth generation after Jacob (cf. Ruth 4:20; 1 Chronicles 2:4–10), and Aaron, according to this list, to the fourth generation (but see commentary on v. 18). For Nadab and Abihu see Leviticus 10:1–2. Eleazar succeeded Aaron as high priest, Phinehas (whose name seems to be of Egyptian origin and means "black man") in turn succeeded Eleazar (cf. Num. 20:26; Deut. 10:6; Judg. 20:28).

6:26–27 *It was this same Aaron and Moses to whom the LORD said, "Bring the Israelites out of Egypt by their divisions." They were the ones who spoke to Pharaoh king of Egypt about bringing the Israelites out of Egypt. It was the same Moses and Aaron.*

These verses indicate that Moses and Aaron were the reason for including this genealogy. In verse 26 Aaron is mentioned first, in verse 27 Moses, since this verse leads back to the story of the Exodus, in which Moses plays the prominent role. "Their divisions," cf. also 7:4 (KJV: "hosts"; note the military allusion). Verse 26 refers back to verse 13 and resumes the narrative.

14. *Moses and Aaron Are Sent Again to Pharaoh. Their First Sign: Aaron's Staff Turned into a Large Snake* (6:28–7:13)

The last three verses of chapter 6 and the first five verses of chapter 7 restate and elaborate on 6:10–13. The narrative then continues with the first miracle before Pharaoh (7:6–13). This miracle differs from those that follow in that it does not have the character of a plague.

6:28–29 *Now when the* Lord *spoke to Moses in Egypt, he said to him, "I am the* Lord. *Tell Pharaoh king of Egypt everything I tell you."*

These verses refer back to verses 10–11. "In Egypt" argues against the idea that Moses returned to Horeb (see 5:22). "I am the Lord" (cf. v. 2). "Everything I tell you" can be reduced to the essential statement in verse 11.

6:30 *But Moses said to the* Lord, *"Since I speak with faltering lips, why would Pharaoh listen to me?"*

This verse is a partial restatement of verse 12 (see commentary on that verse).

7:1–5 *Then the* Lord *said to Moses, "See, I have made you like God to Pharaoh, and your brother Aaron will be your prophet. You are to say everything I command you, and your brother Aaron is to tell Pharaoh to let the Israelites go out of his country. But I will harden Pharaoh's heart, and though I multiply my miraculous signs and wonders in Egypt, he will not listen to you. Then I will lay my hand on Egypt and with mighty acts of judgment I will bring out my divisions, my people the Israelites. And the Egyptians will know that I am the* Lord *when I stretch out my hand against Egypt and bring the Israelites out of it."*

These verses elaborate on what was said in 6:13. Note that Aaron had been given to Moses to be the spokesman before the Israelites. Note also the marked parallels between 4:16 and 7:1, and 4:14–16, 27–31. Up to this point Moses had been the one who spoke before Pharaoh; that is at least the impression we get from chapter 5. But now that Moses appealed to his own inadequacy also when it came to speaking before Pharaoh, Aaron became the prophet and Moses the god here (cf. note on 4:16; cf. also Acts 14:12). Moses was invested with divine authority over Pharaoh and the sequel shows that he could bring many disasters on Pharaoh.

Moses had to relate the Lord's instructions to Aaron (although it is not necessary to add with the LXX "to him," i.e., Aaron, in v. 2), and Aaron was to present the demand of 6:11 (cf. also 5:1–3) to Pharaoh.

In verses 3–5 the Lord predicted again that He Himself would harden Pharaoh's heart (cf. commentary on 4:21–23). The word used for "harden" in 4:21 is not the same as the one in verse 3; the latter emphasizes more the "making heavy" of the heart (cf. Ps. 95:8; Luke 21:34, where it refers to the making heavy as of sleep) and is related to the word "heavy" used of labor in 1:14 and 6:9. ("Signs," see 4:8–9; "wonders," see commentary on 4:21.) The "multiplying" of the signs and wonders indicates that the hardening of Pharaoh's heart had the purpose of glorifying God (cf. also 3:19–22; 4:21–23; 6:1). But even these signs and wonders would not achieve their purpose, so that Moses and Aaron were prepared for Pharaoh's refusal to listen (v. 4, cf. 4:21–23; 6:12; 1 Peter 4:12–13). "My divisions," a term with military connotations, is a remarkable expression in reference to an oppressed people. (For "my people," see 3:7; 6:7; "bring out," see 3:10–12; 6:26–27; "with mighty acts of judgment," see commentary on 6:6.) For verse 5a see commentary on 5:2: then they will know who the Lord is and that it is He they are dealing with (cf. 3:13–15). "Stretch out my hand against Egypt," see 3:19; 5:24; 6:5–7. Verse 5 shows that Pharaoh's refusal to listen brings disaster on his people: "the Egyptians will know" (solidarity, cf. 3:20).

7:6–7 *Moses and Aaron did just as the LORD commanded them. Moses was eighty years old and Aaron eighty-three when they spoke to Pharaoh.*

Verse 6 is a general statement emphasizing the fact that Moses and Aaron had carried out the Lord's instructions to the letter. They, and especially Moses, no longer argued. Verse 7 states that Moses was eighty and Aaron eighty-three years old when they dealt with Pharaoh. Moses was forty years old when he fled to Midian, according to Stephen in Acts 7:23 (cf. commentary on 2:11). Moses thus lived in Midian for forty years (cf. Acts 7:30 and commentary on 3:1), and since he was 120 years old when he died (Deut. 34:7) he led Israel for forty years. Their ages are given because now the decisive battle between the Lord and Pharaoh began.

7:8–9 *The LORD said to Moses and Aaron, "When Pharaoh says to you, 'Perform a miracle,' then say to Aaron, 'Take your staff and throw it down before Pharaoh,' and it will become a snake."*

The Lord probably said what is mentioned here at the same time as, or perhaps somewhat later than, what He had said earlier, but in any case before Moses and Aaron went again before Pharaoh. "Perform a miracle," i.e., to back up your words (cf. RSV: "prove yourselves by working a miracle"; KJV: "show a miracle for you"). "Wonders," see commentary on verse 3. The change to the second person singular in "say to Aaron," as well as the context of the verse indicate that the Lord considered Moses the more important of the two. When Moses spoke to Aaron about "your staff" it was the same staff used by Moses (or by Aaron on Moses' behalf, cf. 4:30) before the Israelites (but cf. 4:2–5, 17, 20, 30; Num. 17). The sequel also gives the impression that there was only one "staff of God" (cf. v. 15; 4:20; 7:15, 19). "Throw down," see 4:3. It is curious that neither in the command nor by its execution mention was made of Aaron's picking up the snake so that it once again became a staff (cf. 4:4). The only purpose of the wonder was to convince Pharaoh.

The root of the word translated "snake" (KJV: "serpent") means "large, powerful, mighty." The context must determine what it was that was strong or mighty. In the Old Testament the word occurs as the name of an animal. In Genesis 1:21 it is a "great creature of the sea," or "sea monster" (RSV; KJV: "whale"), as it is in Psalm 148:7 (KJV: "dragon"). In Deuteronomy 32:33 it cannot mean anything but a "large snake" or "dragon" because of the reference to poison and cobras in the immediate context. In Job 7:12 it may also mean a "monster of the deep" or "sea monster," but it is not impossible that it refers there to a crocodile, which fits the context and makes the image very vivid. In Psalm 91:13 and Jeremiah 51:34 it is translated "serpent" (KJV: "dragon"), although it is unclear what kind of monster is meant, and we must think of a monster or dragon in general. The word is used in the expression "the monster of the sea" or "the monster in the waters" (Isa. 27:1; 51:9; Ps. 74:13; Ezek. 29:3; 32:2) as a symbol of Egypt and Pharaoh, and we could think of a crocodile or a hippopotamus. Since Egypt has a large river, we can easily understand why the Pharaoh of Egypt would be called a river or sea monster and the Egyptians "monsters in the water" (Ps. 74:13; the NIV translates the Hebrew plural as a singular).

After much hesitation I decided on "large serpent" as the correct translation here, but we must remember that in 4:2–4 another word is used for serpent, the same as in e.g., Genesis 3. Since the choice as to the specific kind of monster is open, and in other instances we must think of a crocodile or a hippopotamus, the translation "crocodile" is also possible, especially since the setting here is Egypt. Should this be correct, then the magicians worked undoubtedly with young animals (see commentary on vv. 11–12). But snake charming was more common, and a staff looks more like a snake than like a young crocodile. We should keep in mind that a large, monstrous snake is meant, and a different word is used in 4:2–4 (see also v. 15).

7:10 *Then Moses and Aaron went to Pharaoh and did just as the LORD commanded. Aaron threw his staff down in front of Pharaoh and his officials, and it became a snake.*

Moses and Aaron still had access to Pharaoh. Again the emphasis was on the exact carrying out of the Lord's instructions (cf. v. 6). The following wonder is prophecy, not magic. "Officials," lit. "servants" (KJV, RSV; the translation "officials" reflects the idea that the "servants" of Pharaoh's immediate entourage were those who had positions of influence, cf. also commentary on 1:9.

7:11–12 *Pharaoh then summoned wise men and sorcerers, and the Egyptian magicians also did the same things by their secret arts: Each one threw down his staff and it became a snake. But Aaron's staff swallowed up their staffs.*

But Pharaoh was undaunted. He probably knew the story, well-known among the Egyptians, of King Cheops and the magician. According to this story Cheops (ca. 3000 B.C.) was told the following about one of his predecessors, Nebka: the magician Uba-oner made a crocodile out of wax, which came to life when thrown into the water. When the king became afraid, Uba-oner bent down and picked up the crocodile, which once again became wax in his hand (cf. 4:2–4). Whatever the case, Pharaoh summoned the wise men (his counselors; cf. Gen. 41:8; Exod. 7:22; 8:7, 18–19; 9:11; Dan. 1:20; 2:2, 10, 27; 4:7, 9; 5:11) and the sorcerers, as well as the magicians, those versed in the occult writings (Yahuda; cf. Gen. 41:8, 24; Exod. 8:6, 18, 19; 9:11; Dan. 1:20; 2:2). These people thus were not enabled by the Lord to perform this miracle, yet they did the same thing as Moses and Aaron (as v. 11 clearly indicates) by their magic and secret arts. Indeed, each one of them succeeded in duplicating the miracle. In the oral tradition that was transmitted from father to son in Israel, or in a lost apocryphal book, the names of the two leaders of these magicians were preserved for Paul, who called them Jannes and Jambres (2 Tim. 3:8; cf. Bouma's commentary on 2 Timothy in this series). Moses and Aaron were undoubtedly disappointed; but both their disappointment and Pharaoh's gloating were short-lived: Aaron's staff devoured those of the magicians.

I do not want to elaborate on the possibility of these feats of magic. We could think of sleight of hand. Even today Egyptian magicians can, through hypnosis or by other means, bring a snake or crocodile into a rigid state, so that they can be picked up by the tail like a stick. But the text seems to indicate a genuine transformation, in which case we must think of satanic power, especially here, where Moses and Aaron pleaded for the release of the seed of the woman (Gen. 3:15; 1 Thess. 2:9; Rev. 13:12–15). The magicians could succeed because God allowed them to. Their normal occupation was not to change a stick into a serpent, but rather make a serpent look like a stick.

7:13 *Yet Pharaoh's heart became hard and he would not listen to them, just as the LORD had said.*

Pharaoh was not led to repentance by seeing the staffs of his magicians devoured. His "heart became hard." "Just as the LORD had said" has an almost triumphant ring. From now on the wonders come as plagues (cf. Introduction, pp. 16–21).

15. *The First Plague: Water Changed Into Blood* (7:14–25)

The first plague is also mentioned in Psalms 78:44 and 105:29, both of which are dependent on this section.

7:14–18 *Then the LORD said to Moses, "Pharaoh's heart is unyielding; he refuses to let the people go. Go to Pharaoh in the morning as he goes out to the water. Wait on the bank of the Nile to meet him, and take in your hand the staff that was changed into a snake. Then say to him, "The LORD, the God of the Hebrews, has sent me to say to you: Let my people go, so that they may worship me in the desert. But until now you have not listened. This is what the LORD says: By this you will know that I am the LORD: With the staff that is in my hand I will strike the water of the Nile, and it will be changed into blood. The fish in the Nile will die, and the river will stink; the Egyptians will not be able to drink its water.""*

Moses was addressed and thus remained the prominent figure (see v. 1). In verse 14 still another word was used for Pharaoh's hardening of the heart (cf. 4:21 and 7:3) meaning "to be heavy, to be dulled." His heart was dull, insensitive, "deaf." "Refuse," cf. 4:23; 8:2; 9:2; 10:3–4. "Let go," cf. 3:20; 4:21, 23; 5:1–2, 24; 6:10; 7:2. "The people," cf. 1:22.

Verse 15 indicates that Pharaoh's palace was close to the Nile (cf. 2:5). The Pharaohs of the eighteenth dynasty, to whom Amenhotep II belonged (who in my opinion is meant here, see commentary on 2:23), had their residence in Thebes in southern Egypt, far from the Nile delta. It is possible that the pharaoh lived in a place closer to the delta during the period of the plagues and the Exodus, although we do not know where. Psalm 78:43 speaks of "miracles in the region of Zoan." Numbers 13:22 indicates that Zoan or Tanis was an old city, the capital of the Hyksos, in the vicinity of Goshen, the area allotted to the Israelites (see 1:11). Since Zoan was prominent during the time of the author of Psalm 78 he could appropriately use "region of Zoan" to refer to Egypt and especially northern Egypt. In any case, Psalm 78:43 shows that the Scriptures place the scene of the plagues in northern Egypt.

It was apparently Pharaoh's (daily?) habit to go to the Nile to bathe (see also 2:5—note the contrast—and 8:20). But it is also possible that verse 15 refers to Pharaoh's going to the Nile to worship the Nile god. Festivals in honor of the Nile god were held especially as the season of the annual flooding of the Nile approached. "Wait to meet him," cf. 5:20. "The staff,'' by now well-known to Pharaoh, cf. 4:2–4, 17, 20; 7:9–12. The reference at the end of verse 15 is to 4:2–4 rather than to 7:8–13, since the word for "snake" is the same as in 4:2–4.

The Lord instructed Moses to remind Pharaoh of his sin of refusing to listen (5:1–14; 7:8–13). "Hebrews," cf. 1:15; 3:18; 5:3. "Let go," see above. "My people," cf. 3:7; 6:7; 7:4. "That they may worship me in the desert," cf. 3:18; 5:1, 3. Thus far Pharaoh had neither listened nor obeyed, yet he now got another chance.

Verse 17 is formally introduced to impress Pharaoh: "This is what the LORD says" (KJV: "Thus saith the LORD"), which is later to become a favorite expression of the prophets, and proof that Moses was a prophet. "By this you will know that I am the LORD," cf. 5:2; 7:5. It reminded Pharaoh particularly of his arrogant remark in 5:2 and was in this respect a call to repentance, threatening, designed to persuade. Moses and Aaron indeed asserted themselves with authority (cf. 7:1), a marked change from their attitude in chapter 5.

The threat Moses had to convey is reminiscent of 4:9, except that what was promised there was more limited in nature, merely a sign and not a plague, since it was intended for Israel. The "serpent" for the Israelites (4:2–4) became a "large serpent" for the Egyptians (7:8–13). But now Moses had to inform Pharaoh that not merely some, but all of the water in the Nile, and even all of the waters of Egypt (cf. v. 19) would be changed into blood. Thus this wonder also took on larger dimensions for the Egyptians and became a true destructive plague. It was no longer a demonstration but became an attack. The text clearly indicates that real blood was meant and not merely the annual phenomenon of the so-called "Red Nile." It could not have made much of an impression on the Egyptians if all that happened was merely what happened every year from June through October or December, when the Nile before and during its flooding took on a red color, probably due to chalk particles that gave the water a blood-red color, especially when the sun shone on it. Besides, the "Red Nile" was to Egypt's advantage, since this period of flooding was what made the land fertile. Verse 18 indicates that the fish in the Nile would also die, which did not happen during the "Red Nile." It was rather the "Green Nile," caused by plant remains in the water immediately prior to the Red Nile that was harmful, although even then the fish did not die, certainly not *en masse*.

On the other hand, Joel 2:31 and Revelation 6:12 prophesied that the moon would be changed into blood, so that the Scriptures themselves seemed to use the word "blood" figuratively, but in those cases we are dealing with a prophetic and an apocalyptic book respectively. In Egyptian literature (in the so-called "Exhortations of a Prophet," written centuries before the first plague) the complaint was made: "the river is blood; when one drinks from it as a human being one has to refuse it, for one thirsts for water." But there the reason was that many dead had been buried in the river, and thus the phenomenon referred to was not the Red Nile either.

The fish (a common food in Egypt, cf. Num. 11:5; Isa. 19:8) would die, so that the Nile would stink, and of course this stinking blood could not be drunk by the Egyptians, whose main source of water was the Nile. The Egyptians would try to drink the abominable water in vain, as indicated by their attempts to find drinking water (v. 24).

7:19 *The Lord said to Moses, "Tell Aaron, 'Take your staff and stretch out your hand over the waters of Egypt—over the streams and canals, over the ponds and all the reservoirs'—and they will turn to blood. Blood will be everywhere in Egypt, even in the wooden buckets and stone jars.'"*

Between verses 18 and 19 Moses and Aaron carried out the Lord's instructions and Pharaoh ignored the threat. Verse 20 indicates that, while they still stood before the king and his court, Moses received the command from the Lord to say to Aaron: "Take your staff . . ." (cf. 7:9, where Moses and Aaron stood in the same relationship). Aaron had to stretch his hand (with the staff) over the waters of Egypt: "streams and canals" both referred to the Nile and its delta, and the irrigation canals and rivulets. "Their ponds" were mainly the marshy areas left by the Nile after flooding. "All the reservoirs" (KJV: "pools of water") included lakes, wells, springs, etc.

At this critical moment the Lord confirmed His promise to Moses that all those waters would turn into blood and that there would be blood everywhere in Egypt, even in the "wooden buckets and stone jars" (lit.: "in wood and in stone"). The water stored in, or dipped with, these would also become blood from then on (cf. v. 22). The Lord would plague Egypt with thirst, since the entire water supply was affected. The plagues thus show us the Lord's methods of warfare, which were both modern (cf. Rev. 8:8; 11:6; 16:4) and ancient.

7:20, 21 *Moses and Aaron did just as the Lord had commanded. He raised his staff in the presence of Pharaoh and his officials and struck the water of the Nile, and all the water was changed into blood. The fish in the Nile died, and the river smelled so bad that the Egyptians could not drink its water. Blood was everywhere in Egypt.*

See 7:6, 10. Here again Moses' and Aaron's obedience is mentioned (cf. v. 10). "He" is Aaron (v. 19). Only the water in the Nile is mentioned here, since it was the most important body of water (but see v. 19). Aaron struck the water before the eyes of Pharaoh and his officials (cf. v. 10 and commentary v. 19).

What the Lord had threatened to do (vv. 17–19) took place (Pss. 78:44; 105:29). Verse 21 indicates that what the Lord had promised was fulfilled literally (see especially v. 18).

7:22 *But the Egyptian magicians did the same things by their secret arts, and Pharaoh's heart became hard; he would not listen to Moses and Aaron, just as the* Lord *had said.*

But the Egyptian magicians (see 7:11) did the same (see commentary on vv. 11–12) "by their secret arts" (cf. v. 11). We must assume that water that was drawn before Aaron and Moses carried out their threat had remained water. As a result Pharaoh's heart was hardened and he did not listen to them, as the Lord had predicted (see v. 13).

7:23 *Instead, he turned and went into his palace, and did not take even this to heart.*

Pharaoh, strengthened in his opposition by the "magicians," returned to his palace and "did not take even this to heart," ignored the mighty sign as he had ignored the earlier one (vv. 6–13).

7:24, 25 *And all the Egyptians dug along the Nile to get drinking water, because they could not drink the water of the river. Seven days passed after the* Lord *struck the Nile.*

The Egyptians (*they* were the ones who were suffering from Pharaoh's refusal, cf. 3:20; 7:5) began to dig for water since they could not drink the Nile water, although we are not told what the results were (cf. vv. 18, 21). Perhaps verse 18 expresses the fact that the efforts failed, since this "digging for water" may mean that the Egyptians dug sandpits to filter the Nile water. The LXX reads: "and all the Egyptians dug around the river to drink the water from the river." In the case of the Red Nile digging filtration pits ten to fifteen feet deep was effective, but here it was not and this was another indication that the water not merely changed color, but changed into blood.

This situation continued for seven days (lit.: "and seven days were fulfilled"). The phenomenon of the Red Nile lasted from four to six months. The Lord struck the Nile (cf. vv. 16–17); the conflict was between Him and Pharaoh, who saw the mighty Nile, worshiped as a god, stricken.

16. *The Second Plague: Frogs* (8:1–15)

The second plague is also mentioned in Psalms 78:45; 105:30; the latter is dependent on the description in this chapter. The second plague, like the first, was something loathsome, but not deadly. It was somewhat more serious than the first one in that Pharaoh and his officials were now attacked in their own homes (cf. 7:23 with 8:3–4, 9, 11, 13), which is probably the reason why Pharaoh asked Moses to intercede that the frogs be taken away (v. 8). But as soon as Moses' prayer was answered Pharaoh returned to his stubborn attitude (v. 15).

8:1–4 *Then the LORD said to Moses, "Go to Pharaoh and say to him, "This is what the LORD says: Let my people go, so that they may worship me. If you refuse to let them go, I will plague your whole country with frogs. The Nile will teem with frogs. They will come up into your palace and your bedroom and onto your bed, into the houses of your officials and on your people, and into your ovens and kneading troughs. The frogs will go up on you and your people and all your officials.' "*

The impression is given that the Lord commanded Moses to return to Pharaoh immediately after the first plague had ended with the demand to let His people go to worship Him (cf. commentary on 7:16). For "This is what the Lord says," see commentary on 7:17; for verse 2, see commentary on 7:14.

The Lord threatened Pharaoh through Moses that his entire country would be plagued with frogs. These amphibians who lived in the rivers, streams, and marshes of Egypt (cf. v. 5) and were especially numerous after the annual flooding (but were eaten by other animals such as e.g., the ibis) would now become so numerous that the Nile would teem with them (cf. Gen. 1:20). They would leave the river and the delta and come into Pharaoh's palace, his bedroom, and his bed. His officials (see commentary on 7:20) and the Egyptian people would also suffer (again the concept of soldiarity, cf. commentary on 7:24). Even Pharaoh's oven and kneading troughs (perhaps also: boxes or sacks for the storage of grain, flour, or bread) would not be safe; and the king himself, his people, and his officials would not be spared (see ZPEB, "Frogs" 2:609; in ancient times plagues of frogs were not uncommon).

Through this plague the Lord, the God of the Hebrews, again attacked the gods of Egypt. Not only the Nile, but also frogs represented gods in Egypt. The frog was worshiped from ancient times, and there were even a god and a goddess who were believed to have had a part in the creation of the world and who were depicted with frog's heads. But now the Lord spoke, and it was. Perhaps we must assume here, as in 7:16–18, that Aaron was the spokesman (7:1–2; but cf. vv. 9–10).

8:5, 6 *Then the LORD said to Moses, "Tell Aaron, 'Stretch out your hand with your staff over the streams and canals and ponds, and make frogs come upon the land of Egypt.'"*

So Aaron stretched out his hand over the waters of Egypt, and the frogs came up and covered the land.

Between verses 4 and 5 we have to insert the carrying out of the Lord's command by Moses and Aaron, as was the case in 7:18–19. Verse 5 is similar to 7:19 (see commentary). The stories of the plagues seem to follow a pattern. Yet verse 6 differs from 7:20. Aaron again carried out Moses' instructions. Egypt was covered with frogs. The miracle of this lies in the abnormal multiplication of these animals.

8:7 *But the magicians did the same things by their secret arts; they also made frogs come up on the land of Egypt.*

Verse 7 is roughly the same as 7:22a (cf. also 7:11). Again we do not know how the magicians were able to do this.

8:8–11 *Pharaoh summoned Moses and Aaron and said, "Pray to the LORD to take the frogs away from me and my people, and I will let your people go to offer sacrifices to the LORD."*

Moses said to Pharaoh, "I leave to you the honor of setting the time for me to pray for you and your officials and your people that you and your houses may be rid of the frogs, except for those that remain in the Nile."

"Tomorrow," Pharaoh said.

Moses replied, "It will be as you say, so that you may know there is no one like the LORD our God. The frogs will leave you and your houses, your officials and your people; they will remain only in the Nile."

Note that the magicians seemed to be losing their influence over Pharaoh. This time we do not read that their imitation resulted in the hardening of Pharaoh's heart. This may well have been due to the fact that the magicians were unable to make the frogs disappear. The text says only that Pharaoh summoned Moses and Aaron and asked them to pray to the Lord to take the frogs away from him and his people. He even added the promise that he then would allow the people to go and offer sacrifices. Thus Pharaoh did not harden his heart as he did during the first plague, and his response was different from that described in 7:22–23, probably because he himself had to suffer under this plague as well (cf. v. 3 and the words "the Egyptians" in 7:24). It was thus egotism rather than repentance, even though he did mention the people. "Let go," cf. v. 2. "The people," cf. commentary on 1:22.

Note that according to verses 9–10 Moses spoke (cf. 6:30–7:2). He literally said to Pharaoh: "have honor over me," meaning "command me" in regard to the time when Moses would pray for Pharaoh, his officials, and his people. I would translate "I am at your disposal." It is a courtesy on Moses' part; he declared himself prepared to act as intercessor, while at the same time expressing the certainty that his prayer would result in the elimination of the frogs, so that they would remain only in the Nile.

Pharaoh set the time for Moses' prayer for the next day, perhaps to give Moses as little time as possible to prepare for this great miracle. Moses agreed, so that he could face Pharaoh with the fact that the Lord, Israel's God, had no peer (cf. Deut. 33:26; Ps. 86:8; Jer. 10:6–7; cf. also 7:17). The frogs would leave Pharaoh, his officials, and his people, and their homes, and they would remain only in the Nile.

8:12–14 *After Moses and Aaron left Pharaoh, Moses cried out to the LORD about the frogs he had brought on Pharaoh. And the LORD did what Moses asked. The frogs died in the houses, in the couryards and in the fields. They were piled into heaps, and the land reeked of them.*

Moses (mentioned first since he played the prominent role) and Aaron left Pharaoh, and Moses called to the Lord ("crying," cf. 3:7) about the frogs "he had brought on Pharaoh" (the LXX reads incorrectly "as Pharaoh had commanded"; RSV: "as he had agreed with Pharaoh").

Verse 13, cf. v. 11; James 5:16–18. "Courtyards" may also mean "villages" (cf. KJV). The Lord did not betray Moses' confidence. The frogs were utterly destroyed and the piles of dead frogs reeked (v. 14).

8:15 *But when Pharaoh saw that there was relief, he hardened his heart and would not listen to Moses and Aaron, just as the LORD had said.*

But rather than seeing this new proof of the power of Israel's God bring the Pharaoh to repentance, we notice that he hardened his heart (cf. note on 7:14) after realizing that relief had come, proving that he was not worthy of the Lord's patience (cf. Eccl. 8:11; 1 Peter 3:9). He ignored the words of Moses and Aaron "just as the LORD had said" (cf. commentary on 7:22).

17. *The Third Plague: Gnats* (8:16–19)

The third plague is also mentioned in Psalm 105:31. Note that here for the first time Pharaoh was not warned in advance and that for the first time also the magicians failed in their attempts to imitate the wonder. But Pharaoh was not impressed with either the plague itself or their failure. This plague was again not lethal, but very annoying.

8:16 *Then the LORD said to Moses, "Tell Aaron, 'Stretch out your staff and strike the dust of the ground,' and throughout the land of Egypt the dust will become gnats."*

See 7:9–10, 19–20; 8:5–6. This time Aaron had to strike the dust of the ground with his staff. The Lord said that the dust throughout Egypt would turn into gnats. The word most English version translate "gnats" is sometimes also translated "lice" (ASV, Josephus, Luther, Calvin), or "mosquitoes." "Gnats" seems preferable, since it is broader than "mosquitoes." We must think especially of the family of stinging gnats that lay their eggs in standing water such as was left behind when the Nile receded. They were small, had a very painful sting, and crawled into the nose and ears. Their sting caused unbearable itching. They were common in Egypt, sometimes in such large numbers that they darkened the sky. They bred especially in inundated rice fields. But here they appeared from the dust of the ground. This could not be explained in natural terms, as the magicians realized. (v. 19. See ZPEB, "Lice," 3:925).

8:17 *They did this, and when Aaron stretched out his hand with the staff and struck the dust of the ground, gnats came upon men and animals. All the dust throughout the land of Egypt became gnats.*

The LXX reads: "and he (i.e., Aaron) did this" rather than "and they did this." This is an unnecessary change: Moses and Aaron both carried out the Lord's command of verse 16. For the first time Pharaoh was not warned in advance to let Israel go (cf. 7:14–18; 8:1–4). He and his people were struck without notice: people, cattle, all of Egypt (cf. commentary on 8:1–4). The relationship between the Lord and Pharaoh, who again and again hardened his heart, was coming to a head. "Throughout the land of Egypt," cf. 7:19; 8:5.

8:18 *But when the magicians tried to produce gnats by their secret arts, they could not. And the gnats were on men and animals.*

This verse presents a translation problem. Literally it reads: "the magicians did the same thing by their secret arts, to produce gnats, but they could not." From the following statement, "and the gnats were on men and animals," some have concluded that the magicians tried to get rid of the gnats but failed. But this would necessitate reading "cause to disappear" instead of "produce." Besides, in the case of both earlier plagues the magicians accomplished something similar to what Aaron did, but we read nothing of any attempts to get rid of the plague. Why would the failure of such an attempt in this case make such an impression on the magicians? This verse thus tells us of the failed attempt (perhaps this was not part of their repertoire? cf. commentary on 7:11–12) of the magicians (see commentary on v. 7) to imitate Moses and Aaron and of the continuation of the plague on man and beast.

8:19 *The magicians said to Pharaoh, "This is the finger of God." But Pharaoh's heart was hard and he would not listen, just as the L*ORD *had said.*

The magicians were now very impressed (cf. Isa. 18:11). It is not impossible that they meant: "this is the finger of *a* god," indicating that they saw merely a supernatural power at work ("finger" here means "power," cf. Ps. 8:4; Luke 11:20). Yet neither their statement nor the miracle itself impressed Pharaoh (cf. commentary on 7:13–14, 22; 8:15).

18. *The Fourth Plague: Flies* (8:20–32)

This plague is also mentioned in Psalms 78:45 and 105:31, both of which are dependent on this narrative.

Pharaoh again received advance warning (cf. 7:15–18; 8:1–4). As was the case with the second plague Pharaoh asked Moses and Aaron that he be delivered from the plague (cf. 8:8–11, 25–29) and when Moses' prayer was answered Pharaoh again hardened his heart (cf. 8:12–15, 30–31). Here for the first time mention is made of the separation the Lord made between Egypt and the land of Goshen, where His people lived (v. 22).

8:20–23 *Then the L*ORD *said to Moses, "Get up early in the morning and confront Pharaoh as he goes to the water and say to him, 'This is what the L*ORD *says: Let my people go, so that they may worship me. If you do not let my people go, I will send swarms of flies on you and your officials, on your people and into your houses. The houses of the Egyptians will be full of flies, and even the ground where they are.*

*"'But on that day I will deal differently with the land of Goshen, where my people live; no swarms of flies will be there, so that you will know that I, the L*ORD*, am in this land. I will make a distinction between my people and your people. This miraculous sign will occur tomorrow.'"*

Verse 20, see commentary on 7:15–16. Note the difference between these verses. "This is what the LORD says," cf. 7:17. Verse 20b, cf. 8:1.

"Let go" and "send" in the first part of verse 20 are forms of the same verb: the Lord would "let go" swarms of flies if Pharaoh did not let the people go (cf. also commentary on 7:16 and 8:1). Moses again had to announce a nonlethal but very annoying plague: flies. The LXX uses a word meaning literally "dog flies" *(kunomuia),* flies whose sting caused bloody swellings on cattle. Some translate "stable-flies"; the Vulgate translates "all kinds of mosquitoes," while others think of beetles. Aquila and Luther translate "all kinds of vermin," which would include all kinds of insects and even mice, etc. This is not impossible, since the Hebrew word means "mixture" or "swarm," but the text gives the impression that we must think of a specific insect. The translation "flies" seems to be the most appropriate one to me, whereby we must think especially of dog flies or gadflies who lived on the blood of men and animals. Flies, brought in by the south wind, were common in Egypt, and were even used as a symbol of the Egyptians in Isaiah 7:18, although another, more common word is used there. They caused serious eye diseases and even blindness, since they landed on the eyelids and around the eyes. Through Moses the Lord threatened Pharaoh that if he did not let Israel loose, He would "let loose" those flies on him, his officials (cf. commentary on 7:20; again the concept of solidarity, cf. commentary on 7:24), the people, the palaces and the homes of the Egyptians (cf. 8:4, 9, 11). Even the ground would be teeming with flies.

In verse 22 the Lord said that He would set apart the land of Goshen, so that there would be no flies there when the plague came the next day ("tomorrow," v. 23). The purpose of this separation was to convince Pharaoh that the Lord, the God of Israel "is in this land," i.e., that He ruled and that He as sovereign could appoint the flies their place. No matter how numerous (v. 21), they were set a limit beyond which they could not go (cf. 5:2; 7:5, 17; 8:10; Ps. 104:9). Concerning the location of Goshen, see commentary on 1:11; cf. also Genesis 46:34; 47:11.

Most versions follow the LXX and the Vulgate in verse 23. The Hebrew reads: "I will set a redemption" (cf. NIV, RSV margins); the LXX reading involves the change of one letter which results in "I will make a distinction," which makes better sense than the Hebrew. The Lord's people would be distinguished from Pharaoh's people. The Hebrew has a perfect tense ("I have made a distinction") with the meaning of a future tense ("I will make"). The people shared in the blessing of its king, even as the Egyptians shared in the curse of having Pharaoh as their ruler. Again it becomes clear here that the battle was between those two kings: the Lord and Pharaoh (cf. commentary 1:6–22). Moses had to announce that this miraculous sign would happen the next day, an indication of the Lord's power. "Miraculous sign," cf. commentary on 4:8, 9, 17, 21, 28, 30; 7:3.

The plagues thus belonged to the category of "signs," intended to draw attention to and lead to faith in the words Moses spoke to Pharaoh on the Lord's behalf (cf. 8:18: "this is the finger of God").

8:24 *And the LORD did this. Dense swarms of flies poured into Pharaoh's palace and into the houses of his officials, and throughout Egypt the land was ruined by the flies.*

Between verses 23 and 24 Moses (and Aaron, see 8:1–4, 25) carried out the Lord's instructions, and Pharaoh refused to comply with the Lord's demand conveyed by Moses (see 7:18–19; 8:4–5). Then the Lord did what He had threatened to do (cf. v. 21), "and the land was ruined by the flies" (cf. Ps. 78:45). For the first time it is not stated that Moses and Aaron used the staff (cf. 7:20; 8:5–6, 16–17).

8:25 *Then Pharaoh summoned Moses and Aaron and said, "Go, sacrifice to your God here in the land."*

The situation must have been serious indeed, for Pharaoh again summoned Moses and Aaron. But there is a change from 8:8: Pharaoh's first words were not a request for intercession, but a statement of willingness, almost a command: "Go, sacrifice to your God here in the land." He was willing to let Israel hold their festival, but in Egypt, rather than let them go into the wilderness. Pharaoh was less and less prepared to make major concessions (cf. 8:8), and the plagues had not brought him to the point of readiness to give in to the Lord's demand; instead, his stubbornness increased. But he must have been bothered by the flies, since he proposed this compromise to Moses and Aaron. He clearly showed that he did not believe Moses' and Aaron's words; he wanted to keep his slaves under control, even when they worshiped their God.

8:26, 27 *But Moses said, "That would not be right. The sacrifices we offer the LORD our God would be detestable to the Egyptians. And if we offer sacrifices that are detestable in their eyes, will they not stone us? We must take a three-day journey into the desert to offer sacrifices to the LORD our God, as he commands us."*

If Pharaoh was clever, Moses (who also had an excellent education, cf. 2:1–11) was his match. He told Pharaoh that this would not be wise and added a strong argument: the sacrifices Israel would bring would be detestable to the Egyptians. Moses' argument was thus that he did not want to offend the Egyptians. If the Israelites sacrificed oxen, here called literally "the abomination of the Egyptians," (cf. KJV), i.e., "the idol of the Egyptians" (cf. 2 Kings 23:13), then the gods of the Egyptians would be attacked since the Egyptians worshiped bulls (Apis) and rams, and thus they would see the sacrifices of the Israelites as a sacrificing of their gods to the God of Israel. Similarly the Hindus are frequently insulted today because the cow, which they consider holy, is not treated properly by Christians and Muslims. Moses' argument was especially appropriate since we know from excavations that this Pharaoh, Amenhotep II, worshiped bulls (see also commentary on 9:1–7). Hence Moses could ask Pharaoh personally: "If we would sacrifice the abomination of the Egyptians before their eyes, would they not stone us?" And he then repeated the original demand to let them go into the wilderness. Pharaoh was not to tamper with this.

8:28 *Pharaoh said, "I will let you go to offer sacrifices to the LORD your God in the desert, but you must not go very far. Now pray for me."*

Now Pharaoh said that he was prepared to let the people go into the desert, but he tried to negotiate a shorter journey, again showing his basic unwillingness; and he also requested Moses' and Aaron's intercession.

8:29 *Moses answered, "As soon as I leave you, I will pray to the LORD, and tomorrow the flies will leave Pharaoh and his officials and his people. Only be sure that Pharaoh does not act deceitfully again by not letting the people go to offer sacrifices to the LORD."*

Moses displayed the same certainty of faith as in 8:10–11. But because of his past experience he felt compelled to admonish Pharaoh boldly not to act deceitfully again by breaking his promise. Moses, who increasingly overcame the timidity he expressed in 6:30, did have Pharaoh's interest at heart. But he let it be clearly known that he no longer trusted Pharaoh, even though he was prepared to act as intercessor for him with the Lord.

8:30–32 *Then Moses left Pharaoh and prayed to the LORD, and the LORD did what Moses asked: The flies left Pharaoh and his officials and his people; not a fly remained. But this time also Pharaoh hardened his heart and would not let the people go.*

See 8:12–14. The statement that Pharaoh again hardened his heart is this time not followed by "as the LORD has said" (cf. 7:13, 22; 8:15, 19). This argues against the idea that the plague narratives were constructed along the lines of a fixed scheme. The same word for "harden" is used here as in 8:15 (cf. commentary on 8:15 and 7:14).

19. *The Fifth Plague: Pestilence on Livestock* (9:1–7)

As with the first, second, and fourth plagues, Pharaoh was warned in advance of the consequences if he refused to let the people of Israel go (cf. 7:15–18; 8:1–4; 20–21). The Lord again made a distinction between the Egyptians and the Israelites as in the case of the fourth plague (cf. 8:22; 9:4, 6). This time the distinction did get Pharaoh's attention (v. 7) although once again he hardened his heart in the end.

This plague has a definite religious character (see below) and is therefore a sign that the gods of the Egyptians were nothing compared to the God of the Hebrews (v. 1).

9:1–4 *Then the LORD said to Moses, "Go to Pharaoh and say to him, 'This is what the LORD, the God of the Hebrews, says: "Let my people go, so that they may worship me." If you refuse to let them go and continue to hold them back, the hand of the LORD will bring a terrible plague on your livestock in the field—on your horses and donkeys and camels and on your cattle and sheep and goats. But the LORD will make a distinction between the livestock of Israel and that of Egypt, so that no animal belonging to the Israelites will die.' "*

The first verse is similar to 8:1 (cf. commentary on that verse). "The God of the Hebrews," cf. commentary on 1:15; 3:18; 5:3; 7:16. As in the case of the previous plagues the Lord spoke to Moses only (cf. commentary 8:1–4, 9–10), but here for the first time Aaron is not mentioned.

Verses 2 and 3 can be compared with 8:2, 20–21. "Hold," "hold back," (v. 2b), cf. Judges 7:18; 19:4. If Pharaoh continued to hold back God's people (v. 1) by force from worshiping the Lord in the desert, Pharaoh's people (v. 4) would have to suffer the consequences in the form of a new plague (v. 3). See also commentary on 7:24; 8:23.

"Behold" (KJV, omitted in NIV) calls for attention (cf. 7:17; 18:2). "The hand of the LORD" (cf. 7:5) is an image of His power; the expression "the hand of god" was also known to the Egyptians to whom it meant the power of the godhead that protected them and punished the sinner. The irony is thus that the Lord announced here that *His* hand, the hand of the God of the Hebrews, would subdue the hand of the gods who protected Egypt, and that it would punish the Egyptians as sinners. To Egyptian ears this statement must therefore have been offensive.

Pharaoh's "livestock in the field" is further specified: horses, donkeys, etc. The horse was brought to Palestine from Egypt in Solomon's time. Even today horses are frequently victims of contagious diseases in Egypt, but otherwise cattle plague seems to be fairly uncommon in Egypt. It has been claimed that the Egyptians did not acquire camels until much later, since they are not mentioned in the inscriptions of this period. The implication then is that the author was not familiar with conditions in Egypt, and that consequently the historicity of Exodus is in question. But it is not impossible that camels were already found in Egypt at this time and even earlier (cf. Gen. 12:16). The donkey was used primarily as a riding animal.

Verse 3 literally reads: "the hand of the LORD will be on your cattle . . . a very heavy plague" (cf. KJV). The power of the Lord would thus turn against the livestock of Pharaoh and of the Egyptians (cf. Heidelberg Catechism, A. 27). The word for "heavy" is the same word that is translated "dense swarms" in 8:24.

I already pointed out (8:26–27) that the Egyptians and the Pharaoh who is addressed here, Amenhotep II, worshiped oxen. The golden calf in the wilderness (ch. 32) was made perhaps under the influence of the bull worship in Egypt. The second commandment (20:4–6; Deut. 5:8–10; see also Deut. 4:15–18) warns against animal worship such as the people had seen in Egypt, where (since it was believed that the gods and goddesses revealed themselves in certain animals) the Israelites had encountered sacred calves, sacred bulls, a cow goddess, and the ram, which was considered to be the incarnation of the sun god. Animal cemeteries (e.g., of Apis bulls) have been found. Thus the plague on all livestock was a direct, fundamental attack on the sacred animals and gods of the Egyptians, all the more so because Israel's livestock, none of which the Israelites considered sacred, was spared down to the last one (vv. 4, 6–7). The lesson of this plague for the Egyptians lies in the fact that their gods were struck by the God of the Hebrews, a terrible blow against the polytheism and idolatry of the Egyptians (cf. 15:11).

But this threat also had political implications, since the battle was directed primarily against Pharaoh. Amenhotep II surpassed all his predecessors in his fanatical devotion to the worship of animals, and especially the bull. In 1906 a statue made of sandstone was excavated representing a cow and Amenhotep II leaning his head under its head; he is also depicted kneeling under a cow, drinking its divine milk. He is thus seen as child and slave of the cow goddess. What a threat this must have been to him! He ignored Moses' warning, and an investigation shows that after the disaster struck not one of the cows of the Israelites was affected (v. 7).

Verse 4, cf. 8:22–23. The Lord announced that He would make a distinction between the livestock of Israel and that of Egypt, so that none of the animals of the Israelites would die.

9:5 *The LORD set a time and said, "Tomorrow the LORD will do this in the land."*

This separation points to the sovereign power of the God of the Hebrews, further expressed in verse 5, where the Lord set the following day as the time when this would be fulfilled (cf. 8:23). "In the land" is Egypt (cf. 8:22). The God of the Hebrews was more powerful than the Egyptian gods were in their own land!

9:6, 7 *And the next day the LORD did it: All the livestock of the Egyptians died, but not one animal belonging to the Israelites died. Pharaoh sent men to investigate and found that not even one of the animals of the Israelites had died. Yet his heart was unyielding and he would not let the people go.*

Pharaoh appears to have ignored Moses' warning (cf. 7:18–19; 8:4–5, 23–24). The next day (the time He had set) the Lord did what He had threatened to do. It is not impossible that the gnats and flies transmitted the infection to the cattle. That "all the livestock of the Egyptians died" must be understood as hyperbole in view of the fact that the next two plagues again affected the livestock of the Egyptians (cf. 11:5; 12:29; 13:15). This may be a reflection of the Egyptian language that had a similar expression ("not one remained"). See also verse 3: "your livestock *in the field.*" But the livestock of the Israelites was not affected at all. This got Pharaoh's attention when it was reported to him; it is possible that when Moses said that this would happen when he announced the plague Pharaoh had decided to have it checked out. A representative, or perhaps a commission of inquiry, was sent to Goshen and had to report that ("behold," KJV, RSV, expresses the amazement) not one of Israel's animals had died. Nevertheless, Pharaoh's heart was unyielding, deaf to the miracle of this separation (cf. commentary on 7:14) and he refused to let the people go.

20. The Sixth Plague: Boils (9:8–12)

The sixth plague is mentioned only here (in my opinion Ps. 78:50 refers to the tenth plague). The description is most reminiscent of that of the third plague (cf. 8:16–19). Once again the magicians entered the picture. For the first time they were specifically called victims of the plague, and therein lay Moses' complete victory over them; they were not mentioned again in the subsequent narrative. The effects of this plague were more serious for the people than those of the previous plagues.

9:8, 9 *Then the LORD said to Moses and Aaron, "Take handfuls of soot from a furnace and have Moses toss it into the air in the presence of Pharaoh. It will become fine dust over the whole land of Egypt, and festering boils will break out on men and animals throughout the land."*

Aaron is mentioned again in verse 8, along with Moses (cf. 6:12; 7:8). Both were to take handfuls of soot, but only Moses was to throw it in the air in the presence of Pharaoh. Note in this connection 4:30; 7:9, 19–20; 8:5–6, 16–17. The word for "toss" (KJV: "sprinkle") is also used for seed (Isa. 28:25) and for the sprinkling of blood (e.g., 24:6; 29:16).

"Fine dust" was dust that drifted in the wind, like ashes, as opposed to the heavier dust that stayed on the ground (see also Isa. 5:24; 29:5). Thus a rain of fine dust would come over all of Egypt. "Festering boils" (lit.: "boils breaking out in sores") were fiery, burning sores covered with blains. The so-called Nile pox was common in Egypt; its main characteristic was unbearable itching. But this could not be what was meant here, since it would be nothing unusual to the Egyptians, and the text indicates a disease of a more serious nature. It is difficult to determine exactly which disease "festering boils" refers to (cf. Deut. 28:27, 35, 60). Some even think of leprosy in the light of Leviticus 13:18–20, but this is unlikely. See also 15:26; Deuteronomy 7:15. In my opinion the text does not allow for a disease or pestilence caused by the rotting carcasses left in the wake of the fifth plague, since the soot and the rain of fine dust then would have no meaning. Skin diseases were common in Egypt, but this disease had a miraculous origin. The word for "boils" was borrowed from the Egyptian where it also seemed to have meant "abcess"; it is also found in the illness of Job (Job 2:7) and of Hezekiah (Isa. 38:21).

9:10, 11 *So they took soot from a furnace and stood before Pharaoh. Moses tossed it into the air, and festering boils broke out on men and animals. The magicians could not stand before Moses because of the boils that were on them and on all the Egyptians.*

Moses and Aaron immediately carried out the Lord's instructions, and men and animals were struck with the extremely painful and annoying plague. It is likely that Goshen was spared, although it is not explicitly stated (cf. also v. 11b, which mentions only the Egyptians). The magicians could not stand before Moses because of the boils, a strong proof of the power of the God of the Hebrews. "All Egyptians": the plague was pandemic.

9:12 *But the LORD hardened Pharaoh's heart and he would not listen to Moses and Aaron, just as the LORD had said to Moses.*

"Hardened," cf. 4:21. "As the Lord had said to Moses," cf. 7:13, 22; 8:15, 19. Neither the warning (8:19) nor the effect on the magicians could break Pharaoh's stubbornness.

21. *The Seventh Plague: Hail* (9:13–35)

The seventh plague is mentioned also in Psalms 78:47–48 and 105:32–33. Both poets knew the very detailed description given here. The plague was preceded by a warning (v. 14), which indicated that the plagues that followed were of a very serious nature.

Here for the first time the Lord told Pharaoh and his officials to find a place of shelter for man and beast (vv. 19–20). Goshen was again spared (v. 26). Pharaoh asked Moses and Aaron to intercede for him (vv. 27–28) and they agreed (vv. 29–30), but when the plague ended Pharaoh again hardened his heart (vv. 34–35). This plague was lethal (v. 25).

9:13–19 *Then the* LORD *said to Moses, "Get up early in the morning, confront Pharaoh and say to him, 'This is what the* LORD, *the God of the Hebrews, says: Let my people go, so that they may worship me, or this time I will send the full force of my plagues against you and against your officials and your people, so you may know that there is no one like me in all the earth. For by now I could have stretched out my hand and struck you and your people with a plague that would have wiped you off the earth. But I have raised you up for this very purpose, that I might show you my power and that my name might be proclaimed in all the earth. You still set yourself against my people and will not let them go. Therefore, at this time tomorrow I will send the worst hailstorm that has ever fallen on Egypt, from the day it was founded till now. Give an order now to bring your livestock and everything you have in the field to a place of shelter, because the hail will fall on every man and animal that has not been brought in and is still out in the field, and they will die.' "*

The Lord commanded Moses to announce the plague to Pharaoh. The carrying out of this command is not stated but is assumed in the following verses (cf. 8:1–4, 23–24).

Verse 13, cf. commentary on 8:20. Moses probably met Pharaoh again by the Nile. For the expression "God of the Hebrews" cf. commentary on 1:15; 3:18; 5:3; 7:17; 9:1. In verse 14 the Lord clearly expressed His impatience. "This time" refers to the period of the plagues that would follow. "My plagues" (lit.: "all my plagues," KJV, RSV) means here: "the full extent of my plagues." The word for "plagues" was the same word used in 7:25, from a verb "to strike," hence "blow." "Let go," see commentary on 8:20–21. Pharaoh's officials (cf. commentary on 1:9 and 7:10) and his people would be stricken (cf. 3:20). The purpose of the Lord's "letting loose" all His plagues was to bring Pharaoh to a knowledge of the fact that there was none like Him in the entire earth, including the gods of the Gentiles. This was also the punishment for Pharaoh's arrogance in 5:2, expressed as well in 5:24; 7:3, 5, 17; 8:20, 22. "In all the earth" was the most emphatic statement of the Lord's incomparable greatness made to Pharaoh yet. In verses 15–16 the Lord informed Pharaoh that it was not His lack of power, but rather His restraint that allowed Pharaoh to continually oppose Him. The Lord could have stretched out His hand and struck Pharaoh with a pestilence (which will be the final plague) that would have wiped him and his people off the earth; the only reason that the Lord had not done this was that He wanted to show Pharaoh His power, and that His name was to be ''proclaimed in all the earth.'' The seed of the serpent was created and spared for a purpose (cf. 10:1–2; Prov. 16:4). The Lord accomplished the purpose stated in verse 16 (cf. Josh. 2:10), and the plagues are indeed still known and proclaimed.

In verse 15 the KJV follows the LXX, the Vulgate, and other versions: ''for now I will stretch out my hand . . .'' which gives a different meaning than the Hebrew text: ''for by now I could have stretched out my hand . . .'' (NIV, RSV). In verse 16 the KJV again follows the LXX when it translates ''to show in thee'' rather than the more accurate ''that I might show you.''

''But I have raised you up'' (v. 16): the Hebrew means ''I have spared you'' (RSV: ''I let you live''), which fits the context very well. Elsewhere the verb of verse 16 can also be translated ''I have appointed you'' (cf. Ezra 2:63; Eccl. 4:15; Dan. 8:23; 11:2–4). The verb Paul uses in Romans 9:17 can also mean ''to appoint.'' We have thus in Romans 9:17 a possible translation of Exodus 9:16 and a further indication of God's purpose behind the words Moses was to convey to Pharaoh.

The Lord states in verse 17 that Pharaoh ''raises himself up'' against His people to keep them from leaving; the verb indicates that Pharaoh raised himself up as a mound or obstacle. ''My people,'' cf. 3:7; 5:1; 6:7; 7:4, 16; 8:1, 20–23; 9:1, 13.

Because Pharaoh continued to resist, Moses had to announce a new plague: very heavy hail (v. 18). The Lord wanted to let Pharaoh know that He had authority over the forces of nature, first by saying that *He* would send the hail, and then by telling Pharaoh exactly *when* it would fall (cf. 8:9–10, 23, 29; 9:5–6). ''Behold'' (KJV), see commentary on 9:3. This hail would be so severe that there had never been a hailstorm like it since Egypt was founded, i.e., inhabited. According to Yahuda this is a literal translation of an Egyptian expression which characterizes something as unusual, odious, unheard of. It hails rarely in Egypt, except occasionally early in the year.

Verse 19 contains the command to Moses to advise Pharaoh to bring his livestock and everything he had in the field to a place of shelter. Added to this was the ominous prediction that every man and animal that was not indoors (in Egypt the livestock is in the field from January to April) would be killed by the hail. The Lord thus showed clearly that the announcement of the plague was an act of mercy, that He had the power to save from destruction. He accentuated the thought already expressed in verse 15, that He could and would destroy even more than He had thus far. Those who ignored the warning and who failed to take measures against the impending hail had only themselves to blame for the loss of people and livestock, and they could even be destroyed themselves.

9:20, 21 *Those officials of Pharaoh who feared the word of the* Lord *hurried to bring their slaves and their livestock inside. But those who ignored the word of the* Lord *left their slaves and livestock in the field.*

There appear to be two groups among the Egyptians, as among all unbelievers who receive a warning from the Lord. Some of the officials (cf. commentary on v. 14) feared the word of the Lord because of their previous experiences. They brought their livestock to safety. But others ignored the warning (cf. 7:23) and made the mistake of leaving their slaves and livestock on the open field.

9:22–26 *Then the* Lord *said to Moses, "Stretch out your hand toward the sky so that hail will fall all over Egypt—on men and animals and on everything growing in the fields of Egypt." When Moses stretched out his staff toward the sky, the* Lord *sent thunder and hail, and lightning flashed down to the ground. So the* Lord *rained hail on the land of Egypt; hail fell and lightning flashed back and forth. It was the worst storm in all the land of Egypt since it had become a nation. Throughout Egypt hail struck everything in the fields—both men and animals; it beat down everything growing in the fields and stripped every tree. The only place it did not hail was the land of Goshen, where the Israelites were.*

The plague followed the announcement. Moses was instructed to stretch out the staff; the thunderstorm broke and the hail came down. In verse 22 Moses (rather than Aaron, cf. 7:19–20; 8:5–6, 16–17) is told to stretch his hand (with the staff, cf. v. 23) to the heavens (Job 38:22–23). Moses was also the executor in the narrower sense of the previous plague (cf. vv. 8–10). Egypt was struck, but not Goshen (v. 26). Verse 22 takes us to the day following Moses' speech to Pharaoh (v. 18). Moses thus knew of the impending hailstorm two days in advance. Besides men and animals "everything growing in the field" is also mentioned in verse 22 (cf. also v. 25).

According to verse 23 Moses carried out the instructions and the Lord did not disappoint him: the prediction was fulfilled. He sent thunder (lit.: "voices," "sounds"; the Egyptian word for "thunder" is also "voices" or "voices of a god"), and hail, the actual plague, while "the fire ran down to the earth'' (RSV), a vivid description of lightning (cf. also Pss. 78:47–48; 105:32–33). The thunder is mentioned first, although the lightning must have preceded it, indicating that the sound of the thunder had not yet subsided when the lightning flashed again. The heavy thunder and hailstorm are further described in verse 24. Hail fell while the fire, the lightning, flashed back and forth without pause, ominously interrupting the darkness and illuminating the hail. The hail was so heavy (v. 24b, cf. v. 18b) that in all of Egypt's history as a nation nothing like it had occurred. According to the Egyptians, who also knew the expression used in the text, the establishment of the kingdom of Upper and Lower Egypt was the beginning of their history; at that time the rule of the gods was transferred to their kings and Egypt became a nation.

Verse 25 describes the results of the storm. Men and animals, plants and trees (cf. Pss. 78:47; 105:33) were beaten down and stripped (lit.: ''shattered''), as had been predicted (v. 19, 22). Only Goshen was spared (v. 26, cf. 8:22–23; 9:4, 6–7).

9:27–30 *Then Pharaoh summoned Moses and Aaron. "This time I have sinned," he said to them. "The LORD is in the right, and I and my people are in the wrong. Pray to the LORD, for we have had enough thunder and hail. I will let you go; you don't have to stay any longer."*

Moses replied, "When I have gone out of the city, I will spread out my hands in prayer to the LORD. The thunder will stop and there will be no more hail, so you may know that the earth is the LORD's. But I know that you and your officials still do not fear the LORD God."

See 8:8–11, 25–29. Pharaoh sent messengers to summon Moses and Aaron. He acknowledged that this time (when he had been so emphatically warned beforehand) he had been in the wrong; ''The LORD is in the right, and I and my people are in the wrong'' (lit,: ''I and my people are the wicked ones, the ungodly,'' cf. commentary on 2:13–14). Pharaoh thought that he could get by with the minimum. He asked Moses and Aaron to pray to their God, since he believed that there had been enough thunder and hail (''voices of God,'' cf. commentary on v. 23; this is another indication that the conversations between Moses and Pharaoh were held in Egyptian). He promised to let the Israelites go; they ''don't have to stay any longer.'' The latter implied not only Pharaoh's sense of his own power (his word determined Israel's freedom), but also the implicit acknowledgment that Israel's continued stay in Egypt was harmful to Pharaoh and his people.

Moses, who was the spokesman, was once more willing to grant Pharaoh's request. It is not certain which city was meant (cf. commentary on 7:14–18). The fact that Moses first wanted to leave the city shows that he and Aaron were not afraid that they would be struck by the hail; this, even more than Goshen's being spared, showed the Lord's omnipotence in protecting His people. Second (and this is also expressed in Moses' posture while praying), Moses wanted to show that they sought the Lord in solitude, in that part of Egypt that was hardest hit: the open field. Moses again had great faith: the hail and thunder *would* cease so that Pharaoh would know that the earth belonged to the Lord (cf. Ps. 24:1; commentary on v. 14). Pharaoh was still being called to repentance, but Moses did not want Pharaoh to think that he was naïve. He therefore let him know explicitly (v. 30) that he saw through Pharaoh and his officials (cf. v. 34). He knew that the reason for this request was not a true fear of the Lord, the only God, but only fear for his own life and his own interest (cf. Isa. 26:10), so that Pharaoh was still not inclined to give in to the demand of Israel's God.

9:31, 32 *(The flax and barley were destroyed, since the barley had headed and the flax was in bloom. The wheat and spelt, however, were not destroyed, because they ripen later.)*

These verses must be considered a footnote describing the situation when Pharaoh summoned Moses and Aaron. Flax was grown in Egypt to make linen for clothing (linen was also used to wrap mummies). Spelt is a type of coarse wheat and is harvested after the barley. The Egyptians used spelt to bake bread. The seventh plague thus took place in late January or early February, since in Egypt barley is sown in November and harvested in March. Wheat and spelt ripen a month later than flax and barley.

9:33 *Then Moses left Pharaoh and went out of the city. He spread out his hands toward the LORD; the thunder and hail stopped, and the rain no longer poured down on the land.*

Moses kept his promise and his faith was not put to shame. After (or during) his prayer the hail stopped (cf. 1 Kings 17:1).

9:34–35 *When Pharaoh saw that the rain and hail and thunder had stopped, he sinned again: He and his officials hardened their hearts. So Pharaoh's heart was hard and he would not let the Israelites go, just as the LORD had said through Moses.*

Pharaoh did not keep his promise (cf. 8:12–15, 30–32), but was glad that the rain, hail, and thunder had stopped; he continued to sin: he hardened his heart (cf. commentary on 7:14; 8:15), as did his officials, something that had not been mentioned before. Pharaoh had a negative influence on his surroundings, which in turn reinforced him. "Hardened," cf. commentary on 7:13. "Just as the LORD had said" (cf. commentary on 7:13) refers back to verse 30 as indicated by "through Moses."

22. *The Eighth Plague: Locusts* (10:1–20)

The eighth plague is mentioned also in Psalms 78:46 and 105:34–35; the latter is dependent on the description here.

The Lord explicitly stated the purpose of the hardening of the hearts of Pharaoh and his officials in verses 1–2: His own glorification through these plagues and their remembrance. Again Pharaoh was threatened first (vv. 3–6). For the first time there was also pressure from his officials to give in; Pharaoh yielded to their pressure to the extent that he called Moses and Aaron back. But his refusal to fully comply with the Lord's demand ended the meeting with Moses and Aaron being thrown out (vv. 7–11). When the plague came (although not explicitly stated, it is likely that Goshen was again spared) Pharaoh's usual game followed: his request for intercession and his induration after Moses agreed and the plague ended (vv. 16–20). The Lord used natural means in bringing about this plague: the east and west winds (vv. 13, 19).

10:1, 2 *Then the LORD said to Moses, "Go to Pharaoh, for I have hardened his heart and the hearts of his officials so that I may perform these miraculous signs of mine among them that you may tell your children and grandchildren how I dealt harshly with the Egyptians and how I performed my signs among them, and that you may know that I am the LORD."*

See commentary on 9:1; 8:1. "Officials," cf. commentary on 9:14. "I have hardened," cf. commentary on 4:21; 9:12. The word used here is not the same as in 4:21 and 9:12 (cf. commentary on 8:32). Again the officials are mentioned (cf. commentary on 9:34–35). The Lord told Moses in advance (cf. commentary on 4:21) that He had hardened the hearts of Pharaoh and his officials so that He could perform His miraculous signs among them[11] (cf. commentary on 8:20–23) and Moses (addressed as the representative of the Israelite fathers) would be able to tell his children and his grandchildren of all the signs the Lord performed in Egypt, so that the people would know that He was the Lord. The purpose of the hardening of Pharaoh's heart was thus the Lord's own glorification, while that hardening

---

[11]Hebrew "in his midst," "before him" (KJV). The NIV and RSV follow the LXX and Syriac: "among them" which gives better sense in the context.

in turn justified the sending of the plagues, which were to be the subject of Israel's lore; thus not only *Egypt* but also *Israel* would know that God was the Lord (cf. commentary on 6:7, 29; concerning the Egyptians 7:5, 17; 8:10, 22; 9:14, 16). For the thought that the Lord "plays" with Egypt, cf. Psalm 2:4.

10:3–6 *So Moses and Aaron went to Pharaoh and said to him, "This is what the L*ORD*, the God of the Hebrews, says: 'How long will you refuse to humble yourself before me? Let my people go, so that they may worship me. If you refuse to let them go, I will bring locusts into your country tomorrow. They will cover the face of the ground so that it cannot be seen. They will devour what little you have left after the hail, including every tree that is growing in your fields. They will fill your houses and those of all your officials and all the Egyptians—something neither your fathers nor your forefathers have ever seen from the day they settled in this land till now.'" Then Moses turned and left Pharaoh.*

"The God of the Hebrews," cf. verse 3b and commentary on 9:13. Pharaoh was called to repent, to humble himself before the Lord (cf. James 4:10; 1 Peter 5:6). For the construction of verse 4, cf. 8:2, 21; 9:2–3, 17–18. Locusts are a serious plague that still strikes Egypt occasionally today, when modern methods such as flamethrowers are used against them. It frequently depends on the wind direction whether a given area is spared or not, and only the wind can effectively get rid of them. (cf. Ps. 109:23). They usually arrive in thick swarms. Meant here was probably the Egyptian migratory locust.

This plague probably took place in February or early March, which was the usual time for the locusts to appear. The young hatch in the spring when the sun has warmed the sand in which the eggs are laid. The earliest this can happen is mid-March. Then they go through four stages of development and are extremely voracious in all four stages. Moses threatened Pharaoh that they would cover the face (lit.: "eye") of the ground so that it could not be seen (cf. Num. 22:5, 11). This disaster would be all the more serious because it would complete the destruction inflicted by the hail. The locusts would even enter the houses of Pharaoh, his officials, and his subjects, and "fill them" (cf. 8:3, 21, 24; Joel 29). Nothing like this had happened since time immemorial in Egypt (for this expression in v. 6 cf. commentary on 9:18, 24; "something neither your fathers nor your forefathers have seen" seems to have been a common expression in Egypt. We must remember that the Egyptians referred to the fathers of the Pharaohs as "the gods," but Moses did not let this empty form bother him). Moses did not wait for Pharaoh's answer, or else we must assume a refusal not mentioned here (cf. 8:4–5, 23–24; 9:5–6, 21–22).

10:7–11 *Pharaoh's officials said to him, "How long will this man be a snare to us? Let the people go, so that they may worship the* L ORD *their God. Do you not yet realize that Egypt is ruined?"*

Then Moses and Aaron were brought back to Pharaoh. "Go, worship the L ORD *your God," he said. "But just who will be going?"*

Moses answered, "We will go with our young and old, with our sons and daughters, and with our flocks and herds, because we are to celebrate a festival to the L ORD*."*

Pharaoh said, "The L ORD *be with you—if I let you go, along with your women and children! Clearly you are bent on evil. No! Have only the men go; and worship the* L ORD*, since that's what you have been asking for." Then Moses and Aaron were driven out of Pharaoh's presence.*

Note that Pharaoh's officials tried rather sharply to convince him to give in. The words they used are striking: they asked how long Moses would be a "snare" (or possibly "bait") to them. Pharaoh had to "let the people go" (NIV, LXX) or "let the men go" (KJV, RSV). The Hebrew word allows for both translations. "People" would make the officials' statement a suggestion to give in to the Lord's demand. "Men" would mean that Pharaoh followed their suggestion by allowing only the men to go, while the women and children were to stay behind as hostages (vv. 9–11). "Worship" meant the festival Moses demanded (cf. 3:18; 5:1, 3). Their last question implied the unequivocal acknowledgment of Egypt's defeat. After the magicians (8:19) the officials now had also reached the breaking point and at their urging Pharaoh called Moses and Aaron back and made them a proposition. He ostensibly gave in to Moses' request, but pretended not to know that it involved *all* of Israel: "But just who will be going?" Moses answered that everyone and everything had to go, not only the men, but also the women; not only the young, but also the old; not only sons, but also daughters; not only the small livestock, but also the cattle. For it was a festival to the Lord for *all* of Israel.

Verse 10 is somewhat difficult. Pharaoh said: "The L ORD be with you—if I let you go along with your women and children" (lit.: "little ones"). The intention is ironic: "May your own God, the Lord, be with you in the same way that I let you go, i.e., not at all. But I warn you both, the fact that you insist on going without leaving security behind indicates that your request to go three days into the desert is merely a pretense to leave for good." For the question as to whether Moses (and thus the Lord) indeed used this tactic and Israel would have left permanently, see commentary on 3:18. Verse 11 indicates that Pharaoh entered into further negotiations with Moses and Aaron only to oblige his officials. "Have only the men go" (lit.: "go now you men," cf. KJV. The word for "men" is not the same as in v. 7); the women and children were to stay behind. Moses and Aaron were ignominiously chased away on Pharaoh's command without being allowed a reply. Pharaoh's guilt was all the more pronounced since in Egypt the women also participated in religious worship.

10:12–15 *And the Lord said to Moses, "Stretch out your hand over Egypt so that locusts will swarm over the land and devour everything growing in the fields, everything left by the hail."*

So Moses stretched out his staff over Egypt, and the Lord made an east wind blow across the land all that day and all that night. By morning the wind had brought the locusts; they invaded all Egypt and settled down in every area of the country in great numbers. Never before had there been such a plague of locusts, nor will there ever be again. They covered all the ground until it was black. They devoured all that was left after the hail—everything growing in the fields and the fruit on the trees. Nothing green remained on tree or plant in all the land of Egypt.

Now Moses received the Lord's command: stretch your hand (with the staff, cf. v. 13) over Egypt "for the locusts" (KJV), indicating that the locusts were in readiness: Moses had only to give the sign. The Lord promised again that they would come and complete the work the hail had begun (cf. 7:19; 8:5, 16; 9:22). Moses stretched out the staff (cf. 7:20; 8:6; 9:23) and the east wind came from the desert east of Egypt, between the Nile and the Gulf of Suez, and from Arabia. It blew a full day and a full night and when morning came "the wind had brought the locusts" (KJV: "the east wind brought the locusts," which would mean that they arrived that morning and had possibly been blown in from Arabia). The Lord thus used natural means. The locusts were extremely numerous (v. 14; Ps. 105:34: "without number"). Nothing like this had ever happened before, nor would it ever happen again. See 9:24 where the same expression, translated here "in great numbers," is used of the hail ("very heavy").

In verse 15 we have a choice. The Hebrew reads: "so that the land was darkened," which could mean that the daylight was obscured. But I prefer to take it to mean that the ground was dark with locusts, based on the preceding lines and the prediction in verse 5a. An eyewitness says that the young locusts that do not yet have wings travel along the ground in tight clusters and cover it entirely, so that there is not even enough room for a horse's hoof. But the adult locusts do the same and those are referred to here. Anything green that survived the hail was now eaten by the locusts.

10:16–20 *Pharaoh quickly summoned Moses and Aaron and said, "I have sinned against the Lord your God and against you. Now forgive my sin once more and* *pray to the LORD your God to take this deadly plague away from me."*

Moses then left Pharaoh and prayed to the LORD. And the LORD changed the wind to a very strong west wind, which caught up the locusts and carried them into the Red Sea. Not a locust was left anywhere in Egypt. But the LORD hardened Pharaoh's heart, and he would not let the Israelites go.

Pharaoh was very frightened and (on his own initiative) summoned Moses and Aaron. There appears to be a progression in the confession of his sin. The expression "this time" is not mentioned with the sin (as in 9:27), but rather in connection with the request to take away the plague. But the conclusion shows that he was primarily concerned with the destruction of what was left in the fields, rather than that he had changed. He even forgot to say that he was prepared to let the people go! Moses seems to have said nothing more to Pharaoh; he probably did not deign him worthy an answer.

Verse 18 is virtually identical to 8:30. Only Moses is mentioned. See also 8:12. The Lord answered Moses' prayer immediately: He changed the east wind to a strong west wind (lit.: "sea wind," possibly from the Mediterranean Sea, thus a northwest wind), which carried the locusts into the Red Sea. The name "Red Sea" is the LXX's translation of the Hebrew name "Sea of *Sup.*" The origin of the name is uncertain. Outside this name *sup* is used for "reeds" or "rushes"; the name thus may be derived from the reeds that used to grow on its shores, or perhaps from a city (cf. Deut. 1:1). Others take *sup* to refer to aquatic plants or seaweed (cf. Jonah 2:5). The Red Sea includes the sea and both its arms, the Gulf of Suez and the Gulf of Akaba. The Egyptians had a number of names for the Red Sea: "the large green sea," referring to both the Red Sea and the Mediterranean Sea; "the ocean of the Easterners," "the sea of the rising of the sun," "sea of navigation," "the great sea of the circular water," "the sea."[12] Note that the name "Sea of Reeds" is not found in Egyptian. It frequently happened that swarms of locusts were blown into the sea. Verse 19b, cf. 8:31b. But again the Lord hardened Pharaoh's heart (cf. 4:21; 9:12, 35) as He had predicted (v. 1), and Pharaoh refused to let Israel go.

23. *The Ninth Plague: Darkness* (10:21–29)

This plague is also mentioned in Psalm 105:28. This time it is clearly stated that Goshen was spared (v. 23). Pharaoh's hardening after Moses refused to accept his compromise that the livestock stay behind (vv. 24–26) was so severe that he forbade Moses under penalty of death to

---

[12]Wilhelm Spiegelberg, *"Die ägyptischen Namen für das Rote Meer"* Zeitschrift für Ägyptische Sprache und Altertumskunde, Vol. 66, No. 1 Leipzig, 1930, (pp. 37–39).

come back to him (vv. 27–28). Moses responded that he would indeed not see Pharaoh again (v. 29).

10:21–23 *Then the LORD said to Moses, "Stretch out your hand toward the sky so that darkness will spread over Egypt—darkness that can be felt." So Moses stretched out his hand toward the sky, and total darkness covered all Egypt for three days. No one could see anyone else or leave his place for three days. Yet all the Israelites had light in the places where they lived.*

Verse 21, cf. 9:22; 10:12. The staff is not mentioned at all, although it is likely that Moses had it in his hand. Moses immediately carried out the Lord's command. This plague came without an advance warning for Pharaoh (cf. 8:16). Verse 22, cf. 9:23. "Total darkness" (KJV: "thick darkness"; lit.: "darkness [of] darkness"), a darkness that lasted three days (the Israelites could still observe day and night and thus count the days). It is miraculous and unexplainable that the Israelites were not affected in their houses and in the places where they lived. We must probably think here of the wind that is today called "el-hamsin" in Arabic. "Hamsin" ("fifty") is the name of the fifty-day period between Easter and Pentecost in Egypt; hence the name for the hot south wind that often blew during that period in Egypt. It is worth noting that pestilence (cf. the tenth plague!) usually struck Egypt during the time of the hamsim. But even more intense than the hamsin is the so-called "samum" ("hot, deadly wind"), which, however, rarely lasts more than fifteen or twenty minutes. It blows from the southeast or south-southeast and carries clouds of dust and sand that obscure the sunlight. It is possible that in this case the samum lasted three days, making its duration the miracle. If this wind was what caused the darkness, then the fact that the Israelites had light where they lived can also be explained (v. 23, which also argues against an eclipse of the sun. The hamsin also causes darkness in parts of Egypt, while other parts remains unaffected. "A darkness that can be felt" (v. 21), see preceding remarks (the blowing dust and sand that accompanied and indeed caused the darkness would be tangible). The LXX translation of verse 22 points in the same direction: "and there came gloom, darkness, whirlwind in all of Egypt."

Egypt here was a symbol of God's enemies, but God's people had light (cf. Amos 4:13). This plague was in itself not harmful, but it spoke of God's wrath, cf. the three hours' darkness on the cross (Matt. 27:45; Mark 15:33; Luke 23:44) and Revelation 8:12. This plague, brought on by the servant of another God, must have impressed especially a pagan people: a God who could take away the sunlight entirely had to be powerful, especially to the Egyptians who considered the sun to be a god. The characteristic element of this plague was thus that the hamsin or samum was brought on by the God of Israel.

10:24–29 *Then Pharaoh summoned Moses and said, "Go, worship the LORD. Even your women and children may go with you; only leave your flocks and herds behind."*

But Moses said, "You must allow us to have sacrifices and burnt offerings to present to the LORD our God. Our livestock too must go with us; not a hoof is to be left behind. We have to use some of them in worshiping the LORD our God, and until we get there we will not know what we are to use to worship the LORD."

But the LORD hardened Pharaoh's heart, and he was not willing to let them go. Pharaoh said to Moses, "Get out of my sight! Make sure you do not appear before me again! The day you see my face you will die."

"Just as you say," Moses replied, "I will never appear before you again."

Pharaoh once again summoned Moses (some manuscripts, the LXX, and the Vulgate add "and Aaron": it is indeed possible that Aaron was also present). The statement in verse 23 that "no one could leave his place for three days" thus must not be taken literally, since otherwise Pharaoh could not have summoned Moses until after the plague was over, which is unlikely in the light of Pharaoh's attitude after the previous plagues were taken away, as Calvin already observed. Pharaoh's offer was now broader than in verses 8–11. There he was willing to let only the men go; now he was willing to let the women and children go as well, but the livestock had to stay behind as security (the expression used here means "to keep behind" and may mean "to detain under guard"). But Moses did not deviate from the original demand, something that must have struck Pharaoh as stubbornness. But there was no bargaining; God's dealings with men do not know compromise. Moses' remark in verses 25–26 was very apropos. Pharaoh must have perceived it as insolence that not only *all* their livestock must go with them ("not a hoof must remain behind") since they did not know what sacrifices and which animals the Lord would demand for His worship (cf. 8:27), but that he himself ("you" is emphatic) had to provide sacrifices (those that were partially sacrificed and partially eaten) and burnt offerings (those that were burnt entirely on the altar) for the Israelites. Pharaoh became angry, since he was unwilling to acknowledge the Lord, who as the only true God had the right to full control over His own property (cf. Ps. 24:1) as God. "There" (v. 26): three days into the desert. But Pharaoh's anger had to be attributed primarily to the fact that the Lord hardened his heart (cf. v. 20). On these terms he would not let them go; on the contrary, he chased Moses away as he did in verse 11, but this time permanently, with the threat that if Moses dared come again in his presence he would die. God must have restrained Pharaoh and kept him from issuing this threat until now. Moses, who remained calm, said that he would indeed never again appear before Pharaoh. The plague still ended after three days.

The text indicates that this was the last meeting between Moses and Pharaoh. The relationship had gradually deteriorated because of Pharaoh's stubborn refusal and deceit. The Lord now had to resort to the most drastic measure to bring about the release of the seed of the woman. This would be the tenth plague. A major problem is that Moses still announced the tenth plague to Pharaoh (11:8) after his statement that he would never appear before Pharaoh again. The best solution is to take the verb in 11:1 as a perfect tense ("had said," NIV) rather than an imperfect ("said," KJV). The conversation in 11:4–8 then was a continuation of the meeting in 10:24–29.

24. *The Announcement of the Tenth Plague* (11:1–10)

In chapter 11 the Lord through Moses announces the tenth plague, the death of the firstborn. This plague is also mentioned in Psalms 78:51; 105:36; 135:8; 136:10.

11:1–3 *Now the* LORD *had said to Moses, "I will bring one more plague on Pharaoh and on Egypt. After that, he will let you go from here, and when he does, he will drive you out completely. Tell the people that men and women alike are to ask their neighbors for articles of silver and gold." (The* LORD *made the Egyptians favorably disposed toward the people, and Moses himself was highly regarded in Egypt by Pharaoh's officials and by the people.)*

Verses 1–3 must be considered parenthetical, to inform the reader of the situation and to explain why Moses could stand up to Pharaoh as he did.

I already stated at the end of the previous section why the perfect tense ("had said") is preferable in verse 1. It is unlikely that a redactor so carelessly pieced together his sources that we must read here "and the LORD said. . . ," indicating that Moses was sent back to Pharaoh immediately after 10:29. Grammatically there is no objection to the pluperfect tense here. Some believe that Moses heard an inner voice from the Lord while he was standing before Pharaoh (cf. Matt. 10:19–20; Mark 13:11; Luke 12:12). "Plague" actually means "stroke" from a verb "to touch, strike." Different words are used in 9:14 and 12:13. The Lord had told Moses that he would give Pharaoh the final blow in order to liberate the seed of the woman. "After that, he will let you go," cf. 3:20b. The Lord reminded Moses of what He had said when He appeared to him at Mt. Horeb. "Drive out," cf. commentary on 5:24, 12:31, 33, 39.

On the basis of the certain fulfillment of His word the Lord instructed Moses to tell the Israelites that each one had to ask for gold and silver objects from his neighbors (v. 2; cf. 3:22; 12:35). In 3:22 only the women were mentioned, but now the men are also included.

To the Lord "*the* people" is Israel, cf. 1:22; 3:12, etc. Verse 3, cf. 3:21; 12:36. The Lord had fulfilled the promise of 3:21.[13] "Favorably disposed" must probably be understood in terms of servile fear, after what had happened to them and their country; and once again the threat did not affect only Pharaoh, but also Egypt (v. 1). The officials (cf. 10:7), who hardened their hearts by a previous plague (cf. 9:30, 34), are now said to "highly regard" Moses. Verse 3b ("and Moses . . . by the people") must be a post-Mosaic observation, since it refers to Moses in the third person and in a favorable sense. The observation explains why Pharaoh had spared Moses for so long. His officials seem to have had much influence on him (cf. also 10:7), but their attitude was based on pure fear (cf. 9:30, 34). "And by the people," i.e., the Egyptians, which indicates that this is a later addition (cf. v. 2).

11:4–8 *So Moses said, "This is what the Lord says: 'About midnight I will go throughout Egypt. Every firstborn son in Egypt will die, from the firstborn son of Pharaoh, who sits on the throne, to the firstborn son of the slave girl, who is at her hand mill, and all the firstborn of the cattle as well. There will be loud wailing throughout Egypt—worse than there has ever been or ever will be again. But among the Israelites not a dog will bark at any man or animal.' Then you will know that the Lord makes a distinction between Egypt and Israel. All these officials of yours will come to me, bowing down before me and saying, "Go, you and all the people who follow you!" After that I will leave." Then Moses, hot with anger, left Pharaoh.*

Verse 4 continues the narrative after the parenthetical observations of verses 1–3. Moses formally announced the tenth plague to Pharaoh: the death of the firstborn. He carried out the instructions given in 4:22–23 and repeated in verses 1–2. The end of the battle between the Lord and Pharaoh was drawing near. The announcement was still a call to repentance, but would later be carried out (cf. 12:29). It is not stated which night was meant. The Lord Himself would go out to do battle and every firstborn would die. "At her hand mill" (lit.: "behind the two mill stones"): this

---

[13]The LXX and the Samaritan Pentateuch add: "and they loaned them." This is probably an attempt to remove the impression of impropriety that could be attached to the Israelites' request in verse 2 (cf. commentary on 3:21–22).

expression indicates the lowest class, since the work behind the mill stones was considered degrading and in Egypt was done by prisoners (cf. 12:29; Judg. 16:21; Isa. 47:2; Lam. 5:13). The hand mill consisted of two round stones, the bottom one attached to the ground, while the top stone was turned by one or sometimes two women (cf. Matt. 24:41). "Wailing" (v. 6) is the same word used for the "crying out" of the Israelites in 3:7, 9. Verse 6b, cf. 9:18, 24; 10:6, and especially 10:14. Egypt (again the concept of solidarity) would be plunged into mourning, but Israel would be spared, as stated in the curious expression that "among the Israelites not a dog will bark" (lit.: "sharpen its tongue," indicating hostile growling or barking); a similar expression is found in Joshua 10:21. Verse 7b, cf. 8:22-23; 9:4.

It has been thought by some that the tenth plague was actually pestilence, but this is not mentioned here or in chapter 12. It is striking that only the firstborn were struck, while all others were still spared. But 9:15 and Psalm 78:50 make pestilence probable, since the best translation of Psalm 78:50 is: "He did not spare their soul from death, but gave them over to the plague (pestilence)." However, the emphasis is not on the means, but rather on the fact that the Lord Himself "goes out" (cf. 2 Sam. 24:15ff.; 1 Chron. 21:13ff.; 2 Chron. 19:25; 32:21; Isa. 37.36). The story of Sennacherib especially presents a striking parallel, since the Bible does not mention that in that case the secondary cause was pestilence as nonbiblical sources indicate.[14]

It is worth noting that Thutmose IV (1421-1412 B.C.), who succeeded Amenhotep II (the Pharaoh whose firstborn was killed) was not himself the firstborn. Thutmose IV claimed that when he was still a prince he had a dream in which the sun god promised him the throne; this implies that he was not the one who would be expected to succeed to the throne under normal circumstances. Concerning the terrible nature of this plague I refer to Calvin's remark that we must not dispute with curiosity the question why God demanded the penalty from the sons, when the guilt of the fathers was the more serious, since it was sinful to prescribe to God, whose unfathomable wisdom transcends all human understanding, what the measure of His judgment should be.

In verse 8 the story reached a climax. Moses predicted to the proud Pharaoh that "all these" (he probably pointed to the officials standing around the throne) officials would come to him (lit.: "come down to me," indicating that the palace was situated on high ground, or referring to the lower elevation of Goshen) and would bow down before him, who in vain asked Pharaoh to let Israel go, and they would ask him and all the people

---

[14]Cf. van Gelderen, *Sanherib,* pp. 39-40.

who followed him to leave; which is exactly what happened (12:31–33). Moses left Pharaoh "hot with anger." This was not a sinful anger and foreshadowed the coming outbreak of the Lord's anger (cf. Ps. 78:50). The negotiations were over and had ended in a complete break between Moses, the Lord's representative, and Pharaoh. The fault lay with Pharaoh who repeatedly reneged on his promises.

11:9 *The LORD had said to Moses, "Pharaoh will refuse to listen to you—so that my wonders may be multiplied in Egypt."*

To calm down the angry Moses the Lord once again repeated the purpose that would be achieved by Pharaoh's refusal to listen (cf. 10:1–2). "Wonders," cf. 4:21; 7:3, 9.

11:10 *Moses and Aaron performed all these wonders before Pharaoh, but the LORD hardened Pharaoh's heart, and he would not let the Israelites go out of his country.*

With verse 10 the actual story of the plagues (which possibly existed earlier as a separate narrative) ends. In 12:1 a new section begins (as indicated especially by "in Egypt"): the description of the Exodus as the result of the tenth plague. "Before Pharaoh," cf. 7:10. "Hardened," cf. 10:20.

25. *The Institution of the Passover* (12:1–28)

This section describes the institution of the Passover (cf. also vv. 29–50; 13:3–16; 23:14–19; 34:18–25; Lev. 23:4–8; Num. 28:16–25; Deut. 16:1–8, 16–17; Ezek. 45:21–24). The text indicates that everything described in verses 1–28 happened in one day (cf. "this night," vv. 8, 12; "this day," vv. 14, 17). We must therefore distinguish between what the Lord commanded on the eve of the Exodus (only the slaughtering and eating of the Passover lamb in haste, and the application of the blood on the doorframes, vv. 1–13), and what Israel had to do each year in commemoration of this day (the Passover and the Feast of Unleavened Bread, from the fourteenth to the twenty-first day of each month, vv. 14–20). Neither feast could be celebrated at this time in the form in which the Lord instituted it, since the Passover lamb had to be taken into the house four days before the Passover, on the tenth day of the month, which could not be done in this case, since the Lord apparently spoke here on the fourteenth day (v. 12). Furthermore, the Israelites were forbidden to do any work on the first and seventh days (v. 16), something that was impossible at the time of the Exodus. Moses also instructed the elders to prepare the Passover lamb (vv. 21–24), but not to celebrate the Feast of Unleavened Bread.

114

Verses 24–25 may allude to the fact that this feast could be celebrated only after they had arrived in Canaan. Also, verses 27–28 speak only of the Passover, while verse 25 and 13:5 clearly indicate that the Feast of Unleavened Bread could not be celebrated until after they had reached Canaan. Verses 3–4, 14–20 are therefore instructions for the future. Yet we must assume that the instructions for the Feast of Unleavened Bread are part of the Lord's instructions to Moses on the eve of the Exodus from Egypt (v. 1).

The Passover, which, like the Feast of Unleavened Bread, is based on an historical event, links the Exodus with the idea of sacrifice (v. 27). In the case of the Passover the Lord explicitly stated the historical basis before the event, but the author provided the historical foundation of the Feast of Unleavened Bread after it had been established (v. 39); in verse 8 the reason for the eating of the unleavened bread is still lacking. The Passover has reference especially to the being spared by the blood of the lamb in the Lord's judgment on Egypt (the tenth plague), the Feast of Unleavened Bread refers to the haste of the Exodus (cf. Deut. 16:3) and thus to the Exodus itself. This is why the Feast of Unleavened Bread begins with and follows the Passover. If Egypt is seen as the image of the slavery of sin the symbolism is striking (cf. 1 Cor. 5:7).

Both the Passover and the Feast of Unleavened Bread are commemorations (cf. vv. 14–27). The later Jews made a distinction between the instructions for the celebration of the Passover in Egypt and those that remained valid forever (see above). They considered unique to Egypt the choice of the lamb on the tenth day, the application of the blood to the doorframes, and the eating of the Passover meal in travel clothing and in anxious haste.[15]

12:1 *The LORD said to Moses and Aaron in Egypt,*

Once again Aaron is mentioned. Because of the expression "in Egypt" (which also excludes the possibility that Israel would have derived the Feast of Unleavened Bread from the Canaanites) this verse gives the impression of a new beginning. Perhaps it served at one time as the introduction of a separate narrative. The legal provisions that now follow are the only ones that were given in Egypt.

12:2 *"This month is to be for you the first month, the first month of your year."*

---

[15]Cf. the author's "De oorsprong van het Pascha en van het Massothfeest," *Gereformeerd Theologisch Tijdschrift* (1943), pp. 33–64; and his *Commentaar op Leviticus* (1950), pp. 322–326.

"This month" is the month Abib (cf. 13:4; 23:15) or Nisan, as it was called after the Captivity (cf. Exod. 34:18; Deut. 16:1; Neh. 2:1; Esth. 3:7), i.e., late March or early April. It must be "the head of months" (as the expression literally reads) for the Israelites, i.e., the first one, the beginning. This implies that it was not considered the first month prior to the Exodus. The Exodus marked the beginning of a new era for Israel and was of fundamental importance both nationally and religiously. According to Josephus this change affected only the so-called religious year, while the civic and economic year still began in the fall.

12:3, 4 *"Tell the whole community of Israel that on the tenth day of this month each man is to take a lamb for his family, one for each household. If any household is too small for a whole lamb, they must share one with their nearest neighbor, having taken into account the number of people there are. You are to determine the amount of lamb needed in accordance with what each person will eat."*

The "whole community of Israel" that Moses and Aaron were to address was represented by the elders (cf. v. 21). According to the rabbis the instructions in verses 3 and 6a were kept only on the occasion of this particular Passover, in which case verse 1 should be translated "the LORD *had* said. . . ." Perhaps the tenth day had a special significance, since the Day of Atonement also fell on the tenth day (of the seventh month; cf. Lev. 23:27). "Family," see commentary on 6:14. The male head of every household had to take a lamb; he had to determine how much he would need, based on the number of people in his household and on how much each one could eat. If the number of people was too small (later traditions set the minimum number at ten), then he was to share with his nearest neighbor in order to prevent as much as possible anything being left over. The emphasis was thus on the family unit, represented by the father who functioned as priest, a function later taken over by the priests and Levites. The Passover sacrifice was a communal act—it pointed to the communion between the members of each household and among all Israelites (cf. v. 6).

12:5, 6 *"The animals you choose must be year-old males without defect, and you may take them from the sheep or the goats. Take care of them until the fourteenth day of the month, when all the people of the community of Israel must slaughter them at twilight."*

The lamb itself was to be a male, one year old, without defect (its age guaranteed unbroken strength), either a sheep or a goat. According to Deuteronomy 16:2 sheep and oxen were also permitted, but this may refer to the bringing of other sacrifices. Animals for burnt offerings also had to be male and without defect (cf. Lev. 1:3; 22:19ff.), so that the Passover animal was an animal consecrated entirely to the Lord. It was to be kept for four days (from the tenth until the fourteenth), then it was to be slaughtered. There is no indication as to why it had to be kept for four days; perhaps seeing the animal was intended to focus Israel's attention on the meaning of their redemption and on God's mercy; it also would prevent its becoming unclean, which again expresses the sacredness of the Passover animal. Although it was a family feast, every household participated as a member of the community of Israel ("community," lit.: "assembly of the congregation"; "assembly" is a narrower concept than "congregation"). "At twilight," lit. "between the two evenings." I agree with the traditional Jewish view that the time referred to here is when the sun begins to set; the first evening thus began immediately after noon, the second when the sun had set. In the second temple the slaughtering usually took place at 2:30 in the afternoon.

Verse 6, cf. Leviticus 23:5; Numbers 9:3, 5; 28:16; Deuteronomy 16:6; Joshua 5:10; Ezekiel 45:21.

12:7 *"Then they are to take some of the blood and put it on the sides and tops of the doorframes of the houses where they eat the lambs."*

The purpose of the application of the blood to the sides and tops of the doorframes is given in verses 13, 23, 27; the manner in which it was to be applied in verse 22. The blood has atoning power and points to the blood of the Lamb that will take away the sin of the world (John 1:29, 36).

12:8 *"That same night they are to eat the meat roasted over the fire, along with bitter herbs, and bread made without yeast."*

The unleavened bread points to the haste with which they had to leave Egypt, the land of the slavery of sin (cf. v. 39). The Hebrew word for unleavened bread is *masot* from the root *masas,* meaning "to suck" (Isa. 66:11, KJV: "suck," NIV: "nurse"). *Masot* then indicates that those loaves of bread were as it were "sucked out," without moisture, which points to the being purified of the leaven of sin, the hasty (cf. Gen. 19:3) and willing breaking with sin (whereby the leaven symbolizes decay and contaminating impurity; leaven could not be present in any of the sacrifices, cf. 23:18; Lev. 2:11; 6:14–18; except in the Fellowship Offering, traditionally called the Peace Offering, which was eaten by the priests, Lev. 7:13; 23:17; Amos 4:5). Others interpret *masot* as "sweet," since the unleavened bread tasted sweet, in contrast to the bitter herbs (e.g., wild endive) which reminded the Israelites of the bitter oppression by and in Egypt (cf. Num.

117

9:11; Lam. 3:15). The remembrance was to be a deterrent from ever returning voluntarily to the land of slavery (cf. 1 Cor. 5:7–8, where Paul links the Feast of Unleavened Bread with the life of sanctification and gratitude and calls Christ the Passover Lamb slain for the church). See also Romans 6:21 where Paul speaks of the bitter memories that are to keep us from becoming once again slaves of sin.

12:9 *"Do not eat the meat raw or cooked in water, but roast it over the fire—head, legs and inner parts."*

The lamb was to be eaten in its entirety, expressing once again the idea of unity. It could not be eaten raw or cooked in water. Only primitive people ate raw meat, and then frequently out of superstition. Cooked meat had to be cut into pieces beforehand, while the Passover lamb was to remain intact. In Deuteronomy 16:7 the addition "in water" is omitted, and there we can translate "cooked" (i.e., in the fire) and hence "roasted," cf. 2 Chronicles 35:13. The roasting brought the animal in contact with the fire, which would all the more give it the appearance of a sacrificial animal. It also could remain intact, reflecting the unity with one another and with God (cf. 1 Cor. 10:17), and contact with anything else could be avoided as much as possible. Again, roasting (on the spit) under-lines the sacredness of the Passover animal. Jewish custom was to bend the head and shanks toward the abdominal cavity and to place the cleaned intestines inside. John later saw the requirement that not a bone could be broken fulfilled in Christ (cf. John 19:36; Ps. 34:21).

12:10 *"Do not leave any of it till morning; if some is left till morning, you must burn it."*

The head of the household had to do his best to prevent any of the lamb from being left (v. 4). If, in spite of his precautions, some was nevertheless left over it had to be burned before morning (34:25; Deut. 16:4; also Exod. 23:18). The reason for this was that the Passover refers to only the one night of the Exodus during which the tenth plague took place. From a practical standpoint it also prevented the meat from being used as common food, and also prevented spoilage.

12:11 *"This is how you are to eat it: with your cloak tucked into your belt, your sandals on your feet and your staff in your hand. Eat it in haste; it is the LORD'S Passover."*

The manner in which the Passover sacrifice had to be eaten indicates the great haste with which they would leave Egypt: the cloak was to be tucked into the belt, which was customary when a person had to walk fast, so that he would not trip over it (cf. 1 Kings 18:46; 2 Kings 4:29; Isa. 5:27). The staff had to be in their hand, and the sandals that were worn for traveling were to be on their feet. "Eat in haste" is explicitly added (cf. Deut. 16:3). This instruction also seems to apply only to the first Passover, and was not kept later (cf. Jesus and His disciples, but modern Samaritans celebrate the Passover wearing a white belt, ceremonial shoes, and some have a staff in their hand; at least, this was the case in 1931). But it was only secondarily a meal: it was in the first place a Passover for the Lord. "Passover" comes from the word *pasah,* meaning "to jump past," "to pass by," "to spare." Thus the Passover can best be seen as "the Feast of the Lord's passing over and sparing His people" (cf. v. 12), as is also expressed in its English name, "passover." It was to be an expression of gratitude toward the Lord.

12:12 *"On that same night I will pass through Egypt and strike down every firstborn—both men and animals—and I will bring judgment on all the gods of Egypt; I am the Lord."*

The Lord further explained that this night He would slay every firstborn in Egypt, whether it was man or beast (cf. 11:4–7). "This night" indicates that the Lord spoke to Moses and Aaron on the preceding day. The Lord ("I am the Lord" or "I, the Lord") would thereby also bring judgment on all the gods of Egypt (cf. Num. 33:4; "judgment," 6:6; 7:4). This statement can best be explained on the basis of the religious significance of the plagues, including this final one (see Introduction, p. 20). In the case of some of the plagues this religious significance can readily be seen; but the entire background of the plagues was the battle between the Lord, the God of Israel, and the gods of the Egyptians, who had to be exposed in their nonexistence and impotence. Therefore, "I will bring judgment on all the gods of Egypt, I, the Lord." The gods of Egypt were insignificant in His almighty hand.

12:13 *"The blood will be a sign for you on the houses where you are; and when I see the blood, I will pass over you. No destructive plague will touch you when I strike Egypt."*

Israel, on the other hand, would have the blood as a sign (v. 7), marking their houses as those to be spared by the Lord. When the Lord saw the blood He would pass them over (see commentary on v. 11 for *pasah,* which is used here). The Lord spoke anthropomorphically to make Himself understood by the Israelites, since God of course did not need this sign to recognize the Israelites, as verse 23 indicates. Hence the statement "a sign *for you*." The blood was thus a visible sign and seal. Israel's firstborn ones were spared by the blood of an animal, which thus had substitutionary significance. The Passover was a reminder that this being spared was not a matter of course.

12:14 *"This is a day you are to commemorate; for the generations to come you shall celebrate it as a festival to the Lord–a lasting ordinance."*

This day would also be a commemoration and the Passover a commemorative feast in honor of the Lord (cf. v. 11b). "Celebrate" indicates that the passover was a joyous feast. The word "lasting" (KJV: "forever") means "into the far future"; some also think of the Lord's Supper, the New Testament Passover.

12:15, 16 *"For seven days you are to eat bread made without yeast. On the first day remove the yeast from your houses, for whoever eats anything with yeast in it from the first day through the seventh must be cut off from Israel. On the first day hold a sacred assembly, and another one on the seventh day. Do no work at all on these days, except to prepare food for everyone to eat–that is all you may do."*

Verses 15–20 describe the institution of the Feast of Unleavened Bread (cf. 23:15; 34:18). Some have tried to find the origin of this feast not in the historical setting presented here, but in Canaanite or even pre-Mosaic influences. The Israelites then would have adopted a harvest festival from the Canaanites after they settled in Canaan, or perhaps knew such a feast in Egypt. But to the best of our knowledge nothing is known of the eating of unleavened bread, or of such a festival, among the Canaanites. It would be easier to trace the Passover to a Babylonian custom, which consisted of applying the blood of a lamb to the door frame to ward off evil spirits or to effect atonement (although the sacrificing of firstborn sheep or goats is not an integral part of this custom).[16] We must therefore assume that the Feast of Unleavened Bread (see commentary on v. 8) was of purely Israelite origin and instituted by the Lord without pressing an established custom into His service.

"Seven days" reflects the influence of the idea of the Sabbath on Israel's feasts. The Sabbath was instituted at creation (Gen. 1–2); the Feast of Unleavened Bread also carried the divine imprint of the number seven; it was instituted by the Lord, it was to His glory. The removal of the yeast (the leaven or "sourdough," which was kept in a small clay pot to be used

---

[16]Cf. *Gereformeerd Theologisch Tijdschrift,* 1943, pp. 51–52.

later in the preparation of bread) from the houses points to the breaking with sin (see commentary on v. 8). In Judaism the father went around collecting pieces of bread containing yeast that had been placed around the house earlier. Verse 15b shows how completely God hates sin, also in His people: anyone eating anything with yeast during the seven days would be cut off from Israel; we must think of a divine judgment that may be accompanied or preceded by the expulsion from the tribal, national, and cultic community. The feast was to begin and end with a religious gathering, again indicating the glorification of God, which was to leaven this entire feast. All "servile labor" (as the LXX translates the word used for "work"), i.e., the work of every day, and especially all occupational work, had to come to a halt. On the first and seventh day only the preparation of food was allowed (cf. Lev. 23:7–8; Num. 28:18, 25). In this respect the first and seventh day of the Feast of Unleavened Bread were thus equal to the Sabbath (cf. 20:8–11), except that on the Sabbath and on the Day of Atonement the lighting of a fire, cooking and roasting were also prohibited (cf. 16:23; 35:3; Lev. 23:26–32). Redemption, like creation, is exclusively the work of the Lord (cf. Isa. 43:15–17).

12:17 *"Celebrate the Feast of Unleavened Bread, because it was on this very day that I brought your divisions out of Egypt. Celebrate this day as a lasting ordinance for the generations to come."*

Verse 17 presents a minor problem. The Hebrew reads: "You shall keep the unleavened bread," which would be an unusual way of expressing "You shall keep the Feast of Unleavened Bread." The LXX and the Samaritan Pentateuch change one letter of the Hebrew *masot* ("unleavened bread") and read *miswah* ("commandment"): "You shall keep the (LXX: 'this') commandment." This may be the correct reading, but we cannot be certain. The day of the Exodus is the fifteenth day of the month of Abib or Nisan. "Brought out," cf. commentary on 3:10–12; 6:13, 26, 27; 7:4. This is a perfect tense: "I have brought out," pointing to the possibility that the commandment concerning the Feast of Unleavened Bread was given at a later time (see above). "Your divisions," cf. 6:26; 7:4. Verse 17b, cf. verse 14b.

12:18–20 *"In the first month you are to eat bread made without yeast, from the evening of the fourteenth day until the evening of the twenty-first day. For seven days no yeast is to be found in your houses. And whoever eats anything with yeast in it must be cut off from the community of Israel, whether he is an alien or native-born. Eat nothing made with yeast. Wherever you live, you must eat unleavened bread."*

In verses 18–20 the instructions concerning the Feast of Unleavened Bread are reiterated. In verse 18 the exact date is given (cf. also v. 2). The beginning of the Feast coincides with the Passover; the Passover lamb was to be slaughtered on the fourteenth day of the first month as well. It ended on the evening of the twenty-first day of that month, so that the seven days were counted from the evening of the Passover. Verse 19 restates the severe penalty of verse 15, but here is added that neither an alien (KJV: "sojourner"; cf. 2:22) nor a native-born (born in the land, i.e., Canaan) could eat anything containing yeast. "Community" is the same word used in verse 6. This commandment is repeated in verse 20. For the institution of the Feast of Unleavened Bread see 13:6–7; 34:18; Deuteronomy 16:3. The importance of the demand of total rest from sin, the celebration of the inward Sabbath to which the Feast of Unleavened Bread points, was underscored by the importance the Lord placed on total abstention from anything containing leaven.

12:21–23 *Then Moses summoned all the elders of Israel and said to them, "Go at once and select the animals for your families and slaughter the Passover lamb. Take a bunch of hyssop, dip it into the blood in the basin and put some of the blood on the top and on both sides of the doorframe. Not one of you shall go out the door of his house until morning. When the LORD goes through the land to strike down the Egyptians, he will see the blood on the top and sides of the doorframe and will pass over that doorway, and he will not permit the destroyer to enter your houses and strike you down."*

In verses 21–28 the Lord's command is carried out, first by Moses and then by the Israelites who received it from Moses. In verse 21 (as in v. 1) only Moses is mentioned, since he was the central figure. "Summoned the elders of Israel," see commentary on 4:29. The author of Hebrews sees Moses' role in the institution of the Passover as an act of faith, cf. Hebrews 11:28. "Go" can also mean "acquire," but this is already expressed in "select." "Slaughter the Passover lamb": lit.: "kill the Passover" (cf. KJV); the term "Passover" here thus acquires the meaning of "passover animal." "Animals" are sheep and goats (cf. v. 5).

Moses probably said more to the elders than what is recorded in verse 21, since otherwise the instructions would have been rather unclear. Verse 21 seems to support the impression that the instructions of verses 3 and 6 were not implemented on the occasion of the first Passover (which incidentally shows that the Scriptures do not slavishly repeat themselves). Besides, Moses was a practical man and showed how the Israelites could apply the blood to their houses (cf. v. 7). A brush made from a bundle of hyssop was very suitable for the purpose; hyssop was later used for cleaning purposes (cf. Lev. 14:4; Ps. 51:9). Hyssop was probably marjoram, a shrub with many small branches and small, soft leaves. The command that during the night of the Passover (cf. v. 42) the Israelites were not to leave their homes was not part of what we are told the Lord originally said to Moses and Aaron. But it may have been, and probably was, included, since their salvation depended on their being in a house marked with the blood. The example of Jesus, who went to Gethsemane after eating the Passover meal, shows that this particular directive did not apply later (cf. Matt. 26:30; Mark 14:26; Luke 22:39; John 14:31). The reason for this injunction was that the Lord would go through the land to strike down the Egyptians (v. 23; cf. also vv. 12–13. "strike," cf. 8:2). "The destroyer" has been interpreted in different ways. Some think of a destructive power that raged in the night, others of a particular avenging angel who always carried out the Lord's judgment (cf. 2 Sam. 24:16; 2 Kings 19:35; 2 Chron. 32:21; Isa. 37:36). Still others translate the word impersonally: "the destruction." I see in "the destroyer" an indication that in this plague the Lord worked again indirectly, and am thus most inclined toward the first view: a destructive force (cf. also commentary on 11:4–8).

12:24–27 *"Obey these instructions as a lasting ordinance for you and your descendants. When you enter the land that the LORD will give you as he promised, observe this ceremony. And when your children ask you, 'What does this ceremony mean to you?' then tell them, 'It is the Passover sacrifice to the LORD, who passed over the houses of the Israelites in Egypt and spared our homes when he struck down the Egyptians.'" Then the people bowed down and worshiped.*

In these verses Moses carried out the Lord's instructions of verse 14. The instructions that had to be obeyed, according to verse 24, were those concerning the Passover (vv. 21–23). This ceremony had to be observed also when they reached Canaan (cf. 13:5). Some exegetes feel that the application of the blood to the door frames was meant only for the night of the Exodus and did not have to be repeated annually, which is likely since the tenth plague occurred only once. If this is the case, then only the second part of the originally twofold sacrificial act (the application of the blood and the sacrificial meal, see below) remained in effect after the first Passover. The Samaritans still apply blood to the doors of their tents each year during the Passover on Mt. Gerizim.

In verse 25 Moses reminded the Israelites indirectly of the Lord's promise to Abraham, Isaac, and Jacob. The fulfillment of this promise was the purpose of the Exodus that was about to take place (cf. 2:24; 3:6–10, 14–17; 5:2–8). If, after entering the land, their children (lit.: "sons") asked for the meaning of this ceremony, the Israelites were to explain it by saying that it was a Passover sacrifice to the Lord, who passed over the houses of the Israelites and spared them when He struck down the Egyptians (vv. 26–27). This clearly states that the Lamb was a sacrifice, although in this case the altars were the homes of the Israelites and the priests were the fathers. The blood (which in a similar custom in Babylon also had a propitiating significance and served to ward off evil, see commentary on vv. 15–16) had propitiating power.

On the basis of these and similar instructions (cf. 10:1–2; 17:7–8, 14–15; Deut. 4:9; 6:6–7, 20–25; 11:18–21; Josh. 4:4–9, 20–24) the Jewish custom has developed whereby after the annual seder dish one of the children, usually the youngest, asks the father "Why is this night different from all other nights?" The child then recites several questions from the Haggadah (lit.: "Narrative") and receives answers, also from the Haggadah. "The establishment of the Passover festival is again enjoined, and at the same time there is connected with it an injunction to instruct children concerning it. The Israelitish child will not unthinkingly practice a dead worship; he will ask: What does it mean? And the Israelitish fathers must not suppress the questions of the growing mind, but answer them, and thus begin the spiritualizing of the paschal rite."[17]

The conclusion of verse 27 shows that the people had come to fear the Lord, after they saw what Moses had done by the power the Lord granted him (cf. 6:9).

12:28 *The Israelites did just what the LORD commanded Moses and Aaron.*

Verse 28 states that the Israelites acted in strict accordance with the Lord's instructions to Moses and Aaron.

The first complete Passover (the Passover and the Feast of Unleavened Bread; cf. also Num. 9:1–14) was celebrated in Canaan (cf. Josh. 5:10–11). But in the night following the day during which the Israelites had prepared and eaten the Passover in Egypt the terrible tenth plague was visited on the Egyptians, followed finally by Israel's exodus from Egypt.

26. *The Tenth Plague: Death of the Firstborn. Israel Leaves Egypt* (12:29–42)

12:29, 30 *At midnight the LORD struck down all the firstborn in Egypt, from the firstborn of Pharaoh, who sat on the throne, to the firstborn of the prisoner, who was in the dungeon, and the firstborn of all the livestock as well. Pharaoh and all*

---

[17]Lange, *Exodus,* p. 39–40.

his officials and all the Egyptians got up during the night, and there was loud wailing in Egypt, for there was not a house without someone dead.

There is a marked parallel between these verses and 11:4–6 (see commentary on 11:4–6 for the tenth plague). The Lord's prediction to Pharaoh was literally fulfilled. "Struck down" here means "killed." "The firstborn of the prisoner" (lit.: "of imprisonment," "of him who is in the house of the pit," or prison; cf. Gen. 39:20; Isa. 24:22; Jer. 37:16) is on the same level as "the firstborn of the slave girl who is at her hand mill" (cf. commentary on 11:5). Verse 30 describes the impression this terrible plague made on the Egyptians. There was, as predicted, "loud wailing." Pharaoh, his officials (cf. e.g., commentary on 10:7) and all the Egyptians got up: no one was spared. Egypt paid along with its godless king. Once again we have here the solidarity principle that is seen repeatedly in the story of the ten plagues.

12:31, 32 *During the night Pharaoh summoned Moses and Aaron and said, "Up! Leave my people, you and the Israelites! Go, worship the LORD as you have requested. Take your flocks and herds, as you have said, and go. And also bless me."*

Pharaoh's summons of Moses and Aaron, the leaders of Israel (cf. 5:1), seems to contradict what Moses said in 10:29. But rather than accusing Moses here of a personal error, it is best to assume that Pharaoh gave his permission for Israel to leave not in person, but through his officials (cf. 11:8). This permission was not stated in friendly terms; it was wrested from him by the severe blow. They had to get up, get ready. "Leave," cf. 3:10–12; 6:13, 26–27; 7:4; 12:17, where the same verb is used. "Leave my people" indicates that he considered them harmful to his people, so that their original fear (1:10b) had now become the desire of Pharaoh and especially of his people. Such is the power of the Lord! This time Pharaoh no longer qualified his permission (cf. e.g., 10:8–11), but explicitly stated that his permission included Moses and Aaron as well as the Israelites. But he could not refrain from reminding Moses and Aaron of their initial request, which involved only a journey into the desert to worship the Lord (cf. 4:23; 5:1–3; 7:16; 8:1, 20, 27; 9:1, 13; 10:3). In all his sorrow he still had not come to the point where he never wanted to see Israel again, and he hoped that after their journey they would voluntarily return to be useful to him and the Egyptians as slaves. Verse 32 also indicates that he only thought of the festival, since he granted permission to take along their flocks and herds as Moses and Aaron demanded (cf. 10:8–11, 24–26). Pharaoh had been so impressed by the power of Israel's God that he asked

Moses and Aaron to bless him, that is to say, the people were to ask their God during the festival in the wilderness to bless Pharaoh (cf. 8:28). What Moses predicted in 11:8 was fulfilled!

12:33, 34 *The Egyptians urged the people to hurry and leave the country. "For otherwise," they said, "we will all die!" So the people took their dough before the yeast was added, and carried it on their shoulders in kneading troughs wrapped in clothing.*

Verse 33 shows that what the Lord had promised to Moses in 5:24 and 11:1 was also fulfilled. "The people," see commentary on 11:2. "Hurry," cf. 10:16. The Egyptians wanted to be rid of Israel as soon as possible since they felt that they were "dead men" (kjv), that they had been led to their death. It happened in such a hurry that it could be considered an expulsion rather than an exodus, and the people had to pack up their dough before they had time to add the yeast. They carried the dough in kneading troughs on their shoulders, wrapped in clothing (cf. commentary on 8:3). Verse 34, cf. also verse 39. Clothing was used on occasion to carry things in, cf. Judges 8:25; Ruth 3:15; 1 Kings 4:39; Haggai 2:13. The clothing referred to here was the outer garment, a large square cloth, worn over the underclothing.

12:35, 36 *The Israelites did as Moses instructed and asked the Egyptians for articles of silver and gold and for clothing. The Lord had made the Egyptians favorably disposed toward the people, and they gave them what they asked for; so they plundered the Egyptians.*

For verse 35, cf. commentary on 3:22; 11:2. Again it is striking how the fulfillment exactly matched the promise. "Clothing" (the same word as in v. 34) is now mentioned along with articles of gold and silver, as in 3:22. For verse 36 cf. commentary on 3:21–22; 11:3. The fact that the Egyptians granted their requests is sometimes explained by saying that they gladly paid for the land of the Israelites in Goshen, but the text does not make any mention of this. On the contrary, both 3:22 and 36b speak of "plundering," which also excludes the possibility of payment of wages for their slave labor. The text gives the impression that the Egyptians were willing to give the Israelites what they asked for simply because they were glad that Israel finally left. Indeed, with so many dead it would probably matter little to them whether they kept or gave away a few material possessions. Nor must we forget that verse 36a says that the Lord was the One who prepared the hearts of the Egyptians to give (cf. Ps. 105:27, 38). These treasures were to be used in the wilderness for the outfitting of the tabernacle (cf. Num. 7).

12:37, 38 *The Israelites journeyed from Rameses to Succoth. There were about six hundred thousand men on foot, besides women and children. Many other people went up with them, as well as large droves of livestock, both flocks and herds.*

Now follows the route the Israelites took when they left Egypt (cf. Num. 33:3). Rameses was the starting point (cf. commentary on 1:11; the location of Rameses is uncertain, but it was most likely a city east of Goshen). It is striking that the point of departure for the Exodus was one of the cities that they themselves built. As I mentioned (commentary on 1:11), some identify Succoth with Tell el-Maskuta, which Neville claims to be Pithom. Succoth is then believed to be the profane, and Pithom the sacred name of that city. Succoth ("huts") then indicates both the city itself and the area east of the city. Some also identify only Pithom, but not Succoth, with Tell el-Maskuta. The Israelites traveled from Rameses via Pithom to the East, through the Wadi Tumilat, toward Mt. Horeb. They did not follow the caravan route to Gaza, not so much because it was blocked by Egyptian fortifications (after all, they had Pharaoh's permission), but rather because Sinai was their first goal, and because the Philistines, who would have tried to block their entry had they gone through Gaza, were formidable opponents (cf. 13:17).

The number given here, 600,000 men besides "the little ones," i.e., women and children, who did not all travel on foot (cf. 4:20) has often been derided, but wrongly so. Ancient history mentions other migrations of enormous numbers of people and movements of large armies, and we have no reason to doubt the accuracy of those reports. Furthermore, this number is confirmed in 38:26; Numbers 1:46; 2:32; 11:21. Noordtzij proposes a solution in his exegesis of Numbers 1.[18] I have no solution for the problem this large number presents. It is true that the Amarna letters reflect small numbers of people; but on the other hand the Mari letters show that in Hammurabi's time armies were used consisting of tens of thousands of soldiers.

Verse 38a paves the way for verses 43–51. "Many other people" (KJV: "mixed multitude") refers to non-Israelites, aliens, probably largely Egyptians (cf. Lev. 24:10; concerning their influence on the Israelites, cf. Exod. 20:5–10; Amos 5:25–26), although it is not impossible that others also "went up with them" The term "went up" is used because Egypt's elevation is lower than that of the desert toward which they traveled. The way in which the term "other people" is used hints at the fact that the

---

[18]In his commentary on *Numbers* in this series. For a critique of Noordtzij's solution, see J. G. Aalders, *Gereformeerd Theologisch Tijdschrift* (1950), p. 3–9.

caliber of these people was generally rather low, and Luther translates it "a great rabble" (cf. also Num. 11:4; Neh. 13:3). Among the "other people" may also have been those with a criminal record who now took advantage of the confusion. "Mixed" (KJV) refers to the variety of their origins. The desire for a better place than Egypt to live, devastated as it was by the plagues, must have been a major motivation. And the fact that these "other people" joined Israel indicates that they, unlike Pharaoh (cf. vv. 31–32), did not consider this a temporary journey to worship. The "large droves of livestock" are emphasized to give the impression that they were not lacking for animals to sacrifice (cf. 9:1–7).

12:39 *With the dough they had brought from Egypt, they baked cakes of unleavened bread. The dough was without yeast because they had been driven out of Egypt and did not have time to prepare food for themselves.*

See commentary on verse 34. This verse gives the historical antecedent of the Feast of Unleavened Bread (cf. commentary on 12:1–28). "Driven out," cf. commentary on verse 33. The first unleavened loaves, baked in hot ashes or in the sun, were thus eaten because the dough with which Israel left Egypt was unleavened (v. 34). Calvin observed that God's blessings are always accompanied by some inconvenience so that the souls of the devout will not be spoiled by too much pleasure.

12:40, 41 *Now the length of time the Israelite people lived in Egypt was 430 years. At the end of the 430 years, to the very day, all the LORD's divisions left Egypt.*

These verses indicate the length of Israel's stay in Egypt: 430 years. The LXX reads "in Egypt and in Canaan 430 years"; the Samaritan Pentateuch as well as some manuscripts of the LXX read: "And the time of the sojourn of the Israelites and their fathers in Egypt," while the Samaritan Pentateuch also adds: "and in Canaan." Thus both the LXX and the Samaritan Pentateuch count the 430 years from Abraham's stay in Canaan. Comparison with Genesis 12:4; 21:5; 25:26; 47:9 shows that this would give 215 years for the patriarchs' stay in Canaan and 215 years for Israel's stay in Egypt. This is much too short for the period in Egypt, as is apparent from the 600,000 men mentioned in verse 37. Genesis 15:13 speaks of 400 years in Egypt, as does Acts 7:6. Paul appears to follow the LXX and Samaritan Pentateuch in Galatians 3:17, as do Josephus and many Jewish and early Christian exegetes, e.g., Eusebius, Augustine, and Calvin. We prefer to retain the reading of the Masoretic text (cf. also Introduction, pp. 21–24). Verse 41, see commentary on verse 17. "Left," cf. verse 31. "To the very day," cf. verse 17.

12:42 *Because the Lord kept vigil that night to bring them out of Egypt, on this night all the Israelites are to keep vigil to honor the Lord for the generations to come.*

Verse 42 is sometimes interpreted as meaning that the Lord kept vigil that night to protect Israel from the destroyer (v. 23) to lead them out of Egypt unharmed (NIV, RSV). The Hebrew literally reads: "A night of celebration (or, a night to be observed) is this unto the Lord, for leading them out of Egypt; this night is for the Lord, a celebration (or, to be observed) by all the children of Israel in their generation" (cf. KJV). I prefer the latter interpretation which also provides a transition to verses 43–51.

27. *Instructions Concerning the Celebration of the Passover by Foreigners* (12:43–51)

The instructions concerning the celebration of the Passover by foreigners were necessary because of the "many other people" (v. 38a) who went with Israel.

12:43–45 *The Lord said to Moses and Aaron, "These are the regulations for the Passover:*
"No foreigner is to eat of it. Any slave you have bought may eat of it after you have circumcised him, but a temporary resident and a hired worker may not eat of it."

In verse 43 the Lord excluded every foreigner (lit.: "every son of a foreigner") from participation in the Passover meal. The word "foreigner" refers to descent (LXX: "of another race, or tribe," cf. 2:22). However, the foreigner who was bought as a slave was permitted to eat of the Passover as a member of the family, on the condition that he had been circumcised. Abraham had to circumcise his slaves (cf. Gen. 17:9–14), but it seems that the Israelites did not do this, and the command may have been applicable to Abraham only, which is likely in view of the fact that the noncircumcision of slaves was not criticized here. The Dutch Authorized Version adds in the margin of verse 44: "With the understanding that they have accepted the true religion after having been instructed in it." See Genesis 18:19. Thus the Gentiles could also participate in Israel's blessing; Israel was not better by nature but they had been elected by grace. And the time will come when all nations will participate in Israel's privileges (cf. Gal. 3:28). "Bought" (KJV: "for money") is in contrast to those "born in the household" (Gen. 17:12; cf. Gen. 17:23, 27). The children of slaves who were already part of the household were probably always circumcised, and they had to be raised in the fear of the Lord (cf. Lev. 22:10ff.). The Passover was only for those who belonged to the covenant. A "temporary resident" (KJV: "sojourner"), someone living in Israel without citizenship or landownership (who usually lived under the protection of an Israelite on his property, like the "alien" in v. 48), or a hired worker, in this case of foreign descent, could not partake of the Passover meal (v. 45).

12:46, 47 *"It must be eaten inside one house; take none of the meat outside the house. Do not break any of the bones. The whole community of Israel must celebrate it."*

Verse 46, cf. verses 3–4, 9–10. In this verse the emphasis is on the fact that the Passover lamb had to be eaten inside one house (cf. v. 9), although more than one household could share in the meal (cf. v. 4). See commentary on verse 9 and Numbers 9:12. No one in Israel could refuse to participate (v. 47; cf. v. 6).

12:48, 49 *"An alien living among you who wants to celebrate the LORD's Passover must have all the males in his household circumcised; then he may take part like one born in the land. No uncircumcised male may eat of it. The same law applies to the native-born and to the alien living among you."*

It also could happen that an alien (cf. 2:22), who lived among the Israelites (some believe that this could include both the temporary resident and the hired laborer of v. 45) would express a desire to celebrate the Passover to the Lord, the God of Israel, in the awareness of the god-glorifying meaning of the feast. In that case he and all the males in his household had to be circumcised and thus become part of Israel, the people of the covenant. He then was allowed to (and indeed had to) celebrate the Passover and was considered to be like "one born in the land" (cf. v. 19). This expression indicates that the Lord was thinking of the future, when Israel would live in the Promised Land. The circumcision, and thus becoming part of Israel, was the *sine qua non* for participation in the Passover (v. 48b). In this respect the alien had no more rights than that native-born Israelite (v. 49, cf. Lev. 24:22; Num. 9:14; 15:15, 16, 29). He also had to accept the sign of the covenant and with it its obligations if he wanted to share in the privileges of the covenant.

12:50 *All the Israelites did just what the LORD had commanded Moses and Aaron.*

See verse 28. This refers to the celebration of the Passover in Egypt.

12:51 *And on that very day the Lord brought the Israelites out of Egypt by their divisions.*

See Psalm 136:11. "By their divisions," cf. commentary on verse 17. The instructions in verses 43–49 were apparently given on the day following the Exodus, as verse 51 indicates (cf. v. 41). It is also possible that verses 43–49 were inserted later, and that verses 50–51 originally followed verse 42. Verse 51, cf. verse 41.

28. *Consecration of the Firstborn* (13:1–16)

The author intends to convey the fact that these instructions were also given on the day after the Exodus (cf. vv. 3–4) in Succoth (cf. 12:37). They concern the consecration of the firstborn of both man and animal in Israel, based on the fact that the tenth plague killed the firstborn of Egypt, while those of Israel were spared (vv. 14–15). It is apparent that because of the Exodus the Lord considered Israel His property, His firstborn (4:22). The firstborn are here the representatives and stand-ins for the entire people. First the instructions are given without a rationale (vv. 1–2). Then Moses uses this opportunity to convey to Israel what the Lord had commanded him and Aaron in 12:15–20 (vv. 3–10). The instructions given in verse 2 are then augmented, and the rationale is added (vv. 11–16). The Lord had a right to the firstborn, but He spared them by grace because they were consecrated to Him; the firstborn of the cattle had to be sacrificed. This sparing grace was already seen in the tenth plague. For the consecration of the firstborn, cf. also 22:29–30; 34:19–20; Leviticus 27:26–27; Numbers 3:11–13, where the Levites took the place of the firstborn of the other tribes; 8:16–19; 18:15–18; Deuteronomy 15:19; Luke 2:23. Child sacrifices were a common practice among the Arabs and the Canaanites.

It has been maintained that among many nations, including Israel, the practice of the consecration of the firstborn was already found before the tenth plague, and that Moses now related this already existing, or now adopted, custom to that plague. The existing custom (the attempt to promote fertility by consecrating or sacrificing the firstborn) then would be invested with a historical motivation or rationale. But the Scriptures only present the historical reason, and even if Israel was not the only nation that consecrated its firstborn, only Israel did it because the Lord slew the firstborn of Egypt.

13:1, 2 *The Lord said to Moses, "Consecrate to me every firstborn male. The first offspring of every womb among the Israelites belongs to me, whether man or animal."*

131

Some translations connect verse 1 with verse 51 of the previous chapter: "And on that very day, when the Lord brought the Israelites out of Egypt by their divisions He said to Moses. . . ." Although this is grammatically not impossible, it is not obvious. It would however express even more strongly the fact that the consecration of the firstborn was commanded on the day of the Exodus. Aaron is not mentioned. "Consecrate" here means "set aside from its normal use and dedicate to the Lord." The Lord emphatically stated His right of ownership to every firstborn (cf. v. 15).

13:3–6 *Then Moses said to the people, "Commemorate this day, the day you came out of Egypt, out of the land of slavery, because the LORD brought you out of it with a mighty hand. Eat nothing containing yeast. Today, in the month of Abib, you are leaving. When the LORD brings you into the land of the Canaanites, Hittites, Amorites, Hivites and Jebusites—the land he swore to your forefathers to give you, a land flowing with milk and honey—you are to observe this ceremony in this month: For seven days eat bread made without yeast and on the seventh day hold a festival to the LORD."*

Moses first gave the people instructions concerning the Feast of Unleavened Bread (12:8, 15–20). In practice this would only have been possible by calling together the elders, who in turn spoke to the people (cf. e.g., 12:21, 27–28). The day of the Exodus was the fifteenth day of the month Abib (12:6, 17). Egypt was characterized as the "land of slavery" (lit.: "house of slaves"). This day had to become a day of commemoration for Israel (cf. 34:18; Deut. 16:3), because the Lord led them out with a strong hand (cf. 3:19–20). "Out of it" (lit.' "out of here," KJV: "out of this place") indicates that Moses said this in Egypt (cf. 12:1). The expression "with a mighty hand" (here and in vv. 14–15 the expression is lit. "with strength of hand") is frequently used in the Scriptures in connection with the Exodus (cf. 5:24; 13:9; 32:11; Deut. 4:34; 5:15; 6:21; etc.). On the day that commemorated the Exodus nothing could be eaten that contained leaven (cf. 12:15–20).

In verse 4 Moses drew their attention specifically to the day and month of their leaving (cf. 12:2), lit.: "this day you are leaving" (cf. also 23:15; Deut. 16:1).

Verse 5 uses the singular "you"; Moses here spoke to the people as a whole (cf. v. 3) or perhaps also to the individual Israelite. See commentary on 3:8 for an explanation of this verse. The Lord had sworn to the fathers that He would give the land to Israel, cf. Genesis 12:7; 13:15, 17; 15:7, 18; 17:7–8; 22:15–18; 24:7; 26:3–4; 28:13–15; 35:9–13; 50:24; Exodus 6:4–5, 8; 12:25; 32:13; 33:1; Deuteronomy 1:8; 6:10, 18; 34:4; Psalm 105:11. Verse 5 indicates that the Feast of Unleavened Bread did not have to be celebrated until after they reached Canaan (cf. v. 11). "This ceremony" refers to verses 6ff. Verse 6, cf. 12:15–20. Here the emphasis is on the seventh day as a festival to the Lord.

13:7–9 *"Eat unleavened bread during those seven days; nothing with yeast in it is to be seen among you, nor shall any yeast be seen anywhere within your borders. On that day tell your son, 'I do this because of what the LORD did for me when I came out of Egypt.' This observance will be for you like a sign on your hand and a reminder on your forehead that the law of the LORD is to be on your lips. For the LORD brought you out of Egypt with his mighty hand."*

These verses contain the command to transmit the reason for this feast orally, similar to the instructions in 10:1–2; 12:24–27, and 13:14–15. In verse 8 the text is mutilated; the "I do this" (KJV: "this is done") was added to complete the sentence. During the seven-day period ("on that day") in which the unleavened bread was eaten the Israelite father had to tell his son: this eating of unleavened bread and removal of anything containing yeast is because of what the Lord did for me when I came out of Egypt. This is thus a command to give an oral explanation of the annual Feast of Unleavened Bread (cf. commentary on 12:24–27). Each father was to give this explanation to his children, so that the acts of the Lord during the Exodus from Egypt would be kept in living memory. The striking aspect here is that the explanation was to be given even if the sons did not ask (cf. 12:25; 13:14). Moses was to give this command to the people of Israel in the name of the Lord.

Verse 9 clearly states that continued instruction concerning the Feast of Unleavened Bread (and thus also concerning other laws of the Lord) could only be given, and that the father could only speak about this, if the commandment was placed as a sign on the hand and as a reminder on the forehead (lit.: "between the eyes"). Must this be taken literally or figuratively? The literal interpretation has led the Jews to wear "tefillin" or phylacteries. But this literal interpretation has problems. The first words of verse 9 literally read "and it shall be" (KJV, RSV). "It" then may refer to either the explanation or instruction, or to the observance itself (NIV). The former is supported by that which immediately follows "that the law of the LORD is to be on your lips." It is certain that Moses wanted to impress on the Israelites that they had to continually remember and pass on the teaching concerning the Lord. He has made Himself worthy of this by leading them out of Egypt with a mighty hand (cf. commentary on v. 3). It was to be part of their life of gratitude as a delivered nation. Only if that law was part of their daily lives would it be passed on and could the command to give oral instruction be fulfilled. Verse 9 thus gives the necessary condition and preparation for the instruction of the children concerning the acts of the Lord: taking the commandment into the heart and continuously implementing it. "Law of the Lord," both given by the Lord and concerning the Lord. Only he who did not forget His law but lived with it and in it could speak of it to others. Verse 9b, cf. verse 3.

13:10 *"You must keep this ordinance at the appointed time year after year."*

Verse 10 instructs Moses to keep the ordinance (cf. 12:43) of the Unleavened Bread "from days until days," or year after year, at the appointed time (cf. 12:17). Moses had accurately passed on the command of the Lord given in 12:15–20.

13:11, 12 *"After the LORD brings you into the land of the Canaanites and gives it to you, as he promised on oath to you and your forefathers, you are to give over to the LORD the first offspring of every womb. All the firstborn males of your livestock belong to the LORD."*

In verses 11–16 Moses passed on the ordinance concerning the firstborn (cf. v. 2). Verses 11–12 indicate that the consecration of the first offspring of every womb (cf. v. 2) did not have to be practiced until they reached Canaan. This law applied only to the firstborn males (cf. also 22:30; Deut. 15:21–23).

13:13 *"Redeem with a lamb every firstborn donkey, but if you do not redeem it, break its neck. Redeem every firstborn among your sons."*

An exception was made for the firstborn of donkeys, who were unsuitable for sacrifices since they were unclean animals and are mentioned here in lieu of all unclean domestic animals (cf. Num. 18:15). It could be redeemed with a lamb, or else its neck had to be broken so that it could not be used for ordinary purposes (cf. also Lev. 27:27). The Lord did not require human sacrifices, and thus every firstborn son of the Israelites could be redeemed. Later the tribe of Levi took the place of those who would otherwise have had to serve the Lord directly, although the other tribes still had to pay money to redeem their firstborn (cf. Num. 3:11–13; 8:16–19; 18:16).

13:14, 15 *"In days to come, when your son asks you, 'What does this mean?' say to him, 'With a mighty hand the LORD brought us out of Egypt, out of the land of slavery. When Pharaoh stubbornly refused to let us go, the LORD killed every firstborn in Egypt, both man and animal. This is why I sacrifice to the LORD the first male offspring of every womb and redeem each of my firstborn sons.'"*

These verses are similar to verse 8. "With a mighty hand," cf. commentary on verse 3. The word for "stubbornly refused" is the same as "hardened his heart" in 7:3 (lit.: "when Pharaoh hardened himself against letting us go"). "Let go" occurs frequently in Exodus in connection with Pharaoh (cf. e.g., 3:20; 4:21, 23; 5:1–2, 24; 6:11; 7:2, 14, 16; 8:1, 20–21, 29, 32; 9:1–2, 7, 13, 17, 28, 35; 10:3–4, 7, 10, 20; 11:1, 10). It is thus a word that belongs in the answer that the Israelite fathers were to give their sons when they asked about the custom of sacrificing the firstborn livestock and of redeeming the firstborn sons. This custom is here related to the tenth plague (cf. 12:29) and thus kept alive the memory of the Lord's miraculous help against Israel's enemy.

Verses 14–15 and 12:26–27 are very similar. We have again the command to transmit orally: the father was to answer the son when he asked about this religious custom; it also specified what the father was to answer, the most important aspect being that the tenth plague served to accomplish the miracle of Israel's deliverance from Egypt (v. 15 is linked to v. 14b by "for," cf. RSV). The ultimate purpose was thus to make known from generation to generation the deliverance from Egypt, to the glory of the Lord. The Exodus was for Israel as a nation, and as the church of the Old Testament dispensation, of fundamental importance, a symbol of God's leading His people out of the house of slavery of Satan.

13:16 *"And it will be like a sign on your hand and a symbol on your forehead that the LORD brought us out of Egypt with his mighty hand."*

The relationship between verse 16 and verses 14–15 is the same as that between verse 9 and verse 8. See commentary on verse 9, and for verse 16b, cf. commentary on verse 3. The word "symbol" (lit.: "frontlet") is also used in Deuteronomy 6:8; 11:8, Others think of a mark, sign, or tattoo. Here, as well as in verse 9, the literal interpretation of such expressions is problematic.

29. *The Crossing of the Red Sea* (13:17–14:31)

The crossing of the Red Sea is one of the most beautiful stories in the Scriptures, both from a religious and a literary standpoint. The destruction of the Egyptians is described with a masterly hand. For Israel this was an event of the highest importance, both nationally and spiritually, while for the church redeemed on Calvary it foreshadowed the ultimate victory over all its enemies. It is frequently mentioned elsewhere in the Bible (cf. Josh. 2:10; 4:23; 24:6–8; Neh. 9:11; Pss. 66:6; 77:17–21; 78:13; 106:9; 114:3; 136:13–15; Isa. 63:12–13; 1 Cor. 10:1–2; Heb. 11:29; Rev. 15:3).

The hardening of Pharaoh's heart and his decision to pursue Israel were necessary since he still thought of a temporary release of Israel (cf. commentary on 12:31). Because of this attitude Pharaoh lost any right to Israel's return, and the Red Sea formed the gateway to Israel's existence as a nation.

No sound arguments can be brought against the historicity of this event. Apart from the fact that this indirect miracle (the immediate cause was the east wind) cannot be explained, similar events are known from ancient history. Herodotus tells that during the siege of Potidea in the Persian war the ebbtide lasted unusually long, so that the Persian troops were able to reach the city through the shallow water. But when two-thirds had reached the other side the tide turned and drowned the others. The Persians attributed this catastrophe to the desecration of the temple and statue of Poseidon. Herodotus states that the real cause was a volcanic eruption. Similarly, Scipio was able to take New Carthage in 209 B.C. because of a low tide, apparently caused by a north wind. And there are other examples from later history as well that provide parallels to what happened at the Red Sea.

We should stay with the text of Exodus for both the facts and their explanation; and then there can be no question of a volcanic eruption as Gressmann suggests. He feels that the pillar of cloud and fire points in that direction, and that this pillar separated itself from Mt. Sinai, which he believes to be a volcano. But he only arrives at this by declaring the pillar of cloud and fire going before Israel and the miracles in this story to be unhistorical.

The exegesis can also go astray by applying the source hypothesis to a story such as this: the sources are separated on the basis of who divided the water, the Lord (by means of an east wind) or Moses (with his staff). Nor is this story based on two traditions, one dealing only with the battle between the Israelites and the Egyptians (which the Egyptians lost), the other only with a crossing of the Red Sea by the Israelites.

Closely related to this is the question of the exact geographical location of the crossing, a problem that remains unresolved even if we accept the story as it is presented in Exodus. The primary point is that it was a crossing of the Red Sea (concerning the name, see commentary on 10:19). The only place that can qualify as the location of the crossing is the northern part of the western inlet of the Gulf of Suez, which in ancient times probably extended further than it does today. But it is questionable whether this inlet included the Bitter Lakes or even Lake Timsah, in which case the Red Sea would have been close to Pithom. The Gulf of Suez actually used to be called "Gulf of Hieropolis," the name of Tell el-

Maskutah, which Neville excavated and identified with Pithom. Others, however, believe it to be Succoth. In any case, this arm of the Red Sea was navigable only from Suez on during the time of Darius (fifth century B.C.), which, of course, does not preclude the possibility that it actually stretched up to the region of Pithom (however, the northernmost memorial of Darius has been found three to four miles north of Suez, thus not too far north of the present-day end of the Gulf of Suez).

Some who adopt this view believe that the crossing took place between the Bitter Lakes and Lake Timsah, or in the southern region of the Bitter Lakes. But I am of the opinion that, even if the Gulf of Suez was still connected with the Bitter Lakes and the Lakes were thus part of the Gulf, the statements in the text more fully agree with a crossing through the Gulf of Suez where it is deeper, thus in the vicinity of present-day Suez. We must not forget that the Bitter Lakes received much more water from the Mediterranean Sea after the Suez Canal was dug than before, when they were (at least in the nineteenth century) salty marshes. Little remains of the miracle when during Moses' time this part of the Red Sea on occasion blew dry and Moses speculated that this might happen. Also, how could the Egyptians assume that Israel was lost in the wilderness when it was actually on its way to Sinai? In my opinion the text does not refer to either Lake Timsah, the Bitter Lakes, or Lake Menzaleh; but the places where Israel camped cannot be identified with certainty (see below).

Brugsch's opinion is in direct conflict with the text; he feels that Israel traveled north of Lake Serbonis, along the coast of the Mediterranean Sea. Shortly before the Egyptians perished the Israelites then turned south at Mt. Casius (which Brugsch identifies with Baal-Zephon), toward the Bitter Lakes and then into the desert. Brugsch also believes Etham to be a fortress (see commentary on 13:20), but he does not mention Israel's turning at Etham, even though the text states this (14:2). Another argument against Brugsch's view is 13:17, since in his view Israel would have gone through Philistine country. And if we assume that this road was not the usual military road to Syria, the problem remains that Lake Serbonis is never called the Red Sea in the Bible. The identification of Baal-Zephon (14:2, 9) with a location on the coast of the Mediterranean Sea is uncertain (cf. *The Westminster Historical Atlas to the Bible,* which states that the location of Baal-Zephon is unknown). The biblical data point to the Gulf of Suez, not to the Mediterranean Sea. It would also be difficult to imagine that Solomon's fleet was stationed on Lake Serbonis (cf. 1 Kings 9:26).

Nor is the eastern inlet of the Gulf of Akaba (mentioned in 1 Kings 9:26) possible, although proponents of the volcanic theory (e.g., Pythian Adams) have considered this.

A final note: the present distance between the southern tip of the Bitter Lakes and the northern end of the Gulf of Suez is ten miles; this sandy area was once a sea. It is not surprising that Egyptian sources do not mention the crossing, since unsuccessful military campaigns were usually glossed over.

13:17, 18 *When Pharaoh let the people go, God did not lead them on the road through the Philistine country, though that was shorter. For God said, "If they face war, they might change their minds and return to Egypt." So God led the people around by the desert road toward the Red Sea. The Israelites went up out of Egypt armed for battle.*

The narrative, which was interrupted by legal instructions, now resumes. According to 12:37 the Israelites went from Rameses to Succoth, which we believe to have been Pithom and the region east of Pithom. Now we have the explanation why God ("Elohim," the name used in this and the following verse) did not lead them on the road through the land of the Philistines (cf. commentary on v. 15). This was the caravan road that led directly north to Gaza and followed wherever possible the coast line of the Mediterranean Sea. The Pharaohs used this road for their expeditions to Syria, both during Moses' time and afterward; it was the most direct link between Egypt and Canaan. Yet God avoided it, since the Philistines were outstanding soldiers, and God did not want His people to lose heart and change their mind when they were attacked by chariots in the open plains and would prove inferior to the Philistines in military equipment. First, Israel had to be tested on the wilderness journey. During that forty-year period Egypt's hold over Canaan weakened considerably, after Egyptian raids prior to that time had impoverished the inhabitants of Canaan and ravaged their defenses. We thus see that verses 17–18 contain general statements, and that especially verse 18 must be understood as such. Verse 19 continues the narrative. Verse 20 does not indicate a major change of direction at Succoth. If verse 18 indicated a turning at Succoth toward the road of the Red Sea desert then this verse would be a conclusive argument for seeking Etham south of the Bitter Lakes. I am inclined to see verse 18 as a preliminary indication of the turning back at Etham that the Lord commanded in 14:2. This would be supported if the Gulf of Suez during Moses' time was still linked with the Bitter Lakes. In that case it is unlikely that Etham would be sought between the Bitter Lakes and the Gulf of Suez, although it is not impossible that Etham, if it is indeed the Egyptian defense line, would end south of the Bitter Lakes. Ebers also assumes this, although he seeks the place mentioned in this narrative north of the Bitter Lakes.

The mention of the Philistines has been used as an argument against the factual accuracy of this narrative; it is claimed that the Philistines did not yet live in the southern coastal plains of Canaan at this time and did not settle there until after 1200 B.C., while the Exodus took place around 1445 B.C. (see Introduction, p. 23). However, the Philistines were already mentioned in Genesis 26 as living in Canaan, and Gerar was called "the land of the Philistines" in Genesis 21:32, 34. The Philistines are also mentioned in 15:14 and 23:31. Noordtzij has offered plausible reasons why the Egyptian inscriptions before 1200 B.C. are silent about the Philistines.[19] Up to that time they had remained loyal to the Egyptians who had conquered them, so that their name could not possibly be mentioned in the reports of victories; furthermore, it took a long time to assimilate the semitic civilization as we find it among the Philistines of Samson's time and their fusion from various tribes into one nation required more time than the period from 1200 B.C. to Samson. Excavations, especially those at Gerar, where pottery from the period 2000–1500 B.C. has been found similar to that of the later Philistines, also support Noordtzij's opinion. It is thus correct to speak here of the land of the Philistines.

Rather than leading Israel on the road to the Philistines the Lord let Israel turn south at Etham (cf. 14:2), toward the road of the Red Sea desert, which is west of the Bitter Lakes in the direction of the present Gulf of Suez. The statement that the Israelites left Egypt "armed for battle" (some think that the word used here is related to the Egyptian word for "lance," others that it means "arranged in battle units," cf. commentary on 12:38) serves to explain their subsequent readiness to do battle with e.g., Amalek (ch. 17). The Israelites took not only jewelry, but also arms out of Egypt!

13:19 *Moses took the bones of Joseph with him because Joseph had made the sons of Israel swear an oath. He had said, "God will surely come to your aid, and then you must carry my bones up with you from this place."*

Moses, who was very familiar with the history of his people, also remembered to take the bones of Joseph. He knew of the oath that Joseph had the children of Israel swear when he was dying (cf. Gen. 50:24–25; Josh. 24:32; Heb. 11:22). Moses' act reminded the Israelites that Joseph's faith was not put to shame, and these bones were an encouragement in their undertaking. Calvin states that this shows that in spite of their adversity the people had never forgotten the memory of the promised redemption. "Come to your aid" (KJV: "visit you"), cf. commentary on 3:16; 4:31. "Carry up," causative of "to go up" used in verse 18.

---

[19] A. Noordtzij, *De Filistijnen* (Kampen: J. H. Kok, 1905).

13:20 *After leaving Succoth they camped at Etham on the edge of the desert.*

This verse states that the Israelites traveled from Succoth, where they probably gathered from all parts of Goshen, to Etham (cf. commentary on 12:37). Numbers 33:6 confirms this. It is best to think here of the Egyptian defense line of Chetam. Since that line stretched from Pelusium in the North to (perhaps) south of the Bitter Lakes, the desert east of the Gulf of Suez can also be called the desert of Etham (cf. Num. 33:8). Since the isthmus has changed little in historical times it is possible to seek Etham north of the Gulf of Suez and south of the Bitter Lakes, so that at Etham the Israelites could turn either to the east or to the west of the Red Sea. But, as we saw above, the text mentions the first major change in direction at Etham and not at Succoth. The journey then took them from Rameses via Succoth east to the defense line, perhaps to the north of Lake Timsah.

13:21, 22 *By day the Lord went ahead of them in a pillar of cloud to guide them on their way and by night in a pillar of fire to give them light, so that they could travel by day or night. Neither the pillar of cloud by day nor the pillar of fire by night left its place in front of the people.*

These verses mention the pillar of cloud and fire in which the Lord led and guided Israel (cf. v. 17). This pillar of cloud and fire is mentioned on several occasions during the wilderness journey, cf. 40:38; Numbers 9:15–23; 14:14; Deuteronomy 1:33; Nehemiah 9:12, 19; Psalms 78:14; 105:39; 1 Corinthians 10:1. This pillar, the proof of the Lord's presence, expressed His love and care for Israel (cf. Gen. 15:17). The view, mentioned above, that the pillar showed Israel the way to the volcano Sinai must be rejected, since Sinai was not a volcano (cf. commentary on 3:1). In this view Sinai was one of the mountains in northwest Arabia or in the southern part of what used to be Edom. Some have also thought of the fire signals carried by guides, which were taken to the rear to mislead the Egyptians (14:19–20), but this was not the custom, although Herder and others have maintained this. Besides, the text indicates something entirely different, viz. a miracle.

14:1–4 *Then the Lord said to Moses, "Tell the Israelites to turn back and encamp near Pi Hahiroth, between Migdol and the sea. They are to encamp by the sea, directly opposite Baal Zephon. Pharaoh will think, 'The Israelites are wandering around the land in confusion, hemmed in by the desert.' And I will harden Pharaoh's heart, and he will pursue them. But I will gain glory for myself through*

Pharaoh and all his army, and the Egyptians will know that I am the LORD." So the Israelites did this.

In Etham the Lord commanded Moses to tell the Israelites to turn back and not continue their journey through the wilderness of Etham to Sinai. They now had to go in a southeasterly direction, so that the sea (the northern part of the Gulf of Suez, see above) and Pi Hahiroth and Baal-Zephon lay before them, and Migdol behind them. Migdol means "tower," "fortress," and was the name of more than one Egyptian city (cf. Num. 33:7; Jer. 44:1; 46:14; Ezek. 29:10; 30:6). It is not certain where Migdol was located. Pi Hahiroth (the LXX probably read *haserot* since it translates the word as "dwelling") occurs without "Pi" in Numbers 33:8. Its exact location is also unknown (some think of Agrud, northwest of Suez; Neville, who places the crossing between Lake Timsah and the Bitter Lakes, identifies it with Pi Keheret at Lake Timsah). Some translate Pi Hahiroth as "mouth of the channel or canal," others as "entrance to the abysses," cf. Brugsch's opinion above. Baal-Zephon ("Lord of the North" is also unknown (cf. Num. 33:7), see above. If Israel encamped by the Sea opposite Baal-Zephon (which lies on the other side), then Pharaoh would think that they were confused or had lost their way, and did not know their way in the wilderness east of Egypt and west of the Red Sea. This was an obvious conclusion from the rather curious route Israel followed. Then the Lord would harden Pharaoh's heart (cf. 4:21; 9:12; 10:20, 27; 11:10; 14:8, 17; Josh. 11:20) so that he would pursue Israel, and the final outcome would be that the Lord would gain glory for Himself through Pharaoh and his entire army, so that the Egyptians would know that He was the Lord (cf. e.g., 10:2). Verses 2–4 give us an impression of Pharaoh's reprobation and of God's omnipotence (cf. 9:15; Rom. 9:17, 22–23). From a human standpoint this hardening of Pharaoh's heart was necessary to give Israel complete freedom and to release it from any obligation to return, since Pharaoh had broken his promise (cf. commentary on 12:31).

14:5–9 *When the king of Egypt was told that the people had fled, Pharaoh and his officials changed their minds about them and said, "What have we done? We have let the Israelites go and have lost their services!" So he had his chariot made ready and took his army with him. He took six hundred of the best chariots, along with all the other chariots of Egypt, with officers over all of them. The LORD hardened the heart of Pharaoh king of Egypt, so that he pursued the Israelites, who were marching out boldly. The Egyptians—all Pharaoh's horses and chariots, horsemen and troops—pursued the Israelites and overtook them as they camped by the sea near Pi Hahiroth, opposite Baal Zephon.*

Pharaoh received the report of Israel's curious backward movements, which the Egyptians saw as a flight or panic, occasioned perhaps by the threat of the fortifications, although they had permission to pass these. Pharaoh's disposition toward Israel, and that of his officials (cf. commentary on 10:7; they once again agree with Pharaoh) changed. They were not forced to sin, but made a voluntary choice in the wrong direction. And what was seen in the first chapter was repeated: greed and the desire for gain once again came to the fore, now that the plagues had been gone for a few days. They asked themselves and each other what could have induced them to let their cheap labor go. But the mistake could be corrected. Pharaoh let his own chariot be made ready for battle and mobilized his people. He took 600 crack chariots as well as the ordinary chariots of Egypt. Each chariot normally was manned by two people, the charioteer or driver, and the archer. In this case each chariot carried a third man, called here the "officer" (KJV: "captain").[20] Verse 8 states once again emphatically that this was the Lord's doing, the result of His hardening of Pharaoh's heart. The Israelites went out boldly (RSV: "defiantly"), lit.' "with high hand," which may also mean "under the protection of a high hand"; the latter is probably correct. That high hand then became apparent in what followed (cf. v. 31; Num. 33:3–4). Although the Egyptians had already seen that high (or mighty) hand of the Lord during the Exodus, they nevertheless pursued Israel and thus completed their godlessness (cf. Isa. 26:11). They overtook the Israelites while they were encamped near Pi Hahiroth (v. 2). There, with the sea before them, Pharaoh's cavalry and chariots caught up with them. It has been said that Pharaoh did not have a cavalry, since ancient Egyptian documents do not make mention of it. But it is not impossible (cf. also commentary on 9:1–4; Josh. 24:6).

14:10–14 *As Pharaoh approached, the Israelites looked up, and there were the Egyptians, marching after them. They were terrified and cried out to the LORD. They said to Moses, "Was it because there were no graves in Egypt that you brought us to the desert to die? What have you done to us by bringing us out of Egypt? Didn't we say to you in Egypt, 'Leave us alone; let us serve the Egyptians'? It would have been better for us to serve the Egyptians than to die in the desert!"*

Moses answered the people, "Do not be afraid. Stand firm and you will see the deliverance the LORD will bring you today. The Egyptians you see today you will never see again. The LORD will fight for you; you need only to be still."

The narrative now becomes very vivid and gripping. As Pharaoh approached, the Israelites noticed the swirling clouds of dust and saw the

---

[20]Cf. van Gelderen on 1 Kings 9:22 in this series.

Egyptians in the distance (cf. 13:20). To the east was the sea, to the south and west were the mountains, and the north was blocked by Pharaoh's armies. They became terrified and cried to the Lord (cf. commentary on 3:7), not in faith but in fear, and the first (but by no means the last) grumbling began, and Moses took the brunt of it. They considered themselves as good as dead, although the Egyptians did not intend to destroy them (v. 5). "Lead out," cf. e.g., 12:17, 51. They reminded Moses of what they told him in Egypt (v. 12, cf. 6:9), or at least what they now claimed they told him. Even then they considered slavery in Egypt preferable to death in the wilderness, something that does not speak of them as a people. Verses 13–14 beautifully show the strength of Moses' faith; he trusted in what the Lord had revealed to him in verses 2–4. He therefore admonished the Israelites not to be afraid or flee, but to stand firm (cf. 2:4). By faith he knew that the Egyptians would be destroyed. In verse 14 follows the well-known promise and admonition to be still (cf. Isa. 30:15).

14:15–18 *Then the Lord said to Moses, "Why are you crying out to me? Tell the Israelites to move on. Raise your staff and stretch out your hand over the sea to divide the water so that the Israelites can go through the sea on dry ground. I will harden the hearts of the Egyptians so that they will go in after them. And I will gain glory through Pharaoh and all his army, through his chariots and his horsemen. The Egyptians will know that I am the Lord when I gain glory through Pharaoh, his chariots and his horsemen."*

In these verses the Lord told Moses what had to be done. Moses also seemed to have cried to the Lord after his statement of faith. He had to tell the Israelites to march on in the direction of the sea. He had to raise his staff, which had already performed so many miracles, over the sea and thus divide it so that the Israelites could pass through on dry land. Again the Lord promised that He would harden the hearts of the Egyptians and cause them to pursue, and He then would glorify Himself and make them know that He was the Lord (cf. v. 4). Moses would have to wait and see how this would happen.

14:19, 20 *Then the angel of God, who had been traveling in front of Israel's army, withdrew and went behind them. The pillar of cloud also moved from in front and stood behind them, coming between the armies of Egypt and Israel. Throughout the night the cloud brought darkness to the one side and light to the other side; so neither went near the other all night long.*

"The angel of God" (see commentary on 3:2) thus was present in the pillar of cloud and fire (cf. 13:21) and placed Himself behind Israel in the

143

pillar of cloud, between them and the Egyptians. In the meantime (v. 20) night had come, and on the side of the Egyptians there were clouds and darkness, while on the side of the Israelites the pillar of fire provided light. The Egyptians could not reach the Israelites in the darkness, but had to wait until daybreak, while the Israelites could carry on. All night long darkness and light were the two sides of the same pillar.

14:21–25 *Then Moses stretched out his hand over the sea, and all that night the Lord drove the sea back with a strong east wind and turned it into dry land. The waters were divided, and the Israelites went through the sea on dry ground, with a wall of water on their right and on their left.*

The Egyptians pursued them, and all Pharaoh's horses and chariots and horsemen followed them into the sea. In the morning watch the Lord looked down from the pillar of fire and cloud at the Egyptian army and threw it into confusion. He made the wheels of their chariots swerve so that they had difficulty driving. And the Egyptians said, "Let's get away from the Israelites! The Lord is fighting for them against Egypt."

During the night, while the Egyptians were forced to be idle, Moses stretched his hand over the sea, and the Lord sent a strong east wind that divided the water and turned the sea into a wide stretch (because of their large numbers) of dry land in front of the Israelites. The Lord thus used natural means. Travelers reported that the tide in the Gulf of Suez depends to a large degree on the direction of the wind, and that a northeasterly wind pushed the water to the south. But it was never possible to cross the Gulf on foot, even during prolonged periods of low tide. When night fell the Israelites were already well on their way across the dry land in the middle of the sea, with walls of water on both sides. At daybreak the Egyptians saw that Israel was close to reaching the opposite shore and they did not hesitate a moment. Pharaoh's entire army took the same path through the sea. Pharaoh himself probably did not follow (cf. commentary on 2:23). In the last watch of the night (the Jews divided the night into three watches of four hours each), the so-called morning watch between two o'clock and six o'clock, it happened. The Lord looked down on the army of the Egyptians from the pillar of cloud and fire and threw it into confusion, perhaps by means of a thunderstorm (cf. Ps. 77:18–19). He made the wheels of their chariots swerve. It is unlikely that He "took them off" (KJV), since then they would not have had difficulty driving, but could obviously not have driven at all. But the wheels did not grip the ground that was possibly drenched by rain, if we think of a thunderstorm causing their confusion, or perhaps because the sea bottom was too wet to support the narrow wheels. The Egyptians (lit.: "Egypt") wanted to flee when they realized that the

Lord was fighting for the Israelites. They had forgotten all too soon, and now it was too late.

14:26–28 *Then the Lord said to Moses, "Stretch out your hand over the sea so that the waters may flow back over the Egyptians and their chariots and horsemen." Moses stretched out his hand over the sea, and at daybreak the sea went back to its place. The Egyptians were fleeing toward it, and the Lord swept them into the sea. The water flowed back and covered the chariots and horsemen—the entire army of Pharaoh that had followed the Israelites into the sea. Not one of them survived.*

The Lord's command to Moses, to stretch out his hand over the sea to let the waters return, rang out (v. 26). Moses did this, and at daybreak (the Israelites could watch this happen) the sea returned (the wind turned to a westerly or southeasterly direction, cf. 15:10), and the Egyptians fled directly into the returning sea. Chariots and horsement were covered by the waves. Verse 28 gives the impression that Pharaoh himself did not follow the Israelites into the sea. The mummy of Amenhotep II was found in 1898. Psalm 136:15 must be considered a poetic statement. "Not one of them survived" (see commentary on 10:18). See also Psalms 78:53; 106:11. The Dutch Authorized Version has the following marginal note here: "This was a just punishment of God for the Egyptians, who had thrown the little children of the Israelites into the water and drowned them."

14:29–31 *But the Israelites went through the sea on dry ground, with a wall of water on their right and on their left. That day the Lord saved Israel from the hands of the Egyptians, and Israel saw the Egyptians lying dead on the shore. And when the Israelites saw the great power the Lord displayed against the Egyptians, the people feared the Lord and put their trust in him and in Moses his servant.*

The Israelites on the other hand had walked on dry land in the middle of the sea (v. 29, cf. v. 22). Verse 30 states that Moses' expectation of verse 13 was fulfilled. Israel even saw the bodies of the Egyptians wash up on the shore of the Red Sea (cf. Ps. 74:13–14). Now Israel saw (lit.) "the mighty hand the Lord had raised against the Egyptians" and, like Thomas many centuries later, believed after having seen. Israel feared the Lord and believed (the word used here expresses firmness) the Lord and His servant Moses, whom they saw as the Lord's instrument, His spokesman. Indeed, they sang His praise (Ps. 106:12).

30. *The Song of Moses* (15:1–21)

The song of Moses and the Israelites by the Red Sea with the response of Miriam and the Israelite women has sometimes been considered a later elaboration on the short song Miriam sang and which now served as the response (v. 21). The text argues against this idea. It is also contrary to the text to consider verses 1–18 a psalm that did not originate at the time of the crossing, but was inserted here after it had existed separately as a part of Israel's liturgy (Hans Schmidt). The primary reason for assigning a later date to the song is in verses 11–18, which are thought to presuppose Israel's being settled in Canaan. But verses 1–10 (or 1–12) are not complete in themselves. Furthermore, verses 13–18 can be explained as a prophetic vision of the future received by Moses.

The song itself is found in verses 1–18. Verse 19 restates the occasion, and verses 20–21 continue with the response to the song of the men by Miriam and the women. The song was transmitted orally and was very popular in Israel, as is evident from the fact that it is frequently quoted in the Psalms (v. 1, cf. Pss. 66:6; 68:18; 106:12; v. 2, cf. Ps. 118:14, 21, 28; v. 3, cf. Ps. 24:8; v. r, cf. Ps. 136:15; vv. 5–17, cf. Ps. 78:52–54; vv. 5–13, cf. Ps. 77:14–21; vv. 5–10, cf. Ps. 106:11; v. 7, cf. Ps. 78:49; v. 8, cf. Ps. 78:13; v. 11, cf. Pss. 66:3, 5; 78:4, 12; 86:8; vv. 13–17, cf. Pss. 44:2, 4; 74:2; v. 17, cf. Ps. 80:9, 16; v. 18, cf. Ps. 146:10). This is all the more proof that the crossing of the Red Sea was considered the fundamental fact of Israel's history. Moses sang the song by way of confirmation and remembrance.

For the Christian church this song, and the Israelites standing victoriously at the Red Sea, are a prophecy of those who will have been victorious over Satan and the Antichrist and who will then sing "the song of Moses the servant of God and of the Lamb" (cf. Rev. 15:1–4). For them the song is an expression of the true background of their struggle or "wilderness journey," seen in the light of Golgotha and the victories over Satan and his instruments that God has granted His people.

I have not been able to divide this song into smaller segments or strophes. The best division is into two sections according to content: verses 2–12 and verses 13–18 (see commentary on v. 1, which is the theme of the song). The rabbis call this song the "song of the sea."

15:1 *Then Moses and the Israelites sang this song to the LORD:*

"I will sing to the LORD,
for he is highly exalted.
The horse and its rider
he has hurled into the sea."

The words "Then Moses sang" and "I will sing" indicate that Moses was the actual author of the song. Verse 1 states the theme, repeated by

Miriam in verse 21. The first thing redeemed Israel did was to sing to Jahweh. "I will sing," cf. also Judges 5:3. First His exaltedness was praised, an exaltedness above all men and human display of power, proven by the fact that He had, without any effort, hurled Egypt's horse (chariots and horses) and rider (their riders) into the sea. The remaining verses elaborated on this exaltedness, which is expressed both in Egypt's defeat (vv. 2–12) and in the favor that had been, and was yet to be, bestowed on His people (vv. 13–18). "Rider," cf. 14:9.

15:2 *"The LORD is my strength and my song;*
he has become my salvation.
He is my God, and I will praise him,
my father's God, and I will exalt him."

Moses (and Israel with him) called this exalted God (in this verse the Hebrew for Lord is "Yah," probably a shortened form of Yahweh) his strength and his song, the subject of his song because He had helped and saved him (cf. 14:13). He had experienced the personal bond with that God, and he now glorified and exalted Him. He attributed to the Lord the virtues that He had proven to be His, even from the days of old, and he praised and exalted Him (cf. v. 1; Isa. 12:2). "My father's God," cf. commentary on 3:6. But since Moses spoke here on behalf of all of Israel, and all Israelites joined in, "father" is here a collective term for all ancestors, and especially the three patriarchs, Abraham, Isaac, and Jacob.

15:3–5 *"The LORD is a warrior;*
the LORD is his name.
Pharaoh's chariots and his army
he has hurled into the sea.
The best of Pharaoh's officers
are drowned in the Red Sea.
The deep waters have covered them;
they sank to the depths like a stone."

Jahweh (the name used in this song, see note on 3:14–15) was a warrior (cf. 14:14; Ps. 24:8; Isa. 42:13), and Jahweh was His name. He had proven to be a warrior by hurling Pharaoh's chariots and his army (cf. commentary on 14:4, 7, 9, 17, 28) into the sea. "Officers," see commentary on 14:7. "Red Sea," see commentary on 10:19. Note that the drowning of Pharaoh's chariots and army are mentioned, but not the drowning of Pharaoh himself. Verse 5 argues against the assumption that the Red Sea referred to a shallow marsh (see commentary on previous section): the

147

"deep waters" (lit.: "abyss," "depths," cf. KJV) covered them, they disappeared into the "depths of the sea." See Nehemiah 9:11.

15:6, 7 *"Your right hand, O LORD,*
was majestic in power.
Your right hand, O LORD,
shattered the enemy.
In the greatness of your majesty
you threw down those who opposed you.
You unleashed your burning anger;
it consumed them like stubble."

The "right hand" of the Lord represented His omnipotence, which revealed itself gloriously in His mighty deeds. It shattered and crushed the enemy. Moses then sang of the greatness of His majesty, which threw down and destroyed His opponents. The same word was used of the demolition of buildings. They were "consumed like stubble" (or "straw," cf. commentary on 5:12) when the Lord unleashed His burning anger (cf. 14:24; Isa. 5:24).

15:8–10 *"By the blast of your nostrils*
the waters piled up.
The surging waters stood firm like a wall;
the deep waters congealed in the heart of the sea."

"The enemy boasted,
'I will pursue, I will overtake them.
I will divide the spoils;
I will gorge myself on them.
I will draw my sword
and my hand will destroy them.'
But you blew with your breath,
and the sea covered them.
They sank like lead
in the mighty waters."

Moses relived what had just happened. He saw the wind as the breath of Jahweh's nostrils (cf. 14:21), which piled up the waters. The "running waters" of the sea stood like a wall or dike (cf. 14:22, 29), and the "deep waters" ("depths," cf. v. 5) congealed in the middle of the sea. He saw the enemy, burning with rapacity, standing ready to take the path through the sea. They said: "I will gorge myself on them" (lit.: "my soul shall be filled or satisfied with them." KJV: "my lust shall be satisfied upon them"; the soul was considered the seat of desire or lust, cf. Deut. 23:24; Ps.

78:18; etc.), and "my hand will destroy them"; I prefer the translation "my hand will capture them"; cf. 14:5. "Pursue" and "overtake," cf. 14:9. The spoils were the purpose of military enterprises, cf. Judges 5:30; Psalm 68:13; Isaiah 9:2. But then the Lord blew with His breath, indicating a wind from a different direction (cf. commentary on 14:27), and the sea covered them, they sank like lead in the mighty waters (cf. commentary on v. 5).

15:11, 12 *"Who among the gods is like you, O Lord?*
Who is like you—
majestic in holiness,
awesome in glory,
working wonders?
You stretched out your right hand
and the earth swallowed them."

The song now rises in profound gratitude. No one was like Jahweh, the gods of Egypt had been defeated, none among the gods of the nations could do what He had done. He glorified Himself (cf. v. 6) by showing Himself to be holy, separated from all those gods, exalted above all people and enemies, destroying His enemies (v. 12) but blessing His people (cf. v. 13). Because of His holiness God was above all that was created and all that was sinful. He revealed His holiness in the punishment of sin and the redemption of His people (and the world) from the power of sin (cf. Rev. 15:3–4). That is why He was feared with trepidation among all nations, and why the songs that were sung to His glory spoke of the impotence of all gods before His omnipotence and because He worked wonders that amazed the nations. Once more Moses came back to this special wonder. It was as if the earth itself (of which the sea is considered to be a part) swallowed the Egyptians, because Jahweh merely stretched out His hand and showed His power effortlessly.

15:13–18 *"In your unfailing love you will lead*
the people you have redeemed.
In your strength you will guide them
to your holy dwelling.
The nations will hear and tremble;
anguish will grip the people of Philistia.
The chiefs of Edom will be terrified,
the leaders of Moab will be seized with trembling,
the people of Canaan will melt away;
terror and dread will fall upon them.

149

> *By the power of your arm*
> *they will be as still as a stone—*
> *until your people pass by, O LORD,*
> *until the people you bought pass by.*
> *You will bring them in and plant them*
> *on the mountain of your inheritance—*
> *the place, O LORD, you made for your dwelling,*
> *the sanctuary, O Lord, your hands established.*
> *The LORD will reign*
> *for ever and ever.''*

Finally Moses turned his thoughts to the present and future of Israel, of the people who stood around him and sang with him. They had been led by God's grace thus far, and tended like a flock (cf. 13:17; Ps. 77:21) after the Lord delivered them (cf. commentary on 6:6). Moses, by faith, saw the people already there where by the Lord's power they had yet to go: to His holy dwelling place, to the pasture He had prepared for them, to Canaan. Yes, he already saw the nations tremble after they heard of the crossing and the Exodus (the tense used here is the ''perfectum confidentiae,'' which states a future event in the perfect tense as if it had already taken place). Anguish (as in childbirth), fear and trembling had seized the people of Philistia (cf. commentary on 13:17). The chiefs of Edom (cf. also Gen. 36:15; 1 Chron. 1:51ff.) would be terrified when they heard of this. The leaders (lit.: ''rams''; Moab had much livestock, cf. 2 Kings 3:4, hence perhaps this image) of Moab would be seized with trembling. Edom was Israel's arch enemy; Edom and Moab were the first nations the Israelites would meet at the borders of Canaan. The fact that Edom later refused to let Israel pass (cf. Num. 20:18ff.' 21:4; Deut. 2:1, 3, 8) indicates that Moses spoke these words and that there is no reason to consider this a later addition. ''The leaders of Moab will be seized with trembling'' (cf. Num. 22:2ff.), and the Canaanites would ''melt away.'' This restlessness and anxiety is illustrated historically in the Amarna letters: during the fifty years following the time that Moses sang this song the inhabitants of Canaan repeatedly sent anxious letters to Pharaoh before the invasion of the Hapiru (who were not necessarily the same as the Israelites). It was a period of anxiety, cf. Joshua 2:9ff.; 9:9ff. ''Terror'' in verse 16 is a poetic form, as this song is full of poetic forms and euphonic expressions. Moses already saw all these nations paralyzed by terror and dread because of the Lord's power that could forcibly make room for the people that He had bought for Himself by leading them out of Egypt, the house of slavery.

Verse 17 expresses the certainty that the Lord would bring the Israelites into Canaan, would plant them there like a vine (cf. Ps. 80:9ff.) on His mountain, a symbol of the Promised Land, mountainous Canaan (cf. Deut. 3:25; Isa. 11:9; Ps. 78:54). It was the special property of the Lord and thus could be called His dwelling, made and established by Him. The entire land had become the sanctuary of the Lord (Adonai), who ruled over all things. It had become His sanctuary because He promised it and would give it to the people among whom He wanted to dwell. Note that Moses clearly states the purpose of Israel's exodus and journey in this song (cf. ch. 3–4; 6:8; 13:19). Moses here was a prophet and his words were later fulfilled in the Lord's choice of Zion as the place where He dwelled. We cannot be sure that Moses thought of Mt. Moriah (cf. Gen.22). But he knew that the Lord dwelled among His people in the pillar of cloud and fire and could anticipate that this would be replaced in the Promised Land by the Lord's dwelling on a mountain. But the Holy Spirit had a deeper meaning for these words: there the Lord would be King, and all those things would be fulfilled because He was King. He will reign "forever and ever" over His enemies by the display of His power, over His people with grace (cf. Ps. 146:10).

The suggestion has been made that verse 18 indicates that this song belonged to the psalms, and was sung on the occasion of the celebration of the Lord's accession to the throne. Once a year in the fall the Lord, or rather the ark, then was supposed to have been carried out of the temple and after a symbolic play returned to the temple as the Conqueror over the powers of darkness. On that occasion the people then sang of the fact that He had become King, and numerous expressions in the Psalms supposedly refer to this (cf. e.g., Pss. 93, 97, 99). But neither the historical sections nor the legal sections of the Old Testament mention such a celebration; a similar feast was known in Babylon, however. It is then thought to be *probable* that Israel also had such a feast and the expressions in the Psalms and in verse 18 are used to support this assumption. The proof is thus not very strong. It is also difficult to imagine that the ark, which stood in the Most Holy Place, where only the high priest entered once a year, would have participated in such an annual procession and festival. For the now demonstrated kingship of the Lord over Israel, see commentary on 6:6–8.

15:19 *When Pharaoh's horses, chariots and horsemen went into the sea, the LORD brought the waters of the sea back over them, but the Israelites walked through the sea on dry ground.*

Some consider this verse to be part of the song. Once again Moses stated the occasion for this beautiful song (cf. 14:29). Perhaps it was taken from an old collection of songs where it served the purpose of an explanatory postscript. Numbers 21:14; Joshua 10:13; and 2 Samuel 1:18 indicate that such collections existed.

15:20, 21 *Then Miriam the prophetess, Aaron's sister, took a tambourine in her hand, and all the women followed her, with tambourines and dancing. Miriam sang to them:*

> *"Sing to the LORD,*
> *for he is highly exalted.*
> *The horse and its rider*
> *he has hurled into the sea."*

Miriam (see commentary on 2:1–10) is called here "the prophetess" since she was moved by the Lord's Spirit and gave expression to what the Lord inspired in her soul (cf. also Num. 12:2, 6). "Aaron's sister": the reason why Miriam is called Aaron's rather than Moses' sister may be the fact that Aaron was older than Moses, but it also expresses the unique and elevated position Moses occupied. A tambourine was a small drum with bells or pieces of metal that tinkled when the instrument was struck or swung; Egyptian tambourines had handles, as seen in illustrations that have been found of Egyptian dancers and priestesses with tambourines. See Genesis 31:27. The women followed Miriam (lit.: "went out after her," they came out of the crowd) in a dancing chorus. Miriam answered the singing men with the first strophe of their song (v. 1), which she used as a refrain (repeated over and over, cf. Ps. 136?) and turned into an exhortation to them: "Sing." And thus ended Israel's Exodus from Egypt: even the women sang and danced and made music (cf. Judg. 11:34; 1 Sam. 18:7; Ps. 68:26) to the glory of the Lord, Israel's God! For

> "The horse and its rider
> He has hurled into the sea."

Part Two

The Making of the Covenant at Sinai
(15:22–40:38)

1. *Marah and Elim* (15:22–27)

15:22 *Then Moses led Israel from the Red Sea and they went into the Desert of Shur. For three days they traveled in the desert without finding water.*

This section begins the description of the wilderness journey. Moses was now the acknowledged leader (cf. 14:31). After the celebration at the Red Sea ("Red Sea," cf. commentary on 10:19) he led Israel (cf. 12:37; 13:20; 14:15) into the Desert of Shur. "Shur" is found as the name of a place in northeastern Egypt in Genesis 16:7; 20:1; 25:18; 1 Samuel 15:7; 27:8. It may mean "wall," and here probably refers to a wall that protected Egypt against invasions by the Bedouins from Asia (cf. commentary on 13:20). This same desert is called the Desert of Etham in Numbers 33:8.

15:23–26 *When they came to Marah, they could not drink its water because it was bitter. (That is why the place is called Marah.) So the people grumbled against Moses, saying, "What are we to drink?"*
Then Moses cried out to the Lord, and the Lord showed him a piece of wood. He threw it into the water, and the water became sweet.
There the Lord made a decree and a law for them, and there he tested them. He said, "If you listen carefully to the voice of the Lord your God and do what is right in his eyes, if you pay attention to his commands and keep all his decrees, I will not bring on you any of the diseases I brought on the Egyptians, for I am the Lord who heals you."

"Marah" means "bitter" (see Ruth 1:20). The oasis derived its name from the fact that the water was bitter or salty. It is probably the oasis of Ain Hawara, where the water is still bitter. Böhl's opinion that Marah is in Ain Moweileh ("the sweet spring") south of Canaan, is based on his belief that Israel traveled directly to Kadesh Barnea.[1]

Marah was the scene of the second grumbling of the people against the Lord (cf. 14:10–12) when, after three days without water, the water at Marah turned out to be bitter.

Moses cried out to the Lord (cf. 14:15), and the Lord showed him a piece of wood. Some believe that this was a particular kind of wood that could make bitter water sweet, which is not impossible. The miracle then was that the Lord showed Moses the benefit and use of this wood. Calvin shared this opinion, but believed that on this occasion the efficacy of the wood was miraculously increased (cf. also the apocryphal Ecclesiasticus 38:5–6). But Ebers states that the Arabs were not familiar with any kind of wood that had this property. In any case this, like the miracle of the crossing of the Red Sea (14:21), was an indirect miracle, which used the piece of wood as the means. Verse 25b refers to "a decree and a law," a norm for conduct (cf. 21:1), which the Lord (not Moses, as some believe, since Moses was not the one who tested the people) imposed on the people at Marah. This "law" follows in verse 26. Verse 25b also makes it clear that the experience of Israel at Marah was a test: the Lord wanted to test their faith, and their lack of faith became all too obvious. It is also possible to interpret verse 25b to mean that Israel tested the Lord; but this is less probable, since the Lord is the subject of verse 25a.

Verse 26 gives the content of the "decree and law": the requirement that Israel as a nation, and the Israelites as individuals, were to listen to the voice of the Lord, the God of Israel. They were to obey Him and His commands and decrees, rather than do what was right in their own eyes. But the main sentence is a promise: if Israel fulfilled the condition stated in the "decree," then the Lord would not bring any of the diseases on them that He inflicted on the Egyptians. For He was the Lord, Jahweh (cf. ch. 3), who healed them, who was their Physician. The miracle of Marah must express the fact that the Lord would rather heal than inflict illness and disease (cf. 23:25; Deut. 7:15; Pss. 103:3; 107:20; Ezek. 18:23, 32: 33:11).[2]

---

[1] Cf. F. M. Th. Böhl, "Exodus" (in *Tekst en Uitleg*), and *Palestina in het licht der jongste opgravingen* (Amsterdam: H. J. Paris, 1931), pp. 87–88 and plate 17. The *Westminster Historical Atlas to the Bible* (1946) identifies Marah with Ain Hawara.

[2] Some feel that verses 25–26 do not fit here, but should be connected with 17:7, where *massah* is used, which is derived from *nissah* ("to test"); this verb is also found in verse 25. But in 17:7, Israel tested the Lord, while here the Lord tested Israel.

15:27 *Then they came to Elim, where there were twelve springs and seventy palm trees, and they camped there near the water.*

Elim (lit.: "trees," "palm trees"), on the other hand, showed that on the wilderness journey the Lord could also provide full relief directly; the oasis had twelve springs and seventy palm trees, and the people camped near the water. Israel's journey foreshadows the believer's journey on earth (cf. Rev. 12:6). Elim is located in the Wadi Gharandel, not far from Marah; according to Ebers, it was slightly less than two hours from Marah to Elim by camel. It is a large, deep valley, where today a few palm trees, tamarisks, and acacias are still found, as well as a brook and springs, although in the past the oasis was probably much more luxuriant. The numbers "twelve" and "seventy" may have a symbolic meaning in this context. A connection between these numbers and the number of the tribes and of the elders has sometimes been suggested, but the latter is incorrect. It is perhaps best to think rather of the numbers as symbolizing the fullness of the blessings God bestowed on His people.

2. *Manna and Quail* (16:1–36)

16:1 *The whole Israelite community set out from Elim and came to the Desert of Sin, which is between Elim and Sinai, on the fifteenth day of the second month after they had come out of Egypt.*

The entire Israelite community (cf. 12:3) set out (cf. 12:37; 13:20; 14:15; 15:22) from Elim and came to the Desert of Sin, between Elim and Sinai. The name Sin is related to "Sinai," and may mean "bramble-bush" (cf. commentary on 3:1f.). Another view is that this name, and the name Sinai were derived from the moon-god Sin, who was worshiped in the Sinai peninsula. The location is uncertain; it has been identified with the barren desert and coastal plains of El-Qaa, north of the present Tor, or with the region of Wadi Magara. It should probably be identified with Debbet er-Ramleh, a sandy tract north of the Gebel Musa. Ebers (cf. commentary on 3:1f.) locates the Desert of Sin in the region between Abu Zelime and Wadi Magara, while Bodenheimer places it at the edge of the oasis Feiran. But the expression "from place to place" in 17:1 argues against this, if we assume that the oasis Feiran is the same as Rephidim. Numbers 33:10–11 states that Israel camped by the Red Sea before it came to the Desert of Sin, so that this desert was probably located in the interior of the peninsula rather than along the coast. The detour that this involves can be explained by the fact that more water was available along this route, which coincides with the route the Egyptians followed to their copper mines in the Sinai Peninsula.

The second month after their departure from Egypt (cf. 13:3–4) is the month that was later called Iyyar (April–May).

16:2, 3 *In the desert the whole community grumbled against Moses and Aaron. The Israelites said to them, "If only we had died by the LORD's hand in Egypt! There we sat around pots of meat and ate all the food we wanted, but you have brought us out into this desert to starve this entire assembly to death."*

The Israelites grumbled a third time (cf. commentary on 15:24). Aaron is again mentioned along with Moses. Verse 3 (cf. 14:12): "You (i.e. Moses and Aaron) have brought us" (cf. 6:26–27). "Assembly" (cf. 12:6). They would rather have died by the Lord's hand than because of Moses and Aaron (cf. 14:11; 2 Sam. 24:14; 1 Chron. 21:13). Their hunger caused them to idealize their life in Egypt (cf. 2:23–25; Num. 11:5), and they contemptuously spoke of "this desert." They preferred a natural or even a sudden death (cf. the tenth plague) to a slow death by starvation. Up to this point, the plain they traversed had probably provided sufficient food. They also had brought provisions from Egypt (cf. 12:34, 38–39), but they could not slaughter all their cattle. Their complaint was premature.

16:4, 5 *Then the LORD said to Moses, "I will rain down bread from heaven for you. The people are to go out each day and gather enough for that day. In this way I will test them and see whether they will follow my instructions. On the sixth day they are to prepare what they bring in, and that is to be twice as much as they gather on the other days."*

The Lord immediately gave Moses a revelation (note the difference between this and 14:15; 15:25). Aaron is not mentioned, although the complaint was also directed against him. When the Lord spoke directly, it was almost always to Moses alone. He promised something amazing (KJV: "behold"): He himself would rain down bread from heaven (cf. Deut. 8:3; Neh. 9:15; Pss. 78:23–25; 105:40—the authors of these Psalms probably were familiar with this chapter—John 6:31ff.; Rev. 2:17). The wording of this promise does not allow for any other interpretation than that the manna, which is described later, came down from above, from the sky (cf. also the references cited above), and excludes the possibility that it was a natural phenomenon, such as the "tamarisk manna" or the "manna moss."

The so-called "Sinai manna" or "tamarisk manna" was identified by Bodenheimer and Theodor in 1927 as the secretion of two species of coccus, of which the best-known is the *Trabutina mannipara* or *mannifera*, which Ehrenberg had already observed in 1823. Bodenheimer observed this production of "manna" also in the coastal plains of El-Qaa. Josephus must have referred to this "manna" when he wrote that in his day manna still fell on the Sinai peninsula. Bodenheimer himself is of the opinion that a natural explanation of the miracle of the manna is out of the question for a Bible-believing Christian; and certain scholars who do not take the Bible to be the inspired Word of God agree. Furthermore, this "manna" is found only in June and July, when it rains, and in such small quantities that it would never have sufficed to feed the large number of Israelites. An additional miracle, as we shall see, is that the manna did not fall on the Sabbath (cf. vv. 5, 22–30). The manna could not be kept overnight (vv. 19–20), except on the Sabbath, while the natural "manna" could be kept in a cool place for a long period of time. Also, the natural "manna" could be boiled, but not baked. And it can hardly be said of this "manna" that "he who gathered much did not have too much, and he who gathered little did not have too little" (v. 18), or that it appeared at the hour appointed by God and announced by Moses. All this points to the fact that this was indeed a miracle, which does not have a parallel in today's natural "manna," although the natural phenomenon of the dew seems to have played a role in the provision of the manna (vv. 13–14).

The "manna moss" that is found in Morocco and the Sahara desert must also be rejected as the source of the manna, although it is worth noting that the seeds of this plant can be carried by the wind over a distance of several miles, so that travelers in those regions have on occasion experienced a "manna rain" that lasted sometimes for several minutes; Ohle believes this to be the biblical manna. But, even apart from the arguments presented above, which also apply to this explanation, this phenomenon has never been observed in the Sinai peninsula.

It has been suggested that the miraculous element in this narrative marks it as a saga, based on the fact that the Israelites (whose number was much smaller than the Bible states) came in contact with and ate the "manna" found in the Sinai region, but this is in direct contradiction to what is written. Calvin already listed eight reasons why it is impossible that the manna of the wilderness journey was the same as the "manna" still found in the Sinai region.

"Go out," i.e. from the camp (cf. vv. 13, 27). "Gather enough for that day": the same expression is used in 5:13. "Gather": the same word is also used of the "gleaning" of grain (cf. Ruth 2:8). The end of verse 4 refers to the regulation that the people were to gather only enough for that day; it was thus a test of trust and obedience. "I will test them" (cf.

15:25). "Instructions," lit. "law," "instruction" *(Torah)*. The Lord attached limiting conditions to His gifts in order to test His people. Others, including Calvin, interpret this in a broader sense: the Lord would test them to see if they would walk in accordance with His directions, now that their needs had been and would be met. He wanted to bring them to obedience to Him through His generosity (cf. also Deut. 8:3, 16–18).

Note the command and the promise regarding the sixth day (v. 5). The promise was that there would be twice as much manna on the sixth day, and that the gathered double portions would not shrink to one omer per person (cf. vv. 17–18, 22–23). They were instructed to prepare the double portion, either by baking or boiling the manna (v. 23, cf. Num. 11:8). The reason for this was that the seventh day was the Sabbath (vv. 23–30), which indicated that Israel knew the Sabbath before the giving of the law at Sinai; this agrees with Genesis 2:2–3.[3] It is doubtful that Israel observed the Sabbath with any degree of care prior to Sinai (cf. vv. 27–28).

16:6–7 *So Moses and Aaron said to all the Israelites, "In the evening you will know that it was the LORD who brought you out of Egypt, and in the morning you will see the glory of the LORD, because he has heard your grumbling against him. Who are we, that you should grumble against us?"*

After Moses had received this revelation, he and Aaron could give an answer to *"all* the Israelites" (cf. vv. 1, 2, 3; apparently all of Israel grumbled). It is likely that Aaron spoke on Moses' behalf. Verses 4–5 do not mention that they would know that same evening that it was the Lord who led them out of Egypt, nor that they would see the glory of the Lord in the morning (v. 7); verses 4–5 are thus apparently a summary of what the Lord said to Moses. Moses and Aaron countered the complaint of the Israelites that the two of them had led Israel out of Egypt with evil intentions (cf. verses 2–3): the emphasis in verses 6–8 is on the Lord as the One who led them out (cf. e.g. 12:17, 42, 51). The "glory of the LORD" in this context (v. 10) is the splendor and majesty that became visible in the pillar of cloud and fire (cf. 24:17). This seeing of His glory is not, however, limited to what is described in verse 10, but includes the experience of God's omnipotence in the gift of the manna "in the morning" (v. 7), after He had shown His glory in the provision of the quail the previous evening (cf. vv. 8, 13). The Israelites would see His glory because they murmured

---

[3]Some recent translations change the sequence of verses 5–13 as found in the Hebrew text. Thus the (Dutch) Leyden Translation reads: verses 5, 11–12, 9–10, 6–7, 13; verse 8 is omitted. Baentsch reads: verses 5, 9–12, 6–8, 13. However, the Hebrew sequence makes good sense.

ultimately against Him, since Moses and Aaron derived their authority from Him (cf. Num. 16:11).

16:8 *Moses also said, "You will know that it was the LORD when he gives you meat to eat in the evening and all the bread you want in the morning, because he has heard your grumbling against him. Who are we? You are not grumbling against us, but against the LORD."*

Moses here also added for the first time the promise of meat (cf. the "pots of meat" in Egypt, v. 3). The Lord provided this meat and bread not because it was His gracious pleasure to do so, but because He had heard the grumbling against Him. *He* answered the challenge directed against His representatives, Moses and Aaron (cf. 1 Sam. 8:7), which was ultimately directed against Him (cf. Ps. 78:19, although the context there is different).

16:9–12 *Then Moses told Aaron, "Say to the entire Israelite community, 'Come before the LORD, for he has heard your grumbling.'"*
While Aaron was speaking to the whole Israelite community, they looked toward the desert, and there was the glory of the LORD appearing in the cloud.
The LORD said to Moses, "I have heard the grumbling of the Israelites. Tell them, 'At twilight you will eat meat, and in the morning you will be filled with bread. Then you will know that I am the LORD your God.'"

In verse 9, Aaron was against Moses' spokesman (cf. 4:14–16, 29–30). "The whole Israelite community" (cf. vv. 1–2). "The LORD . . . has heard your grumbling" (cf. vv. 7–8).

Verse 10 gives us the impression that the pillar of cloud (and fire) hovered above the desert, around the camp, and that the Israelites turned toward the pillar in response to Aaron's exhortation (v. 9). "Behold" (KJV) expresses the sudden, the unexpected, the wonderful. "The glory of the LORD appearing in the cloud," i.e. the pillar of cloud that at this point still concealed so much of that glory that the people were able to watch it. The Lord thus showed His presence, of which Israel had practically lost sight, in a remarkable way. And at the same time He provided support for Moses' and Aaron's authority. Verse 10, cf. Numbers 14:10; 16:19, 42. Verse 11, cf. verses 7–9. "At twilight," cf. commentary on 12:6. "Meat" and "bread," cf. verse 3. "Then you will know that I am the LORD your God," cf. verse 6 and 6:7.

16:13, 14 *That evening quail came and covered the camp, and in the morning there was a layer of dew around the camp. When the dew was gone, thin flakes like frost on the ground appeared on the desert floor.*

The Lord's promise was fulfilled: the quail arrived in such numbers that the ground of the camp was covered with them. Cf. Numbers 11:31–32; Psalms 78:26ff.; 105:40. The quail is a partridge-like bird, which migrates north from Africa and Arabia in the spring, and back south in the fall; it is found especially in the Sinai peninsula. Quail migrate in large flocks, and fly only a few feet above the ground, so that they can easily be caught and killed, which is probably what happened here. The next morning, when the dew was gone, there was a substance on the ground, small (or fine, like dust), "thin flakes" (KJV: "a small round thing," which is also possible). "Desert floor," lit.: "face of the wilderness" (cf. 10:5, 15).

16:15, 16 *When the Israelites saw it, they said to each other, "What is it?" For they did not know what it was.*

Moses said to them, "It is the bread the LORD has given you to eat. This is what the LORD has commanded: 'Each one is to gather as much as he needs. Take an omer for each person you have in your tent.'"

Opinions differ as to the correct translation of what the Israelites said to each other when they saw the manna. The Hebrew reads *man hu,* which is translated "What is it?" (NIV), or "It is manna" (KJV). Strictly speaking, the first translation would require *ma hu* in Hebrew. But it is possible that the Hebrew *ma* ("what") is derived from an older form *mant;* the Aramaic *man* means "who." The Israelites did not immediately give a name to what they saw; the context rather indicates a question: "What is it?" On the other hand, if they immediately said "This is *man* or manna," it may indicate that they thought it to be the Sinai manna (see above). Verse 31 states that the Israelites called the bread "manna," but it seems best to translate *man* as "what," especially in view of the following statement, "for they did not know what it was." Another possibility is to translate *man* as "gift," which is not convincing, if only because Moses' response then would merely restate the same thing. Moses *did* know what it was, and he answered the question. There is no indication in Moses' answer that the manna could have been the "natural manna." Jesus later called Himself the "bread from heaven" (John 6:31ff.).

Verse 16 elucidates verse 4. Moses conveyed the Lord's command that each Israelite was to gather one omer per person (cf. vv. 4–5). For "As much as he needs," see commentary on 12:4. Verse 36 states that an omer is one tenth of a ephah; the ephah was a dry measure, equal to approximately 22 liters, so that an omer is about 2.2 liters or about two quarts. Some think that the omer does not refer to a measure, but rather to a cup or bowl that was carried along in the wilderness to dip water from the wells, and which held approximately one tenth of an ephah.

160

16:17, 18 *The Israelites did as they were told; some gathered much, some little. And when they measured it by the omer, he who gathered much did not have too much, and he who gathered little did not have too little. Each one gathered as much as he needed.*

The Israelites carried out Moses' instructions, but some gathered more, others less than one omer, not from disobedience but rather because they had, of necessity, to estimate how much they gathered. The miracle was that when they measured it by the omer there was exactly enough for each person (v. 18, cf. v. 16; 2 Cor. 8:15).

16:19, 20 *Then Moses said to them, "No one is to keep any of it until morning." However, some of them paid no attention to Moses; they kept part of it until morning, but it was full of maggots and began to smell. So Moses was angry with them.*

Those who, against Moses' advice, left some until the next day, discovered that the manna was full of maggots and that it smelled. This was a punishment for unbelief; Israel had to trust God anew for each day, so that its faith could be strengthened (cf. the fourth petition of the Lord's Prayer). Moses was justifiably angry. In the East, bread that was made the previous day was not considered fit for consumption.

16:21 *Each morning everyone gathered as much as he needed, and when the sun grew hot, it melted away.*

Each morning the manna was gathered (cf. vv. 16, 18), but "when the sun grew hot, it melted away." The same seems to be true of today's "natural manna," which, however, does not spoil when kept in a cool place.

16:22–30 *On the sixth day, they gathered twice as much—two omers for each person—and the leaders of the community came and reported this to Moses. He said to them, "This is what the Lord commanded: 'Tomorrow is to be a day of rest, a holy Sabbath to the Lord. So bake what you want to bake and boil what you want to boil. Save whatever is left and keep it until morning.'"*
So they saved it until morning, as Moses commanded, and it did not stink or get maggots in it. "Eat it today," Moses said, "because today is a Sabbath to the Lord. You will not find any of it on the ground today. Six days you are to gather it, but on the seventh day, the Sabbath, there will not be any."
Nevertheless, some of the people went out on the seventh day to gather it, but they found none. Then the Lord said to Moses, "How long will you refuse to keep

my commands and my instructions? Bear in mind that the Lord has given you the Sabbath; this is why on the sixth day he gives you bread for two days. Everyone is to stay where he is on the seventh day; no one is to go out." So the people rested on the seventh day.

See verse 5. It is probable that Moses had told the people to do this, so that the people were correct when they gathered twice as much on the sixth day, and the leaders who came to complain to Moses were wrong. The fact that the leaders came to complain proves that the Israelites intentionally gathered twice as much as usual. Another possibility is that the leaders simply reported this to Moses as something unusual. Driver states: "Another surprise. On the sixth day, they discover that they have gathered, without knowing it, a double quantity."

"Bread," cf. verses 4, 8, 12, 15. Moses agreed with the people (v. 23). See commentary on verse 5 concerning the Sabbath as the day of rest prior to the giving of the law at Sinai. The celebration of the Sabbath as a day of rest seems to have been neglected, as indicated by the attitude of the leaders and the statement in verse 27. "Bake," cf. 12:39; "boil," cf. 12:9; "save", cf. 12:6. Verse 23 gives the impression that the manna was baked or boiled (cf. Num. 11:8) and that what was left over of this prepared manna could be kept from the sixth until the seventh day, without spoiling (v. 24, cf. v. 20). "Maggots" (v. 24) is derived from the verb "to rise up," i.e. with worms, translated "bred worms" (kjv) in verse 20, where a different word for "maggots" is used. It is possible that the word means "putrify," so that "maggots" (v. 24) could also be translated "spoilage." "Stink" is a stronger form of the verb translated "to smell" in verse 20.

Moses encouraged the people to eat the prepared manna on the seventh day without fear of it being spoiled (v. 25). He also told them that on this day, which was dedicated to the Lord, they would not find manna in the field (cf. Gen. 2:1–3). Verse 26 is stylistically similar to 20:9–10. Again some of the Israelites did not believe what Moses told them, and they returned empty-handed (v. 27). Their attitude aroused the Lord's anger; He considered their action a refusal to keep His commands and instructions (v. 28, cf. vv. 4–5). The plural "you" in verse 28 indicates that the Lord addressed Moses as the leader and representative of the people. Again the Sabbath is referred to as a day that previously had been instituted by the Lord (cf. Mark 2:27), and as the reason for the double portion of manna on the sixth day. The Israelites were to remain in the camp on the seventh day. Verse 30 indicates that after this experience and these instructions, the people rested on the seventh day and celebrated the Sabbath.

16:31 *The people of Israel called the bread manna. It was white like coriander seed and tasted like wafers made with honey.*

See commentary on verses 15–16. The "people of Israel," lit.: the "house of Israel" (some MSS, the LXX, and the Peshitta read instead "the children of Israel"). We would not expect to find this expression until much later, when Israel had become one nation; it is also found, however, in 40:38; Leviticus 10:6; 17:3, 8, 10 (KJV); 22:18 (KJV); Num. 20:29; Josh. 21:45 (cf. Ridderbos on Hos. 1:4). The manna is now described in more detail. It was white like coriander seed, and it tasted like wafers made with honey. The coriander is found in Egypt and Palestine, as well as in Europe and America. The seeds, which are approximately the size of a peppercorn, smell like anise when dried, and are used in baking, while the dried leaves taste like dried orange peel and are used for seasoning. The seeds are used also for the manufacture of oil. The manna is also described in Numbers 11:7–8, where it is said to look like "bdellium" (KJV), which may refer to a gum or resin (NIV), or a pearl or precious stone. The color was probably yellow.

16:32–34 *Moses said, "This is what the LORD has commanded: 'Take an omer of manna and keep it for the generations to come, so they can see the bread I gave you to eat in the desert when I brought you out of Egypt.'"*
So Moses said to Aaron, "Take a jar and put an omer of manna in it. Then place it before the LORD to be kept for the generations to come."
As the LORD commanded Moses, Aaron put the manna in front of the Testimony, that it might be kept.

In verse 32, Moses again conveyed a command of the Lord that had not been mentioned before (cf. v. 16): an omer of manna had to be kept for posterity. This is an additional argument against identifying the manna with the "natural manna" that is still found today. Furthermore, a miraculous element here is that this manna would not spoil. "The bread," cf. v. 15. "I": Moses spoke on the Lord's behalf and quoted His words. "Brought you out," cf. 6:6; 7:4–5; 12:17, 42, 51; 13:3, 9, 14, 16. "Take a jar" (KJV "pot"): the LXX and Hebrews 9:4 refer to the "gold jar" (cf. Grosheide on Hebrews 9:4). Verses 33–34 present a problem: where was Aaron to place the jar with the manna before the tabernacle and the ark had been built, if he was to place it "before the Lord"? Aaron was to place it "in front of the Testimony," which could only refer to the law, which was given later (cf. van Gelderen on 1 Kings 8:9). I therefore believe that verses 33–34 reflect a later event (cf. 25:16; 31:18; Num. 17:7). These verses were inserted here because the author wanted to tell the story of the manna as a unit, which is also supported by the later addition in verses 35–36. Note that Moses' instructions in these verses create a concrete historical reference point; Israel was a nation with an acute and highly developed historical sense.

16:35, 36 *The Israelites ate manna forty years, until they came to a land that was settled; they ate manna until they reached the border of Canaan.*
(An omer is one tenth of an ephah.)

These verses are a later addition, cf. verses 15–16 and Joshua 5:12.

3. *Massah and Meribah* (17:1–7)

17:1 *The whole Israelite community set out from the Desert of Sin, traveling from place to place as the LORD commanded. They camped at Rephidim, but there was no water for the people to drink.*

"Set out," cf. 15:22; 16:1. "The whole Israelite community," cf. commentary on 16:1. "The Desert of Sin," cf. commentary on 16:1. "From place to place," lit: "according to their journeys" cf. Genesis 13:3; Numbers 10:12; 33:2. The journey was thus made in stages, with rest periods in between (cf. Num. 33:12–14), always "as the LORD commanded" by means of the pillar of cloud and fire (or perhaps by means of instructions given to Moses, cf. 14:1–2). "They camped," cf. 14:2. The Israelites thus did not reach Rephidim in one day after they left the Desert of Sin. If the latter is identified with Debbet er-Ramleh, then Rephidim may well be the Wadi Feiran, as Ebers and Palmer suggest, the most beautiful valley of the Sinai peninsula with much vegetation. The Israelites then camped in front of the most fertile part of the valley, which has a stream that never dries up and a large number of springs. The Amelekites probably controlled the stream, the springs, and the palm trees, and they soon came out and attacked Israel (17:8–16). The Israelites thus could not reach the springs but had to be satisfied with the barren part of the wadi, and had no water to drink.

17:2, 3 *So they quarreled with Moses and said, "Give us water to drink."*
Moses replied, "Why do you quarrel with me? Why do you put the LORD to the test?"
But the people were thirsty for water there, and they grumbled against Moses. They said, "Why did you bring us up out of Egypt to make us and our children and livestock die of thirst?"

Irritated by their thirst, and probably also by the nearness of the inaccessible springs, the people began to quarrel with Moses. This is the fourth time the people grumbled (cf. commentary on 16:2). "Quarrel," usually used of a verbal argument or dispute (cf. Gen. 26:20–21; Num. 20:3, 13), is more serious than "grumble." The lesson of the manna and the quail had all too soon been forgotten! Aaron is not mentioned, but was also addressed by implication, since "give" (v. 2) is a plural. It is possible, however, that the plural is incorrect, since many mss and several versions have a singular here. This grumbling resembles the one described in 15:22–26. The words of the people imply that Moses, who had performed many miracles, was able to provide water so that they could drink; but Moses pointed out that while they quarreled with him, their argument was really with the Lord, as indicated by "Why do you put the LORD to the test?" (cf. 15:25; 16:4), with which Moses reproached the people. Moses considered himself powerless: there was no sense in their quarreling with *him*. The Lord could provide water, but to ask Him to do so in such a spirit of discontent and doubt amounted to "testing" (cf. v. 7; Ps. 78:18). Their sin lay in this testing (Massah-"testing") and quarreling (Meribah-"quarreling"), cf. v. 7. Testing as used here means to invoke the Lord's power, not in faith, but with challenge and irreverence, which is precisely what Israel was doing. It was an expression of discontent rather than a prayer. For verses 2–3, cf. Numbers 20:3–4. For "testing," cf. Psalms 95:8–9; 106:14; 1 Cor. 10:9. See also 16:8–9.

Moses' question appears to have had a calming influence for a few hours. But soon (v. 3) the people were grumbling again (cf. 15:24; 16:2, 7–8; concerning Moses' question, cf. 14:11; 16:3). The complaint in verse 3 was directed especially against Moses ("you" is singular). The NIV and KJV follow the LXX, Vulgate, Peshitta, and other versions by using the plural in verse 3: "us . . . our children . . . our livestock"; the Hebrew text has the singular here: "me . . . my children . . . my livestock," which would place the emphasis on the individual speaking in the midst of the general grumbling; the first person singular could also refer to the entire nation, cf. Numbers 20:19. Note the contrast between verse 3 and 15:2. The expression "bring up" is fitting, since the elevation of Egypt is lower than that of the Sinai peninsula. The thirst must have been severe: "the people were thirsty for water," or, as some translate, "yearned for water," water that they could not reach. They believed that they, their children, and their livestock would die of thirst, and their attitude toward Moses became threatening.

17:4–6 *Then Moses cried out to the LORD, "What am I to do with these people? They are almost ready to stone me."*

The LORD answered Moses, "Walk on ahead of the people. Take with you some of the elders of Israel and take in your hand the staff with which you struck the Nile, and go. I will stand there before you by the rock at Horeb. Strike the rock, and water will come out of it for the people to drink." So Moses did this in the sight of the elders of Israel.

Moses now called on the Lord, cf. 14:15. Here, as in 15:25, Moses probably cried out loud. He was at the end of his rope, he did not know what he was to do with "this people" (disparaging?), for they were about ready to stone him (cf. 1 Sam. 30:6). Cf. also Exod. 8:26: now Moses was afraid, albeit for a different reason, that he would receive the same treatment at the hand of the Israelites (cf. Num. 14:10). The Lord instructed Moses to walk on ahead of the people. The fact that Moses was to take some of the elders of Israel with him is in line with 3:16, 18; 4:29; 12:21. Moses was to take the elders as the representatives of the people, since the whole community (cf. vv. 1–2) grumbled, not just a few who were troublemakers (15:24; 16:2, 9–10). Furthermore, the grumbling was directed against Moses, the leader (v. 3), and the elders had witnessed the first miracles that Moses performed with the staff (4:29–30: the staff changed into a serpent, water changed into blood). The elders also were to accompany Moses as reliable witnesses of the reality of the miracle. What follows is, to Israel's shame and Moses' encouragement, a reminder of the first plague: Moses had to take the staff with which he struck the Nile (7:20; there Aaron was the one who carried out Moses' instructions). How could a man who carried that staff be rejected and brought to despair? Note that the Lord continuously used new means to admonish and to put the Israelites to shame, and also to help them. The promise in verse 6 begins with "behold" (KJV, omitted in NIV), which conveys encouragement. The statement that the Lord would stand before Moses by the rock at Horeb is an anthropomorphism, referring to an invisible, yet real presence (cf. 1 Sam. 3:10). "Horeb," cf. commentary on 3:1. The rock appears to have been at some distance from the camp, cf. verse 5. It is likely that most of the people, as well as the elders, followed Moses. Palmer says that he found a rock in the area just before the valley becomes fertile, which Arabic tradition still points to as the rock where this miracle took place; it is called Hesy el Khattatin. Ebers agrees with Palmer, but others prefer to think of a rocky mountain, rather than a specific rock; the text seems to favor a specific rock. "Go" (v. 5), i.e. out of the camp.

The Lord further promised that in His presence water would come out of the rock. In other words, His power would produce the water (cf. Heidelberg Catechism, Lord's Day 10), which does not preclude the possibility that the striking of the rock fractured a thin layer of rock that covered a vein of water. But the text does not state this (cf. on the other hand, 14:21). Moses carried out the Lord's instructions to the letter "in the sight of the elders of Israel" (cf. 4:30; 19:8). If Rephidim is indeed the Wadi Feiran, then the distance to Horeb in the sense of the mountain of the giving of the law is too great. It would thus be better to understand Horeb here in the sense of the entire plateau (cf. p. 50, footnotes, although we would have to include more in this plateau than the monks of St. Catherine do). Ebers, understandably, finds in this text an argument in favor of his identification of the mountain of God with the Gebel Serbal (see pp. 50–51). The name Horeb here does present a problem, and the route that the Israelites followed through the desert to Sinai has not yet been established with certainty. But since all indications point to the identification of Rephidim with the Wadi Feiran, the conclusion we must draw is that Horeb here refers to the entire plateau. The impression given in 19:2 is that Rephidim was not near the mountain of God (cf. commentary on 18:5). The conservative German exegete Keil, who believed the mountain of the giving of the law to be one of the peaks of the Gebel Musa range (see p. 50), places Rephidim at the site where the Wadi es-Sheik enters the plain er-Râhah (see p. 51), close to the mountain of God. Tentatively, however, I believe that I must maintain the view presented above.

17:7 *And he called the place Massah and Meribah because the Israelites quarreled and because they tested the* LORD *saying, "Is the* LORD *among us or not?"*

See commentary on verse 2. Massah means "testing," Meribah means "quarreling" (cf. also Num. 20:13; Num. 20 describes a different event that took place in another location, not the same events described in these verses). Moses probably was the one who gave the place its name. The question stated in verse 7 is not mentioned in verses 3–4 (cf. Ps. 78:18–20). Psalm 78:19 expresses doubt concerning God's power, since this power had not expressed itself by doing what they wanted; in verse 7b the doubt concerned God's presence, for the same reason. For further commentary on verses 1–7, cf. Deuteronomy 6:16; 8:15; 9:22; 33:8; Nehemiah 9:15; Psalms 78:15; 95; 105:41; 114:8; Isaiah 48:21; concerning the rock that provided water, cf. 1 Corinthians 10:4, where this rock is compared with Christ (cf. v. 6a), as Christ compared Himself with the manna and the spring of living water (cf. ch. 16; John 7:37–38). Christ was the source of all the blessings Israel received on the wilderness journey. Psalm 23:5 expresses the situation as it probably existed at that point (Amalek occupying the other part of the Wadi Feiran).

4. *Israel Defeats the Amalekites at Rephidim* (17:8–16)

17:8 *The Amalekites came and attacked the Israelites at Rephidim.*

For the first time on the wilderness journey, Israel was attacked by another nation, the Amalekites, who lived in the southern part of the region that later belonged to the tribe of Judah (cf. Gen. 14:7; Num. 13:29; 14:25, 43, 45; 1 Sam. 15:7; 27:8; 30:1). The people who attacked Israel were thus a group of Amalekites who either lived in the Wadi Feiran, or who had brought their herds to pastures in this region, which was at a higher elevation than their own country (cf. commentary on 3:1). It is unlikely, as verse 13 may imply, that they would have dispatched an army from the southern part of Canaan. The Amalekites were already mentioned in Genesis 14:7, perhaps because the region referred to there was later named after them; it is also possible that the Amalekites were already a nation at that time (see ZPEB, "Amalek, Amalekites" 1:123–125). In Numbers 24:20, Balaam called Amalek "the first among the nations" (cf. also Gen. 36:12, 16). It is possible that part of Amalek was later assimilated by the Edomites. Deuteronomy 25:17–18 provides further information about the manner in which the Amalekites attacked: they came while Israel was traveling and thus "weary and worn out," and attacked the rear, where the weak people traveled. (Cf. also commentary on v. 1 for a description of the situation.) According to Palmer, a desert people like the Amalekites would not dare attack Israel's armies in the open desert. Most likely they attacked them unawares, close to the oasis, before Israel had set up their camp.

17:9 *Moses said to Joshua, "Choose some of our men and go out to fight the Amalekites. Tomorrow I will stand on top of the hill with the staff of God in my hands."*

Moses took the initiative now that it came to combating, together with his people, an enemy from outside. This is the first mention of Joshua in the Bible; he was the one whom Moses told to choose men and to fight the Amalekites. This was a prelude to his future calling (Calvin). His name was originally Hoshea (cf. Num. 13:8, 16). Joshua means "the LORD is salvation," Hoshea means "salvation." "Choose some of our men," lit.: "chose for us men" (cf. KJV), "us" referring to the Israelites, or to Aaron and Moses, although this is less likely, since Hur is also mentioned along with Aaron (vv. 10, 12). The Amalekites appear to have retreated into the fertile part of the wadi after inflicting as much damage as possible on Israel. The next day Moses would stand on the top of "the" hill. Moses' statement that the "staff of God" (cf. 4:20) would be in his hands indicates that he had learned a lesson (cf. v. 5), although he did not yet say what he would do with that staff. In the absence of direct instructions from the Lord (at least, none are recorded) Moses may have thought of the instructions he had received in 8:5; 9:22; and 10:12. Note that Moses' reliance on the staff of God did not exclude Joshua's action.

17:10–13 *So Joshua fought the Amalekites as Moses had ordered, and Moses, Aaron and Hur went to the top of the hill. As long as Moses held up his hands, the Israelites were winning, but whenever he lowered his hands, the Amalekites were winning. When Moses' hands grew tired, they took a stone and put it under him and he sat on it. Aaron and Hur held his hands up—one on one side, one on the other—so that his hands remained steady till sunset. So Joshua overcame the Amalekite army with the sword.*

Hur is also mentioned here for the first time (cf. 24:14). It is unlikely that this is the same Hur as the grandfather of Bezalel (cf. 31:2; 35:30; 38:22; 1 Chron. 2:20; 4:1); according to a later Jewish saga Hur was Miriam's husband.

Joshua obeyed Moses' instructions. Since he was given freedom to use his own judgment in the battle, he must have been considered an able general. Moses seems to have anticipated possible fatigue, which is why he took Aaron and Hur along. Moses held up his hands with the staff (cf. 8:6; 9:22; 10:12, where the stretching out of the hand also implies the hand "with the staff"). We do not read that Moses prayed; rather he asked for the Lord's help by using the staff. He wanted to remind the Lord of His previous miracles, and the raising of the staff expressed the desire that the Lord would continue His miracles. Moses quietly exercised his faith. We might expect that therefore things would go well for Israel; but only as long as Moses held up the staff, as long as he kept the Lord before Israel, did Israel win. When he lowered his hands (v. 11 uses the singular "hand"), probably to rest, then Amalek was stronger. The significance of this is that Israel's strength lay only in a continuous appeal to the Lord's power and a continuous remembrance of what He had already done for them, in other words, a continuous appeal in deed and work (thus also in prayer) to His faithfulness. In this battle with Amalek, Israel could not, even for a moment, do without Moses, who reminded the Lord of His past deeds on Israel's behalf. Once Moses had chosen, on his own initiative, to use the staff, he had to apply it to the fullest extent possible, and both he and Israel had to learn that the entire outcome of the battle depended on the Lord's faithfulness to His own past actions, to His covenant, of which the staff was the temporary symbol. Without Him, they could do nothing (cf. also

v. 16: Moses' hands were placed on the throne of the Lord as the hands of a suppliant). Combat alone was not sufficient; Joshua needed Moses.

Moses' spiritual labor was actually more important and decisive for the outcome of the battle. Moses here is a type of Christ (cf. Heb. 7:25). But Moses' hands grew tired; therefore, they (Aaron and Hur, or others; the text gives the impression that only Aaron and Hur accompanied Moses on the hill, cf. v. 10) took a stone and put it under him so that Moses could sit down. Then Aaron and Hur each took one of Moses' hands and held them up so that they remained "steady" (Heb.: *amuna,* related to our "amen") until sunset. In this manner, Joshua defeated ("weakened," the same word is also used in Job 14:10; Isa. 14:12) Amalek "with the sword" (lit.: "according to the mouth of the sword," i.e. without quarter, without mercy). It was not an extermination of the Amalekites, but a victory over them. "The Amalekite army," lit.: "Amalek and his armed men" (cf. KJV); this phrase may also reflect a "personification" of the Amalekites (cf. "your brother Israel" in Numbers 20:14–21).

17:14 *Then the Lord said to Moses, "Write this on a scroll as something to be remembered and make sure that Joshua hears it, because I will completely erase the memory of the Amalekites from under heaven."*

Only now, after Joshua had defeated the Amalekites, did the Lord address Moses. He instructed Moses to write "this" (the battle with, and victory over Amalek, and also the prediction of Amalek's destruction at the end of this verse) on a scroll "as something to be remembered" (KJV: "for a memorial"). The word for "memorial" is also found in 12:14; 13:9. This verse is important for our understanding of the origin of the Pentateuch (cf. Aalders on *Genesis* in this series, pp. 20–22). This is the first time that mention is made of the fact that Moses had to record the events of the wilderness journey (cf. later Num. 33:2). It is possible to translate *"the* scroll," and then to assume (also in view of Num. 33:2) that Moses was already keeping a journal, so that he had to write this "on *the* scroll." However, the Hebrew uses the definite article even where we would use the indefinite article, so that *"a* scroll" is better, since the existence of such a book has not been mentioned before; it was to be written on a scroll used for this specific occasion. It is possible that this event provided the impetus for starting a journal. Besides writing this down, Moses was also to impress orally on Joshua that the Lord would "completely erase the memory of the Amalekites from under heaven" (cf. Gen. 6:7; 7:4, 23; Num. 24:20; Deut. 25:17–19; 1 Sam. 15:2, 3, 7; 30:1, 17; 2 Sam. 8:12; 1 Chron. 4:43); lit.: "set it in the ears of Joshua." The first time we encounter Joshua in the

Scriptures he already had a prominent position, due in part to his victory. He already seemed destined to become Moses' successor.

17:15, 16 *Moses built an altar and called it The Lord is my Banner. He said, "For hands were lifted up to the throne of the Lord. The Lord will be at war against the Amalekites from generation to generation."*

Moses now built an altar as a memorial, a custom that was already common among the patriarchs (cf. Gen. 12:7; 13:18; 26:25; 33:20; 35:1, 3, 7). The name of the altar stated that the Lord was the banner of Moses and of Israel, on whose behalf Moses spoke (cf. 15:2). They sought His help, His strength, and because Moses clung to Him on that hill, Israel was victorious. He towered above all things, He was their Banner, their Leader (cf. Isa. 5:26 and esp. Isa. 11:10). In verse 16, Moses summarized two things: his own lifting up of his hands with the staff (also in the future Israel would always be victorious if they sought the Lord): "for hands were lifted up to the throne of the Lord"; and the Lord's promise (v. 14): "the Lord will be (or: is) at war against the Amalekites from generation to generation." Although the translation "fight for the Lord against Amalek" is also possible (cf. Judg. 7:18), verse 14 supports the translation given above.

Another interpretation is that the Lord does not sit idly on the throne in heaven, but rules the world; as long as He rules, he will not cease to pursue Amalek with just vengeance (Calvin).

But the first interpretation (the hands on the throne in supplication) does justice to both the silent prayers of Moses and the Israelites and the Lord's promise of Amalek's annihilation. And the hand that is on the throne of the Lord is especially that of the Mediator (Moses as a type of Christ).

The Jews read 17:8–16 at the Purim Feast (Haman may have been a descendant of Agag, the king of the Amalekites, cf. 1 Sam. 15:8f; Esth. 3:1).

5. *Jethro's Visit* (18:1–27)

Chapter 18 describes Jethro's visit to Moses, on which occasion he gave wise counsel to Moses (vv. 13–26). All indications point to the fact that this chapter is placed in the proper historical context, and that the visit did indeed take place between the battle of Rephidim and the giving of the law at Sinai. Verse 5, which states that Israel was camped "near the mountain of God," and Moses' words in Deuteronomy 1:9–18 seem to argue against this; but, on the other hand, Aaron is not yet the high priest (cf. v. 12), and Moses appears to function as judge for the entire nation in all matters, which seems to indicate that the Law had not yet been given. In spite of the phraseology, verses 15–16 thus give the impression that they refer to the period before the giving of the Law. The honesty with which the selection of officials is attributed to the advice of a Gentile is remarkable, and indicates that this narrative reflects the facts. The Gentiles here appear in a more positive light than in 17:8–16. Deuteronomy 1:9–18 presupposes, rather than contradicts, this chapter, although Moses does not mention Jethro's advice there, and "at that time" in Deuteronomy is not specific. Furthermore, the word "near" in the expression "near the mountain of God" (v. 5) is not expressed in Hebrew, and we must therefore be careful not to press the point it seems to make. In the commentary on 2:11–22, I already explained why there is no reason to accept the so-called Kenite hypothesis, in spite of Jethro's advice concerning the administration of justice. Here we can add that according to verse 11 Jethro had come to realize the greatness of Jahweh, which does not agree with the concept that he was the one who had originally instructed Moses concerning Jahweh. The view that places the events of chapter 18 near Kadesh (Deut. 1:46), also called the "Fountain of Judgment" (En Mishpat, Gen. 14:7), rather than in the vicinity of Sinai, is in conflict with the context of this chapter, as well as with 18:5 and Deuteronomy 1:9–18. This chapter is one of the many indications that the Bible describes men "of flesh and blood." It does not make sense to assume that someone would simply have made up this scene that presents the great Moses as dependent on his (otherwise not very prominent) father-in-law, a Kenite, for the regulation of the administration of justice. The chapter, placed between the victory over Amalek and the giving of the law at Sinai, increases the element of suspense in the narrative, since it constitutes a brief interlude. The Holy Spirit also wants to show us that the Lord did not elect Israel from among all other nations because of its moral superiority.

18:1–6 *Now Jethro, the priest of Midian and father-in-law of Moses, heard of everything God had done for Moses and for his people Israel, and how the L*ORD *had brought Israel out of Egypt.*

After Moses had sent away his wife Zipporah, his father-in-law Jethro received her and her two sons. One son was named Gershom, for Moses said, "I have become an alien in a foreign land"; and the other was named Eliezer, for he said, "My father's God was my helper; he saved me from the sword of Pharaoh."

Jethro, Moses' father-in-law, together with Moses' sons and wife, came to him in the desert, where he was camped near the mountain of God. Jethro had sent word to him, "I, your father-in-law Jethro, am coming to you with your wife and her two sons."

"Jethro," cf. commentary on 3:1. "Priest of Midian," cf. commentary on 2:16; 3:1. Israel approaches the region of Midian. Concerning the location of Midian, see commentary on 2:15; 3:1. As Moses' father-in-law, Jethro was also interested in Israel, but Moses is mentioned first: "for Moses and for his people Israel." The report of Israel's exodus and the plagues on Egypt had reached the Midianites and the other nations in the vicinity of Canaan and even those in Canaan itself (cf. commentary on 15:14–16 and Josh. 2:9–11). "Brought out," cf. pp. 1–2. Verse 2, cf. commentary on 4:27–31. Apparently Moses had sent his wife away. Calvin believed that Moses took Zipporah and her two sons with him to Egypt, but that he had allowed them to visit Jethro during the wilderness journey; Jethro then brought them back to Moses. The expression "after sending her away" argues against this view, but it also contradicts the idea that Zipporah voluntarily left in anger to return to her father after the circumcision of her son. Moses had sent them away, and Jethro wanted to return them to Moses, now that the situation for Moses and Israel seemed to be more hopeful than Zipporah might have anticipated. And Jethro knew that Moses and Israel owed this to the Lord, the God of Israel, who had brought them out of Egypt (v. 1, cf. also v. 11). Apparently Jethro had "heard of everything" before he came to visit Moses. Zipporah herself had little to say about what happened to her and her children, in accordance with the place of women in those days. Moses' sons are also mentioned in 1 Chronicles 23:15–17; 26:24–25. "Gershom," see commentary on 2:22. Zipporah's second son, Eliezer, is mentioned here for the first time by name (but see commentary on 4:24–26). "Eliezer" means "my God is helper," cf. Deuteronomy 33:26; Psalm 146:5. Verse 4 indicates that Moses named this son when he felt safe from the sword of Pharaoh (see commentary on 2:5) and remembered that threat. While "Gershom" expresses Moses' feeling that he was an alien, "Eliezer" conveys gratitude. His calling in 3:1ff. thus came unexpectedly.

Note the "her" in verses 3, 6; they were in the first place Zipporah's children, and probably were not close to their father. The Bible does not indicate whether Moses was glad to see them again, and thus does not satisfy our curoisity in this respect. "My father's God," see commentary on 3:6; cf. 15:2. I already discussed verse 5. "The mountain of God," see commentary on 3:1; the LXX here also reads "mountain of God" rather than "Mt. Horeb." "Was camped," see commentary on 14:2; 17:1. Jethro sent a message to Moses to announce his visit; "Jethro had sent word to him," lit.: "and he said to Moses." There are indications of a cooling of the relationship between Jethro and Moses; Moses did not tell his father-in-law the full truth when he left (4:18), and Zipporah's experience in 4:24–26 may also have been a contributing factor.

18:7–12 *So Moses went out to meet his father-in-law and bowed down and kissed him. They greeted each other and then went into the tent. Moses told his father-in-law about everything the LORD had done to Pharaoh and the Egyptians for Israel's sake and about all the hardships they had met along the way and how the LORD had saved them.*

Jethro was delighted to hear about all the good things the LORD had done for Israel in rescuing them from the hand of the Egyptians. He said, "Praise be to the LORD, who rescued you from the hand of the Egyptians and of Pharaoh, and who rescued the people from the hand of the Egyptians. Now I know that the LORD is greater than all other gods, for he did this to those who had treated Israel arrogantly." Then Jethro, Moses' father-in-law, brought a burnt offering and other sacrifices to God, and Aaron came with all the elders of Israel to eat bread with Moses' father-in-law in the presence of God.

Yet when Moses received the message of the impending visit, he went out of the camp to meet Jethro (Zipporah and the children are not mentioned), and he courteously and warmly welcomed him (v. 7). In his tent, Moses told Jethro "about all the good things the LORD had done for Israel in rescuing them from the hand of the Egyptians" ("save," cf. also v. 4; 2:19; 3:8; 5:23; 6:6; 12:27; 18:10). Verse 9, cf. 3:8; the Lord's promise was fulfilled. In verses 10–11, Jethro expressed his joy over all the good things the Lord had done for Israel. "You" (v. 10) is plural. The second part of verse 10 is essentially a restatement of the first part, and is omitted in the LXX; but the wording is slightly different and it is not impossible that Jethro actually said this in the animated discussion.

The translation of verse 11 is more problematic. Jethro declared that he now knew that the Lord was above all gods, a statement that speaks against the Kenite hypothesis. The second part of the verse reads literally: "truly (or: for) in the thing wherein they dealt proudly against them." The KJV translates "for in the thing wherein they dealt proudly (he was) above them," meaning that the Lord punished the Egyptians in those matters in which they were presumptuous in their dealings with the Israelites. I believe the intended meaning to be that the Lord is greater than all the gods precisely in those things where the Egyptians were arrogant against the Israelites, which also establishes a closer connection between the two parts of verse 11 than that found in the KJV or NIV. Some exegetes, especially Jewish, limit this to the destruction of the Egyptians in the water: the Egyptians wanted to annihilate the Israelites in the water, but they themselves perished in the Red Sea (1:22, 14:28); more likely the statement refers to all the proud and presumptuous acts of the Egyptians against the Israelites (cf. Ps. 76:10). It is also possible to think here of the arrogance of the gods, but this is unlikely (cf. Neh. 9:10). Jethro saw in the rescue from the power of the Egyptians and of Pharaoh proof that the Lord was greater than all other gods (cf. 15:11; Ps. 135:5), and, of course, especially the gods of Egypt. He thus perceived the spiritual background of the events of the Exodus and wilderness journey, even though he was a Gentile; his praise was a prophecy of the future recognition on the part of the nations, those who were not descendants of Abraham, that none among the gods was like the God of Israel (cf. Ps. 86:8–10). In Jethro, the Lord showed Israel that, although the law would later be given to Israel alone, He was faithful to His promise of Genesis 12:3 (cf. also Jethro's sacrifices in v. 12; "burnt offering," see Aalders on Gen. 8:20 in this commentary series).

The guests mentioned in verse 12 probably also ate of the sacrifices with which Jethro expressed his gratitude. The idea that Jethro brought a sacrifice to confirm the reestablishment of the relationship between Moses and himself, which had become somewhat strained (see commentary on vv. 1–6), is unlikely in view of verse 11; the meal that followed the sacrifices would better serve this purpose (cf. Gen. 31:53–54). But there is no distinction made here, since the law had not yet been given; nor did Aaron function as high priest or one of his sons as priest. "All the elders," see commentary on 17:5. "Bread" referred to food in general. Calvin observes that the manna was here called "bread" (but cf. 16:4, 8, 12, 15). Jethro was an honored guest, not as priest of Midian, but as Moses' father-in-law (see commentary on 2:16–17). "In the presence of God" (lit.: "before God") probably refers to the nearness of the pillar of cloud and fire, rather than to the thought expressed in 16:33; it seems incorrect to make "in the presence of God" refer to the altar or to the place where the sacrifices were brought. The Dutch Authorized Version (margin) states: "That is, in the fear of the Lord, being mindful of the Lord, or of the majesty of God which appeared in the pillar of cloud; cf. Deut. 12:7 and 27:7." I cannot give any other explanation for the interchanging of "God" and "Lord" in these verses than to see it as a stylistic device.

18:13–23 *The next day Moses took his seat to serve as judge for the people, and they stood around him from morning till evening. When his father-in-law saw all that Moses was doing for the people, he said, "What is this you are doing for the people? Why do you alone sit as judge, while all these people stand around you from morning till evening?"*

Moses answered him, "Because the people come to me to seek God's will. Whenever they have a dispute, it is brought to me, and I decide between the parties and inform them of God's decrees and laws."

Moses' father-in-law replied, "What you are doing is not good. You and these people who come to you will only wear yourselves out. The work is too heavy for you; you cannot handle it alone. Listen now to me and I will give you some advice, and may God be with you. You must be the people's representative before God and bring their disputes to him. Teach them the decrees and laws, and show them the way to live and the duties they are to perform. But select capable men from all the people—men who fear God, trustworthy men who hate dishonest gain—and appoint them as officials over thousands, hundreds, fifties and tens. Have them serve as judges for the people at all times, but have them bring every difficult case to you; the simple cases they can decide themselves. That will make your load lighter, because they will share it with you. If you do this and God so commands, you will be able to stand the strain, and all these people will go home satisfied.''

What follows next shows that Moses could not be called Israel's law-giver because of regulations that he instituted on his own initiative. The organization of the administration of justice was still very inadequate; even the most outstanding leader has his limitations. Division of labor and a proper use of one's energies were necessary also when it came to leading the Lord's people. The reason why the people came only to Moses and not to the elders may well be that the Israelites apparently never had the opportunity to consult the elders on a regular basis in Egypt. Moses was the leader now (cf. 14:31) and the elders did not as yet play an important role. Moses had spoiled the people: only his personal attention to a problem satisfied them. Jethro was surprised by Moses' method and asked him for an explanation (v. 14). He especially noticed the length of the session, ''from morning till evening.'' Moses answered that the people came to him to seek God's will (lit.: ''to inquire of God'') in particular issues. The people thus saw Moses as a prophet, a spokesman who conveyed God's thoughts. Verse 15 is in sharp contrast to 2:14; things had changed for the better! Moses had to wait for the *Lord's* time. ''Decrees,'' see commentary on 15:25. ''Laws'': the word used here *(torah)* also means ''instruction.'' These ''laws'' were not the written laws that were given later at Sinai; Moses here received God's directions and instructions directly (cf. vv. 19–20). After the giving of the law at Sinai, the task of interpreting and explaining the written regulations fell to the priests and Levites (cf. Lev. 10:11; Deut. 17:8–13; 19:17; 33:10; 1 Chron. 23:4; 26:29; 2 Chron. 17:7–9; Mal. 2:7; but cf also Num. 15:33ff.; 27:5ff.). Moses' role as judge thus depended on God's revelation to him. We do not have a collection of his decisions; the so-called Book of the Covenant (20:22–23:33) and the Book of Deuteronomy cannot be considered to be such collections. His pronouncements were probably transmitted orally, but we must not forget that after the giving and recording of the law at Sinai Moses' pronouncements, to the extent that they were not repeated in the law, were superseded by it. This ''judging'' prior to the giving of the law was only an interim procedure. Jethro bluntly disapproved of Moses' approach (v. 17). He expressed his conviction and fear that Moses would "wear out" (the same word is also used for the wilting of leaves and flowers, e.g., Ps. 37:2), as well as the people who had to stand and wait for so long. This was no task for one man (v. 18). And he made a suggestion that he undoubtedly believed to have God's approval: Moses had to be "the people's representative before God and bring their disputes to him" (v. 19) and be their teacher, rather than their judge (v. 20). His duties as judge were to be assumed by capable men who feared God, who were trustworthy (the word here is the same as "steady" in 17:12) and who could not be bribed; they had to be the judges for specific groups of people (thousands, hundreds, fifties, and tens) and take care of routine matters, while Moses himself became only the final "court of appeal." Jethro was convinced that if Moses, subject of course to God's approval, instituted this arrangement, he would "be able to stand the strain" and the Israelites who had disputes would go home satisfied (lit.: "in peace").

18:24–26 *Moses listened to his father-in-law and did everything he said. He chose capable men from all Israel and made them leaders of the people, officials over thousands, hundreds, fifties and tens. They served as judges for the people at all times. The difficult cases they brought to Moses, but the simple ones they decided themselves.*

Moses accepted his father-in-law's advice, and the people voiced their agreement (Deut. 1:14); the day-to-day administration of justice was placed in the hands of the officials. From then on only difficult cases were referred to Moses (cf. Deut. 1:9ff.). The elders, i.e., the heads of the tribes and clans (or some of them), were chosen to be judges or, perhaps, restored to their former office (cf. 3:16; Deut. 1:15–17). We must therefore not take the numbers (thousand, hundred, fifty, ten) literally.

18:27 *Then Moses sent his father-in-law on his way, and he returned to his own country.*

Jethro returned to his own land, Midian, apparently without Zipporah and her two sons, who stayed with Moses, although they are not mentioned again after verse 6. Jethro has been compared to Melchizedek (Gen. 14), but we must not forget that Jethro was a descendant of Abraham. The attempt on the part of some to see in this story a revision, which changes the report of Midian's influence on Israel into advice given during a family visit, is amusing; it is based on the assumption that the idyllic and naïve precedes the strictly historical and legal.

6. *The Lord Appears to Israel at Sinai* (19:1–25)

The Lord's appearance to Israel at Sinai, which was the prelude to the making of the covenant, made a deep impression and is mentioned in other books outside the Pentateuch (cf. e.g., Pss. 18:8–16; 50:1–7; in the Pentateuch, Deut. 4:10–15; 5:2–6). This was a theophany, an appearance of God, which was much more awe-inspiring in its external signs than the theophany in 3:1–4:17. Here the promise of 3:12 was fulfilled, and not only Moses, but all of Israel, delivered from Egypt, was present. Some exegetes consider 19:1 to be the beginning of the so-called Book of the Covenant, which then ends with 24:11 (cf. pp. 2–3 and Aalders on *Genesis* in this series, pp. 20–21). This chapter provides a prime target for proponents of the source hypothesis and for those who want to see Jahweh as a god of thunder, or as the god of a volcano.

19:1, 2 *In the third month after the Israelites left Egypt—on the very day—they came to the Desert of Sinai. After they set out from Rephidim, they entered the Desert of Sinai, and Israel camped there in the desert in front of the mountain.*

Because of the importance of what follows, the date is given in verse 1. According to 12:17 and 13:4, the day of the Exodus was the fifteenth of the month Abib or Nisan. The third month after the Exodus was Sivan (May-June), since we probably have to include Abib in the three months. According to Jewish tradition, the Israelites arrived in the Sinai desert on the first of Sivan, while the law was given during the Feast of Pentecost, which was celebrated on the sixth and seventh of Sivan (cf. van Nes, *Het Jodendom*, p. 171). "On the very day," lit. "on this day," "Left," see p. 3. "Set out" and "Rephidim," see commentary on 17:1. The Israelites thus traveled from the Wadi Feiran to the plain of er-Râhah, which is here called the Desert of Sinai. The objections that have been raised against this view are, as Palmer has shown, not insurmountable. It has been said that it is impossible that a large group of people, who carried all their belongings with them, could have reached the mountain of the giving of the law (assuming that this mountain lies in the Gebel Musa range, see p. 50) in one day's journey from the Wadi Feiran. The camels that carried Israel's possessions then would have had to make a detour through a valley called the Wadi es-Sheikh. But the Desert of Sinai stretches beyond the immediate vicinity of the mountain of the giving of the law, so that Palmer assumes that Israel had reached the Desert of Sinai when they came to the Sinai region at the end of the pass of Nagb Hawa. There they found a suitable place to set up camp, the plain of er-Râhah.

Palmer makes a distinction in verse 2 between the arrival in the desert of

Sinai (at the end of the pass of Nagb Hawa) and the camping in that desert (i.e., in the plain of er-Râhah opposite the mountain of the giving of the law, Ras es-Sufsafeh). He also suggests the possibility that Moses and the most important elders took the shorter route across the pass, while the people and the luggage followed the longer route through the Wadi es-Sheikh. In view of the distance between the Wadi Feiran and the pass, he considers it possible that the journey of that day was extended into the night. This seems to be the most likely view, although we cannot, of course, speak with absolute certainty. "Camped," cf. 14:2; 17:1; 18:5. I thus take "Desert of Sinai" in verse 2 in a broader sense than the "desert" where Israel camped, which I believe to refer to the plain of er-Râhah. The fact that the LXX omits the words "in the desert" after "Israel camped there" supports, in my opinion, Palmer's view. The Israelites remained in front of the mountain for eleven months (cf. Num. 10:11).

19:3–6 *Then Moses went up to God, and the Lord called to him from the mountain and said, "This is what you are to say to the house of Jacob and what you are to tell the people of Israel: 'You yourselves have seen what I did to Egypt, and how I carried you on eagles' wings and brought you to myself. Now if you obey me fully and keep my covenant, then out of all nations you will be my treasured possession. Although the whole earth is mine, you will be for me a kingdom of priests and a holy nation.' These are the words you are to speak to the Israelites."*

Moses "went up to God" (Dutch Authorized Version, marginal note: "to the pillar of cloud on the mountain"), because God had appeared here to him before (cf. also 3:12, from which Moses concluded that God would appear here again, this time to Israel). He was not disappointed: the Lord called him from Mount Sinai. Moses was to relay the message to "the house of Jacob" (Jacob's descendants were the ones who went to Egypt, cf. 1:1) and to "the people (lit.: sons) of Israel" (see commentary on 1:1). In verse 3, the LXX reads "the mountain of God" instead of "God," and "from heaven" instead of "from the mountain." These changes show that the translators of the LXX wanted to avoid the impression the Hebrew text could give that the Lord dwelled on Sinai rather than in heaven. But this actually argues *against* emending the Hebrew text. Verse 11 indicates that the Lord dwelled in heaven rather than on Mount Sinai. Verse 3, cf. Acts. 7:38. Moses first had to remind the people of Israel of the miracles of the Exodus and during the wilderness journey (v. 4, cf. 14:31; cf. also Deut. 29:2ff.; 32:11ff.). God's dealings with them were in sharp contrast to His dealings with Egypt. The image of the eagle is based on the fact that the eagle, when its offspring learns to fly, will catch them on its wings when they fall. "To myself" (v. 4) again gives the impression that the Lord dwelled on Sinai.

After the reminder of verse 4 follows the promise of verses 5–6. These two verses are of tremendous significance (see commentary on 6:7). Verse 4 showed that the promise, given in 6:6, had been fulfilled. What remained to be realized was the Lord's taking Israel as His own people, and Israel's reaching Canaan (6:7–8). The Lord now would adopt Israel as His people; the only condition was that Israel had to obey the Lord fully and keep His covenant (v. 5a). Then Israel would be the Lord's "treasured possession," out of all nations (cf. Amos 3:2; 9:7). The Lord emphasized His sovereign election: "the whole earth is mine," including all nations (cf. 9:29). It was therefore grace that moved God to make Israel His "treasured possession" His people. The word translated "treasured possession" (KJV: "peculiar treasure") seems to have meant originally "private possession" as opposed to the possessions of a family or larger community; hence "treasure," cf. 1 Chronicles 29:3; Ecclesiastes 2:8 (KJV). It was thus possible that Israel could lose its privilege when it did not fulfill the stated condition. And the Lord emphasized Israel's wonderful destiny and solemn responsibility: it was to be a kingdom of priests (the service that was required of them as subjects of God's kingdom was thus priestly in nature) and a holy, separated, and pure nation, consecrated to God. Then Israel would be a kingdom also in the sense that they would rule with Him (Gen. 17:6; Rev. 1:6). These were words spoken out of unfathomable love, which have been considered the center and theme of the entire Pentateuch (e.g., by Rupprecht, a conservative German Old Testament scholar, and Dillmann, who calls vv. 3–6 "the classic pronouncement of the Old Testament concerning the nature and purpose of the theocratic covenant"). These words are even more profound after all that has happened since the Exodus (v. 4); the Lord did not remind Israel of these things, except indirectly (vv. 5a, 6a). Verse 4, cf. 15:26; Deuteronomy 4:20; 7:6; 10:14–15; 14:2; 26:18; 28:9; Pss. 24:1; 135:4; Isaiah 41:8; Titus 2:14. Verse 6, cf. 1 Peter 2:5, 9; 1 Corinthians 3:17; Revelation 1:6. In spite of the grumblings, the Lord fulfilled His promise of 6:7; He was determined to fulfill Genesis 3:15.

19:7, 8 *So Moses went back and summoned the elders of the people and set before them all the words the LORD had commanded him to speak. The people all responded together, "We will do everything the LORD has said." So Moses brought their answer back to the LORD.*

Moses was the mediator between God and the people. He summoned the elders (see commentary on 17:5; cf. 18:12). The people seem to have listened in (v. 8a), and they were prepared to enter into the covenant with the Lord and to accept the conditions (cf. 24:3). So Moses, as mediator (Acts 7:38; Gal. 3:19), took their response back to the Lord. There were now no more obstacles to the making of the covenant and the giving of the law. The people wanted to be the Lord's "treasured possession," motivated by His words and miracles. The Lord announced to Moses His imminent visible appearance to the people.

19:9–13 *The Lord said to Moses, "I am going to come to you in a dense cloud, so that the people will hear me speaking with you and will always put their trust in you." Then Moses told the Lord what the people had said.*

And the Lord said to Moses, "Go to the people and consecrate them today and tomorrow. Have them wash their clothes and be ready by the third day, because on that day the Lord will come down on Mount Sinai in the sight of all the people. Put limits for the people around the mountain and tell them, 'Be careful that you do not go up the mountain or touch the foot of it. Whoever touches the mountain shall surely be put to death. He shall surely be stoned or shot with arrows; not a hand is to be laid on him. Whether man or animal, he shall not be permitted to live.' Only when the ram's horn sounds a long blast may they go up to the mountain."

The Lord would come to Moses in "a dense cloud." Clouds frequently accompanied His appearance (cf. 13:21; Pss. 87:2; 104:3; Ezek. 1:4; Dan. 7:13; Matt. 17:5; 26:64; Mark 14:62; Rev. 1:7). They covered His glory (cf. 16:10), so that the people could come close enough to be able to hear His voice when He spoke with Moses on the mountain. The purpose of the Lord's speaking within earshot of the people was that the people would always trust in Moses (cf. 14:31; and 4:1). The Lord thus did not need to speak audibly, either here or in the giving of the Ten Commandments; He did it to support Moses' authority, especially after the repeated grumblings and the assaults on his authority, and also to lend divine authority to the laws that were given through Moses. "Always" (v. 9; KJV: "forever") comes probably from a verb meaning "to be hidden"; the term is a composite of *olam* ("hidden thing"), which, when used of time, means literally "hidden, unknown time," either past or future, and hence "time far removed in the past or in the future," or "eternity" (cf. 27:21). The Lord promised here that the Israelites would trust, or believe in, Moses into the far future, and in eternity (in the sense in which we use it) the song of Moses would be sung (Rev. 15:3).

The sequence in verse 9 is striking: Moses did not present the people's response of verse 8 to the Lord until after the Lord had spoken.

Moses now received further instructions concerning the impending theophany. Verses 10–13 describe how the people were to prepare themselves for the Lord's coming down on Mount Sinai. Moses was to go to the people and consecrate them, that is, separate them from anything unclean, so that they were in the appropriate condition for approaching the Lord (cf. Amos 4:12). Even their clothes had to be clean (cf. Gen. 35:2). The word for clothes here means "outer garments" (cf. 3:22; 12:35). Calvin points out that, although these external cleansings are no longer prescribed for us, their truth and essence remain necessary for us: if we want to be admitted to and participate in the heavenly doctrine, we must cleanse ourselves of all contamination of flesh and spirit (cf. Jude 23). For two days Moses was to occupy himself with the consecration of the people. On the third day, they were to be ready, because on that day the Lord would "come down" visibly on Mount Sinai (cf. Gen. 11:5, 7). Moses had to "put limits for the people"; the verb means "to limit, to set boundaries" and must be taken in a literal sense here, rather than in the sense of "restraining verbally" (cf. v. 23; Deut. 19:14; Josh. 18:20; Zech. 9:2). Moses was to "fence off" the mountain (cf. v. 23). The people were not to try to go up the mountain, or even touch the foot of the mountain under penalty of death (the Ras es-Sufsafeh rises abruptly from the plain of er-Râhah; cf. commentary on 3:1), and no one could touch an individual who had touched the mountain; the death penalty had to be carried out from a distance, by means of rocks or arrows. Should anyone, or any animal, approach the mountain, no one could follow and try to bring the person or the animal back (cf. Heb. 12:18–21, and Grosheide's notes on these verses in this commentary series). In verse 13b we read that the Lord indicated when the people (those who are authorized, v. 24) could "go up" the mountain, or, more specifically, could approach the foot of the mountain (cf. v. 17b), although it is also possible that the people abandoned any desire to go up the mountain (cf. 20:18–21). The signal would be a long blast of the ram's horn (cf. Josh. 6:15–16); but the signal would not be a human signal; rather, it would be a sound like that of the ram's horn or of the trumpet (cf. vv. 16, 19). The LXX states that the signal sounded "from the mountain," which is factually correct (cf. Heb. 12:19).

19:14, 15 *After Moses had gone down the mountain to the people, he consecrated them, and they washed their clothes. Then he said to the people, "Prepare yourselves for the third day. Abstain from sexual relations."*

Moses carried out the Lord's commands. Special mention is made of the fact that he told the people to abstain from sexual relations (cf. 1 Sam. 21:4; Joel 2:16; 1 Cor. 7:5). They were to be outwardly clean and inwardly concentrating on the imminent encounter with their God.

19:16–20 *On the morning of the third day there was thunder and lightning, with a thick cloud over the mountain, and a very loud trumpet blast. Everyone in the camp trembled. Then Moses led the people out of the camp to meet with God, and they stood at the foot of the mountain. Mount Sinai was covered with smoke, because the* Lord *descended on it in fire. The smoke billowed up from it like smoke from a furnace, the whole mountain trembled violently, and the sound of the trumpet grew louder and louder. Then Moses spoke and the voice of God answered him.*

The Lord *descended to the top of Mount Sinai and called Moses to the top of the mountain. So Moses went up.*

Then, on the morning of the third day, it happened. A heavy thunderstorm developed with thunder and lightning and a thick (or heavy) cloud (see commentary on v. 9). One of the characteristics that indicate that this phenomenon was more than a thunderstorm was, according to verse 16, the sound of a very loud trumpet blast (cf. 1 Thess. 4:16, van Leeuwen in this commentary series on 1 Thess.). Ebers claims that the sound of the trumpet was similar to what he heard during a thunderstorm on the Sinai peninsula. This was not the eruption of a volcano, as some would like to believe (see p. 51); no lava or ashes are mentioned. We must stick with the facts as they are related to us, and not assume that Moses received the Ten Commandments inwardly while he observed a thunderstorm. There is no question of symbolism here. The sound of the trumpet, which grew louder, the smoke, the fire, and the trembling of the mountain all indicate that the coming down of the Lord was not merely accompanied by a thunderstorm. Verse 9 alone is sufficient to reject the idea that the Lord only spoke to Moses inwardly. The events made a deep impression on the people in the camp: they trembled. Verse 17, cf. Deuteronomy 4:10–11. After verse 17 describes how Moses led the people to the foot of the mountain to wait for the Lord's appearance, verse 18 provides a description of the mountain itself. It was "covered with smoke," and "smoke billowed up from it," not because it was a volcano, but because the Lord "descended on it in fire" (see commentary on v. 11; cf. also the pillar of cloud and fire, and Gen. 15:17). The smoke is here compared to the smoke of a furnace (cf. 9:8, 10). Even the mountain itself trembled (cf. Judg. 5:4; Pss. 68:8; 114:4; Hab. 3:6). The entire event is awesome and terrifying, and is characteristic of the Old Testament dispensation (cf. Heb. 12:18–29). But He who descended was the Lord; He kept His word (v. 13b), and the promised sign was given. Moses then addressed the Lord, who answered in a human voice. God must not be identified with the awesome events that accompanied His coming; He merely used them. Once again, the author states what actually happened (v. 20). Moses was summoned, and went up the mountain.

19:21–25 *And the LORD said to him, "Go down and warn the people so they do not force their way through to see the LORD and many of them perish. Even the priests, who approach the LORD, must consecrate themselves, or the LORD will break out against them."*

Moses said to the LORD, "The people cannot come up Mount Sinai, because you yourself warned us, 'Put limits around the mountain and set it apart as holy.'"

The LORD replied, "Go down and bring Aaron up with you. But the priests and the people must not force their way through to come up to the LORD, or he will break out against them."

So Moses went down to the people and told them.

The conversation between Moses and the Lord showed once again that God, who appeared in majesty, was the Lord, who deeply cared for His people, and who could not be viewed as a blind natural force. He commanded Moses (who apparently did not convey the instructions given in v. 12 to the people) to go down and to warn the people not to try to approach Him out of curiosity, which would have terrible consequences (v. 21). We read in verse 22 that the priests were instructed to consecrate themselves as well, lest the Lord "break out against them." I do not know what to do with this verse, and am inclined to consider it a later addition, since at that time there were still no priests, while the command to consecrate themselves does not fit here (the people were already standing at the foot of the mountain). The Dutch Authorized Version says in the margin: "We must understand this as referring to the firstborn, which God the Lord had consecrated unto Himself, and who served as priests in the families (Ex. 13:2 and 24:5) before the tribe of Levi was set apart for that purpose and took their place (Num. 8:14, etc.)." Calvin assumes that Israel, like the pagan nations, already had priests, although he does not believe that these were the firstborn.

Moses answered the Lord that the people had been adequately warned, since the mountain had been fenced off (see commentary on v. 12, where the same word, "to put limits," is used). Moses thus considered the warning unnecessary—it was still the same Moses who dared make objections even while speaking directly with the Lord (cf. ch. 3–4). But the Lord insisted that Moses go down, and then come back with Aaron; but the priests (see commentary on v. 22) and the people "must not force their way through to come up to the LORD," lest He "break out against them." "And this is the legitimate boundary of knowledge, that we humbly learn from the mouth of God what He freely teaches us, and not run ahead with too much desire, but follow Him who leads" (Calvin).

Moses then carried out (v. 25) the Lord's command (vv. 21, 24), although it is not stated that he went back up the mountain with Aaron.

7. The Ten Commandments (20:1–17)

This important section of Scripture is called the "law of the LORD," the "law of the Ten Commandments," the "Ten Commandments," or simply "the Law." In 34:28 and Deuteronomy 4:13; 10:4 it is called literally "the ten words" (translated "Ten Commandments"), and hence the name "Decalogue" (from the Greek *deka* = "ten" and *logos* = "word"), which was apparently used first by Clement of Alexandria, and is appropriate. The Decalogue is a special part of the extensive Mosaic law, given and written on two stone tablets by God Himself, and presented to the people by Moses (although according to this chapter, the people witnessed its proclamation).

The entire body of laws that we refer to as the "Mosaic law" was given by God through angels (Acts 7:38, 53; Gal. 3:19; Heb. 2:2; see Grosheide on the references in Acts and Hebrews, and Greijdnaus on the reference in Galatians in this commentary series.) The argument that Moses could not possibly have been a lawgiver has been countered by the more recent archaeological finds. Laws of other nations have been found that date from ancient times, and several of the commandments of the second tablet of the Law have been found among so-called primitive nations (possibly even a knowledge of the tenth commandment among some tribes who apparently considered covetousness dangerous for superstitious reasons). But the discovery of the law code of the Babylonian king Hammurabi, who lived long before Moses (around 1700 B.C.), has especially silenced the critics. Hammurabi's law code is engraved on a piece of black diorite 2.25 m. (c. 8 ft.) high, and 45 cm. (c. 1½ ft.) wide at the top and 60 cm. (c. 2 ft.) at the base. The stele was discovered at Susa in 1902, and contains 282 laws, promulgated by the famous Babylonian king three centuries before Moses. Moses, therefore could have done what Hammurabi did.[4] Friedrich Delitzsch went so far as to make Moses totally dependent on Hammurabi (in spite of the fact that there are no parallels between the Decalogue and Hammurabi's code, although there are some similarities between the Decalogue and other Babylonian laws). It is a known fact that the history of Abraham (e.g.,

---

[4]Even the most radical critics must, and generally do, acknowledge this possibility at present. But Wildeboer does not realize that, for us evangelicals, the reliability of the Scriptures never has been dependent on discoveries such as that of the Code of Hammurabi when he writes: "The apologists in their zeal never realized that they overshot their target. Their line of reasoning was apparently based on an argument which no one on our side would ever have used: because a Babylonian king had promulgated similar laws one thousand years earlier [Wildeboer's dating] any obstacle to crediting Moses with such laws had been removed! In their zeal, they sacrificed the unique nature of the Mosaic law, which they used to attribute to divine revelation" (*Nieuw licht over het Oude Testament*, 1911, p. 11).

Sarah's dealings with Hagar) contains traces of Babylonian jurisprudence. But it cannot be denied that from a religious standpoint, Israel's law is of a much higher caliber than Hammurabi's code, as the many books written about this discovery will verify. In the notes on the individual commandments, any similarities with Hammurabi's code will be examined. The main similarity lies in their form, e.g., in the use of the formula ''if someone . . . then. . . .'' The discovery of the Code of Hammurabi has reinstated the previously mentioned ''Book of the Covenant'' (cf. e.g., commentary on ch. 19) and the Decalogue as being of Mosaic origin (e.g., by Sellin, Kittel, Ed. Konig, Eerdmans, Gressmann, etc.). But the Code of Hammurabi stands on a lower level than the Decalogue, if only because the former does not forbid covetousness (cf. 20:17). H. T. Obbink says: ''The entire code of Hammurabi does not contain a single religious idea, not even in the laws concerning temple prostitutes and magic'' (*Inleiding tot den Bijbel,* p. 27). The purpose is not to inculcate godliness, but rather to regulate social relationships. And Israel's laws are, according to Wildeboer, more imbued with a spirit of mercy. But we must not forget that Hammurabi's code was intended to be a legal rather than a religious document.

In both Babylonian and Egyptian texts (such as the Egyptian ''Book of the Dead''), a coherent body of regulations is found, which Jirku calls the ''Ancient Near-eastern moral code.'' This ''moral code'' expresses thoughts that parallel the last six commandments of the Decalogue, but Jirku himself points out that these commandments, which regulate the relationship with the neighbor, express ideas that could have arisen independently in various locations. Furthermore, these ideas are connected in Babylonia and Egypt with magical concepts that are totally absent in the Decalogue. Jirku considers Moses to be the one who consecrated the generally valid human principles of behavior by adding the first four commandments. Although we do not agree with this, since the Lord Himself gave the Ten Commandments, the archaeological discoveries support the thesis that the Ten Commandments are a restatement and clarification of the innate moral law with which man was created (cf. Rom. 2:14–15). In recent years parallels have been discovered between God's covenant with Israel and the so-called vassal treaties of antiquity as found among, e.g., the Hittites (cf. Kline, *Treaty of the Great King,* Grand Rapids: Eerdmans, 1963).

Although we can thus see a change in the opinions concerning the date of the composition of the Decalogue, some believe that it was originally shorter, and acquired its present form due to later additions. Thus, Eerdmans (*De Godsdienst van Israel,* I, pp. 42–44) believes that the

Decalogue as a whole was inserted in Exodus, while verse 4 was a later addition, and that the fourth and tenth commandments were originally shorter. But he does not question that the Decalogue is of ancient origin. Another view holds that the original Decalogue was drawn up for a nation that was still nomadic, and that later additions were made to adapt it to a more civilized agricultural nation. But it is difficult to prove such an expansion of the "original" Ten Commandments, and it is unlikely that such a code, engraved on two tablets (24:12; 31:18; 32:16; Deut. 9:9ff.; 10:5), would later have been expanded. Attempts to reconstruct the original Decalogue are highly subjective and debatable. Goethe already complained that the historical narrative was hampered by the legal sections (cf. also Eerdmans, *De Godsdienst,* p. 42: "In the narrative of Exodus, the Decalog interrupts the continuity and has been added later"), but we must not forget that the Pentateuch reports what took place, and that the giving of the law is part of the historical sequence. The historical setting of the giving of the law on Sinai is much grander than that of the Code of Hammurabi.

The Scriptures as a whole, and especially the New Testament, must determine the significance of the Ten Commandments for us. Paul deals with the relationship between the Mosaic law in general (and the Ten Commandments in particular) and the work of Jesus Christ (e.g., Rom. 5:20–21; Gal. 3:10–14). We can only mention a few highlights here. The division of the law into the ceremonial, civil, and moral law is well-known. Apart from a few minor details, the Ten Commandments summarize the moral law, which is valid for all, because it was given in creation (Rom. 2:14–15). This law is thus still valid for the Christian as a "law of gratitude," that Jesus summarized in the demand that we love God, and our neighbor as ourselves (Matt. 22:37–39; Mark 12:28–34; Luke 10:27; Rom. 13:9; Gal. 5:14; cf. Lev. 19:18; Deut. 6:5; 10:12; 30:6). Our purpose here is not to present an ethic, but rather to provide an understanding of the words and the main points.

Two points require further consideration in these preliminary remarks: the relationship between Exodus 20:1–17 and Deuteronomy 5:6–21, and the division of the commandments. The Decalogue as found in Exodus differs on several points from Moses' restatement of the Decalogue in Deuteronomy, as indicated in the following notes. The main difference is the motivation for the Sabbath law. These differences must be explained on the basis of differences in inspiration: when Moses repeated the law, God gave him different words than those that He Himself spoke on Mount Sinai (cf. J. Ridderbos, *Deuteronomy,* in this commentary series).

There is no agreement as to whether each of the two tablets contained five commandments (Philo, Josephus, Irenaeus, etc), or one four and the other six (Calvin), or one three and the other seven (Augustine). Today some are of the opinion that each of the two tablets contained all ten commandments (e.g., Kline, see above; Ernst E. Ettisch, *Vetus Testamentum,* 14, 1964, pp. 211–215). We do not know the size of the tablets, although we do know that they had to be kept in the ark.[5] The early church, the Greek Orthodox Church, the Socinians, and the churches of the Calvinistic branch of the Reformation follow Philo (who placed the seventh before the sixth commandment, however) and Josephus, and take verses 4–6 to be the second commandment, while the Roman Catholic and Lutheran Churches follow Augustine and others, and consider verses 2–6 one commandment. But some Lutheran exegetes agree that the first view is better, especially since the second one also divides the tenth commandment into two: "You shall not covet your neighbor's house" is Luther's ninth commandment, and "You shall not covet your neighbor's wife" is the ninth commandment of the Roman Catholic Church; furthermore, since the Roman Catholic view follows Deuteronomy, the tenth commandment is: "You shall not set your desire on your neighbor's house," etc. There is no reason for dividing the tenth commandment into two separate commandments, while there is a clear distinction between the first and second commandment (see commentary below). The Jews consider verse 2 to be the first commandment, and combine the first and second commandments.

20:1 *And God spoke all these words.*

Unless the command in 19:24–25 was not carried out, Aaron accompanied Moses back up the mountain (cf. Deut. 5:4–5). "God" is used rather than "the Lord": this law is valid for all people, not just for the Israelites, although it was given to Israel. But the LXX and other ancient versions use "Lord" here, so that the argument cannot be pressed too much, especially since the different names of God are used in the Pentateuch in such a way that it is not always possible to arrive at a satisfactory explanation for the use of a particular name of God in a given instance.

20:2 *"I am the Lord your God, who brought you out of Egypt, out of the land of slavery."*

---

[5]Since the outside dimensions of the ark were 2½ by 1½ by 1½ cubits (25:10), the tablets cannot have been larger than approximately 3 by 2 feet, and were probably smaller, since Moses was able to carry them. (tr.)

Before the Lord commanded Israel what it had to be and do, He first told them who He was and what He had done in His relationship with them: He was "the LORD" (concerning this name, see commentary on 3:13–15, and for the use of this name here, see commentary on 6:1–8). "Your" and "you" are masculine singular. He had proven to be the God of the Israelite by bringing him out of Egypt (cf. Introduction, I), which had become for him a "land of slavery" (cf. 13:3, 14). The Lord thus began with an appeal to the gratitude of each member of the people of the covenant individually: his redemption was to lead to a keeping of God's commandments. This redemption has a typical significance for us: the redemption from the "land of slavery" of Satan by Jesus Christ (cf. 1 Cor. 10:6, 11, and Grosheide on these verses in this commentary series). We must remember that this reminder was superfluous in the sense that "the LORD," as "God," could simply require from every human being that he or she obey His will. But as the God of Israel He gave a reason, He wanted to convince. Although Israel was the heir, it was still a "child"—but God nevertheless treated it as a son (cf. Gal. 4:1; Ps. 81:10; Hos. 11:1). The giving of the law must be seen as part of the making of the covenant (cf. the connection between Deut. 5:2–5 and 6–21; Exod. 19, esp. 19:8, and 24:3–8). The stone tablets are also called the "tablets of the covenant" (cf. Deut. 9:9, 11, 15; 1 Kings 8:9, and van Gelderen's commentary on 1 Kings 8:9 in this series).

20:3 *"You shall have no other gods before me."*

"You" is masculine singular in all the commandments. Eight of the commandments are negative: "you shall not." The Hebrew *lo* makes the prohibitions emphatic: God absolutely did not want the Israelite to do this, and He fully expected that he would not do it.

The commandment reads literally: "there shall not be other gods besides (or, before) My face or person"; the Lord alone was to be Israel's God to the exclusion of all other gods that the Israelites worshiped besides Him in Egypt, and to which they continually wanted to return during the wilderness journey (cf. Josh. 24:14; Ezek. 20:5–10; 23:2–3, 8, 19, 27; Amos 5:25–26). The phrase "besides me" or "before me" can also mean "over me" in the sense of "in preference over me." The first commandment is of fundamental importance. Just as only Israel heard that the Lord was its God, so it had to consider only the Lord to be its God. This did not mean that God accepted the existence of other gods. The patriarchs already believed in one God, and we encounter here a pure monotheism (cf. Deut. 6:4). But it was possible for Israel to have other "gods" or idols besides the Lord, as happened later in the time of Ahab and Elijah (1 Kings 17f.). (Cf. Lev. 26:1; Deut. 16:21–22; 1 Sam. 7:3; Ps. 97:7; Isa. 42:8; Matt. 4:10). Not having any other gods besides the Lord involves total surrender and consecration to the one and only God.

20:4–6 *"You shall not make for yourself an idol in the form of anything in heaven above or on the earth beneath or in the waters below. You shall not bow down to them or worship them; for I, the LORD your God, am a jealous God, punishing the children for the sin of the fathers to the third and fourth generation of those who hate me, but showing love to thousands who love me and keep my commandments."*

The second commandment prohibits the making of any idols (or, images carved from wood or stone; KJV: "graven image") in the form of anything in heaven above (the air and the firmament), or on the earth, or in the waters below ("below" merely indicates that the level of the waters is lower than the land, not that the earth rests on the waters), cf. Deuteronomy 4:18. It is probably best to see this in contrast to the Egyptian religion, which included the worship of the heavenly bodies, especially the sun, and of animals such as birds, cows, frogs, and fish; fish gods were also common among many northern Semitic nations. Only the Lord may be worshiped as God (v. 3), but He may not be represented by any image (v. 4; cf. Aalders on Gen. 1:26 in this commentary series).

A different division of the second commandment has been suggested, based on the assumption that "form" (KJV: "likeness") can never refer to a statue or sculpture: "You shall not make for yourself an idol. And the form of anything . . . , you shall not bow down to them or worship them." But the premise is open to question, and the word "form" or "likeness" makes good sense, especially when translated "an idol *in* the form of" rather than "an idol *or* a likeness" (cf. KJV). See also Deuteronomy 4:15–20, and Leviticus 26:1. Since the second commandment was spoken directly by God Himself, it could not contain a Babylonian or other primitive near-Eastern world view. Verse 11 supports this viewpoint. Verse 5a indicates that honoring or worshiping such idols or likenesses is forbidden. We can draw the conclusion, therefore, that the second commandment forbids the making of any images of God, rather than the making of images of birds, bulls, fish, etc. in general.

Calvin considered this last view foolish and not worthy of refutation. The first view is indeed confirmed by what God Himself commanded concerning the ceremonial objects (e.g., the cherubim on the ark, 25:18; 37:7; cf. 26:1) and by the things Solomon made for the temple and for his own palace (lions, bulls, cherubim, cf. 1 Kings 7; 10:18–20); cf. also the bronze snake, Numbers 21:8. The intent of verse 4 is thus further clarified by the prohibition: ''you shall not bow down to them or worship them.'' This is the basis for the statement that the second commandment concerns the cultus. And we agree with Calvin that we must determine what is commanded on the basis of what is prohibited, and also realize that this commandment deals with a whole group or category of sins. ''Bow down and worship'' (the combination is found elsewhere in the Scriptures, e.g., Deut. 4:18; 8:19; 11:16; 17:3; 29:26; 30:17) may indicate a progression: the latter may refer to a regular, daily dependence on such idols, while the former may refer to a more incidental relationship. It has been claimed that before the time of Amos and Hosea the worship of an image of the Lord was not considered to be contrary to the law, but if this is true, then e.g., 1 Kings 12:28; 13 (the condemnation of the sin of Jeroboam the son of Nebat) and Exodus 32 must be considered later additions, which is precisely what proponents of this view say. In other words, the Bible is then distorted on the basis of presuppositions that take precedence over the statements of the Bible itself. The examples used to support the view that the use of images in the worship of the Lord was permitted (e.g., Micah and the Danites, Judg. 17–17; Michal, 1 Sam. 19:13, 16) are in reality nothing more than illustrations of a practice that the Scriptures sometimes reject outright, and certainly never approve (cf. e.g., Judg. 18:1, and the fact that Michal was not a shining example of religiosity, 2 Sam. 6:20).

The reason for this prohibition is given in verses 5b–6: the Lord calls Himself emphatically ''I, the LORD your God.'' The reason is not that God is a Spirit (cf. John 4:24) and thus cannot be represented by any image, but rather that He is a jealous God (the name of God used here, *El,* may point to His power). The word for ''jealous'' combines the concepts of ''zeal'' and ''jealousy'' (LXX: *zēlotēs*). He will not allow the Israelites to bow down to, or worship, something that represents a creature, made by their own hands, even if that image represents Him, and the worship is thus ultimately intended for Him (cf. 34:14, 17; Deut. 4:24; 6:15; Josh. 24:19; Nah. 1:2; Isa. 42:8; 48:11). If they nevertheless disobey this commandment, then they will know that He is a God who punishes (lit. ''visits,'' cf. KJV; cf. also 3:16; 4:31; 13:19; ''visit'' is used in a negative or hostile sense here, hence ''punish''). Yet the Lord's jealousy with regard to images that are to represent Him shows love: He Himself wants to be the object of the worship and service of the Israelites, and He wants to make Himself an image (cf. e.g., the image of the Lord as Israel's Husband in the prophets, e.g., Jer. 2:2; Hos. 1–3).

The Lord does notice the guilt, the sin of the fathers, and will punish the children to the third and fourth generation of those who hate Him. This sin and "hate," then, expressed themselves in the making and worshiping of images of God, in spite of His explicit prohibition. But on the basis of verse 6, which speaks of "commandments," we must not be too anxious to limit the threat to the second commandment only, although it is worth noting that the threat is attached to this commandment. This is perhaps because of the nature of the sin with which it deals: the attempt to make the worship of the Lord something that relates to the senses rather than to the spirit. Among the other nations, who broke the first commandment as well, this had led to abuses such as temple prostitution, etc. Furthermore, it is easy for someone who breaks the second commandment to move on to a transgression of the first commandment. The sin of Jeroboam, the son of Nebat, led to the worship of Baal Melqart of Tyre (cf. also Jer. 48:13). "For whoever reduces the Deity to a creature by representing it as a calf, must ultimately add its equals to it, like other creatures; by destroying its infiniteness one also destroys its uniqueness" (van Andel, *Handleiding bij de beoefening der gewijde geschiedenis,* p. 147). And as a result generations have often perished, "visited" by the jealous God of the covenant, whose jealousy, however, coincides with His love (cf. v. 6). In connection with this threat we must remember that in the ancient Near East the ties between the individual and the larger context of tribe, nation, and family had not been devalued as it has been among many people today.

A parallel to the concept of the punishment of the children for the sin of the fathers has been thought to exist in the Babylonian-Assyrian wisdom literature, where a statement is found to the effect that a young child receives the punishment for the father, or for the father and mother; the statement is unclear, however. A Hittite prayer says, "It is only too true that man is sinful. My father sinned and transgressed against the word of the Hattian Storm-god, my lord. But I have not sinned in any respect. It is only too true, however, that the father's sin falls upon the son. So, my father's sin has fallen upon me." Of course, the word "sin" here does not have the same meaning as it does in the Bible. Verse 5 does not say explicitly that those children also walk in the sin of their fathers, but in view of verse 6 this seems to be implied. Note also the scriptural distinction between punishment and chastisement. "Love" is an inadequate rendering of the Hebrew word, *hesed.* It does not refer to kindness to which one has no right or claim; the Hebrew has a different word for this. But the word refers to a goodness, a kindness, a mercy to which one is obligated on the basis of a relationship. On the human level this can be the relationship of marriage, friendship, or of a covenant. In the case of God and Israel the obligation was based on the covenant: covenant love, which expressed itself in a mutual relationship of rights and duties, and in which God binds man to himself. He showed this love, based on the relationship with Israel in which He has placed Himself ("I, the LORD your God," v. 5), to those who respected that covenant by loving Him and keeping His commandments, and He showed it most generously: "to thousands." This is the other side of His covenant jealousy (v. 5). "Hate" (v. 5) is thus on the part of the Israelites: breaking the covenant, apostasy; "love" is that to which they were obligated out of gratitude, in fulfillment of the law. Verses 5–6, cf. 34:7; Numbers 14:18; Jeremiah 32:18. Concerning the supposed contradiction between verses 5–6 and Ezekiel 18, see Noordtzij on *Ezekiel* in this commentary series. Ezekiel 18 opposes the abuse of the threat attached to the second commandment, viz. the denial of one's own sins (cf. Ezek. 18:2). Deuteronomy 24:16 discusses a different situation; the command there is directed to the authorities.

20:7 *"You shall not misuse the name of the LORD your God, for the LORD will not hold anyone guiltless who misuses his name."*

The first part of the third commandment literally means "You shall not lift up (or, take up) the name of the LORD, your God for the unreal, vain, frivolous, insincere." The lifting up or taking up of a name also means "to intone, to pronounce" a name. We could therefore also translate: "You shall not pronounce the name of the LORD your God insincerely, or culpably, or thoughtlessly." "Misuse" is indeed the best translation of the word. Concerning the Jewish view of this commandment, see commentary on 3:13–15. The third commandment covers all occasions on which the name of the Lord is used, and includes e.g., perjury (cf. Lev. 19:12), swearing, etc. König translates Deuteronomy 5:11 "with inner insincerity." "Any pronouncing of the Divine name without heartfelt sincerity is thus prohibited." The name is spiritual in nature; even in the absence of images, the name that the Lord has revealed as His makes it possible to have communion with Him, to name Him. That name must be used in a holy manner (cf. the first petition of the Lord's prayer), that is, it must be kept far from that which is sinful, frivolous, or vain. "Name" has a profound meaning: the revelation of that which can be known of God. "Jahweh," or, "the LORD, your God" indicates that implied in that name is the revelation of God as the unchangeable God of the covenant in the history of the patriarchs and of Israel's exodus and wilderness journey. The Lord Himself guards the holiness of His name, as is indicated by the threat that accompanies this commandment. The word translated "to hold guiltless" can also mean "to acquit" or "to leave unpunished" (cf. 1 Kings 2:9; Jer. 30:11; 46:28; cf. also Lev. 24:10–23). In the Sermon on the

Mount the Lord spoke out against the rash oaths of His contemporaries (Matt. 5:33–37). Of course, the phrase "will not hold anyone guiltless" is a litotes, an affirmation expressed by the negation of the contrary, which has a softening effect. But on the other hand Moses received in Leviticus 24:10–23 a special revelation from the Lord telling him what he had to do with a blasphemer. This commandment also has been interpreted and worked out copiously in Reformed ethics (e.g., by Geesink). Between the two extremes (blasphemy against the Holy Spirit and martyrdom for the sake of the faith) is then an entire spectrum, based on the scheme: misuse—disuse—proper use of the revelation.

20:8–11 *"Remember the Sabbath day by keeping it holy. Six days you shall labor and do all your work, but the seventh day is a Sabbath to the Lord your God. On it you shall not do any work, neither you, nor your son or daughter, nor your manservant or maidservant, nor your animals, nor the alien within your gates. For in six days the Lord made the heavens and the earth, the sea, and all that is in them, but he rested on the seventh day. Therefore the Lord blessed the Sabbath day and made it holy."*

The fourth and fifth commandments are the only true *commandments,* unlike the others, which are negative in form, and thus prohibitions. "Remember" the Sabbath day indicates that the Sabbath already existed (see commentary on 16:4–5, 22–30). It has been claimed that the sabbath was also known as a day of rest among the Babylonians (cf. e.g., Geesink, *Van's Heren Ordinantiën,* III, pp. 437–438). But it seems that the Babylonians did not call the seventh, fourteenth, twenty-first, and twenty-eighth days of their lunar month "sabbath." These days were indeed days of rest, but were not called *shabatu;* this name was given to only one particular day (according to Böhl the fifteenth day of the month) and this Shabatu (according to Böhl *sha patu,* i.e., day of the middle, or the boundary of the month) was called "the day of the stilling of the heart," i.e., the heart of the gods. We should note that the seventh, fourteenth, twenty-first, and twenty-eighth (and, according to Jirku, also the nineteenth) days were days of rest because they were considered evil or unlucky days; the custom was thus based on superstitious fear. Jirku considered it possible that the *name shabatu* was adopted by Israel to designate the already existing day of rest (cf. Noordtzij on Ezek. 20:12 in this commentary series). The general thesis that Israel, being a nomadic people, could hardly have had a weekly day of rest is untenable, especially since Israel was not nomadic in the usual sense of the word. Deuteronomy 5:12 uses the more common "observe" instead of "remember," and adds a reference to the fact that Lord had commanded the observance of the Sabbath here: "as the Lord your

God has commanded you." The Sabbath was to be kept holy, i.e., to be set apart for the Lord's service (cf. Aalders on Gen. 2:3 in this commentary series).

It is incorrect to conclude from the fact that only the Sabbath is mentioned here, and not e.g., the Passover, that only the Sabbath is definitely of Mosaic origin, while the other feasts had their origin in Canaan. "Sabbath" means "rest," from the verb *shabat,* "to rest", which is also used in Genesis 2:2–3. It is thus in the first place a "negative" concept. Another view is that Sabbath means "period, portion of time," and hence "time of rest." Still others believe that the word "Sabbath" is related to "seven": the Israelite had six days to labor and to do all his work (see commentary on 12:16, where the same word is used, indicating both the daily task and occupational as well as servile labor), but the seventh day was the day of rest in honor of the Lord, his God. "By keeping it holy": "That is, set it apart from your usual work, or daily work, which belong to this temporary life, and use it to serve God with holy works, which concern God's honor, eternity, and the spiritual life" (marginal note, Dutch Authorized Version).

Verse 10 indicates how seriously the Lord took this prohibition of all work, especially occupational and servile work. Not only could the Israelite not do "any work," but neither could any member of his household (son, daughter, manservant, maidservant; the wife is included with the husband), and even the livestock. The references at the end of this paragraph give an indication of some of the specific tasks that were prohibited. Even the "alien" was included (see commentary on 2:22; 12:48; 18:3). The addition "within your gates" shows that the Lord assumed that Israel would live in cities in the near future. Deuteronomy 5:14 differs in several respects from verse 10: after "maidservant" is added "nor your ox, your donkey, or any of your animals," and the motivation for the observance of the Sabbath is also different (for the motivation given in Exodus, cf. Gen. 2:1–3 and Aalders' comments on those verses in this series). The reasons for the observance of the Sabbath given in Exodus and Deuteronomy are not mutually exclusive, but the one in Exodus is broader and is valid for mankind in general: God Himself rested on the seventh day. The word used for "rested" has as its primary emphasis the idea of "relaxing, taking a rest" (cf. the more elaborate phrase in 31:17). Deuteronomy places the emphasis more on the neighbor, Exodus more on the service of God and the following of His example: God made the Sabbath day a day of rest for man, and blessed it and made it holy because He Himself rested on the seventh day. Deuteronomy 5:14–15 also places full emphasis on the Sabbath as a day of rest (as well as on its holiness, cf. v. 12). It should be noted that Israel was the only nation in antiquity that had such a day of rest that was considered an obligation as well as a blessing. Attempts to prove that the books of the Old Testament that predate the captivity do not mention the Sabbath must be considered a failure. The conclusion has been drawn correctly (e.g., by Calvin) that the basis for the Sabbath given in Exodus instructs man to follow God's example, and that His example of six days of work and one day of rest must be the rule for mankind. The question as to the extent to which the Sabbath day as the *seventh* day belonged to the "shadows" of the Old Testament dispensation, which has been replaced in the New Testament by the *first* day, the day of the resurrection, has been dealt with in Reformed literature, e.g., by van Nes, *Het Jodendom*, pp. 326ff.; B. J. Esser, *Schriftuurlijk Anti-Sabbathisme* (Colportage Boekhandel Magelang, 1930). Concerning the Sabbath, cf. 23:12; 31:12–17; 34:21; 35:3; Leviticus 23:3; Numbers 15:32–36; 28:9–10; 2 Kings 4:23; 11:5; 16:18; Nehemiah 13:15–22; Isaiah 1:13; Jeremiah 17:21–22; Ezekiel 20:11–12, 19–20; 46:1; Amos 8:5–6; Galatians 4:9–11; Colossians 2:16–17. Jesus' attitude toward the view of the Sabbath held by His contemporaries is also of great importance.

20:12 *"Honor your father and your mother, so that you may live long in the land the* LORD *your God is giving you."*

With the fifth commandment the Law shifts to the relationship with the neighbor. But some feel that the fifth commandment still belongs to the first tablet, and believe that the difference between the first five and last five commandments lies in the fact that the first five contain obligations toward God and toward those who occupy a higher position, while the second set of five commandments regulate the relationship with those who are equals. Paul calls this commandment "the first commandment with a promise" (Eph. 6:2–3; cf. Greijdanus on those verses in this series). "Honor" is from a verb that means "to be heavy" (cf. 5:9; 9:7; and in causative form 8:15, 32; 9:34; 10:1; 14:4, 17), and hence also "to be rich, to be honored," and here "to consider important, to honor." This commandment is also best translated in the second person masculine singular (cf. Ridderbos, *Deuteronomy):* every Israelite was commanded to honor not only his father, but also his mother, which shows that the woman in Israel did occupy a place of honor in her family. Deuteronomy 5:16 adds "as the LORD your God has commanded you": after "honor your father and your mother," probably in reference to Exodus 20.

In the Babylonian-Assyrian wisdom literature the saying is found "(if a person) does not honor his father, he soon perishes" (cf. Deut. 27:16).

Adoption documents also contain the requirement that parents be honored. An adopted son who lacks respect for his parents can be shorn and sold for money without legal process. The Bible uses the names "father" and "mother" not only for the physical parents, but also for those in authority, such as prophets, teachers, etc. (cf. Gen. 45:8; Judg. 5:7; 2 Kings 2:12; 13:14; cf. also the use of "son" in the Book of Proverbs, and the Heidelberg Catechism, Lord's Day 39). For the Israelite the result of honoring his parents, which expresses itself in obedience (Eph. 6:1; Col. 3:20), will be a long life in the land that the Lord his God is in the process of giving him; this is the reason why the Israelite must keep this commandment. The promise includes both a long life and a long period of being settled in Canaan, which would be possible in part because of an orderly society. Deuteronomy 5:16 adds the promise of prosperity: "and that it may go well with you."

The first five commandments, as well as verse 2, speak of "the LORD your God" ("me" in the first commandment refers back to this); a repeated appeal is thus made to Israel's gratitude. By using the same expression in the fifth commandment the Lord makes the question of honoring the parents His business, as was naturally the case in the first four commandments, which dealt with His service, His name, and His day. He would give the Israelite lasting possession of the Promised Land if he kept the fifth commandment. Concerning the validity of this promise for us, the New Testament church, see Greijdanus on Ephesians 6:3. Cf. also Exodus 21:15, 17; Leviticus 19:3; 20:9; Proverbs 20:20; 30:11, 17; Matthew 10:37; 15:4–6; Mark 7:10–13; Luke 14:26; 2 Timothy 3:2–3.

20:13 *"You shall not murder."*

The Vatican codex of the LXX places verse 13 after verses 14–15, while Philo places it between verse 14 and verse 15. Mark 10:19, Luke 18:20, and Romans 13:9 also list the commandments rather freely. The sixth commandment forbids killing or murder, the violent and unauthorized taking of life. The respect for life, reflected in this commandment, and for the neighbor who is made in the image of God (cf. Gen. 9:5–6), is far reaching (cf. Gen. 9:6; Lev. 19:17ff.; Job 2:4; Matt. 5:21–22; Rom. 13:4; 1 John 3:15; and Heidelberg Catechism, Lord's Day 40). Suicide is also forbidden, since the verb has no specific object. See also Ridderbos on Deuteronomy 5:17 in this commentary series.

20:14 *"You shall not commit adultery."*

The seventh commandment concerns marriage (cf. Lev. 18:20; 10:10; Deut. 22:22) and sexual behavior in general. Joseph had high standards in this respect (cf. Gen. 39:7–12), and many pagan nations also disapproved of adultery. The married man is forbidden to have sexual intercourse with someone else's wife, and the married woman may not have intercourse with any man other than her husband (cf. Lev. 20:10). But here again, we must go beyond what is explicitly stated, and see this as a prohibition of a whole range of sexual sins. The full depth of this commandment is elucidated in the New Testament (cf. Matt. 5:27–32; 1 Cor. 6:19–20).

20:15 *"You shall not steal."*

The eighth commandment forbids theft and robbery, the surreptitiously and fraudulently taking of something. The conclusion has been drawn that the Scriptures support respect for private property, which is correct, provided that we pay attention to the further regulations concerning property in the Pentateuch. Just as the seventh commandment covers the entire sexual realm, in the same way this commandment covers the whole sphere of material life, commerce, etc. (cf. Lev. 19:11). The Lord is the absolute Owner of all things (Ps. 24:1); man is His steward. Any society that takes into account His laws as they relate to material things will prosper.

20:16 *"You shall not give false testimony against your neighbor."*

The ninth commandment protects not the life, wife, or property of the neighbor, but his name. The giving of false witness is forbidden. The Israelite may not give a "witness of falsehood" (cf. 5:9) against his neighbor to a judge or to anyone else. Deuteronomy 5:20 uses the same word found in verse 7 ("frivolous, vain") instead of "falsehood" (cf. 23:1; Deut. 19:16–21; Prov. 14:5; 19:5; 25:18). When we realize that here also the most serious sin of this type is mentioned, then we see that this commandment condemns the whole spectrum of sins of the tongue: gossip, slander, flattery, etc.

20:17 *"You shall not covet your neighbor's house. You shall not covet your neighbor's wife, or his manservant or maidservant, his ox or donkey, or anything that belongs to your neighbor."*

The tenth commandment goes beyond sins in word and deed to their source: evil desires, the wrongfully striving after, lusting after, desiring, of our neighbor's house, wife, manservant, maidservant, ox, donkey, or anything else that belongs to our neighbor. The word used for "covet" can also refer to a good rather than an evil desire (cf. Ps. 19:10 KJV, where a passive participle of this verb is used; Ps. 68:16 KJV). But here it is used in a negative sense. In this verse especially it becomes evident that the Ten Commandments are more than a common, civil law and that they go deeper than all other laws promulgated by earthly kings (e.g., Hammurabi of Babylonia). (Cf. Rom. 7:7.) Because man, and thus also the Israelite, cannot restrain his evil desires, he is faced with his misery by means of the law, so that he might seek everything outside himself, in God: the Lord his God, who has performed other miracles (cf. v. 2). The many differences between verse 17 and Deuteronomy 5:21 are well-known; there the tenth commandment reads "You shall not covet your neighbor's wife. You shall not set your desire on your neighbor's house or land, his manservant or maidservant, his ox or donkey, or anything that belongs to your neighbor." The reversal of the sequence that places "wife" before "house" in Deuteronomy 5 indicates that we cannot place a great deal of emphasis on the sequence in Exodus 20:17, except to say that, after her husband, the wife occupied the most important place in the house. "Land" looks toward the imminent settling in Canaan. The sense of Exodus 20:17 and and Deuteronomy 5:21 is thus the same.

The last four commandments in Deuteronomy 5 begin with "and not" in Hebrew. I already noted that some scholars are of the opinion that traces of the tenth commandment can also be found among primitive nations. But, apart from the objections to the use of "primitive" in this context, the reason why covetousness is prohibited is different there: the person who covets is in danger, a danger that finds its source in the coveted object or in the jealous gods. The Lord protects the neighbor, and goes beyond the outward expression of covetousness. Yet it is striking that the memory of the moral law, however corrupted it may be, remains. The depths of man's corruption must be laid bare by this tenth commandment and by God's entire law (cf. Rom. 7:7).

8. *Israel's Fear and Moses' Approach* (20:18–21)

Some interpreters, especially among adherents of the so-called source hypothesis, believe 20:18–21 to be out of place here; they consider these verses to be a continuation of 19:18 or 19:19, in which case they precede the Ten Commandments. But Deuteronomy 5:22ff. records the same sequence of events, and this view cannot be supported with proof. Furthermore, verse 19 (which states that the Israelites requested that God would no longer speak to them, but rather Moses) argues against this view: the Ten Commandments preceded this request. These verses are where they are supposed to be.

20:18, 19 *When the people saw the thunder and lightning and heard the trumpet and saw the mountain in smoke, they trembled with fear. They stayed at a distance and said to Moses, "Speak to us yourself and we will listen. But do not have God speak to us or we will die."*

Verses 18–19 describe the impression the theophany of chapter 19 made on the people of Israel (cf. 19:8). See commentary on 19:9–13, 16–20 concerning the thunder and lightning (the word for "lightning" can also mean "torches"), the sound of the trumpet, and the smoking mountain. Thunder and trumpet blasts cannot be seen, so that the word "saw" here is used in the sense of "perceive, observe." The participle "was seeing" is used, indicating that the people observed these things for some time, numb with fear, while the Lord proclaimed the Ten Commandments. Now, however, fear and trembling ("trembling," cf. Isa. 7:2; 19:1) got the better of them, and they lined up at a distance, away from the mountain. Verse 18b reads literally "and the people saw and they trembled and they stood from a distance" (cf. KJV); the translation "and the people feared and trembled" (NIV: "trembled with fear") follows the Samaritan Pentateuch, the LXX, and the Vulgate, and involves only a change in the vowel signs of the Hebrew. Israel was afraid of God. Through its leading men and elders (Deut. 5:12) it asked Moses, who probably had not gone far up the mountain and had rejoined them, to stand between them and the Lord. Compare these verses with Deuteronomy 5:23ff., which gives the impression that this fear and trembling became evident, and this request was made, *after* Moses returned to the people with the two stone tablets; but this is not a necessary implication of Deuteronomy 5:22 (cf. Deut. 9:10f.). God's speaking made a tremendous impression on them (cf. Heb. 12:19). They requested that Moses, and not the Lord, speak to them. They were afraid that they would die. "Listen" implies obedience to what they heard (cf. Deut. 5:27).

20:20 *Moses said to the people, "Do not be afraid. God has come to test you, so that the fear of God will be with you to keep you from sinning."*

Moses tried to quiet them; he said that God (the name *Elohim* is used in these verses probably because it was His majesty that was in the foreground, cf. also v. 1) had come to test them (cf. 15:25; 16:4; 17:2; Deut. 8:2), so that the fear of Him would be with them (or, according to others, seize them) to keep them from sinning. We must think then specifically of the sin that they had already committed repeatedly, viz. grumbling (see commentary on 19:9–13).

20:21 *The people remained at a distance, while Moses approached the thick darkness where God was.*

The people stayed at a distance (cf. also Deut. 5:30), but Moses approached the dark clouds (cf. 19:19; Deut. 4:11; 5:22; Ps. 18:9) where God was: a significant event, which shows us again Moses, the mediator (cf. Deut. 18:15f.).

9. The Book of the Covenant (20:22–23:33)

A. Laws concerning worship (20:22–26)

Here begins, in all probability, the so-called Book of the Covenant (see p. 2; Aalders, *Genesis*, pp. 20–21). At one time this book existed separately, as 24:4–8 indicates; it derives its name from 24:7. One reason for assuming that the Book of the Covenant begins with verse 22 is the use of the covenant name "LORD" (in contrast to v. 1). The contents of the book are of a strictly legal nature. The Lord gives regulations, which Moses must relate to the people. These regulations contain several allusions to the Ten Commandments, without any discernible pattern in their sequence. Concerning the distinction between "words" and "laws," see commentary on 21:1 and 24:3.

Adherents of the source hypothesis generally ascribe this book to E (Elohist; see Aalders, *Genesis*, pp. 6–7). It is then considered one of the oldest remnants of Israelite literature as well as the oldest Israelite law, dating from the time of the settling in Canaan and applicable to the more complex social conditions during the later period of the kings. E then has included this document in his work, which dates at the latest from the time of Solomon. There is no agreement as to the proper place of the Book of the Covenant. Kuenen believed that it had been ousted from its proper place by Deuteronomy, while others felt that it should be included in Joshua 24. But such views lack an adequate basis.

20:22, 23 *Then the LORD said to Moses, "Tell the Israelites this: 'You have seen for yourselves that I have spoken to you from heaven: Do not make any gods to be alongside me; do not make for yourselves gods of silver or gods of gold.'"*

If we assume that the Book of the Covenant begins here, then it does not have to have a direct connection with the preceding verses. The Lord addresses Moses, but what He says is intended for the Israelites (v. 22, cf. v. 19; 19:3). In verses 22–23 "you" is masculine plural. "Seen" must be taken in the general sense of "observed" (see commentary on v. 18). The

201

thought expressed is this: "You, the Israelites, know that I cannot be compared with gods made of silver and gold, since you have heard Me speak from heaven, invisible, terrible, with tremendous signs." Thus a connection exists between these verses and verses 18–21 in terms of content (cf. also ch. 19; Deut. 4:12, 15–19, 36). Verse 23 repeats the content of verses 3–5a. "Gold" and "silver" are mentioned specifically to make clear that even the most precious and valuable things could not be compared to Him who spoke from heaven. It does not mean that simple images made of wood or stone were permissible. The Israelites were not to have these idols of gold and silver, even if they would worship the Lord as well.

20:24 " 'Make an altar of earth for me and sacrifice on it your burnt offerings and fellowship offerings, your sheep and goats and your cattle. Wherever I cause my name to be honored, I will come to you and bless you.' "

Even the altar was to be as simple as possible, to avoid breaking the first and second commandments. "Earth": the Hebrew is *adama* (Gen. 1:25; cf. "Adam"), and refers here to the soil or clay, probably placed in a low mound in the shape of a bench or table. A distinction has been made between regular altars, which "lay persons" were allowed to erect, and the large altars in the sanctuaries; but this is not the intended contrast here (see below). Excavations at Shechem have brought to light an altar for burnt offerings made of clay tiles. "You" is once again masculine singular, as in verses 2–17 (the LXX has a plural here). "Burnt offerings" are offerings that are completely consumed by the fire (cf. Aalders on Gen. 8:20 in this series; Exod. 10:25; 18:12; cf. also the later regulations in Lev. 1; and Deut. 33:10; 1 Sam. 7:9; Ps. 51:19). "Fellowship offerings" is the plural form of a word that probably means "peace" or "unity," although others believe that it is derived from a word that means "to pay." (See ZPEB, "Sacrifice and Offerings," 6:194–210.) These offerings were brought by the Israelite ("you") before they were regulated by the law (cf. Lev. 3; 7:11–21, 28–34). Animals from the flock or from the herd were later prescribed for both these offerings. Although the word translated "sacrifice" can also mean "slaughter," the context points to its technical meaning "to sacrifice." Verse 24 complements verses 4–5a, the second commandment. (Cf. also Deut. 27:5; Josh. 8:30–31.)

The Lord promised His presence and blessing if this law was kept. "Wherever" (lit. "in every place," cf. KJV) could mean "in the whole place," since the definite article is used, in which case it would refer to "the whole place" of the sanctuary; those who accept this translation then assume that this is an emendation, since "wherever" was offensive because it would allow worship in many locations rather than only in the one central sanctuary. But this is not necessary, since in Hebrew a definite article can be used where we would use the indefinite article; or, the definite article could be used here because the word for "all" or "every" can also mean "totality." Similarly, in 1:22 the definite article is used, but the correct translation is "every boy" or "every son." The identical phrase is used in Genesis 20:13, where it is translated "everywhere." It is not necessary that "place" here mean "holy or sacred place"; the Lord will come to him who sacrifices and will bless him wherever He will cause His name to be remembered, and wherever He will bring to life or keep alive the memory of His revelation. It is therefore not necessary to take the statement "I will come to you and bless you" as the motivation for honoring the Lord's name. Rather, the recollection of the Lord's revelation comes first, and then the Lord will grant the one who sacrifices the experience of His nearness and blessing (an example of such a place is Bethel, Gen. 35:1–15).

This was the situation as it stood at this moment: an altar could be built, not in just any place, but in every place where the Lord would bring to mind His revelation as the God of the covenant. In this way there is indeed agreement between this verse and Deuteronomy 12:13. But apart from this agreement, the regulations in Deuteronomy 12 deal with the centralization of the worship, probably in one particular location, appointed by God (cf. e.g., Deut. 12:11). We must not forget that Samuel (1 Sam. 9:12–14) and Elijah sacrificed outside of the central sanctuary, or rather (at least where Samuel is concerned) in the absence of a central sanctuary (see van Gelderen on 1 Kings 3:2–3), as was the case here. "Come" is an anthropomorphism (cf. Gen. 11:5).[6]

20:25 *"'If you make an altar of stones for me, do not build it with dressed stones, for you will defile it if you use a tool on it.'"*

An altar made of stone was not forbidden, as long as it was made for the service of the Lord. But only rough, unhewn stones could be used by the Israelite ("you" is masculine singular), not dressed stones, because the use of a metal chisel or other tool (lit. "sword" or "knife") would desecrate or

---

[6]Concerning Exodus 20:24 in relation to Deuteronomy 12, see Hoedemaker, *De Mosaïsche oorsprong van de wetten in de boeken Exodus, Leviticus en Numeri*, pp. 190–191, 209–210. "The regulation in Exod. 20:24 fits the situation, it was given before the breaking of the Covenant and before the tabernacle was built" (p. 190). But Deuteronomy 12 was given thirty-eight years later, when Israel was about to enter Canaan. Cf. also Orr, *Het oude Testament beschouwd met betrekking tot de nieuwere critiek*, pp. 123ff.

profane the stone. Thus e.g., Joshua (Josh. 8:30–31) and Elijah (1 Kings 18:30–32) made altars of stones which, in accordance with this regulation, were not dressed; this was intended to prevent any breach of, and even the first step toward any breach of the second commandment. There is no basis for the idea that hitting or beating the stone with tools would drive away the deity that resided in the stone (Cf. van Gelderen on 1 Kings 6:7 and Isa. 65:3.) It is possible that the unhewn stones were considered clean or pure, as some suggest. (Cf. also Deut. 27:5; Judg. 6:20; 13:19; 1 Sam. 6:14.)

20:26 *"'And do not go up to my altar on steps, lest your nakedness be exposed on it.'"*

In order to understand this regulation we must remember that the Israelites did not wear pants, but only an undergarment and an outer garment, and sometimes a shirt (but cf. 28:42). Again the intent was to prevent the first step on the road toward the immorality in worship that was found among other nations. The building of steps leading toward the altar was prohibited, not merely going up these steps, although altars with steps dating from later times have been excavated in Palestine.

B. The rights of Hebrew servants (21:1–11)

After the regulations concerning worship the Lord first gave His attention to servants.[7] Moses was to show the people how to behave toward their neighbor in specific cases. Verses 1–11 deal with the obligations of a master toward his Hebrew servants.

21:1 *"These are the laws you are to set before them:"*

The Lord announced what follows as "laws" (cf. 15:23–25; van Gelderen on 1 Kings 2:3). The marginal notes of the Dutch Authorized Version say "namely, civil laws on the basis of which the judges were to judge God's people"; Israelite jurisprudence had to conform to these laws.

Verses 22–26 of the preceding chapter are not part of these laws; it is thus possible that sections such as 20:22–26 belong to the "words" (see

---

[7]The Hebrew *eved* is variously translated as "servant," "manservant" (KJV, ASV) or "slave" (RSV). The NIV uses both "slave" and "servant," depending on the context (cf. Exod. 21:20, 26). Similarly, *'amah* is translated "maidservant" (KJV, ASV) or "female slave" (RSV), while the NIV uses both. Neither "slave" nor "servant" is an adequate translation, since the position of the *eved* and *'amah* does not fully correspond to the position implied in either our term "slave" or our term "servant." The author uses "slave"; the translation follows the usage of the NIV. (tr.)

Introduction pp. 12–13 and commentary on 24:3). The question is whether all of 21:1–23:33 should be included in these "laws." I think 23:20–33 should not be included, since 23:21, 25, 32–33 deal with Israel's relationship with the Lord, and the entire section is of a promising and warning nature. But if we do not include 20:22–26 in these "laws," although these verses were most likely part of the Book of the Covenant, then we can go one step further and also exclude 23:13–19; but this is as far as I dare go. There is not sufficient reason for limiting the "laws" to 21:2–22:17, although 22:18ff. differs in style. The "laws" were thus those ordinances that regulated the relationship with one's neighbor and animals, which was the purpose of 23:10–12; 22:29–31; and 22:18–20. The poor, wild animals, the ox and donkey, the slave, and the alien are mentioned in 23:10–12; the firstborn of both man and beast and animals torn by wild beasts are mentioned in 22:29–31. In 22:18–20 those in authority were told how to deal with a sorceress, bestiality, and idolatry. This view has the advantage that the "laws" then formed a single unit, viz. 21:1–23:12, and it does full justice to the word "these" in verse 1. A corrolary is that the "words" (cf. 24:3) are then found in 20:22–26 and 23:13–33. The "words" then detail the Israelite's obligations toward God, although we must think of the entire law of the Ten Commandments, rather than of the first tablet only. The idea that on the basis of 20:1 "the words" refers to the Ten Commandments is contradicted by the fact that the Ten Commandments are a separate unit, inscribed on two stone tablets. But the expression in 20:1 does support my view that we must not try to carefully limit the term "the words" in the Book of the Covenant to an elaboration on the commandments of the first tablet of the Law. Moses was again the mediator between the Lord and the people (cf. commentary on 20:22). He had to present these laws to them, literally "put them before their face" (cf. 19:7).

21:2–6 *"If you buy a Hebrew servant, he is to serve you for six years. But in the seventh year, he shall go free, without paying anything. If he comes alone, he is to go free alone; but it he has a wife when he comes, she is to go with him. If his master gives him a wife and she bears him sons or daughters, the woman and her children shall belong to her master, and only the man shall go free.*

"But if the servant declares, 'I love my master and my wife and children and do not want to go free,' then his master must take him before the judges. He shall take him to the door or the doorpost and pierce his ear with an awl. Then he will be his servant for life."

The Hebrew uses two different conjunctions to introduce the various laws; the NIV and KJV obscure this distinction by translating both conjunctions with "if." One *(ki)* introduces the general principle or law, the other *('im)* the specific instances. Thus, "if" in verse 2 *(ki)* introduces the general law that Hebrew servants were to be set free after six years, while in verses 3, 4, 5 "if" *('im)* introduces statements concerning the application of the general law under specific circumstances. The RSV translates *ki* "when," *'im* "if." The Code of Hammurabi (cf. commentary on 20:1–17 and 21:7–11) uses the same formula.

The first law concerns the setting free of a Hebrew servant. "You" is again masculine singular (cf. 20:24). ("Hebrew," see commentary on 1:19. Cf. also 22:3; Lev. 25:39). Leviticus 25:44–46 deals with alien-born slaves. The setting free prescribed in our passage under consideration is not one of the privileges that are part of the sabbatical year (cf. 23:10–11; Lev. 25:1–7; Deut. 15:1–11; etc.), since the period of servitude was set at six years for each individual. Neither the servant nor his family was to pay anything for the servant's freedom (cf. also Deut. 15:12ff.; Jer. 34:14). "Go" is the same word used of the Israelites' going out of Egypt. (Cf. p. 1).

The specific instances are given in verses 3–6; the first instance is "if he comes alone" (lit. "with his body or person"), in which case he also was to leave alone. But if he came with a wife, then both he and his wife were to go free after six years. The third instance strikes us as somewhat odd, but we must not forget that the woman referred to here was the maidservant of the master, and in a sense his property. Thus Hagar was the property of Sarai, Zilpah of Leah, and Bilhah of Rachel (Gen. 16:2; 29:24, 29; 30:3–13), although these examples are not quite parallel to this situation. The Israelite of that time found nothing objectionable in this. The Lord did not abolish slavery in Israel, but He regulated it and made it more humane, while at the same time looking after the interests of the master, who would otherwise be at a disadvantage. Verse 7 and Leviticus 25:44 indicate that this situation concerned a non-Israelite woman. The Samaritan Pentateuch, the Peshitta, the Codex Vaticanus of the LXX, and the Vulgate read "shall belong to her master" instead of "shall belong to his master"; but the latter reading makes good sense, especially in view of my remarks above, and as the more difficult reading of the two, is to be preferred. Unfortunately we do not know whether many servants took advantage of the right established in verse 4. Furthermore, this law was not always observed (cf. Jer. 34). An indirect implication of verse 4 is that those who were born in slavery from non-Israelite female slaves remained slaves.

Verses 5 and 6 (cf. Deut. 15:16–17) give a fourth instance: the servant who loved his master, the wife his master had given him, and the children born of this marriage, and who declared ("truly said") that he did not want to go free. In that case the master was to honor his decision and take him "before the judges." The Hebrew literally says "before (or, to) God," referring to the one true God, rather than the house gods or the family god (which would be in direct contradiction to 20:2, 23). The LXX reads "to the judgment-seat of God." The NIV translation is possible, especially in the light of e.g., Psalm 82:1, 6, but the literal translation "before God" also makes good sense. "Before God," together with the following "to the door or the doorpost" could give the impression that a sanctuary of God was referred to, a place where He caused His name "to be honored" (20:24; Deut. 15:17 then would drop this requirement; a journey to the one central sanctuary would not be necessary). I believe this view to be acceptable, especially in view of 22:9. But the repetition of "must (shall) take him" seems to indicate a twofold action. "Door" or "doorpost" (cf. 12:7) can only refer to the house of the master and the servant since the servant was not God's, but his master's servant for life (*leolam,* into the remotest, hidden future; Lev. 25:39–46 is probably a later exception). This is symbolically represented by temporarily attaching the servant's ear (probably the right ear, as in the ceremonies in Lev. 8:23ff.; 14:14, 17; with the ear one hears, and thus obeys, someone else) to the door or doorpost of his master's house with an awl. If this is correct, then we must in all probability limit the phrase "take him before God" (lit. "cause to approach in the direction of God," cf. Gen. 48:10, 13; 1 Sam. 13:9; 14:34; 15:32; etc., which indicates that that which was caused to approach was usually already near) to be an action *in* God's house: otherwise there is no indication as to what was to be done with the slave in God's presence, which would be strange, although we could easily imagine that it would consist of a declaration under oath (see below). There would then be a gap in the text, although Hebrew, like other semitic languages such as Arabic, can jump from one action to a later action, i.e., the "taking before God" could actually have taken place *after* the "taking to the door or the doorpost." We do not know whether in later times a door or doorpost in the tabernacle or temple was used for the purpose described in these verses, but see the remark on Deuteronomy 15:17 above. If we translate "judges" rather than "God," then the door or doorpost would probably refer to the city gate. But what, then, would be the meaning of the piercing of the ear? I therefore adopt the following interpretation (with some hesitation and not necessarily rejecting the interpretation given above, which is entirely possible): the servant was to be "taken before God" to solemnly restate his declaration of verse 5, with God as his witness.[8] He whose ear was

---

[8]If we assume that the servant was taken to the sanctuary, then we must keep in mind that this provision was specific to the Book of the Covenant (cf. 20:22–26 and Deut. 15:17), and was not repeated prior to the entry into Canaan. See footnote on p. 203.

pierced was a servant of his master "forever." Psalm 40:6 uses a different verb (cf. Noordtzij, *Psalms;* cf. also Heb. 10:7 and Grosheide on those verses in this series): these two verses therefore do not allude to Exodus 21:5–6.

21:7–11 *"If a man sells his daughter as a servant, she is not to go free as menservants do. If she does not please the master who has selected her for himself, he must let her be redeemed. He has no right to sell her to foreigners, because he has broken faith with her. If he selects her for his son, he must grant her the rights of a daughter. If he marries another woman, he must not deprive the first one of her food, clothing and marital rights. If he does not provide her with these three things, she is to go free, without any payment of money."*

The second law regulated the setting free of a Hebrew female servant, to be understood here probably in the sense of "concubine" (cf. Gen. 20:17; 21:12; although the term cannot always be translated in this way, cf. 2:5; 20:10). The female servant whose duty was the performance of manual labor falls under the regulations for servants in general (cf. v. 7b; vv. 1–6; and the later regulations in Deut. 14:12, 17). The first "if" in verse 7 again introduces the general case, while in the following verses "if" introduces the specific instances (see commentary on vv. 2–6). "Go free," see commentary on verse 2. A father thus had, according to verse 7, the right to sell his daughter as a servant. But since this was done on the assumption that she would become the concubine of the buyer, it would be unfair if she were to be sent away after six years as was supposed to happen to Hebrew female servants. She had to stay. The first specific instance is given in verse 8. "Does not please," literally, "is evil, bad"; this could have a variety of causes, since it speaks here of not being pleasing in the eyes of her master: he could find her appearance or her character unattractive, etc., so that he would not take her, although he had selected her for himself.[9] But this would be a humiliating position for the servant. The Lord therefore stipulated that in that case the master was to give her relatives the opportunity to redeem her, to "buy her back" (cf. 13:13, 15). But he could not sell her to "foreigners" (see commentary on 2:22), since he had "broken faith with her," i.e., had reneged on his promise that she would be his concubine. It is also possible to translate "when he has broken faith with her." A second specific instance, which may (but does not have to) come out of

---

[9]The Hebrew reads "who has not chosen her." The verb means "to appoint, assign, designate as wife or concubine." Some manuscripts, e.g., LXX, Codex Vaticanus, Targum, and Vultage read, with a very minor change, "for him (self)" *(lo)* instead of "not" *(lo')*. This is probably the correct reading; if the Hebrew reading referred to the choosing of a bride for "his son" (cf. v. 9) both "not" *(lo')* and "for himself" *(lo)* would be required.

the first one is given in verse 9: the master "selects her for his son," in which case she was to be granted the rights of a daughter.

Verse 10 gives a third specific instance: the master later decided to take another woman besides the first one; in that case the rights of the first woman were not to be abrogated. Mentioned are specifically clothing, marital rights, and food (lit. "meat"; the Israelite referred to here was wealthy and could thus afford to eat meat daily; cf. Job 31:31. We can also think of "meat" as referring to eating during feasts, cf. 1 Sam. 1:5, although Hanna and Peninnah were not concubines). From our perspective we do not envy the Hebrew female servants; but we must not forget that the Lord intervened here with regulations designed to eliminate excesses and to gradually restore the general validity of the monogamous marriage in Israel.

The fourth specific instance (v. 11) gave her the right to go free (probably in the seventh year) without any payment of money (e.g., to reimburse the master for his initial investment) if the three things mentioned in verse 10 were not provided.

The Code of Hammurabi says (117): "If an obligation came due against a seignior and he sold (the services of) his wife, his son, or his daughter, or he has been bound over to service, they shall work (in) the house of their purchaser or obligee for three years, with their freedom reestablished in the fourth year."[10]

C. Laws concerning the life of the neighbor (21:12–36)

Verses 12–36 deal with the life of the neighbor (which was protected, but was also forfeited in certain cases), the life of his property (bull, etc.), and the life of male and female servants.

21:12–14 *"Anyone who strikes a man and kills him shall surely be put to death. However, if he does not do it intentionally, but God lets it happen, he is to flee to a place I will designate. But if a man schemes and kills another man deliberately, take him from my altar and put him to death."*

---

[10]Quotations from the Code of Hammurabi are from Meek's translation in *Ancient Near Eastern Texts,* James B. Pritchard, ed. (Princeton, 1950). Cf. also Jirku, *Altorientalischer Kommentar zum Alten Testament* (Leipzig-Erlangen, 1923), pp. 93ff., and Wilhelm Eilers, *Die Gesetzstelle Chammurabis (Gesetz und die Wende des dritten vorchristlichen Jahrtausends)* (J. C. Hinrich'sche Buchandlung, Leipzig, 1932). See also M. David, "De Codex Hammoerabi en zijn verhouding tot de wetsbepaling in Exodus," *Tijdschrift voor Rechtsgeschiedenis,* 1939, pp. 73ff., and *Oudtestamentische Studien,* VII, 1950, pp. 149–178. David concludes that Exodus 21ff. and the Code of Hammurabi are independent from one another. M. A. Beek, *Aan Babylons stromen* (Amsterdam, 1950), pp. 97–101, places various laws from Exodus and from the Code of Hammurabi side by side for comparison.

Verse 12 speaks of striking someone so that the individual dies; this may refer only to a case where the individual dies immediately (cf. v. 21). Otherwise this law would apply to any inflicting of bodily harm that would result in death. The offender was "surely" to be put to death. But not all cases were alike; in verse 13 the Lord (20:22) made provision for someone who did not intend to kill his neighbor, but who accidentally inflicted an injury that resulted in death. "God lets it happen"; we might call it "happenstance." The Lord promised to designate a place where this man could go; this was a promise of the "cities of refuge" (cf. Num. 35:9–34; Deut. 4:41–43; 19:1–13; Josh. 20:1–9). Sometimes a distinction is made between this law and the law concerning the cities of refuge, since verse 14 mentions the altar as the place of refuge. Verse 13b reads literally "a place which I will designate for you" (cf. KJV), "you" again masculine singular as in the Decalogue. Unintentional injury that resulted in death thus did not carry the death penalty, but flight was necessary because of blood revenge (see ZPEB, "Cities of Refuge," 1:869–871). There were thus exceptions to the rule of Genesis 9:6; Leviticus 24:17; etc., which shows again the merciful standpoint of the Lawgiver in this Book of the Covenant. We must not build a theory on the interchangeable use of "God" and "I," which is also found elsewhere, as Eerdmans does. He assumes that "God" refers to one of the gods, without specifying which one, while "I" refers to the God of Israel (Eerdmans, *De Godsdienst van Israel,* 1930, I, p. 20). "If" (v. 14) is the same word used in verses 2, 7 (see commentary on vv. 2–6). "Schemes," see commentary on 18:11; if someone "with guile" (KJV) committed premeditated murder (cf. Num. 35:16f.; Deut. 19:11) and then fled to the altar as a place of refuge, he was to be taken away from the altar and put to death (again, masculine singular; cf. 1 Kings 2:28–34). Verse 12 gives the general rule, verse 13 the exception, while verse 14 is designed to prevent abuse of the exception. The Code of Hammurabi prescribed a fine for unpremeditated murder.

21:15 *"Anyone who attacks his father or his mother must be put to death."*

A new case: physical abuse of father or mother by their child. Here (in contrast to v. 12) the death penalty was required for the mere striking of the parent, which shows how important Israel's lawgiver considered respect for the parents. The Code of Hammurabi states that if a son struck his father, his hand was to be cut off (cf. 20:12; Deut. 21:18–21).

21:16 *"Anyone who kidnaps another and either sells him or still has him when he is caught must be put to death."*

The LXX reverses the sequence of verses 16 and 17. Verse 16 imposes the death penalty for kidnapping. This agrees with the Code of Hammurabi (14): "If a seignior has stolen the young son of a(nother) seignior, he shall be put to death." Jirku explains the fact that this law was restricted to young persons because adults were not kidnapped in Babylon. After "another" the LXX adds: "of the sons of Israel and having done him violence," but this addition can be explained on the basis of Deuteronomy 24:7. The neighbor's liberty (the Hebrew does not limit the "neighbor" to the fellow Israelite) was thus protected, as well as his life. The motive for such a crime was probably primarily the pursuit of gain. It is therefore striking to read that at the beginning of Israel's existence as an independent nation the Lord imposed the death penalty in its absolute form for this crime (the Hebrew reads "shall surely be put to death," cf. KJV). Cf. Amos 1:9.

21:17 *"Anyone who curses his father or mother must be put to death."*

The transposition of verses 16 and 17 in the LXX is understandable, since verses 15 and 17 are closely related (but cf. Hoedemaker, *Mosaïsche oorsprong,* p. 252). A serious transgression of the fifth commandment was also punishable by death. "Curses" (from a root that means "being small, insignificant") is the direct opposite of "honor" (see commentary on 20:12 and the references cited there; also Deut. 27:16). A Sumerian law states that in the case of a similar offense against the father, the father was to sell his son as a slave; if the offense was against the mother the son was to be expelled from the house.

21:18, 19 *"If men quarrel and one hits the other with a stone or with his fist and he does not die but is confined to bed, the one who struck the blow will not be held responsible if the other gets up and walks around outside with his staff; however, he must pay the injured man for the loss of his time and see that he is completely healed."*

"If" is the same word used in verses 2, 7, 14 (see commentary on verses 2–6). "Quarreling" refers to a verbal argument. The word "fist" (also used in Isa. 58:4) is translated by some as "clod, lump of earth" or "stone from the ground," by others as the tool with which the clods were pried loose, i.e., a shovel, or a small pick, or also as "cudgel" or "stick." The meaning of the word is uncertain. We assume that the translators of the LXX, who rendered it "fist," were in the best position to know the original meaning of the word. The Code of Hammurabi states that if someone injured another party in a quarrel, he had to swear that the injury was not intentional, and he had to pay the doctor's fee. The parallels between these verses and the Code of Hammurabi are marked, although the question of intentionality is not raised in these verses, and the Book of the Covenant is more flexible. "If" (v. 19) is the same word used in verses 3, 4, 5, 8, 9, 10, 11 (see commentary on vv. 2–6). Should the injured person die after getting up and walking around outside, then the one who hit him was not liable; the injured person perhaps got out of bed too soon. But should he die in bed, before he was able to walk outside, then verse 12 was of course applicable. There are insufficient grounds to place verses 23–25 immediately after verse 19.

21:20, 21 *"If a man beats his male or female slave with a rod and the slave dies as a direct result, he must be punished, but he is not to be punished if the slave gets up after a day or two, since the slave is his property."*

"If" is the same word as in verses 2, 7, 14, 18 (see commentary on vv. 2–6). The life of the slave ("male slave" and "female slave" are the same Hebrew words translated "servant" in vv. 1–11 and "manservant" and "maidservant" vv. 26ff. See translator's note on 21:1) is also protected, another example of the humane perspective of Israel's lawgiver. Striking is the distinction made between the case where the slave dies "as a direct result" (lit. "under his hand"), and the case where the slave "gets up after a day or two" (lit. "continues for a day or two") and then dies. In the former situation the master would be punished (lit. "he—i.e., the slave—shall be avenged"; the Samaritan Pentateuch undoubtedly renders the meaning of this expression accurately: "he shall surely be put to death," although others think of a fine or punishment imposed by a judge); in the latter case he would not be avenged (the Samaritan Pentateuch again applies this to the master: "he shall not be put to death").

In the Roman republic a citizen could kill his slave with impunity. "Since the slave is his property" (lit. "for he is his money"), i.e., he had been paid for with silver or money. Physical punishment was allowed, but it was not to be too severe. The marginal notes of the Dutch Authorized Version add, "That is, he has bought him with his money, and thus he is his property, wherefore it is reasonable to assume that he merely wanted to punish, and not to kill him." The loss of his slave was sufficient punishment for the master. "If" (v. 21) introduces the specific instance (see commentary on vv. 2–6).

21:22–25 *"If men who are fighting hit a pregnant woman and she gives birth prematurely but there is no serious injury, the offender must be fined whatever the* *woman's husband demands and the court allows. But if there is serious injury, you are to take life for life, eye for eye, tooth for tooth, hand for hand, foot for foot, burn for burn, wound for wound, bruise for bruise.''*

"If'' (v. 22) again introduces the general, "if'' (v. 23) the specific instance (see commentary on vv. 2–6). "Fighting,'' see commentary on 2:13. "Hit,'' cf. 8:2 (KJV) and 21:35. The Lord even protected the unborn life. If the miscarriage or premature birth was caused accidentally, and the mother survived and recuperated fully, then the woman's husband had the right to impose a fine on the offender or offenders. But this was to be determined by "the court'' (the word used here is somewhat unusual, and is best derived from a verb meaning "to judge, to render a judicial verdict,'' and hence literally "through the judges''). However, if there was serious injury (probably a miscarriage with fatal consequences for the woman), then the well-known law of retribution applied: "take life for life, eye for eye, tooth for tooth,'' etc. This was thus a principle to be used in jurisprudence, since the monetary fine was also to be imposed by the judges (Cf. Lev. 24:20; Deut. 19:21; Matt. 5:38). The assumption that this rule was implemented literally only when the injured party insisted is probably correct (cf. v. 30). "Wound'' and "bruise,'' cf. Genesis 4:23 and Isaiah 1:6. The Code of Hammurabi specifies that he who caused someone else's daughter to have a miscarriage had to pay a fine; if the woman died, the offender's daughter was to be put to death. The rule "an eye for an eye'' is also found in the Code of Hammurabi (see my commentary on Lev. 24:17–22). It is possible that verses 22–25 have in mind a woman who tried to separate the fighting men (cf. Deut. 25:11).

21:26, 27 *"If a man hits a manservant or maidservant in the eye and destroys it, he must let the servant go free to compensate for the eye. And if he knocks out the tooth of a manservant or maidservant, he must let the servant go free to compensate for the tooth.''*

Another law for the protection of slaves. "If'' (v. 26) introduces the general rule, "if'' (v. 27) the special case (see commentary on vv. 2–6). "Let go free' is also used a number of times in connection with Pharaoh and Israel (see p. 2). The destruction of an eye involved in any case the blinding of the servant, as the LXX translates. The setting free then compensated for the blinding; but even the knocking out of a tooth entitled the servant to be set free. The Code of Hammurabi specified in such cases only the payment of a fine.

21:28–32 *"If a bull gores a man or a woman to death, the bull must be stoned to death, and its meat must not be eaten. But the owner of the bull will not be held responsible. If, however, the bull had had the habit of goring and the owner has been warned but has not kept it penned up and it kills a man or woman, the bull must be stoned and the owner also must be put to death. However, if payment is demanded of him, he may redeem his life by paying whatever is demanded. This law also applies if the bull gores a son or daughter. If the bull gores a male or female slave, the owner must pay thirty shekels of silver to the master of the slave, and the bull must be stoned.*

"If" (v. 28) introduces the general rule, "if" (vv. 29–32) the special case (see commentary on vv. 2–6). Verse 28 is a curious law, based on the value of human life (cf. Gen. 9:5). The bull was to be stoned (cf. 19:13), and its meat was not to be eaten (because it was unclean, cf. Num. 35:33f.), even though the owner was not culpable and did not have to be punished; this indicates how high a value the Lord places on human life. But at the same time the idea of punishment for the bull is expressed here. Even after the Middle Ages in Europe, animals that caused human death were put to death. But the owner did not always get off free: if the bull had the habit of goring and the owner had been explicitly warned, but had failed to keep it under guard or penned up, then the owner would lose his own life. But this regulation was immediately relaxed: he was able to redeem his life by means of a payment of money (cf. 30:12; Ps. 49:8, etc.). The deciding factor was apparently whether or not the relatives of the victim were satisfied with the payment of a fine (cf. v. 22). Verses 30 and 32 are exceptions to a regulation that was otherwise strictly upheld (cf. Num. 35:31f.). And this law (see commentary on v. 1) also applied when the bull gored and killed a son or daughter rather than an adult. The Code of Hammurabi does not mention the killing of the bull, but it does speak of the payment of a fine by the owner, when the owner knew that the bull had a habit of goring. The Code of Hammurabi also agrees with verse 32, again with the exception of the stoning of the bull. The value of a slave was thus, according to verse 32, thirty shekels of silver. This is what Judas received for betraying Jesus! (Cf. Matt. 26:15 in connection with Zech. 11:12; cf. also Lev. 27:3f.)

21:33–36 *"If a man uncovers a pit or digs one and fails to cover it and an ox or a donkey falls into it, the owner of the pit must pay for the loss; he must pay its owner, and the dead animal will be his.*

"If a man's bull injures the bull of another and it dies, they are to sell the live one and divide both the money and the dead animal equally. However, if it was

known that the bull had the habit of goring, yet the owner did not keep it penned up, the owner must pay, animal for animal, and the dead animal will be his."

This section concludes with regulations concerning the life of the neighbor's livestock. "If" in verses 33–36 is the same word used in verse 2 (see commentary on vv. 2–6). If a pit was dug, or an existing pit opened up and not covered again, a neighbor's ox or donkey might fall in and die, or have to be destroyed. The owner of the pit was to make restitution to the owner of the animal, but (notice how carefully the Lord regulates everything) the dead animal became the property of the owner of the pit; this is important, because the hide was valuable (cf. also Deut. 14:21). The regulations in verses 35 and 36 are clear and equitable. The beginning of verse 36 reads literally "or it was known . . . ," but since verse 36 presents a slightly different case the translation "However, if it was known . . ." is more appropriate. It has been suggested that the offending bull had to be given instead of the dead bull; there would then not be any payment involved, since the goring bull would have been a stronger bull (and in that sense better) than the dead bull. But it is doubtful that the owner who had suffered loss would be pleased to receive a bull that had the habit of goring. Besides, the text does not say this. An old Sumerian law of the kingdom Eshnunna (20th-century B.C.) states "If a bull gores the bull (of another man), so that it dies, then both owners shall divide (among them) the value of the living and of the dead bull" (see M. David, *Een nieuw-ontdekte Babylonische wet uit de tijd vóór Hammurabi*, Leiden, 1949, pp. 24–25).

D. *Regulations concerning property* (22:1–17)

This section of the Book of the Covenant deals with the neighbor's property. The words used in verses 16–17 indicate that these verses belong in this section.

22:1–4 *"If a man steals an ox or a sheep and slaughters it or sells it, he must pay back five head of cattle for the ox and four sheep for the sheep.*

"If a thief is caught breaking in and is struck so that he dies, the defender is not guilty of bloodshed; but if it happens after sunrise, he is guilty of bloodshed.

"A thief must certainly make restitution, but if he has nothing, he must be sold to pay for his theft.

"If the stolen animal is found alive in his possession—whether ox or donkey or sheep—he must pay back double."

In the Hebrew text our verse 1 is 21:37, and chapter 22 has only thirty verses. "If," see commentary on 21:2–6. "Ox" (the same word is also translated "bull," cf. e.g. 21:28–36) see commentary on 20:17; 21:28f.

"Sheep," cf. 12:3–5; 13:13. "Pay back," see commentary on 21:34: 2 Samuel 12:6; Luke 19:8. Note that the Book of the Covenant does not demand a prison sentence for theft, only liberal restitution (but cf. v. 3b). In the Code of Hammurabi the punishment was much more severe; thirty-fold restitution if the animal belonged to a god or to the court, tenfold restitution if it belonged to a serf; if the thief did not have anything, he was to be put to death. "If a seignior stole either an ox or a sheep or an ass or a pig or a boat, if it belonged to the church (or) if it belonged to the state, he shall make thirtyfold restitution; if it belonged to a private citizen, he shall make good tenfold. If the thief does not have sufficient to make restitution, he shall be put to death" (*Ancient Near Eastern Texts,* p. 166). The Hittite laws spoke of fifteen-fold restitution. Later the Romans required fourfold restitution if the thief was caught in the act. Today the Bedouins also require fourfold restitution for the theft of an animal. "If" in verses 2, 3, 4, is *'im* (see commentary on 21:2–6). "The defender" (v. 2) is a free but correct interpretation of the Hebrew, which reads simply "he." The defender was not guilty of "bloodshed": the Hebrew word is the plural of "blood" which "denotes *blood that is shed,* when it appears as blood-stains (Isa. 1:15) or as bloodmarks (so evidently in Isa. 9:4). But since bloodstains or bloodmarks, as a rule, suggest bloodshed in murder . . . (it) acquired . . . simply the sense of *bloody deed,* and especially of *blood-guiltiness.*[11] (Verse 2, cf. Matt. 24:43.)

"Breaking in," literally "by the digging through," i.e. of a wall. This method is still used in Syria and is relatively easy where walls are made of clay. Others think of breaking into the stable or sheep pen (cf. John 10:1, 10). The meaning of verse 3 is that if the defender caught the thief in the act during daylight, and killed him, he was guilty of bloodshed. The thief was to make restitution, and if he did not have the resources to make the required payment, he was to be "sold to pay for his theft" (the Hebrew reads "sold for his theft"), so that the requirement of verse 1 could be fulfilled. It is also possible that verse 3b indicates what was to be done specifically in the case of a thief caught in the act during broad daylight. These provisions also gave the thief the opportunity to repent. In the Code of Hammurabi, breaking in carried the death penalty. The Athenian law and the Roman law of the Twelve Tables *(lex duodecim tabularum)* also did not consider the killing of an intruder at night punishable. Verse 4 presents a separate case: if a stolen animal was recovered double restitution was sufficient.

---

[11]Gesenius-Kautzsch, *Hebrew Grammar* (Oxford, 1963), p. 400.

22:5 *"If a man grazes his livestock in a field or vineyard and lets them stray and they graze in another man's field, he must make restitution from the best of his own field or vineyard."*

"If" *(ki)*, see commentary on 21:2–6. "Restitution," see commentary on 21:34. The LXX adds to this verse and reads ". . . graze in another man's field, he shall make restitution from his own field, according to what it produces; and if they shall have grazed the whole field, he must make restitution. . . ." Some read "burn" rather than "graze," which is possible, but requires a minor change in the Hebrew, and is unnecessary. Both Hammurabi and the Hittite law prescribed restitution in a case like this. "From the best," perhaps "because . . . after the destruction of the entire field its quality could no longer be determined"[12]; this explanation is suggested by the addition in the LXX, but is not explicitly stated in the Hebrew text. Another explanation is that the best was to be given, since livestock also seeks out the best.

22:6 *"If a fire breaks out and spreads into thornbushes so that it burns shocks of grain or standing grain or the whole field, the one who started the fire must make restitution."*

"If" *(ki)* see commentary on 21:2–6. "Thornbushes" is a general name for all thorny plants; but here it refers to weeds that grew in the cultivated fields rather than to bushes that grew wild everywhere. The word may also refer to the very common thirstle *Carthamus glaucus* (wild safflower), which often forms a dense blue-green carpet from which the violet blooms stick up. Thorns and thistles were the great enemies of the farmer in Palestine. They frequently grew as tall as a man, and had a deep and widespread root system, which made it virtually impossible to get rid of them; they also produced seeds in great quantities. As a result the plants were usually cut off at ground level, while the roots were left in the soil. The plants were then gathered and burned; they had no other use, since they crackled a great deal, but gave off little heat when they burned. If adequate precautions were not taken when burning these thistles, the fire could easily spread to adjacent properties. During the harvest it could also happen that the harvested grain was put in piles, while the dry thorns and thistles were still standing in the fields, so that carelessness with fire could ignite the dry plants and thus also destroy the grain. The text determines

---

[12]Daube, "Zur Fruhtalmudischen Rechtspraxis," *Zeitschrift fur die alttestamentlichen Wissenschaft*, 1932, p. 150.

liability in cases like this.[13] Others think of damage to the thorn hedges that surrounded a field or vineyard, caused by carelessness (cf. Isa. 5:5).

"Shocks of grain" were piles of harvested grain, while "standing grain" was grain that was still in the field. The person who started the fire could be either the owner of an adjacent field, or someone else. "Breaks out" in this case also means "breaks out of its boundaries," "spreads into," literally "finds." The burning of the whole field refers to the temporarily rendering useless of the soil.

These and other regulations make it clear that the Book of the Covenant made provisions also for the time when Israel would live in Canaan; Sinai was not their final destination.

22:7–9 *"If a man gives his neighbor silver or goods for safekeeping and they are stolen from the neighbor's house, the thief, if he is caught, must pay back double. But if the thief is not found, the owner of the house must appear before the judges to determine whether he has laid his hands on the other man's property. In all cases of illegal possession of an ox, a donkey, a sheep, a garment, or any other lost property about which somebody says, 'This is mine,' both parties are to bring their cases before the judges. The one whom the judges declare guilty must pay back double to his neighbor.''*

"If" (v. 7a: *ki;* vv. 7b, 8: *'im*): see commentary on 21:2–6. The stipulation in verse 7 is clear: the thief was to pay double (see commentary on vv. 1–4). The issue was whether or not the thief could be found, because a problem arose when he could not be found. In that case the owner of the house was to appear before the "judges" (the Hebrew word means literally "gods" or "God"; see commentary on 21:6). After long hesitation I prefer the translation "judges" rather than "God" in verses 8–9. The situation was different in 21:6, where I preferred "God" over "judges." The main reason for translating "judges" is that in verse 9b "declare" is a plural in Hebrew (the Samaritan Pentateuch has a singular, but the reading is doubtful). But Hebrew on occasion does use a plural predicate even if the translation requires "God" rather than "gods" (cf. Gen. 20:13; 31:53; 35:7), so that this is not a conclusive argument. Since we do not know how else the determination of guilt was to be made (although it could have been done by casting lots, cf. Josh. 7; 1 Sam. 14:40f.; but even in that case it would have involved a court of law) we must probably think here of a judicial determination. Others explain the plural by the fact that God's decision was mediated by men. In my opinion the idea of a divine judgment is also possible, in which case we must, of

---

[13]The above data were kindly provided by Mr. F. J. Bruyel.

course, translate "God" (thus e.g. the LXX, Ostervald, Böhl, ASV). Regardless of whether we translate "God" or "judges" in verse 8, the idea here is probably that the person under suspicion was to swear to his innocence (cf. Lev. 6:2–5); the LXX and the Vulgate read ". . . must appear before the judges, and must swear that he has not laid his hands on the other man's property." Verse 9 vividly describes the situation where the owner of an ox, a donkey, a sheep, a garment, or any other property that is missing, believes that he recognizes it and exclaims "this is it!" Others interpret it to mean "that it is this (i.e. a criminal offense)." The judge was to decide in such a case (cf. 1 Kings 3:16–28, which, incidentally, supports the translation "judges"). The one declared guilty was to make double restitution; this applies thus also to someone who made a false accusation. Köhler feels that verse 9a refers to contested ownership, rather than illegal possession, because the word that is translated "illegal possession" (KJV: "trespass") is derived from a verb that means "to stand up against."[14] This view deserves serious consideration. The Code of Hammurabi also dealt with possessions entrusted for safekeeping, and required double restitution as well. In case of a break-in or destruction of property the person to whom the possessions were entrusted was to make full restitution. The owner of the house was to search for the lost property and take it away from the thief. Someone who made a false accusation was also to make double restitution.

22:10–13 *"If a man gives a donkey, an ox, a sheep or any other animal to his neighbor for safekeeping and it dies or is injured or is taken away while no one is looking, the issue between them will be settled by the taking of an oath before the* LORD *that the neighbor did not lay hands on the other person's property. The owner is to accept this, and no restitution is required. But if the animal was stolen from the neighbor, he must make restitution to the owner. If it was torn to pieces by a wild animal, he shall bring in the remains as evidence and he will not be required to pay for the torn animal."*

These verses deal with the giving in safekeeping of an animal; since verses 14–15 concern the loaning of animals, these verses refer to the entrusting of animals to a shepherd in the service of the owner. "If" (v. 10: *ki;* vv. 12–13: *'im*), see commentary on 21:2–6. Verse 11 also requires the "oath of cleansing," see commentary on verse 8. It is noteworthy that "Lord" rather than "God" is used here. "While no one is looking" (v. 10): if someone saw it, then his witness would be accepted. The owner had to accept the oath, and no restitution was required. Verses 10–11 deal

---

[14]*Zeitschrift für die alttestamentlichen Wissenschaft,* Neue Folge, 1928, pp. 213f.

with a case of death that could not have been prevented, or an accident that injured the animal, or a case where the animal was carried away by raiders or wild animals (cf. 1 Chron. 5:21; 2 Chron. 14:15; Job 1:15, 17). But verse 12 presents the situation where a thief stole the animal; in that case the shepherd had to make restitution to the owner, since he could have prevented the theft by being more alert. Verse 13, cf. Amos 3:12; Genesis 31:39. The Code of Hammurabi required that if an ox or lamb that had been entrusted to someone's care was lost, restitution had to be made on the basis of an ox for an ox and a lamb for a lamb. If an accident happened in the stable, or a lion killed the animal, then the shepherd was to cleanse himself before the deity, but the owner of the stable was to carry the loss. But if the damage in the stable was the shepherd's fault, then he was to reimburse the owner for the oxen and sheep. The Hittite and Sumerian laws contained similar provisions. The issue was whether or not the shepherd was culpable. Concerning the good shepherd, cf. 1 Samuel 17:34–37; John 10:11–18.

22:14, 15 *"If a man borrows an animal from his neighbor and it is injured or dies while the owner is not present, he must make restitution. But if the owner is with the animal, the borrower will not have to pay. If the animal was hired, the money paid for the hire covers the loss.*

"If" (v. 14: *ki;* v. 15: *'im*) see commentary on 21:2–6. In the case of a borrowed animal a distinction was made as to whether the fatal injury or dying (also due to mistreatment) occurred while the owner was present or not; only in the latter case was the borrower to make restitution (v. 14). But if the animal were hired, and it died while the owner was present, the owner was to receive the money paid for the hire, as expressed in verse 15b, which has been translated in a number of ways. The Dutch Leyden Version says "Then the damages are included in the rental fee," which is similar to our translation. The margin of the Dutch Authorized Version states "The meaning is: he who has hired it shall go free by paying the agreed-upon fee." The owner took this risk, so that restitution was not necessary. Böhl translates "If he is a hireling, then it shall be taken out of his wages"; Buber-Rosenzweig and others agree with this. But the Hebrew reads literally "if it was hired," and it is most natural to refer this back to the animal. Hammurabi succinctly stated that if someone "hired an ox or an ass and a lion has killed it in the open, (the loss) shall be its owner's" (244).

22:16, 17 *"If a man seduces a virgin who is not pledged to be married and sleeps with her, he must pay the bride-price, and she shall be his wife. If her father absolutely refuses to give her to him, he must still pay the bride-price for virgins."*

This provision can also be considered part of the laws concerning the neighbor's property. The virgin who was not pledged to be married is here considered to be the property of the father; the seducer had to marry her (v. 16). If the father absolutely refused to give her to the seducer, then the latter had to give money to the father, the *mohar* or dowry for a virgin. "If" (v. 16: *ki;* v. 17: *'im*), see commentary on 21:2–6. If the virgin was pledged to be married, then the seducer had violated a woman who was considered to be his neighbor's wife. (Cf. also, Deut. 22:23–29.) The price, according to Deuteronomy 22:29, was fifty shekels of silver. "He must pay the bride-price," literally "he must weigh silver according to the bride-price."

An ancient Assyrian law stipulated that the seducer had to pay triple the bride-price to the father; and even then the father could give his daughter to whomever he wanted. A Sumerian law imposed the death sentence in a case like this.

E. *Regulations concerning three abominable sins* (22:18–20)

22:18–20 *"Do not allow a sorceress to live.*
"Anyone who has sexual relations with an animal must be put to death."
"Whoever sacrifices to any god other than the LORD must be destroyed."

See commentary on 21:1. Verse 18, see commentary on 7:11. Sorcery was common in Mesopotamia. The LXX has a masculine plural, rather than the Hebrew masculine singular. There may be significance in the fact that a sorceress was mentioned (cf. the witch of Endor, 1 Sam. 28). In the Code of Hammurabi (2) anyone accused of sorcery had to subject himself to a divine judgment; if he drowned, the accuser got the house of the accused; if he survived the accuser was put to death. Other ancient Near Eastern laws also imposed a penalty for sorcery. But Heinisch points out that in Mesopotamia sorcerers and witches were opposed because they caused harm to people, while in Israel they were threatened with death because they served another god. In Mesopotamia the motivation was thus materialistic, but in Israel it was religious, because Israel's faith in the Lord was to be kept pure. In the ancient Near Eastern world Israel was in danger of falling into this sin; the Lord therefore required the death penalty. I must admit that I cannot find any connection between verse 18 and the preceding section. The form is also different, as especially Jirku and Alt, who distinguished several formulas (the "if" formula, the "thou shalt" formula, etc.), have stressed. Jirku concludes that the Pentateuch therefore contains remnants of a number of different laws, each with their own characteristic formula: one law in which each provision began with "if," another that used the "thou shalt" formula, etc.[15] But this is difficult to prove; there is no reason to assume that the Lord was tied to one particular formula. More important is that these three verses belong together in terms of their content; they deal with three abominable sins. The woman especially would lend herself to sorcery (cf. Ezek. 13:18 and Noordtzij on that verse in this commentary series; 1 Sam. 28:7; but cf. Deut. 18:10; 2 Chron. 33:6; Jer. 27:9; Mal. 3:5); on the other hand, the feminine form used here could indicate the class as a whole (a well-known example is the Hebrew title of Ecclesiastes, *kohelet*, which is a feminine word, but indicates an office or completeness, "preacher"). The severe penalty for the sin of sorcery was in line with the Decalogue. Witch hunts, especially those that took place during the Middle Ages, were a misapplication of this law, which belongs to the laws intended for Israel only. "Do not allow to live" means, according to some, "to outlaw," while Keil believes that it may indicate that only the sorceress who did not give up sorcery after having been told to do so was to be put to death. It is not necessary to try to find any other meaning here than that the Israelite was told to put a sorceress to death; the wording ("do not allow to live" rather than "put to death") may have been chosen for the sake of variation.

Sexual intercourse with an animal (v. 19) was the second abomination of which the inhabitants of Canaan were guilty (Lev. 18:23; a Ugaritic text also points in the same direction), and which was also found among other nations, notably among the Egyptians. And the third abomination was bringing sacrifices to another god (cf. the first commandment). The offender was to be destroyed; the NIV margin adds: "The Hebrew term refers to the irrevocable giving over of things or persons to the Lord, often by totally destroying them."

These three sins would affect Israel's holiness, and would bring Israel down to the same level as the pagan nations; the authorities were to guard against this. The penalties were so severe because the existence of Israel as the Lord's people was at stake. Verse 18, cf. Deuteronomy 18:10–11. Verse 19, cf. Leviticus 18:23; 20:15 and my note on those verses in this series; Deuteronomy 27:21. Verse 20, cf. Leviticus 27:29; Deuteronomy 13:13f.; 17:2–5.

F. *Regulations concerning those in need* (22:21–27)

These regulations show God's goodness (cf. v. 27b). The alien, the widow and orphan, and the poor are protected (cf. Ps. 146:7–9). Although

---

[15] A. Jirku, *Das weltliche Recht im Alten Testament* (Gütersloh, 1927). See Albrecht Alt, *Die Ursprünge des Israelitischen Rechts* (Leipzig, 1934).

these regulations were to be implemented on the wilderness journey, they were given especially in view of the imminent settling in Canaan (cf. v. 21b). Unfortunately Israel did not always keep them (cf. Amos 2:8; 4:1; etc.). But the reproval voiced by the prophets shows that the Lord had never relaxed these regulations. And we must take them into account as well, different as our circumstances may be.

22:21 *"Do not mistreat an alien or oppress him, for you were aliens in Egypt."*

"Alien" *(gēr),* see commentary on 2:20–22; 12:45–49; 20:10. In addition, "alien" can also refer to someone who was not a member of one's own tribe (cf. Judg. 17:7–9; 19:16). Pedersen is of the opinion that the *gērim* ("aliens") whom the laws had in mind were the conquered inhabitants of Canaan who had almost, but not quite, adapted themselves to Israel. As a class they then occupied a position between the free Israelites citizens and the slaves. But it would then follow that this law was given when Israel already lived in Canaan and had established close ties with those they had allowed to live, which is not correct. Furthermore, we get a different impression of the position of e.g. the Gibeonites. In our opinion the *gēr* was someone who did not belong to the nation or to the tribe, but neither to those nations that the Lord commanded Israel to destroy. The protection of the *gēr* in Israel was commanded by Israel's God Himself. The Israelites could not mistreat or oppress the alien, since they once were in the same position in Egypt, and they knew from their own bitter experience how terrible it was to be oppressed in a foreign land. The reason given was intended to make implementation of this law a matter of course for them, and did not mean that otherwise the Lord would not have protected the alien. Cf. also 23:9; Leviticus 19:33–34.

22:22–24 *"Do not take advantage of a widow or an orphan. If you do and they cry out to me, I will certainly hear their cry. My anger will be aroused, and I will kill you with the sword; your wives will become widows and your children fatherless."*

It is not impossible that "orphan" refers in the first place to a fatherless child (cf. Job. 24:9; Lam. 5:3; v. 22, cf. Ezek. 22:7; Zech. 7:10; James 1:27). "If" *('im),* see commentary on 21:2–6. "They" and "their" (v. 23) are singular in Hebrew; the LXX and the Peshitta have the plural reading. Verse 23, cf. commentary on 3:7 and Amos 3:2. Verse 22 states specifically that not a single case of maltreatment of a widow or orphan could occur, which could be an argument in support of the singular in verse 23. The "hearing" would be followed by action: the Lord's anger would be aroused, the enemy would come, and the men who ignored this law, as well as others, would be killed, so that *their* women and children would become widows and orphans (cf. 21:23–25).

22:25 *"If you lend money to one of my people among you who is needy, do not be like a moneylender; charge him no interest."*

"If" *('im),* see commentary on 21:2–6. The "needy" was the person who did not own land. The Lord forbade the charging of interest; the Hebrew can mean both "interest" and "usury," but the former is probably meant here. "Moneylender" can also mean "usurer." (Cf. Lev. 25:36–37; Deut. 23:19–20; 2 Kings 4:1; Pss. 15:5; 109:11 [KJV]; Prov. 28:8; Ezek. 18:8, 13, 17; 22:12 and Noordtzij on the references in Ezekiel in this commentary series.) The Code of Hammurabi permitted the charging of interest, but regulated it. An interest rate of 33% (and later even of 100%) on crops was not uncommon in Babylonia (cf. Böhl, *Tekst en Uitleg* on this verse). Driver notes that "in ancient times money was commonly lent for the relief of poverty brought about by misfortune or debt; it partook thus the nature of a *charity;* and to take interest on money thus lent was felt to be making gain out of a neighbor's need."[16] Today money is commonly lent for commercial purposes, in which case the charging of interest is natural and appropriate. (Cf. also Neh. 5.) Calvin believed that it was permissible to take interest from the rich.

22:26, 27 *"If you take your neighbor's cloak as a pledge, return it to him by sunset, because his cloak is the only covering he has for his body. What else will he sleep in? When he cries out to me, I will hear, for I am compassionate."*

The Israelite wore only an undergarment and an outer garment (see commentary on 12:34). The outer garment served as both cloak and blanket, and was indispensable during the cold nights. Hence the instruction to return it before sundown, for "What else will he sleep in?"

Verse 27b contains a threat in case this commandment was ignored, similar to that in verse 23. "The *people* of the covenant show themselves as lacking in mercy in contrast to the avowed mercy of the *God* of the covenant" (van Gelderen on Amos 2:8). That mercy is seen in these regulations, in a form that indicated that God was moved by the fate of the poor. (Cf. also Deut. 24:6, 12–13; Ezek. 18:12, 16; 33:15; Job 22:6; 24:7; Prov. 20:16; 27:13.) Lending against security or collateral was thus not prohibited.

---

[16]Driver, *Exodus* (Cambridge, 1953), p. 232.

G. *Regulations concerning respect for God and the authorities; the firstborn and torn animals* (22:28–31)

Now follow several regulations that cannot readily be summarized. Verses 29–30 clearly belong together, while verse 28 and verse 31 are unrelated.

22:28 *"Do not blaspheme God or curse the ruler of your people."*

Concerning "blaspheme," see commentary on 21:17. Some, including the Dutch Authorized Version, read "gods" in the sense of "authorities" rather than "God," but this is not the obvious meaning (see also commentary on 21:6). Proverbs 30:9 indicates that in poverty one is in danger of blaspheming God. It is also understandable that under those circumstances one is tempted to curse the "ruler" or head of the tribe (cf. 16:22), or the authorities in general, since besides the guidance that God provides in our life the authorities can hamper us through their measures. Another reason for cursing the ruler is that his position is better. It is strange that the Lord here confines Himself to a simple statement without adding e.g. the death penalty for breaking this law. But this can be explained by the fact that in the first place the individual Israelite is addressed here (vv. 18–20 cannot be used against this argument because they are different in form), who would commit such a sin at first in private. (Cf. also Lev. 24:11f.; 1 Kings 21:13; Prov. 24:21; Acts 23:3–5; 1 Peter 2:17.)

22:29, 30 *"Do not hold back offerings from your granaries or your vats.*
"You must give me the firstborn of your sons. Do the same with your cattle and your sheep. Let them stay with their mothers for seven days, but give them to me on the eighth day."

According to verse 29 the Israelites were not to delay bringing offerings from (lit.) their "abundance" (i.e. their grain; but cf. Num. 18:27; Deut. 22:9) and their "liquids" (lit. "weeping, trickling"), i.e. they were to give of their firstfruits to the Lord without delay (cf. Deut. 14:22f.; 26:1f.). They were also to give the firstborn of their sons to the Lord (see commentary on 13:2, 12, 15). Similarly, the firstborn of their cattle and sheep were to be given to the Lord, but not before the eighth day (since otherwise they would be too small a gift), and then on the altar (cf. 23:19; Lev. 22:27; Ezek. 44:30).

22:31 *"You are to be my holy people. So do not eat the meat of an animal torn by wild beasts; throw it to the dogs."*

Ezekiel 44:30–31 has the same sequence as Exodus 22:30–31 (see Noordtzij on Ezekiel). Cf. Lev. 17:15–16; 22:8. The blood had not been drained from the meat of an animal that had been torn by wild beasts (cf. also v. 13); consequently it was unclean to the Lord's people (cf. also Gen. 9:4 and Aalders on that verse, Deut. 12:16, 23), and was to be thrown to the dogs (cf. van Gelderen on 1 Kings 14:11). According to Bruyel this does not refer to our domesticated dog, but rather to the pariah dog *(canis ferus)*, a dog that had no owner and did not receive any care, but lived around people. In the East, at least in Egypt and Palestine, this dog was found in very ancient times; its remains have been found in Egyptian graves. The pariah dog had a rather pointed nose, ears that stood up, a reddish coat that was never spotted, and a fairly long tail. It frequently roamed in packs, especially in the cities and villages, since it seemed to have a special liking, not for humans, but for human dwellings. It was not seen much during the day, but during the evening and night its whining was frequently intolerable (Ps. 59:15). It also served a useful purpose: anything useless or unclean was thrown into the street, and the pariah dogs cleaned it up.

"Holy people"; cf. 15:11, where God is referred to as "holy." The thought expressed here is that of Israel as separated to the Lord (cf. 19:6).

H. *Regulations concerning the rights of the neighbor* (23:1–12)

See commentary on 21:1. Verses 1–3 deal with the administration of justice, verses 4–5 with the attitude toward enemies and haters, verses 6–8 again with the administration of justice, verse 9 with the alien, verses 10–11 with the seventh year, the so-called sabbatical year, and verse 12 with the Sabbath; the stress in verses 10–12 is on the social aspects.

23:1–3"*Do not spread false reports. Do not help a wicked man by being a malicious witness.*

"*Do not follow the crowd in doing wrong. When you give testimony in a lawsuit, do not pervert justice by siding with the crowd, and do not show favoritism to a poor man in his lawsuit.*"

Verse 1 is reminiscent of 20:7 in terms of the choice of words, and of 20:16 in terms of content. "Spread," lit. "lift up"; the LXX and the Dutch Authorized Version understand this in the sense of "receiving" or listening to a false report; the intended meaning is more likely "lifting up" with the mouth, i.e. spreading. (Cf. also Lev. 19:16.) This applies especially in a judicial setting. The negation in verse 1a is stronger than that in verse 1b. "A wicked man" is here "one who is in the wrong in this particular legal issue" (see commentary on 2:13; 9:27; cf. also 23:7).

"A malicious witness" is literally a "witness of violence, of wrong" (cf. Deut. 19:16; Ps. 35:11), and here thus a witness who intended to do violence or wrong against the innocent by supporting the guilty party.

Verse 2 forbade a sin that was easily committed, especially by a judge (cf. Matt. 27:24).[17] A judge was to be unbiased, and was never to bend justice in the direction of his chosing when he spoke and rendered a verdict. The word "justice" in verse 2 is not in the Masoretic text, but is required by the context; it may refer to an abstract principle, but more likely refers to the principles of justice laid down in the Law (see van Gelderen on 1 Kings 2:3; Exod. 21:1; Deut. 16:19; 24:17; 1 Sam. 8:3; Lam. 3:35). The *vox populi* may never be presented as the *vox dei*.

Gesenius-Buhl's Lexicon (17th ed.) and others prefer to change one consonant in verse 3 in "and a poor man" (lit. "and the lowly"), and read "a great man"; in my opinion there is no basis for this emendation. Leviticus 19:15 does not provide a basis for making this change. The verb translated "show favoritism" may originally have meant "to fear," and hence "to honor," and in a negative sense "to show partiality." This law reflects psychological insight, since showing favoritism to the "lowly," the weak, and the unimportant in order to gain a reputation for being a lenient judge was a great temptation, in line with verse 2. Today we would call it "false democracy." In the Code of Hammurabi (3 and 4) the death penalty was imposed on a false witness in a case that involved life and death; if the lawsuit involved grain or money the false witness was to be punished with the same punishment the accused would have received. (Cf. Deut. 19:16:21.)

23:4, 5 *"If you come across your enemy's ox or donkey wandering off, be sure to take it back to him. If you see the donkey of someone who hates you fallen down under its load, do not leave it there; be sure you help him with it."*

Some feel that these verses interrupt the continuity between verses 1–3 and verses 6–9, and would therefore fit better after 22:24 or 24:27.[18] "Ox," cf. 20:17; 22:30 (KJV). The laws in verses 4–5 command manifestations of love toward a personal enemy (cf. Lev. 19:17–18; Deut. 22:1–4; Matt. 5:44; Luke 6:27; Heidelberg Catechism, Answer 107). Both verses are directed against a potential sin of omission (cf. Luke 10:31–32). This is

---

[17]The author takes *'anah,* "to speak," in the sense of "pronouncing a verdict" rather than "giving testimony" (tr.).

[18]Against this view, see e.g. Hoedemaker, p. 254: "Justice: in everything, above all else, whatever it may cost you, and how great the temptation may be to bend or violate justice," etc. The same thought is expressed by Keil. Neither the crowd, nor personal animosity, etc. was to lead to injustice.

more probable than the (possible) interpretation that e.g. verse 4 would refer to theft. The text of verse 5 presents some problems. The Hebrew reads literally ''you shall refrain from leaving (it) to him; you shall surely loose (it) from him,'' whereby ''leaving'' and ''loose'' are forms of the same verb. Some prefer to consider the second verb as deriving from a different root, which means ''to assist,'' ''to help.'' But it is possible to interpret the two verbs as ''leaving the work to the one who hates you,'' and ''loosing, setting free, unloading of the donkey'' respectively. The margin of the Dutch Authorized Version says: ''Even as he must leave what he is doing in order to save his donkey, so you also must on his behalf leave what you are doing.'' When the burden slid off a donkey, according to Dalman, the driver was unable to replace the burden by himself, so that he was dependent on the help of others; the same applied to an animal that had fallen down under its burden. Laws such as this made social relations more pleasant and facilitated the first step toward reconciliation. It would be strange indeed if such action would not result in closer relations (cf. 1 Sam. 24:17).

23:6–8 *''Do not deny justice to your poor people in their lawsuits. Have nothing to do with a false charge and do not put an innocent or honest person to death, for I will not acquit the guilty.*

''Do not accept a bribe, for a bribe blinds those who see and twists the words of the righteous.''

Concerning the perversion of justice in verse 6, cf. commentary on verse 2. Here the meaning moves in the direction of one's rights rather than justice as laid down in the law, although the rights of the poor had been established by the Lord (cf. Deut. 1:17; 27:19). ''Your poor people'' indicates that the poor person had been entrusted to the judge in the legal matter at hand, and points to Israel's responsibility toward those who were, socially speaking, weak (cf. Deut. 15:11; Matt. 26:11; Mark 14:7; John 12:8; and the wrong attitude of the judge in the parable in Luke 18:4–5). ''False charge'' (v. 7), lit. ''false matter''; it is possible that this refers to plotting by means of false witness against an innocent party (cf. e.g. 1 Kings 21; Lev. 19:16). In verse 7b the Lord prohibited the putting to death of an innocent or honest person (cf. Deut. 27:25; Ps. 94:6, 21). The LXX connects the end of verse 7 with the beginning of verse 8 and reads, ''You shall not justify the wicked for a bribe,'' which involves changing the subject of the verb, as well as changing ''and'' at the beginning of verse 8 (not translated in the NIV) to ''for.'' The obvious meaning of the verse refers to a judicial verdict in a case between a ''wicked'' or guilty person and a "just" or innocent person (cf. Deut. 25:1). The Lord pointed out that justice was rendered in His name, and that He did not condone judicial murder: He would punish the guilty person (see commentary on v. 1). In the long run the wicked or guilty person thus did not gain any advantage. God was to be followed also in the administration of justice. The ultimate transgression of the commandment in verse 7b was committed against Jesus.

Verse 8 forbade the accepting of bribes, which is still a common practice in the East. The reason given for this commandment reflects great wisdom. "Twist," lit. "to turn upside-down," of a field that was plowed. "Bribe" can also simply mean "gift": the wording indicates that the giver did not even intimate that there was a connection between the "gift" and the legal issue, but the judge himself was to make this connection. Accepting "gifts" was nowhere absolutely prohibited, but it must be kept in mind that the giver and the recipient, although perhaps not yet in a position where they had to make a decision or testify in a specific legal matter, could well find themselves in such a position in the future; and the giver usually knew this sooner and better! (Cf. Deut. 10:17; 16:19; 27:25; 1 Sam. 8:3; Pss. 15:5; 26:10; Prov. 17:8, 23; 19:6; Eccl. 7:7; Isa. 1:23; 5:23; 33:15; Ezek. 22:12; Mic. 3:11; Acts 24:26).

23:9 *"Do not oppress an alien; you yourselves know how it feels to be aliens, because you were aliens in Egypt."*

Concerning "alien," see commentary on 22:21. "Oppress," cf. 3:9; 22:21. "Yourselves" and "you" are plural. The Israelites could enter into the feeling (lit. "soul") of the alien because of their own experience. This motivation was in agreement with the rule "love your neighbor as yourself" (Lev. 19:18; see also commentary on 22:21). This law was already given in 22:21, in a context that stressed social responsibility (cf. 22:22). Here it is restated in a context that deals with justice. This repetition indicates that the Lord was deeply concerned with the treatment of the alien (cf. also Lev. 19:33–34; Deut. 10:18–19; 24:17; 27:19; Mal. 3:5).

23:10, 11 *"For six years you are to sow your fields and harvest the crops, but during the seventh year let the land lie unplowed and unused. Then the poor among your people may get food from it, and the wild animals may eat what they leave. Do the same with your vineyard and your olive grove."*

"Your fields" (lit. "your land") refers, of course, to Canaan. The Lord anticipated the time when Israel would live there. This is the first mention made of the Sabbatical year (see comments on Lev. 25:1–7 in my commentary on Leviticus and also the comment on 21:1 in this book). Every seventh year the Israelite was to let his land lie fallow after (this must be noted) having sown and harvested it for six years. The law here emphasized its benefit for Israel's poor, and even for the wild animals. Vineyards and olive groves also fell under this regulation, which thus covered both agriculture and horticulture. Opinion differs as to whether the seventh year was the same year throughout the land, or whether it varied from field to field, depending on the year in which it was first cultivated. Leviticus 25:1–7 clearly shows the former view to be correct.

23:12 *"Six days do your work, but on the seventh day do not work, so that your ox and your donkey may rest and the slave born in your household, and the alien as well, may be refreshed."*

Cf. 20:8–10. The emphasis here is on the care for that which was dependent on the Israelite: the ox and donkey, the slave born in the household (see commentary on 12:43–45), and the alien (see above). After six days of effort there would be rest, a "breather." Prominent here is thus the social importance of the Sabbath law.

I. *Regulations concerning the relationship to the Lord* (23:13–33)

See commentary on 21:1 concerning the divisions of the Book of the Covenant. I consider verses 13–33 to belong to the same category as 20:22–26; these verses also form the conclusion of the Book of the Covenant. See also commentary on 20:22–26.

23:13 *"Be careful to do everything I have said to you. Do not invoke the names of other gods; do not let them be heard on your lips."*

The parallel with 20:22–23 is striking. While those verses also contain a warning against other gods, here the Israelites were forbidden to invoke (lit. "mention") their names. The Israelites were to be careful in all things the Lord had said to them, which included everything from 20:1 on, although we must also think of the Lord's earlier pronouncements (cf. e.g. 15:26). The "mentioning" of the name of other gods involved more than merely pronouncing their name; it referred to the use of that name in worship, in an oath, in a curse, in prayer, etc., and is thus properly rendered "to invoke." Psalm 16:4 is probably dependent on this verse. (Cf. Deut. 12:2–3; Josh. 23:7; Hos. 2:17; Zech. 13:2; and possibly also Num. 32:38.) This warning was especially important in view of their future life in Canaan (cf. also vv. 24 and 27).

23:14–17 *"Three times a year you are to celebrate a festival to me.*

"Celebrate the Feast of Unleavened Bread; for seven days eat bread made without yeast, as I commanded you. Do this at the appointed time in the month of Abib, for in that month you came out of Egypt.

"No one is to appear before me empty-handed.

"Celebrate the Feast of Harvest with the firstfruits of the crops you sow in your field.

"Three times a year all the men are to appear before the Sovereign Lord.*"*

Leviticus 23 deals more extensively with the festivals. Three festivals are mentioned here: the Feast of Unleavened Bread (v. 15), the Feast of Harvest, and the Feast of Ingathering (v. 16). See ZPEB, "Feasts," 2:521–526. The "celebration of a festival" was already mentioned in 5:1; 10:9; 12:14. Verse 15, cf. 12:15–20. Concerning the month of Abib, see 12:2; 13:3–4. The Lord reminded Israel of the commandments given earlier. "Came out," cf. 11:8. The statement "no one is to appear before me empty-handed" (v. 15) is also found in 34:20, where it relates to the redemption of the first-born (cf. 13:1–16), and in Deuteronomy 16:16, where it refers to all three feasts. "Before me" (lit. "before my face") here probably implies that a sanctuary would be established, so that this phrase points to the celebration of these three festivals at this future sanctuary. In Assyrian the expression "to see the face of a god" means "to visit him." "At the appointed time," cf. 9:5; 13:10. These verses thus also constitute by implication the basis for the pilgrimages of the Israelites to Jerusalem (cf. 1 Sam. 1:3). Note that the Lord attaches great importance to the Exodus from Egypt, not only in verse 15 but through the Scriptures.

In verse 16 the Feast of Harvest (i.e. the wheat harvest) is instituted (which was also called the Feast of Weeks, and later the Feast of Pentecost; cf. Acts 2:1), and the Feast of Ingathering (or, the Feast of Tabernacles). Pentecost fell on the fiftieth day, seven full weeks from the time when the sickle was first put to the standing grain (Deut. 16:9). Concerning the Feast of Pentecost, cf. 34:22; Leviticus 23:15–21; Numbers 28:26–31; Deuteronomy 16:9–12; concerning the Feast of Tabernacles, cf. 34:22; Leviticus 23:34–36, 39–43; Deuteronomy 16:13–15. The men thus were obligated to appear before the Lord on these three festivals; for the women and young children this was difficult (but cf. Hannah and Peninnah in 1 Sam. 1; and Luke 2:41f.). Jesus complied with these regulations, although He also abrogated them by appearing before the Lord (but not "empty-handed!"). "At the end of the year," see commentary on 12:2. In verse 17 the Hebrew reads *'adon jahweh,* or "lord Lord," which is appropriately rendered "Sovereign Lord" in the NIV. The Lord was the

Sovereign God, and the people had to reckon with His commandments. Verses 17–19 are virtually the same as 34:23, 25–26.

23:18, 19 *"Do not offer the blood of a sacrifice to me along with anything containing yeast.*
"The fat of my festival offerings must not be kept until morning.
"Bring the best of the firstfruits of your soil to the house of the LORD your God.
"Do not cook a young goat in its mother's milk."

Verse 18 forbade the use of anything containing yeast with the sacrifices (cf. Lev. 2:11; 7:12). See commentary on 12:8 for the basis for this prohibition. "My festival" in verse 18b probably refers to the Passover Feast (cf. 34:25), in which case it is related to 12:10.

In verse 19 the Israelites were instructed to bring the best (lit. "the first") of the firstfruits of the soil to the house of the Lord their God (cf. 22:29–30; 34:26; Deut. 26). The intent of verse 19a is: they were to bring this offering to the Lord, who had given them the soil (cf. Rom. 11:16). The command in verse 19b may strike us as strange; it is also found in 34:26 and Deuteronomy 14:21. Eerdmans sees the reason for this commandment in "the belief that this use of the mother's milk would render the mother goat barren, so that she would no longer give milk. The nourishing milk, which made the animal grow, may not be used to prepare it as food. It would have been impossible for us, with our western way of thinking and our radically different view of nature, to discover how such a commandment could have come into being, if similar ideas were not still found today among African tribes" (*De Godsdienst,* I, p. 46). Eerdmans also notes that this injunction became the basis for the prohibition in Judaism against eating meat and dairy products together. Yet Eerdman's explanation is not satisfactory, since the young goat was emphasized rather than the mother (cf. Lev. 22:27). Besides, the idea found among African tribes was (as far as we know) unknown in Israel, and it is unworthy of God to assume such a reason for His injunction. The idea that this verse prohibits an existing pagan fertility rite is more acceptable than Eerdman's view. An allusion to such a rite is thought to have been found in a text from Ras Shamra (Ugarit), which says: "Cook a young goat in milk" (see Gordon, 52:14). The Canaanites thought that milk contained the seed of life, and they therefore sprinkled the ground with it. If a young goat was boiled in milk its vitality was doubled, and when this special milk was sprinkled on the ground one could be even more certain of its positive influence on the fertility of fields and plants. But the Lord says in this verse, "Acknowledge Me as the Giver of the fruits of the field by bringing me the firstfruits of your soil, but do not follow that foolish pagan custom.'' I prefer to seek the solution in this direction, rather than in the repulsive nature of such an act (similar to the slaughtering of a cow or sheep and its young on the same day, Lev. 22:28). Van Andel (*De Mozaïsche Wet*, p. 81) relates this prohibition to the fact that the Law so strongly inculcated the idea of purity that it forbade the Israelite any action that involved a mixing of things that belonged to separate categories in the original order of things; he refers to Leviticus 19:19; Deuteronomy 22:5, 10–11. In my opinion the explanation given above provides the most satisfactory interpretation of the verse as a whole.

23:20–23 *"See, I am sending an angel ahead of you to guard you along the way and to bring you to the place I have prepared.*

Pay attention to him and listen to what he says. Do not rebel against him; he will not forgive your rebellion, since my Name is in him. If you listen carefully to what he says and do all that I say, I will be an enemy to your enemies and will oppose those who oppose you. My angel will go ahead of you and bring you into the land of the Amorites, Hittites, Perizzites, Canaanites, Hivites and Jebusites, and I will wipe them out.''

Verse 20 begins the last part of the Book of the Covenant (see commentary on 21:1). Verses 20–33, cf. Leviticus 26. The Lord called Israel's attention to the fact that He was sending an angel ahead of them, who would protect them along the way, and bring them to Canaan, the place that the Lord had prepared for them. Verses 21–22 clearly indicate that this was the Angel of the Lord (see commentary on 3:2), in contrast to 33:2. Only of the Angel of the Lord could be said that the Lord's ''Name is in him'' (v. 21), i.e. that the Lord Himself in His self-revelation was actually present in the Angel. This is also supported by the transition in verse 22 from ''what *he* says'' to ''all that *I* say.'' This might refer to two different speakers, but ''listen'' and ''do'' stand side by side and are complementary. This is the great promise that the Lord Himself, in the Angel of the Lord (the Samaritan Pentateuch, the LXX, and the Vulgate read ''my angel'' in vv. 20 and 23) protects and accompanies His people. The Israelite (v. 21 uses the singular) had to pay attention and obey, and not rebel against the Lord. The reason why the Angel would not forgive their rebellion (lit. ''transgressions,'' which in the context refers to the specific transgression of rebellion) is that the Lord's Name was in him (cf. 34:5–7; also 20:5). Forgiveness and retribution are the two aspects of the Lord's revelation of Himself as the God of the covenant (cf. Nah. 1:2–3). ''If you listen carefully to what he says,'' cf. 15:26; 19:5. The rest of the wilderness journey (e.g. Exod. 32–33) shows us what this meant for Israel: it meant living near a consuming fire. On the other hand, obedience brought with it the promise that the Lord would oppose Israel's enemies and opponents and "drive them to the wall" (v. 22). Much thus hinged on Israel's obedience: the Angel of the Lord would then go before them and lead them to the nations already mentioned in 3:8, 17, and the Lord would "wipe them out" (cf. 9:15). The nations are listed in a different order in 3:8, 17, which argues against the assumption that such lists reflect standard formulas, and in favor of the fact that the Lord Himself spoke. "Do not rebel against him," cf. Numbers 20:24; Psalms 78:40.

23:24–33 *"Do not bow down before their gods or worship them or follow their practices. You must demolish them and break their sacred stones to pieces. Worship the Lord your God, and his blessing will be on your food and water. I will take away sickness from among you, and none will miscarry or be barren in your land. I will give you a full life span.*

"I will send my terror ahead of you and throw into confusion every nation you encounter. I will make all your enemies turn their backs and run. I will send the hornet ahead of you to drive the Hivites, Canaanites and Hittites out of your way. But I will not drive them out in a single year, because the land would become desolate and the wild animals too numerous for you. Little by little I will drive them out before you, until you have increased enough to take possession of the land.

"I will establish your borders from the Red Sea to the Sea of the Philistines, and from the desert to the River. I will hand over to you the people who live in the land and you will drive them out before you. Do not make a covenant with them or with their gods. Do not let them live in your land, or they will cause you to sin against me, because the worship of their gods will certainly be a snare to you."

These verses contain exhortations, warnings, and promises relating to Israel's future life in the Promised Land. Verse 24, cf. 2:22–23; Leviticus 18:3. Israel could adopt neither the religion nor the morals of the nations that had been mentioned. The commandment to exterminate the people and to destroy the sacred stones was to be carried out relentlessly. Excavations have brought to light many such sacred stones, e.g. in Gezer (see my commentary on Leviticus for Lev. 26:1). But Israel later also ignored this commandment, and suffered the sad consequence, God's punishment (see also Aalders on Gen. 28:18–19 in this commentary series). Verse 25 states the positive demand "Worship the Lord your God" ("your" and the verb are both plural); this is tied to a promise concerning temporal things: food and water, and the removal of sickness. This promise is continued in verses 26–31. Verse 25, cf. 15:26; Deuteronomy 7:15. The promised blessing had an earthly character: the absence of miscarriage and barrenness (the feminine form of "barren" is used), and a long life. We know from various examples (Hannah, Elizabeth) that childlessness was considered a severe disgrace. Israel never fully carried out the demand of verses 24–25a; consequently, the promises given here were never fully realized in Israel. (Verse 26, cf. 20:12; Deut. 7:14; Ps. 55:23; Isa. 65:20. The promise in verse 27 is elucidated in 15:16; Josh. 2:11; cf. 14:24.) The end of verse 27 reads literally "and I have given all your enemies to you (as) the neck," indicating that the Lord would make them see only the neck of their enemies. A curious means to achieve this is mentioned in verse 28, the "hornet." It has been thought that this referred to the *Rhinoestrus purpureus,* which was 15–20 mm. long, and could descend on humans in swarms. This hornet had the dangerous habit of depositing its eggs in the human face by means of its ovipositor, so quickly that it was difficult to prevent it; and this could result in serious eye diseases. But this cannot be correct, since these dangerous insects were found only in the steppe of central Asia. Neither can the "hornets" be identified with the gadfly, which was found in Egypt and Palestine, and caused unrest among cattle, but was harmless to humans, since it did not sting. The "hornet" was more likely the feared wasp *Vespa cobra,* a large, brightly colored wasp, with a sting that was harmful to humans. Garstang (*Joshua-Judges,* London, 1933) discusses Joshua 24:12 in detail and says that the hornet was a "large insect of the wasp family, inflicting serious sting." The title page of Garstang's work shows a representation of the hornet found on Egyptian monuments, since this insect was the symbol of the rule over Lower Egypt. Colored representations of the hornet are known, which show variations in the wings, but always depict the typical characteristic of wasps, a yellow abdomen with black bands, and a primitive representation of a sting. Dalman also refers to this text when he speaks of hornets that were attracted by ripe figs; hornets, like all wasps, are fond of ripe fruit, while gadflies eat at most some honey. (See Goslinga on Josh. 24:11–12 in this commentary series concerning the significance of hornets in this context.) We must add, however, that Garstang thinks of the Egyptians when he speaks of hornets (*Joshua-Judges,* pp. 112–115); he points out that before and during the time when Israel settled in Canaan the Pharaohs raided the cities of Canaan. The victories of the Egyptians prior to Israel's arrival in Canaan meant that the land was completely destroyed, and explains the fact that the power and civilization of Canaan had declined. And Joshua and his people appeared on the borders of the Promised Land at the precise moment when the Egyptian armies retreated temporarily. God then used Egypt in two ways: it had to let Israel go after being defeated; and secondly, its long-standing policy of conquest had weakened the enemies in Canaan, so that the burden did not fall primarily on Israel's sword and bow.

I present this view because it correctly points out that God used Egypt to weaken the inhabitants of Canaan. But, attractive as this view may be, I believe that verse 28b argues against it: the three nations mentioned there were still in Canaan when Israel arrived (cf. commentary on 3:8; Deut. 7:20). It is also unlikely that the Egyptians would be called ''hornets,'' while all other nations were identified by their usual names. (Note that 7:18 mentions Egypt.) Köhler derives the Hebrew word for ''hornet'' from an Arabic word meaning ''discouragement,'' ''disheartenment.''[19] The Lord sent fear and terror ahead of Israel; the Egyptians, who had terrorized the inhabitants of Canaan, were themselves defeated by the Lord. (See Josh. 2:9–11.)

But this fear would not be such that the Lord would drive them out in a single year (v. 29). This would not be in the best interest of the Israelites themselves; rather, it would be a gradual process (v. 30). This promise must have been given before Israel entered Canaan; otherwise it would be rather ridiculous, since it would cover up the less favorable course of events that followed and even present it under the guise of a favor. As it stands we can only admire the divine wisdom, but also understand the necessity of warnings such as those in verses 24–25, 32–33 (cf. Deut. 7:22.)

Verse 31 contains a promise concerning the extent of Israel's future territory: from the Red Sea to the Sea of the Philistines, i.e. the Mediterranean, and from the desert, the southern steppe, to the river, i.e. the Euphrates (cf. Gen. 15:18). And this is possible only because the Lord would give the inhabitants into the hands of the Israelites, so that they could drive them out. This promise was also linked to the demand of verses 24–25a (see above), and was not fulfilled until the time of David and Solomon (cf. 1 Kings 4:21). ''Red Sea,'' see commentary on 10:20. (Verse 31, cf. Gen. 15:18; Num. 34:3–4; Deut. 11:24; 2 Sam. 8:5f.; 10:6, 15–19; 1 Kings 4:21, 24.)

Verses 32–33, which constitute the end of the Book of the *Covenant,* contain a warning against making a *covenant* with the gods of the inhabitants of the land; we thus see a return to the thought expressed in 20:22–23, which argues for the existence of the Book of the Covenant as a separate book. (Concerning the content of verses 32–33, cf. 34:12, 15; Deut. 7:2; Josh. 13:13; Ps. 106:34–39.) ''Snare,'' cf. 10:7. The nations listed in verse 28 would lead Israel to destruction if they were allowed to live in the land; they would be a snare that Israel would not be able to resist. Van Gelderen, in discussing Amos 3:5 in his commentary on Amos, points out

---

[19]*Zeitschrift für die alttestamentliche Wissenschaft,* Neue Folge, 1932, p. 183.

that the more refined culture and sensual cultus of the Canaanites would be the snare that would lead Israel astray.

10. *The Confirmation of the Covenant* (24:1–18)

Chapter 24 resumes the narrative. In 20:21 we read that Moses approached the Lord in the thick darkness, where God gave him the contents of the Book of the Covenant (20:22–23:33). Verse 4 indicates that Moses did not write these things down until he descended from the mountain; at that time he also wrote other sections of Exodus, e.g., chapters 25–31. Chapter 24 describes the ceremony with which the covenant was made at Sinai. The Lord invited representatives of the people into His presence on the mountain. Moses erected an altar and twelve stone pillars at the foot of the mountain, read the Book of the Covenant, sprinkled blood, and the people once again solemnly accepted the covenant of the Lord. Proponents of the source hypothesis reject, of course, the unity of this chapter; verses 3–8 are usually ascribed to E, the rest to J or to J and P. But this is of little importance for our purpose.

24:1, 2 *Then he said to Moses, "Come up to the Lord, you and Aaron, Nadab and Abihu, and seventy of the elders of Israel. You are to worship at a distance, but Moses alone is to approach the Lord; the others must not come near. And the people may not come up with him."*

Moses was still on the mountain (cf. 20:21). After the preceding "words" and "laws" had been revealed, the Lord commanded him to "come up to the Lord" together with Aaron and his two eldest sons, Nadab and Abihu (cf. 6:22; 28:1; Lev. 10:1ff.); the sequel and the context indicate that this means that they were to ascend the mountain. Aaron and his sons were summoned because of their future calling as priests. They were to worship (lit. "bow") at a distance. Then Moses himself, but not the others, was to approach the Lord. There were thus three degrees of approach: (1) Moses, (2) the elders with Aaron, Nadab, and Abihu, and (3) the people. The number seventy was not accidental; it pointed to the holiness of Israel as the Lord's people (19:6). Also, the representation was to be as broad as possible. The Lord made the covenant with all His people (cf. Num. 11:16).

24:3–8 *When Moses went and told the people all the Lord's words and laws, they responded with one voice, "Everything the Lord has said we will do." Moses then wrote down everything the Lord had said.*

He got up early the next morning and built an altar at the foot of the mountain and set up twelve stone pillars representing the twelve tribes of Israel. Then he sent young Israelite men, and they offered burnt offerings and sacrificed young bulls as fellowship offerings to the Lord. Moses took half of the blood and put it in bowls, and the other half he sprinkled on the altar. Then he took the Book of the Covenant and read it to the people. They responded, "We will do everything the Lord has said; we will obey."

Moses then took the blood, sprinkled it on the people and said, "This is the blood of the covenant that the Lord has made with you in accordance with all these words."

The purpose of the instructions in verses 1–2 was to illustrate the state of peace, the covenant, between the Lord and Israel, and involved a high honor bestowed by the Lord on the representatives of Israel. But first we read in verses 3–8 what Moses did on his own initiative. He went down from the mountain and related to the people all the Lord's "words" and "laws" (see commentary on 21:1; concerning "covenant," see Aalders on Gen. 6:18 in this commentary series). The unanimous response of the people was similar to that in 19:8. Unlike Moses, the people did not distinquish between "words" and "laws" (see Introduction, pp. 12–13); they spoke of "words" in general ("Everything the Lord has said," lit. "all the words of Jahweh"). This refers to the Book of the Covenant, since Moses received the two tablets of the Testimony that contained the "Ten Commandments" from the Lord later on the mountain (cf. v. 12; 31:18; 32:15–16). "Everything" (lit. "all the words") in verse 4 also refers to the Book of the Covenant, and like verse 3b, ignores the distinction between "words" and "laws" made in verse 3a. But this does not mean that this distinction is unfounded (see commentary on 21:1).

Early the next morning Moses built an altar at the foot of the mountain (cf. 20:24–26). "Stone pillars," cf. 23:24; Josh. 4:5, 20; 1 Kings 18:31. "Young Israelite men": the young men who served as Moses' servants (see Aalders on Jer. 1:7 in this commentary series). Moses used them to slaughter and sacrifice young bulls (cf. Ps. 50:5; Zech. 9:11). "Burnt offerings" and "fellowship offerings," see commentary on 20:24; 10:25. We must explain Moses' actions from his joy over the imminent covenant of the Lord. First he sprinkled blood on the newly built altar (v. 6); the nature of the offerings indicates that the emphasis here was on dedication or consecration to the Lord. According to Hebrews 9:19 the Book of the Covenant was also sprinkled with blood. It is too far-fetched, however, to see the altar as representing the Lord (on the basis of Gen. 15:9–10, 17), which then, as the other party to the covenant, was sprinkled with the same blood with which later the people would be sprinkled. We can limit ourselves to consecration (v. 6) and cleansing (v. 8). The altar bore Israel's offerings, but the Lord was enthroned on the mountain, and was thus nearby. The consecration and cleansing together prepared the people for the celebration of the making of the covenant. Again the people expressed their agreement with everything that the Lord had said (v. 7). "Obey," lit. "hear"; but "hearing" implies obedience (cf. Deut. 5:27).

Moses then sprinkled the blood on the people; the verb suggests that Moses scattered the blood so that the drops fell on the people. It was the blood of the covenant that the Lord had made with them in accordance with (or, on the basis of) all the words of the Book of the Covenant (v. 8); in other words, if Israel kept these "words" and "laws," the covenant would remain in force. But the fact that the people as well as the altar was to be sprinkled with blood indicates that even the keeping of the words and laws was to be based on the sacrificial blood; Hebrews 9:19–20 explains what this means (see Grosheide on Hebrews in this commentary series; also 1 Peter 1:2). The blood cleansed so that the "hearing" and "doing" became possible. But also, Moses did not dare carry out the Lord's instructions of verses 1–2 without first making propitiation by means of the shedding of blood, thereby ratifying the covenant. Again, Moses the mediator!

24:9–11 *Moses and Aaron, Nadab and Abihu, and the seventy elders of Israel went up and saw the God of Israel. Under his feet was something like a pavement made of sapphire, clear as the sky itself. But God did not raise his hand against these leaders of the Israelites; they saw God, and they ate and drank.*

Then arrived the great moment in the lives of Aaron, Nadab, Abihu, and the seventy elders: the ascent of the mountain. The representatives saw Him, who was pleased to be Israel's God. We are not told what His appearance was like (cf. 33:18ff.; Isa. 6:1; Rev. 4:2–3); most likely He appeared as a king sitting on His throne, since verse 10 mentions His feet. Under His feet was something like a pavement made of sapphire; the word for "pavement" is the same as the word translated "brick" in 1:14; 5:7f. The Hebrew literally says "sapphire stone," which must be understood as "lapis lazuli," an opaque, blue precious stone speckled with gold, which is also found in Egypt. The specks are pyrite, which assumes a golden yellow color when the stone is polished. J. Bolman,[20] to whom I am indebted for much of the information on the precious stones mentioned in Exodus, notes that the true sapphire, the crystalline transparent blue variety of corundum, was unknown in Egypt around 1400 B.C. Lapis lazuli was used by the Egyptians in the manufacture of royal ornaments. The true

---

[20]J. Bolman, *De edelsteenen uit den Bijbel gezien in het licht der hedendaagsche edelsteenkunde* (Amsterdam, 1938).

sapphire was found only in relatively small crystals, while the lapis lazuli was found in pieces of sometimes considerable size so that it was not unusual to find pillars or tables made of lapis lazuli. Here the stone was "clear as the sky itself." We have here an indication of the exaltedness of Israel's God (cf. Ezek. 1:26). The manner in which this God revealed Himself shows at the same time the enormous distance between Him and even the elite of His people. They did not see the Lord Himself; they looked up at a blue "pavement," clear as the sky itself. Yet we must note with gratitude that the Lord did not raise His hand (lit. "stretch out His hand," see commentary on 9:15; 22:8) against those "leaders" or "select ones" of the Israelites (others understand this word, which in this sense is found only here, to mean "corners," the "supports" of the Israelite community, on the basis of Isa. 41:9). On the contrary, they saw God and ate and drank, a meal that consisted probably of the meat of the fellowship offering (cf. v. 5); not only did they live, they were allowed to sit down to a feast on the mountain. This is indeed something worth mentioning (cf. commentary on 3:6; 19:12; 20:19; and the use of the meat of the offerings in Gen. 26:30; 31:44–54; Exod. 18:12). The parallel with the Lord's Supper obviously suggests itself: there also is fellowship with God after atonement has been made by the blood of Christ (vv. 3–8; cf. also Matt. 26:28; Heb. 12:18–24). Keil believes that this meal took place by the altar, rather than on the mountain, which is possible, but not likely in view of verses 1–2, which contain a single commandment. Keil *(Archaeologie)* correctly points to Luke 14:15; 22:30 in connection with sacrificial meals in general. (Cf. Rev. 19:7–9; Isa. 25:6–8.)

24:12–18 *The Lord said to Moses, "Come up to me on the mountain and stay here, and I will give you the tablets of stone, with the law and commands I have written for their instruction."*

Then Moses set out with Joshua his aide, and Moses went up on the mountain of God. He said to the elders, "Wait here for us until we come back to you. Aaron and Hur are with you, and anyone involved in a dispute can go to them."

When Moses went up on the mountain, the cloud covered it, and the glory of the Lord settled on Mount Sinai. For six days the cloud covered the mountain, and on the seventh day the Lord called to Moses from within the cloud. To the Israelites the glory of the Lord looked like a consuming fire on top of the mountain. Then Moses entered the cloud as he went on up the mountain. And he stayed on the mountain forty days and forty nights.

Moses was now instructed to climb even higher up the mountain, to the Lord, in accordance with verse 2. This is the first time the tablets of stone are mentioned (cf. 31:18; 32:15–16; 34:28; Deut. 4:13; 5:22). "With" in verse 12 is "and" in Hebrew, which can also be translated "namely." These tablets had thus been inscribed and were ready and waiting. "Law" *(torah)* means literally "teaching" (cf. Noordtzij, *God's Woord en der eeuwen getuigenis,* 2nd ed., pp. 326f.). According to verse 13 Joshua, here called "his aide," accompanied Moses further up the mountain (concerning Joshua see commentary on 17:9). "The mountain of God," see commentary on 3:1; the name is here very appropriate, since God descended and was present on this mountain. The elders were to wait "here," i.e., with the people. There is no reason to press the expression to mean that the elders were to wait for Moses for forty days and nights; verse 14b then would not make much sense. Aaron and Hur (cf. 17:10f.) were appointed as Moses' deputies, and were to function as arbiters or judges (cf. ch. 18). It is curious that in the story of the golden calf (ch. 32) Hur is not mentioned. He cannot have been a strong personality, because then he would have restrained Aaron. After these instructions, which were to insure that everything continued properly during his absence, Moses went up the mountain into the cloud (v. 15; the translation "clouds" is also possible, but see commentary on 13:21; 16:10). The "glory of the LORD" (v. 16) refers to the emanation from His innermost Being, from the focal point of His attributes (see Ridderbos on Isa. 6:3 in this commentary series). Here it means that the Lord Himself dwelled temporarily on Mount Sinai (see commentary on 3:1). The number "seven" is the number of holiness. Moses had to wait six days, and then the Lord called to Moses from within the cloud on the seventh day. Verses 17–18a describe what the Israelites were still able to see. "The glory of the LORD looked like," lit. "the appearance of the glory of the LORD (was)"; see commentary on 3:1 concerning "appearance" and also Hebrews 12:29. The Lord showed His glory in the likeness of a consuming fire, which proved that He hated sin and was terrible in His anger (cf. Ps. 97:3; Nah. 1:6; etc.).

When the covenant was made at Sinai, fellowship with the Lord was still only very partial; there was still much that inspired fear. Moses had to wait for six days. The distance was still considerable (cf. v. 10). Yet Moses proceeded. Before the eyes of the Israelites he disappeared in the cloud, steadily climbing higher (v. 18a). Verse 18b notes the length of his stay: the wilderness journey lasted forty years, Jesus fasted forty days and forty nights (Matt. 4:2). This time of testing proved to be too long for Israel (cf. 32:1f.). (Cf also Gen. 7:4, 12, 17; 8:6; Deut. 8:2; 9:9, 11; cf. also Exod. 34:28; Deut. 9:18; 1 Kings 19:8). Keil links the number forty with a period of divine testing, as well as strengthening of faith. But see van Gelderen on 1 Kings 19:8 in this commentary series.

11. *Instructions Concerning the Tabernacle* (25:1–31:7)

A. *The offerings for the tabernacle* (25:1–9)

See Introduction, pp. 13–15, for a summary and general treatment of chapters 25–31. Proponents of the source hypothesis ascribed this section to P.

25:1–7 *The Lord said to Moses, "Tell the Israelites to bring me an offering. You are to receive the offering for me from each man whose heart prompts him to give. These are the offerings you are to receive from them: gold, silver and bronze; blue, purple and sacrlet yarn and fine linen; goat hair; ram skins dyed red and hides of sea cows; acacia wood; olive oil for the light; spices for the anointing oil and for the fragrant incense; and onyx stones and other gems to be mounted on the ephod and breastpiece."*

Moses received all these instructions on the mountain, during the forty days and nights mentioned in 24:18. He was to tell the Israelites that they were to bring an offering; this offering would serve to gather the materials necessary for the building of the Tabernacle and for its service. The word translated "offering" *(terumah)* comes from a root that means "to lift up." This word is sometimes also translated "heave offering" (cf. ASV, margin; KJV: Num. 15:19, etc.), based on the incorrect notion, already found among ancient rabbinical sources, that this was an offering that was lifted up to God. The Dutch Authorized Version translates "heave offering," but states in the margin: "In Hebrew, an offering, or setting apart; as being a gift separated from the rest and consecrated to the Lord." Not a single instance where the word is used in the Bible justifies the translation "heave offering." The marginal notes of the Dutch Authorized Version are correct; the word indicates something that had been set apart from a larger quantity for a sacred purpose, i.e., for the Lord. Here it refers to an offering for Him, and commanded by Him, a "special gift" as the NIV translates *terumah* in e.g., Deuteronomy 12:6, 11, 17; cf. also Ezekiel 45:1–7. The voluntary nature of this "special gift" is emphasized in verse 2b. Not everyone had to contribute; this offering would be received only from every man whose heart impelled him to give (cf. 1 Chron. 29:3, 5, 9; 2 Cor. 8:12; 9:7). "You" (v. 2) is plural and refers to the people as a whole: Israel was to take care of this, and Moses appointed certain men to use the materials collected in the actual construction of the tabernacle (cf. 36:1–7). Verse 2 indicates that most of the materials that were needed for the sanctuary had to come from the private possessions of the Israelites. They had brought gold, silver, and bronze with them from Egypt (cf. 3:22; 11:2; 12:35–36; although none of these verses mention bronze specifically). The Israelites probably learned the goldsmith's art in Egypt. Bolman (*De Edelsteenen,* p. 24) speaks highly of the craftsmanship of the Egyptian goldsmiths. Both gold and silver were found in various locations in Upper Egypt. Copper mines existed in the Sinai Peninsula between Suez and Sinai. The Israelites also were familiar with iron, although this is not mentioned (cf. 20:25; Num. 35:16; Deut. 40:20; 19:5; 27:5, etc.).

"Blue" (Hebrew *tekelet;* LXX *hyakinthos*): yarn colored by means of a dye derived from a shellfish. There is uncertainty as to the exact color: sky-blue, deep dark blue, blue-purple, or violet. Because of this uncertainty it is difficult to assign a specific deeper meaning to the use of this color. The dye was fade resistant. The color was used for the sanctuary because it was extremely expensive. The dye was supplied especially by the Phoenicians, and was also exported to Egypt. The Hebrew reads "blue and purple and scarlet and fine linen" (cf. KJV); the offering probably consisted of dyed "yarn" or perhaps fabric, especially wool (cf. 3:22; 12:35: "clothing").

"Purple" (Heb. *argaman;* LXX *porphyra*): this dye was also derived from a shellfish and supplied primarily by the Phoenicians. The color was actually purple-red.

"Scarlet" (Heb. *tola'at shani,* lit. "worm of brilliancy"). The scarlet or crimson dye was derived from the eggs and bodies of the *coccus ilicis.* Again, the Phoenicians supplied much of this. The color was a brilliant bright red (according to Franz Delitzsch, yellow-red).

"Fine linen" (Heb. *shesh;* LXX *byssos*). The word *shesh* is probably derived from the Egyptian; according to Ezekiel 27:7 the *byssos* came from Egypt, and was probably brought from there by the Israelites. It refers to a fine, woven material, probably linen rather than cotton. The Assyrian *busi* means "linen" (Galling, *Bibilisches Real Lexikon,* Column 122). The color of this linen was usually white.

"Goat hair" (Heb. lit. "goats," which is probably elliptic): most likely black goat hair. This was used to weave tents.)

What about the symbolic significance of the colors? We may assume that white, represented in the "fine linen," was the color of purity, holiness, joy, and victory (cf. Dan. 7:9; Rev. 1:14; 6:2; 7:9; 19:11; and Greijdanus on these references in Rev. in this commentary series); it was the color of light (cf. Matt. 17:2; 28:3). Scarlet or crimson was the color of wrath and of fire. Sin, which caused wrath, was red like scarlet (cf. Isa. 1:18).

The fire of the Lord's wrath stood side by side with the light of love. Purple pointed to the majesty and dignity of the Lord: He was a King (cf. 15:18). Franz Delitzsch, on the basis of 24:10 (cf. Num. 15:38), links the "blue" with God's majesty in its condescension, the scarlet with that majesty in its exaltedness. Red, the color of blood (cf. Num. 19), then was a symbol of fresh, undiminished life. This interpretation is plausible, since it finds support in various places in the Scriptures, although I find his distinction between blue and scarlet somewhat unconvincing. Besides, Bähr and Delitzsch assume that in this case the goat hair was white: since black represents death and darkness they do not believe that it could have been used in the tabernacle. But it is unlikely that the tent coverings, which were to provide protection against rain and the elements, would have been white. Today the Bedouins usually paint the light camel hair black when it is used for the making of tents; white would soon turn dirty. We must thus be very careful in assigning a deeper significance to the colors that are mentioned here, and not go beyond what the Bible itself suggests. The Bible itself must decide, since otherwise our interpretation would become arbitrary (cf. my *De ceremoniële wet,* p. 16; "Zinnebeelden der Wet," *De Heraut,* March and April, 1939).

"Ram skins dyed red" were ram skins from which all wool had been removed, and which then were dyed in bright colors, like our saffron or morocco leather. The inhabitants of the East were advanced in the art of preparing this kind of leather (cf. J. Th. de Visser, *Hebreeuwsche Archaeologie,* Utrecht, n.d., I, 172).

"Hides of sea cows" (Heb. "skins of *techashim*"); the meaning of *techashim* is uncertain (KJV: "badger"; RSV: "goat"; ASV: "seal"). Some believe that the word is of Egyptian origin and refers to fine leather or chrome leather (cf. Ezek. 16:10). Most likely, the *tachash* was the Asiatic or East-African sea cow, which was found especially in the Red Sea; the inhabitants of the Sinai Peninsula used its skin to make sandals. It has been pointed out that the mention of both the *tachash* and acacia wood argues strongly for the historicity of the narrative, since both were materials found typically in the Sinai region (see Dillmann). I believe that it is well possible that the Israelites had purchased such hides and other objects from caravans of merchants.

"Acacia wood" (Heb. *shittim*): this is generally taken to be the wood of the acacia tree *(Mimosa nilotica)* which was especially abundant in Egypt, and was also common in the Sinai Peninsula; this was still true in Jerome's time. Böhl, who identified the tree as the *Spina aegyptica* or *Acacia seyal,* noted that the only tree he found when he visited the oasis of Kadesh in 1926 was an *Acacia seyal*. The wood was light, yet hard. Cf. Keil, *Archaeologie* (second German edition, p. 85, note 2; and ZPEB, "Acacia" 1:31).

"Olive oil for the light," see commentary on 27:20. Olive oil was also used for baking and frying, but here it was used as fuel. The Israelites may have carried this oil with them in vats or in "tarred" sacks made of hides (cf. F. J. Bruyel, "de Olijfboom" *Orgaan van de Christelijke Vereeniging van Natuur- en Geneeskundigen in Nederland,* 1936, pp. 161f.; this article is more detailed than that in the *Gereformeerd Theologisch Tijdschrift,* June 1934, pp. 273–281). The olive tree was common in the region around the Mediterranean Sea; burning olive oil gave off an exceptionally bright light.

"Spices for the anointing oil and for the fragrant incense"; olive oil was used as a body lotion to keep the skin soft. "Sometimes the olives were squeezed between the hands to obtain the oil; sometimes the body was rubbed with olives that had turned soft, which were sold at the entrance to public baths. Thus olive oil acquired the character of an ointment, and treatment with oil was almost always called 'anointing.' Usually the olive oil was mixed with other ingredients that gave the oil a pleasant smell" (Bruyel). Here anointing oil for a sacred purpose is mentioned (cf. 30:22–33). The various spices for the anointing oil are listed in 30:23–24, those for the fragrant incense in 30:34 (see commentary on those verses). "Spices" (Heb. plural of *bosem,* "spice, perfume, sweet odor"), cf. van Gelderen on 1 Kings 10:10. "Fragrant incense," lit. "incense of fragrances."

"Onyx stones" (Heb. *shoham*): there is some uncertainty as to what the *shoham* was. The LXX translates it *beryllion* here, *onyx* in e.g., Job 28:16. I prefer the translation "chrysoprase" (Bolman provides an explanation for the LXX's use of "beryl" here). The chrysoprase is a type of quartz, a variety of chalcedony, which is found in the soft ophite or serpentine; its color ranges from blue-green to yellow-green and apple-green. It is rarer than most other quartz varieties, and was used primarily for seals. Because of its color and scarcity it was highly valued. The Egyptians were familiar with chrysoprase, and the Israelites thus probably brought the stones with them from Egypt.

"Other gems to be mounted on the ephod and breastpiece": see commentary on 28:6–25.

25:8, 9 *"Then have them make a sanctuary for me, and I will dwell among them. Make this tabernacle and all its furnishings exactly like the pattern I will show you."*

In verse 8 the Lord told Moses that the Israelites had to make Him a sanctuary and that He then would dwell among them (cf. 24:16; 29:45–46; Num. 5:3; 35:34; Ezek. 43:7, 9; 48:35; Zech. 2:10–11; 8:3; Rev. 21:3). The "tabernacle" (from the Latin *tabernaculum,* "tent," used in the Vulgate), was thus a sanctuary, a dwelling place for the Lord as Israel's

God, His holy palace (cf. 19:6). The theocracy was thus also reflected in the fact that there was a dwelling place of the Lord; this was *His* tent among all other tents. The meaning of the tabernacle must thus be based on the words that were used to refer to it: "sanctuary" and "dwelling place." The tabernacle was a representation of the heavenly dwelling place (cf. Acts 7:44, 48–50; Heb. 8:5; 9:11, 24; cf. Rev. 11:19 and commentary at the beginning of ch. 26).

Verse 9 reads literally "according to all that I show (or, will show) you, the plan of the tabernacle and the plan of all its furnishings and so you shall do." The following instructions were thus accompanied by a vision in order to give Moses a clear idea of what was to be done (cf. v. 40; 26:30; 27:8, Num. 8:4). He saw the whole as he was given the details. "Exactly like the pattern" is the correct meaning of "and so you shall do" or "exactly thus you shall do." Israel was to follow the pattern that the Lord showed them, not only for the "dwelling place" as a whole, but also for the smaller objects that belonged in the sanctuary, the furnishings. The objects used in Israel's cultus were thus determined down to the smallest detail by the Lord's pattern and instructions (but see commenatry on 31:1–11). The divine plan was the basis of the ministry of reconciliation even in its foreshadowing. The materials, chosen by the Lord and given voluntarily, could be used only in accordance with His will.

B. *The ark* (25:10–22)

The first item in the divine palace, the tabernacle, concerning which Moses received instructions, was the throne on which Israel's king would reside in the midst of His people. (See ZPEB, "Tabernacle," 5:572–583.)

25:10–15 *"Have them make a chest of acacia wood—two and a half cubits long, a cubit and a half wide, and a cubit and a half high. Overlay it with pure gold, both inside and out, and make a gold molding around it. Cast four gold rings for it and fasten them to its four feet, with two rings on one side and two rings on the other. Then make poles of acacia wood and overlay them with gold. Insert the poles into the rings on the sides of the chest to carry it. The poles are to remain in the rings of this ark; they are not to be removed."*

The word "ark" means "chest" (cf. 2 Kings 12:9–10; Gen. 50:26). "Cubit," see van Gelderen on 1 Kings 6:2. The question is whether this was the Babylonian or Egyptian cubit; most likely it was the royal Egyptian cubit (525 or 540 mm.). The name "ark" is derived from the Latin *arca*. ("Acacia wood," see commentary on v. 5; see also 37:1; Heb. 9:4–5.) "Pure gold (v. 11) was gold from which silver and other impurities had been removed more carefully than from ordinary gold. The molding ran probably around the top of the ark on all four sides; it is possible that the lid rested on this molding. However, it is also possible that the molding encased the atonement cover, so that the cover could not slide, e.g., when the ark was lifted up or put down. The word used in verse 12 seems to indicate that the ark stood on feet or legs (not the same word as in v. 26). The four rings of ordinary gold were attached to the feet (see also van Gelderen on 1 Kings 7:30). The carrying poles were overlaid with ordinary gold. Verse 15, cf. 1 Kings 8:8.

25:16 *"Then put in the ark the Testimony, which I will give you."*

The "Testimony" refers to the Ten Commandments, which solemnly declare and affirm God's will and are, so to speak, Israel's constitution. Thus, reference is made to "the ark of the Testimony" and "the tablets of the Testimony" (cf. v. 22; 16:34; 26:33; 31:18; etc.; cf. also Heb. 9:4). Heinisch points out that in Egypt, as well as in Babylonia and the Hittite empire, important documents were deposited in the sanctuary, "at the feet" of the deity. Verse 16, cf. Psalms 89:15; 97:2.

25:17–20 *"Make an atonement cover of pure gold—two and a half cubits long and a cubit and a half wide. And make two cherubim out of hammered gold at the ends of the cover. Make one cherub on one end and the second cherub on the other; make the cherubim of one piece with the cover, at the two ends. The cherubim are to have their wings spread upward, overshadowing the cover with them. The cherubim are to face each other, looking toward the cover."*

Moses had to make an "atonement cover" (KJV: "mercy seat"), again from pure gold (cf. 37:6). The root meaning of the Hebrew verb is "to cover, hide," and hence "to atone." The atonement cover fit exactly on the ark. (Concerning the cherubim, see Aalders on Gen. 3:24, and van Gelderen on 1 Kings 6:23–28; also ZPEB, "Cherub, Cherubim," 1:788–790). The cherubim point to the presence of the Lord who gave His Testimony to Moses, and who could remain present only as long as that Testimony was kept; yet even then atonement had to be made regularly (cf. Lev. 16:14f.). The cherubim most likely were represented in human form. The conclusion has been drawn correctly that the atonement cover was to provide the opportunity to bring the blood of the atonement as closely as possible to the Lord (cf. Rom. 3:25 and van Leeuwen on that verse; Heb. 9:23f.). Moses was to make the cherubim, between whom the Lord dwelled (cf. e.g., Ps. 99:1; Aalders on Gen. 3:24), of hammered gold in such a way that they formed one piece with the cover. It is very possible that we should think here of a relief. Verse 20, cf. 1 Kings 8:7; Hebrews 9:5. The cherubim provided a "protective covering," cf. 33:22. The fact that they looked toward the cover may be related to 1 Peter 1:12, but it also shows reverence for the Lord, who according to verse 22 met with Moses between them and above the atonement cover.

25:21, 22 *"Place the cover on top of the ark and put in the ark the Testimony, which I will give you. There, above the cover between the two cherubim that are over the ark of the Testimony, I will meet with you and give you all my commands for the Israelites."*

In verse 21 Moses was instructed to place the atonement cover, when it was finished, on top of the ark, and to put the Testimony, which the Lord would give Moses, in the ark. The promise in verse 22 concerns *Moses* (cf. also Num. 7:89; and later 1 Sam. 3:1–14). The Lord would meet with Moses in this particular place. Moses was the mediator between the Lord and the Israelites, who appeared before the throne where the Lord came above the atonement cover between the cherubim, to receive the commands for Israel (cf. 20:19). From the beginning the ark was thus both the Lord's throne (1 Chron. 28:2; Pss. 99:5; 132:7; Lam. 2:1: the ark as the Lord's footstool; but see Aalders on Lam. 2:1) and the repository for the Law. Those who reject the historicity of a section such as this must resort to assumptions concerning the origins and original form of the ark. A favorite approach is then to assume an empty throne for the deity (see also commentary on 32:1–6), as well as sacred chests (cf. e.g., Galling, *Biblisches Real Lexikon,* Column 343. This section then represents speculation on the part of P, who supposedly distinguishes between throne and chest; but this distinction does not exist (cf. v. 16 with v. 22). The atonement cover served not merely as a cover for the ark, but had a significance of its own.

C. *The table* (25:23–30)

25:23–29 *"Make a table of acacia wood—two cubits long, a cubit wide and a cubit and a half high. Overlay it with pure gold and make a gold molding around it. Also make around it a rim a handbreadth wide and put a gold molding on the rim. Make four gold rings for the table and fasten them to the four corners, where the four legs are. The rings are to be close to the rim to hold the poles used in carrying the table. Make the poles of acacia wood, overlay them with gold and carry the table with them. And make its plates and ladles of pure gold, as well as its pitchers and bowls for the pouring out of offerings."*

Cf. verses 1–9, 10–22; 37:10–16. Moses was still the one who was addressed. The rim (v. 25) probably went around the one-and-a-half cubits high legs, halfway from the top (cf. the depiction on the Arch of Titus). According to Josephus the upper half of the legs was square, the lower half round. Some (e.g., Schouten) believe that the rim was placed around the table against the table top. I agree with others (e.g., De Visser) that it is more probable that the rim was placed there where the square section ended and the round section of the legs began, which agrees with the illustration mentioned above. Around the outer edge of the rim, as well as around the edge of the table itself, was again a molding of gold. The gold rings were thus placed close to the rim halfway up the legs. "Legs" is literally "feet" (cf. KJV), perhaps referring to "claws" that formed the base of the legs. The "plates" were for use with the bread of the Presence, the "ladles" for the incense, the "pitchers and bowls" for the wine of the drink offerings (cf. Num. 4:7; 7). Tables were relatively rare in the East. The Bedouins used a piece of leather for a table (cf. Ps. 69:22).

25:30 *"Put the bread of the Presence on this table to be before me at all times."*

"Bread of the Presence," i.e., of the Lord (cf. Lev. 24:5–9; Noordtzij on 1 Chron. 9:32; 23:29). Bread was a gift from God; Israel was sustained by its God. This is what the table of the bread of the Presence teaches. Its purpose was not to provide nourishment for the deity, but to remind Israel of its sustaining God. And to remind ultimately of God's greatest gift; Christ, the bread of life (cf. Deut. 8:3).

D. *The lampstand* (25:31–40)

25:31–40 *"Make a lampstand of pure gold and hammer it out, base and shaft; its flowerlike cups, buds and blossoms shall be on one piece with it. Six branches are to extend from the sides of the lampstand—three on one side and three on the other. Three cups shaped like almond flowers with buds and blossoms are to be on one branch, three on the next branch, and the same for all six branches extending from the lampstand. And on the lampstand there are to be four cups shaped like almond flowers with buds and blossoms. One bud shall be under the first pair of branches extending from the lampstand, a second bud under the second pair, and a third bud under the third pair—six branches in all. The buds and branches shall all be of one piece with the lampstand, hammered out of pure gold.*

"Then make its seven lamps and set them up on it so that they light the space in front of it. Its wick trimmers and trays are to be of pure gold. A talent of pure gold is to be used for the lampstand and all these accessories. See that you make them according to the pattern shown you on the mountain."

See also the preceding sections and 37:17–24. Verse 31, see commentary on verse 18. "Base and shaft" (v. 31) could also be translated "its shaft and its branch'' (cf. KJV: "its shaft, and its branches"). In the following verses the word translated "shaft" in verse 31 (NIV) is indeed found in the sense of "branch" or "arm." But the word for "base" means literally "loins, thigh," and probably refers to the base of the lampstand. Although it is somewhat awkward that the word for "shaft" is translated "arm" in the following verses, I agree with the NIV translation (which is also supported by e.g., Keil, Kittel, Dillmann-Ryssel, Böhl, and Heinisch) as being the most probable one. The word for "branch" also means "reed" (e.g., 1 Kings 14:15), or "stalk" (Gen. 41:5, 22). "Flowerlike cups" is the plural of the word used in Genesis 44:2, 12, 16, for "cup." "Buds" is also found in 37:17, 19:22; Amos 9:1; Zephaniah 2:14; in the latter two instances it means "column" or "pillar." In the case of the lampstand it can refer to a fruit; Josephus thought of pomegranates. One of the seven lamps (v. 37) was placed on top of the shaft, while the other six lamps were placed on the six arms; the seven lamps thus formed a straight line. Each branch was decorated with three cups shaped like almond flowers, consisting of a bud and a blossom, while the lampstand itself, i.e., the shaft (v. 34), was adorned with four of these decorations. Concerning the almond flower, see Aalders on Jeremiah 1:11–12. Verse 35 indicates that the branches were attached to the shaft in three pairs (cf. the lampstand depicted on the Arch of Titus, although that lampstand differed slightly from the one described here). Below each pair of branches was to be a bud, while the fourth one (v. 34) was probably below the lamp at the top of the center shaft. It is emphasized that everything was to be of one piece (v. 36). The lamps themselves, the wick trimmers and the trays were to be made separately (v. 37, cf. Num. 8:2). The gold required for all this amounted to one talent, or 34 kg. Finally Moses was reminded that he was to follow the pattern that was shown him on the mountain also where the lampstand and its accessories were concerned (see commentary on v. 9). We are not told how high the lampstand was. The removable lamps had to be filled with oil, and a wick was to be inserted in each. Schouten says "the wick of each lamp was placed toward the front of the lamp which was slightly pointed, rather than in the center" (*De Tabernakel,* 2nd ed., p. 234). The trays were used when the lamps were extinguished; according to some they were filled with water, and the charred wick was dropped in the water in order to avoid an unpleasant stench in the sanctuary (L. Schouten, p. 237).

In the Lord's dwelling place among Israel a lampstand or candelabra could of course not be absent; without light there is no life (cf. Rev. 18:23; 2 Sam. 21:17; Job 18:6; Jer. 25:10). Zechariah 4 and Revelation 1:12, 20 give us an insight into the symbolic meaning of the golden lampstand (see

Ridderbos and Greijdanus on those verses in this commentary series). The golden lampstand with its *seven* branches was a symbol of the Lord's church, fed by the oil of the Spirit (cf. also Greijdanus on Rev. 1:4).

Concerning the making of the golden lampstand, see Heinisch's commentary. Schouten points out that the lampstand was made in such a way that it surpassed normal human skill (p. 228). He sees in the lampstand a foreshadowing of Christ, and refers to Revelation 21:23 etc.; cf. Isaiah 60:19f. But the Scriptures point rather to the Spirit and the church, whose Head, however, is Christ. There is no scriptural reason to seek a mythical symbolism, such as a representation of the world-tree and the seven planets, in the lampstand.

E. *The tabernacle* (26:1–37)

The word "tabernacle" is derived from the Latin "tabernaculum" or tent. This chapter gives us a good idea of what the tabernacle looked like, and how it was to be built, although opinions differ on a few details. Concerning the meaning of the tabernacle, cf. Hebrews 9; concerning the fulfillment of the symbolic meaning of the tabernacle, cf. Revelation 21:3. Even if the division into courtyard (cf. 27:9–18), Holy Place, and Most Holy Place were also found in the temples of other nations such as the Babylonians and Egyptians, the Lord gives an entirely different meaning to this division for Israel. Only the Scriptures can answer the question as to what the tabernacle represented: e.g., the world as we can divide it into the earth (the courtyard), the heaven or firmament (Holy Place) and the "highest heavens" (e.g., Ps. 115:16) where God, the angels and the saints dwell (the Most Holy Place). The Scriptures give the impression that the tabernacle represented that which was found in much greater glory and perfection in the heavens as the dwelling place of God, the angels and the saints (cf. Heb. 9:11, 22–24; 10:19–20; Rev. 1:4–5; see Grosheide on the references in Hebrews, and Greijdanus on Rev. 1 in this commentary series; see also Introduction, p. 13–15). Again, we must remember that Moses saw a model of this tabernacle on the mountain (cf. v. 30), so that he had a clear concept of all its parts. Concerning the events that befell the tabernacle, see van Gelderen on 1 Kings 8:4. When we consider the meaning of this chapter for us as Christians, we must stay with what the Scriptures, and especially the New Testament, say, and look at the tabernacle as a whole, rather than seeking a "deeper" meaning in every loop, clasp, and crossbar.

26:1–14 *"Make the tabernacle with ten curtains of finely twisted linen and blue, purple and scarlet yarn, with cherubim worked into them by a skilled craftsman. All the curtains are to be the same size—twenty-eight cubits long and four cubits wide.*

Join five of the curtains together, and do the same with the other five. Make loops of blue material along the edge of the end curtain in one set, and do the same with the end curtain in the other set. Make fifty loops on one curtain and fifty loops on the end curtain of the other set, with the loops opposite each other. Then make fifty gold clasps and use them to fasten the curtains together so that the tabernacle is a unit.

"Make curtains of goat hair for the tent over the tabernacle—eleven altogether. All eleven curtains are to be the same size—thirty cubits long and four cubits wide. Join five of the curtains together into one set and the other six into another set. Fold the sixth curtain double at the front of the tent. Make fifty loops along the edge of the end curtain in one set and also along the edge of the end curtain in the other set. Then make fifty bronze clasps and put them in the loops to fasten the tent together as a unit. As for the additional length of the tent curtains, the half curtain that is left over is to hang down at the rear of the tabernacle. The tent curtains will be a cubit longer on both sides; what is left will hang over the sides of the tabernacle so as to cover it. Make for the tent a covering of ram skins dyed red, and over that a covering of hides of sea cows."

Verse 1 speaks of *"the* tabernacle," referring back to 25:8–9. For the various materials mentioned in verse 1, see commentary on 25:4; concerning the cherubim, see commentary on 25:18. Verses 1–14, cf. 36:8–19. The "fine linen" of 25:4 had to be twined ("finely twined linen"), made of threads consisting of several twined strands. The skills acquired in Egypt were to be put to use by the Israelites in the making of the tabernacle. "Worked into them by a skilled craftsman": "the work of a craftsman, (31:4) who can weave in golden strands (28:6, 15; 39:3, 8) and work in figures (v. 31; 36:8, 35), and who is distinguished from the embroiderer (v. 36) and the simple weaver (28:32; 39:27)" (Dillmann-Ryssel). These craftsmen were to weave the representations of the cherubim into the fine white linen with colored yarn; all ten curtains of which verses 1–6 speak were to be made in this manner. "Cubit," see commentary on 25:10. The ten curtains or tapestries were to be joined together into two large curtains, each containing five segments. Each piece was 28 cubits long and 20 cubits wide.

"In one set" (v. 4) reads literally "at the juncture"; the meaning is somewhat unclear but the interpretation "in one set" (cf. also RSV) is probably the best. Moses had to attach fifty loops at each end of the two large curtains, a total of one hundred loops per curtain (vv. 4–5). The fifty clasps (v. 6) were thus shaped in such a way that each could hook together two opposite loops, so that the curtains formed a unit. The present-day Bedouins occasionally still make tents in this manner. Some think that this large inner curtain, together with the frames mentioned later, formed both the walls and the ceiling of the tabernacle, in which case the curtain did not hang on the outside, but on the inside, and covered nine cubits of the ten-cubit high frames. The one large piece then was used for the Most Holy Place, the other for the Holy Place. It is unknown exactly how this large curtain then was to be folded and attached. The curtains rather than the frames are mentioned and described first, which proves that they were considered more important, as is still true among the Bedouins. Not all interpreters agree with the view given above. Some let the inner curtain hang on the outside, so that it did not cover the larger part of the gold-covered crossbars. But the counter argument is that in that case the weight of the heavy outer curtains would have been too hard on the thin inner curtains of "finely twisted linen." A point like this can, of course, not be decided with absolute certainty on the basis of the text before us. But verses 12–13 are correctly used as an argument against the first view (cf. also 40:18–19, and Schouten, pp. 202–203).

I believe, therefore, that the curtain of finely twisted linen hung on the outside; no mention is made of hooks and loops which would have been necessary to hang the curtain on the inside. Furthermore, any damage to the inner curtain due to the weight of the curtain made of goat hair could be minimized by stretching the latter tightly. We can also ask why it might not have been the intent to make a new curtain periodically. It is thus best to assume that the frames, overlaid with gold, formed the walls, while the inner curtain was visible only as the ceiling.[21]

According to verse 33 the seam where the two sections of the curtain were joined by means of the loops and clasps was to be located exactly where the curtain that separated the Holy Place from the Most Holy Place was to hang. Since the former curtain was forty cubits long and twenty-eight cubits wide, we must imagine that it was placed over the frame of the tabernacle. The Holy Place, which was twenty cubits long, was thus covered by half the length of the curtain of finely twisted linen, while the other half covered the Most Holy Place, which was ten cubits long, and the back wall, which was probably one cubit thick. This left a section nine cubits long, which then simply hung down. The width of the curtain covered the width of the tabernacle, which measured ten cubits, and the frame, which was probably one cubit thick on both sides. This left sixteen cubits, so that on both sides the curtain hung down eight cubits. Thus, at the back side a one-cubit high section of the frame was exposed at the

---

[21]Gispen holds the view that the "frames" were solid boards (cf. KJV); if the frames were not solid, the curtain would, of course, also have been visible through the frames. See commentary on verses 15–30 (tr.).

bottom, and a section of two cubits high along the sides (cf. e.g., Kittel, P.R.E., 3rd ed., XIX, p. 35; see also commentary on vv. 23–25). The front was thus left uncovered (cf. v. 36).

Verses 7–13 contain instructions concerning the second curtain, made of goat hair (cf. commentary on 25:4 and 36:14–18). This curtain, which was to be the tent over the tabernacle, was also to be made in sections; these sections were to be woven from spun goat hair (cf. 35:26). The eleven sections were then to be joined together into two large curtains, one containing five, the other six sections. The sixth curtain was to be folded double at the front of the tent so that it was only two cubits wide; this made the tent cover slightly higher at the front. Flavius Josephus already assumed that this was to represent the façade and "portico." Furthermore, this insured that the seams of the inner and outer curtains would not be superimposed, and this measure thus helped make the tent tight. Verse 10, cf. verse 5.

The fifty clasps for this curtain were to be made of bronze rather than gold (see commentary on 25:3). The assembled curtain was forty-four cubits long, and thirty cubits wide, four cubits longer and two cubits wider than the curtain of finely twisted linen. But since the sixth curtain was folded double, the total length was forty-two cubits, so that this curtain was two cubits wider and longer than the curtain of finely twisted linen. Verses 12–13 indicate that this curtain was to hang down two cubits at the rear of the tabernacle, and one cubit on both sides. "The half curtain that is left over" (v. 12) thus refers to the two extra cubits that were left after the sixth curtain had been folded double. Verse 13 refers to the extra width, which also amounted to two cubits.[22] Cf. also note on verses 23–25. Verse 14, see commentary on 25:5; 36:19. We do not hear much about these curtains (cf. Num. 3:25; 4:25); they served as protection in bad weather. The various curtains were put up as one tent (cf. 27:19; 35:18; 38:20, 31; 39:40; Num. 3:36–37; 4:25, 32).

26:15–30 *"Make upright frames of acacia wood for the tabernacle. Each frame is to be ten cubits long and a cubit and a half wide, with two projections set parallel to each other. Make all the frames of the tabernacle in this way. Make twenty frames*

---

[22]Verses 12 and 13 indicate that the extra length and width were to hang down at the rear and over the sides of the tabernacle. Given the dimensions of the tabernacle, the outer curtain must have hung down nine cubits on the sides, and eleven cubits at the rear (assuming that the frames were one cubit thick), rather than one and two cubits respectively. Verses 12 and 13 may therefore refer to the extent to which the outer curtain hung down *beyond* the inner curtain. Since the tabernacle was ten cubits high and the curtain at the rear hung down eleven cubits, we can assume that the outer curtain was stretched away from the tabernacle and pegged to the ground, so that it would not touch the soil (tr.).

for the south side of the tabernacle and make forty silver bases to go under them—two bases for each frame, one under each projection. For the other side, the north side of the tabernacle, make twenty frames and forty silver bases—two under each frame. Make six frames for the far end, that is, the west end of the tabernacle, and make two frames for the corners at the far end. At these two corners they must be double from the bottom all the way to the top, and fitted into a single ring; both shall be like that. So there will be eight frames and sixteen silver bases—two under each frame.

"Also make crossbars of acacia wood: five for the frames on one side of the tabernacle, five for those on the other side, and five for the frames on the west, at the far end of the tabernacle. The center crossbar is to extend from end to end at the middle of the frames. Overlay the frames with gold and make gold rings to hold the crossbars. Also overlay the crossbars with gold.

"Set up the tabernacle according to the plan shown you on the mountain."

"Acacia wood," see commentary on 25:5. There is no indication as to the thickness of the wood, but it was probably one cubit thick (see above). The word translated "frames" in the NIV is used only in connection with the tabernacle and in Ezekiel 27:6, where its meaning is uncertain (NIV: "deck," KJV: "benches"). I prefer the translation "boards" (cf. KJV). Kennedy, on the other hand, thinks of wooden frames through which the curtain of finely twisted linen could be seen from the inside (cf. also D. J. Baarslag Dzn., *De Bijbelse Geschiedenis in de omlijsting van de historie van het Oosten*, I, pp. 458–461). But in my opinion this view is not supported by the text, and the arguments for it are not strong. The LXX translates *stuloi* or "pillars." The "projections" in verse 17 are literally "hands." I assume on the basis of verse 19 that these projections were long and narrow, and extended from the base of each of the frames that were then joined by means of a separate band, which would provide stability. Riehm *(Handwörterbuch)* defends the view that each board consisted of two *parts,* joined by bands; hence the two bases for each board. The ends of the boards were pointed, and were stuck directly into the ground through the silver bases. The bases then were square silver plates with a large hole through which the boards were stuck. It is then not necessary to assume that the boards rested on the silver bases, which were placed on the ground; otherwise it would have been necessary to place solid boards under the bases to prevent them from sinking into the ground. But it is preferable to consider these two "hands" to be projections rather than two parts, while Riehm is then correct in the sense that each projection was placed in the ground through a base. It is unlikely that the silver bases were cone-shaped collars that were buried in the ground. But it is clear that we cannot say with certainty that the concept that we believe to be most true to the text is indeed the correct one, since the text allows for a number of interpretations. Moses did not have this problem, since he had also seen the pattern.

Moses had to make twenty frames for the south side, and forty silver bases; and the same number of frames and bases for the north side (vv. 20–21). If we assume that the frames adjoined each other, which is most likely, then each of the long sides measured 30 cubits (20 x 1½ cubits; cf. v. 16). Similarly, the rear measured 9 cubits (6 x 1½ cubits; v. 22). The words for "south" and "west" have led some interpreters to believe that they could have been written by an inhabitant of Palestine, but not by Moses, thus ignoring the question as to whether the Lord Himself used these words. But Johannes de Groot wrote, not about this passage in particular, but about Hebrew in general: "This language as it is known to us from the Old Testament clearly has a Palestinian imprint. Just like our Dutch language, with its many terms derived from agriculture and navigation, reveals the peculiarities of both our land and the people, so the Hebrew language has not only an Israelite, but also a Palestinian character, whereby the Palestinian is primary, the Israelite secondary. That language must have developed long before the Israelites entered Palestine. This is shown by the name for the Mediterranean Sea, which is called the 'hindmost sea'; the term for 'West,' which is simply 'sea,' i.e., the Mediterranean Sea; the word for 'South,' which is nothing but the geographical term for the steppe which borders on Palestine to the South . . ." (*De Palestijnsche achtergrond van den Pentateuch*, 1928). The word for "west" in verse 22 is indeed "sea"; "the southside" is literally "on the side of the *negev* to the right *(teman)*." But neither *negev* nor *teman* were necessarily proper nouns originally, since they also mean "dry land" and "that which is at the right" respectively. But we can even go further than de Groot and assume that Jacob already spoke Canaanite Hebrew. The use of these terms does not argue against the fact that Moses used them or that the Lord spoke these words to Moses, in spite of the fact that they reflect a Palestinian perspective. As for the points of the compass, the Semite turned toward the East as representing that which was ahead of him, to the West as to that which was behind him, while the South was that which was on the right, and the North that which was on the left. The tabernacle was to be oriented with its back toward the West, and its front toward the East, where the sun rises (cf. also 27:13). We must be careful with the assertion that temples usually faced East; in a well-documented article Busink notes: "We cannot consider the question of the orientation as having been solved" ("Tempelbouw in Oud-Mesopotamie," Jaarbericht No. 5 van het *Vooraziatisch-Egyptisch gezelschap Ex Oriente Lux 1937–1938*, p. 416).

The "frames for the corners" are discussed next (vv. 23–25). Verse 24 is especially obscure and has been interpreted in many different ways. Moses had to make two frames for the corners. They were to be double (or "twins," "equal") from top to bottom and be fitted into a single ring.[23]

Thus the rear of the tabernacle had eight boards with sixteen silver bases. The rear of the tabernacle was then ten cubits wide, since to the nine cubits of verse 22 must be added one cubit: one-half cubit for each corner frame. It is also probable that these corner frames were positioned in such a way that they did not add to the overall length of thirty cubits. But it is difficult to gain a clear conception of these corner boards on the basis of the text. I select here the view that is in my opinion the most likely one, that of de Visser: "We imagine that the two corner boards, which were of the same height and width as the other boards, were placed against those of the backside. They thus helped in part, i.e., each with one-half cubit, to close off the Most Holy Place, which was ten cubits wide. The other part, i.e., one cubit on either side, less that portion which rested against the boards of the north and south side, extended outward. This protruding part was cut away from the bottom to the first ring (which is actually the uppermost ring) and the first crossbar, so that the crossbars could be continuous, while the part which still protruded at the top served to prevent that the corners of the curtain would touch the ground. Thus we remain faithful to the most probable reading of v. 24, we have eight boards on the west side, and we do justice to v. 23, which seems to indicate that something special was done to the two boards to make them into corner boards."

In verses 26–29 Moses was told to make fifteen crossbars, five for each of the three sides. The center one, which was halfway between the top and the bottom, was to be continuous from one end to the other. The other crossbars, four on each of the three sides, were thus not continuous. Gold rings were to serve as holders (lit. "house") for the bars (cf. 25:26–27). When all this had been done Moses could set up the tabernacle, so that it would look exactly like the plan that was shown them (or him) on the mountain (cf. 25:9, 40; 27:8; Acts 7:44; Heb. 8:5). "Plan," cf. van Gelderen on 2 Kings 1:7. Moses also had to take care that the tabernacle was properly oriented, with its open side toward the East (cf. ch. 40).

26:31–37 *"Make a curtain of blue, purple and scarlet yarn and finely twisted linen, with cherubim worked into it by a skilled craftsman. Hang it with gold hooks on four posts of acacia wood overlaid with gold and standing on four silver bases. Hang the curtain from the clasps and place the ark of the Testimony behind the curtain. The curtain will separate the Holy Place from the Most Holy Place. Put the atonement cover on the ark of the Testimony in the Most Holy Place. Place the*

---

[23]See RSV for a different interpretation (tr.).

table outside the curtain on the north side of the tabernacle and put the lampstand opposite it on the south side.

"For the entrance to the tent make a curtain of blue, purple and scarlet yarn and finely twisted linen—the work of an embroiderer. Make gold hooks for this curtain and five posts of acacia wood overlaid with gold. And cast five bronze bases for them."

"Blue, purple, and scarlet yarn and finely twisted linen," see commentary on verse 1; 25:4. "With cherubim," "by a skilled craftsman," see commentary on verse 1 (Cf. also 36:35–38; 2 Chron. 3:14.) It was thus a very costly curtain that separated the Holy Place from the Most Holy Place. "The ark of the Testimony" (v. 33), see commentary on 25:16, 21. "Clasps," cf. verse 6. The curtain (cf. Heb. 6:19–20; 9:3, 7–8, 12, 24–26; 10:20) thus hung below the clasps that joined the curtains of finely twisted linen (see commentary on v. 6). Since the curtain hung below these clasps the area behind the curtain, the Most Holy Place, was ten cubits long, while the Holy Place, in front of the curtain, was twenty cubits long. Verses 34–35, cf. 40:20, 22, 24. Verse 34, see commentary on 25:17, 21. Verse 35, see commentary on 25:23–30, 31–40. "Opposite," cf. 14:2. "On the south side," cf. verse 18. Verse 36, see commentary on verse 1 and 25:4. "The work of an embroiderer" (v. 37), cf. "skilled craftsman" in verses 1, 31. Verses 36–37, cf. also 36:37–38. This curtain thus served as a door. We do not know how the posts, mentioned in verses 32 and 37, were placed, nor what they looked like. Note that no mention is made of a floor made of boards; it is unlikely that such a floor existed, although e.g., Schouten assumed this (pp. 47–49).

F. *The altar of burnt offering* (27:1–8)

After the tabernacle itself came the courtyard. In this courtyard there had to be an altar; the instructions as to how it was to be built are found in verses 1–8 (cf. 38:1–7; 20:22–26).

27:1–8 *"Build an altar of acacia wood, three cubits high; it is to be square, five cubits long and five cubits wide. Make a horn at each of the four corners, so that the horns and the altar are of one piece, and overlay the altar with bronze. Make all its utensils of bronze—its pots to remove the ashes, and its shovels, sprinkling bowls, meat forks and firepans. Make a grating for it, a bronze network, and make a bronze ring at each of the four corners of the network. Put it under the ledge of the altar so that it is halfway up the altar. Make poles of acacia wood for the altar and overlay them with bronze. The poles are to be inserted into the rings so they will be on two sides of the altar when it is carried. Make the altar hollow, out of boards. It is to be made just as you were shown on the mountain."*

"An altar," literally "the altar" (cf. RSV; cf. 30:18, 20; 40:7, 32). "Acacia wood," see commentary on 25:5. "Cubits," see commentary on 25:10. "Horns," cf. van Gelderen on 1 Kings 1:50, who believes that the horns represent the sacrificial animal rather than God: "Stated more accurately and adequately the horns symbolize the atoning power of altar and sacrifice. They have a special significance in the atonement ritual, since some of the blood was put on the horns before the rest was poured out at the base of the altar: Exod. 29:12; Lev. 4:7, 18, 25, 30, 34. From the altar of burnt offering the atoning power was also transferred to the altar of fragrant incense, Lev. 4:7, 18." The shape of these horns is unknown to us. The horns had to be of one piece with the altar (cf. 25:18–19, 31; 30:2).

Verse 3, see van Gelderen on 1 Kings 7:40. "Meat forks," cf. 1 Samuel 2:13f. "Firepans" (or "censers," cf. Lev. 10:1; 16:12; 1 Kings 7:50) is the same word used in 25:38 for "trays." "All its utentils," literally "according to all its utensils" or "concerning all its utensils" (for the NIV translation, cf. Gesenius-Kautsch, *Hebrew Grammar,* 2nd English ed., Oxford, 1936, § 117n, 143e; cf. v. 19.) Concerning the cleaning of the altar by removing the ashes, cf. Leviticus 6:10. Bronze grating had to cover the lower half of the altar, and bronze rings were to be attached to the four corners of the grating to receive the carrying poles (cf. 25:13–15, 27–28). The grating then had to be attached to the altar, perhaps at the bottom (?). The ledge of the altar would then be above the grating and was probably formed by dirt that was used to fill in the space between the grating and the altar; we must thus assume that a ramp was built to lead up to that ledge (cf. Lev. 9:22). We can also assume that the altar, which was hollow, was filled with dirt before use, and emptied before it was transported from one place to the next. Böhl points out that similar portable altars were carried along by Assyrian kings on their military campaigns (cf. 20:24). "Boards" (v. 8) is the same word used for "tablets" (cf. 24:12; 31:18; 32:15f.; 34:28–29). Verse 8b, cf. 25:9, 40; 26:30. "It is to be made," literally "they shall make it," i.e., those who were later appointed to carry out the instructions received by Moses. These verses refer to the altar simply as "the altar"; it was later called the "altar of burnt offering" (cf. 30:28; 31:9), as distinguished from the altar of fragrant incense (cf. 30:1–10); since the latter was overlaid with gold, the altar of burnt offering was also called the "bronze altar" (cf. 38:30; 39:39). It probably did not have a bottom or cover so the actual offering was brought on "earth."

G. *The courtyard* (27:9–19)

The courtyard was new evidence of the fact that, although the Lord dwelled among Israel, the Israelites could not freely approach Him. (Cf.

39:9–20; Pss. 100:4; 116:17–19.) The work of Christ has removed the need for this restriction; the Lord now dwells in the hearts of His people. We are privileged above the Israel of the Old Covenant: besides the approach to the Lord's throne through prayer and "falling asleep in the Lord" (cf. 1 Cor. 15:18), which was also open to the Israelites, we no longer have a courtyard beyond which the vast majority of the Israelites could not approach, and which they were not always able or allowed to enter.

27:9–18 *"Make a courtyard for the tabernacle. The south side shall be a hundred cubits long and is to have curtains of finely twisted linen, with twenty posts and twenty bronze bases and with silver hooks and bands on the posts. The north side shall also be a hundred cubits long and is to have curtains, with twenty posts and twenty bronze bases and with silver hooks and bands on the posts.*

"The west end of the courtyard shall be fifty cubits wide and have curtains, with ten posts and ten bases. On the east end, toward the sunrise, the courtyard shall also be fifty cubits wide. Curtains fifteen cubits long are to be on one side of the entrance, with three posts and three bases, and curtains fifteen cubits long are to be on the other side, with three posts and three bases.

"For the entrance to the courtyard, provide a curtain twenty cubits long, of blue, purple and scarlet yarn and finely twisted linen—the work of an embroiderer —with four posts and four bases. All the posts around the courtyard are to have silver bands and hooks, and bronze bases. The courtyard shall be a hundred cubits long and fifty cubits wide, with curtains of finely twisted linen five cubits high, and with bronze bases."

The courtyard was a fenced-in area that extended, according to the description, also along the sides and rear of the tabernacle. The expression "the south side" (v. 9) is also used in 26:18 (see commentary on that verse). The word used for "curtains" is different from that used in 26:36–37; the latter is from a root that means "to cover," while the word used here is derived from "slinging." "Fine twisted linen," see commentary on 26:1. "Posts" (v. 10), cf. 26:32, 37; lit. "its posts," i.e., of the courtyard. "Bases," cf. 26:19. "Hooks," cf. 26:32, 37. "Bands" (cf. v. 17) or binding rings (from a root that means "to bind"). The Hebrew words may also mean "connecting rods" (cf. 38:19), rather than bands or rings (in the latter case the hooks for the curtains were then inserted in the rings).

"West end" (v. 12) and "east end" (v. 13), see commentary on 26:18, 22. "Side" (vv. 14–15), lit. "shoulder" (cf. 28:6, where the word is used for the shoulder pieces of the ephod): the sections of the enclosure between the entrance and the long sides of the courtyard. "Curtain" (v. 16) is the same word as in 26:36–37; see above. "Blue, purple and scarlet yarn and finely twisted linen," see commentary on 25:4. "The work of an embroiderer," cf. 26:36. "Bands" (v. 17), see above. "Bases," see commentary on 26:19. The enclosure was to be half as high as the tabernacle (cf. 26:16). There is no need to assume that more than sixty posts were needed (cf. Keil, and the illustration in his *Archäologie*, 2nd ed.). The posts were placed 5 cubits apart, so that the courtyard was a rectangular area, 100 cubits long and 50 cubits wide.

27:19 *"All the other articles used in the service of the tabernacle, whatever their function, including all the tent pegs for it and those for the courtyard, are to be of bronze."*

Verse 19a, see commentary on 27:3. "Whatever their function," lit. "in all the service thereof" (cf. KJV); the phrase can also refer to the work of making, setting up, and arranging these articles. The pegs and other assorted smaller objects were to be made of bronze. This verse is an indication that we have only a partial listing of what needed to be made for the tabernacle, and it is therefore not surprising if we cannot form a complete picture of how the various components of the tabernacle fit together. With verse 19 end the instructions for the tabernacle and the courtyard.

H. *The oil for the lampstand (27:20–21)*

27:20, 21 *"Command the Israelites to bring you clear oil of pressed olives for the light so that the lamps may be kept burning. In the Tent of Meeting, outside the curtain that is in front of the Testimony, Aaron and his sons are to keep the lamps burning before the Lord from evening till morning. This is to be a lasting ordinance among the Israelites for the generations to come."*

These verses contain instructions concerning the oil for use in the lampstand. "Clear oil of pressed olives," see commentary on 25:6. "The oil for the lampstand and the anointing oil is, in agreement with the original text, described as 'pure beaten olive oil' (Exod. 27:20; Lev. 24:2, the oil for the daily meal offering as 'beaten oil' (Exod. 29:40; Num. 28:5). To obtain this oil the finest olives were selected. These were then squashed into a pulpy mass in a stone pestle, and this mass was placed in a basket. The oil which dripped through this basket, and which, due to the careful process, was not mixed with any other parts of the olive, is the "pure beaten oil.' This oil is clear and does not smoke when it burns. By placing weights (such as rocks) on the contents of the basket, the second kind of olive oil, the 'beaten oil' is produced, which is still of excellent quality" (cf. F. J. Bruyel, "De Olijfboom"). "For the light," see commentary on 25:6. "So that the lamps may be kept burning," lit. "to set up lamps perpetually."

The tabernacle here is called for the first time the "Tent of Meeting." We must in the first place think of the tabernacle as the place where the Lord would meet with Moses and speak with him (25:22), the place where the Lord would reveal Himself to Moses in his role as the mediator between Himself and the people (cf. 20:19ff.). The small dimensions of the court-yard and the tabernacle, as well as the arrangement of the tabernacle, precludes the possibility that the tent was to be a meeting place for the people, or for the people and the Lord. But since the tent was to be a meeting place, albeit in a limited sense, it had to be illuminated during the night (cf. also 30:7-8; 1 Sam. 3:3; 2 Chron. 13:11). Aaron and his sons (note the transition to ch. 28) were responsible for keeping the lamps burning during the night (during the day light came in through the curtains of the Holy Place and of the Most Holy Place); the golden lampstand was placed in front of the curtain that separated the two parts of the tabernacle (cf. 26:35). The invisible God was the *living* God; His dwelling place a *true* dwelling place. (Cf. also Lev. 24:3).

Verse 21b contains an expression that recurs again and again, also in Leviticus: "a lasting ordinance . . . for the generations to come" (cf. also 12:24). The Israelites had to keep this ordinance into the far future (see commentary on 19:9). This, like the provisions of the ceremonial law, was fulfilled by the work of Christ, and therefore abrogated. "Lasting," see Aalders on Genesis 17:7. "The Testimony," see commentary on 25:16. This was another proof of the importance attached to the Law that had been placed in the ark. The living God is the Lawgiver.

I. *The sacred garments* (28:1-43)

This chapter deals with the sacred garments that were to be made for Aaron and his sons, who had been chosen to be priests. Among the many difficulties that this chapter presents, those concerning the ephod and the Urim and Thummim stand out; a consensus on these problems will not soon be reached. Even the impressive book by Hermann Thiersch, *Ependytes und Epod* (Verlag W. Kohlhammer, Stuttgart-Berlin, 1936), has elicited disagreement concerning e.g., its interpretation of the Urim and the Thummim, although it cannot be denied that the book makes a significant contribution toward the solution of the ephod problem. It is best to go through this chapter verse by verse, and to refer to Thiersch's book and other views whenever necessary.

28:1-5 *"Have Aaron your brother brought to you from among the Israelites, along with his sons Nadab and Abihu, Eleazar and Ithamar, so they may serve me as priests. Make sacred garments for your brother Aaron, to give him dignity and honor. Tell all the skilled men to whom I have given wisdom in such matters that they are to make garments for Aaron, for his consecration, so he may serve me as priest. These are the garments they are to make: a breastpiece, an ephod, a robe, a woven tunic, a turban and a sash. They are to make these sacred garments for your brother Aaron and his sons, so they may serve me as priests. Have them use gold, and blue, purple and scarlet yarn, and fine linen."*

The Lord now mentioned by name those who had been chosen to fill the priestly office: Moses' brother, Aaron, and his four sons. "Nadab and Abihu," see commentary on 24:1; after their death (Lev. 10) only Aaron, Eleazar, and Ithamar were left. "Serve me as priests": the root of the verb used here is usually taken to mean "to assist someone"; the priest was then someone who stood before God, serving Him (cf. also Heb. 10:11). In Deuteronomy 10:8 and 18:7 this was applied to all the *Levites,* rather than to only Aaron and his sons (cf. Num. 3:5f.); but here only the latter are mentioned (cf. Num. 18:6-7; Heb. 5:1-6). The Aaronic priesthood was a "step backward": the priesthood in the order of Melchizedek was higher. But Christ also brings the fulfillment of the Aaronic priesthood, so that this "step backward" served to reach a much more glorious dispensation (cf. Hebrews, and especially Heb. 7). The priest was indispensable in the life of fellowship with the Lord: he was (with the prophet, and also with the mediator, Moses) its enduring and unchanging element. The prophet and the priest were initially not antithetical, but rather complementary; at least, this was their intended relationship. The prophets later spoke out against the *sins* of the priests and *sinful* worship (cf. e.g., Aalders on Jer. 7:21-28).

We must understand "Have Aaron your brother brought to you" in the first place in a literal sense (cf. 40:12-14; Lev. 8:6, 13, 24; Num. 3:6. "Eleazar," cf. Num. 20:23-28; Deut. 10:6; Josh. 24:33). In verse 2 Moses was instructed to make sacred garments for his brother Aaron; these were the garments for the high priest. The garments for the regular priests are discussed later (vv. 40-43). "Sacred" and "consecrate" are both from the same root, and mean "set apart" and "to set apart for the Lord's service." These garments showed that those who wore them were not ordinary Israelites, but Israelites who had been "set apart" from the rest of the people (v. 1) to serve as priests. The high-priestly garments especially could be made only by those who were skilled (lit. "wise of heart"), to whom the Lord had given wisdom (lit. "filled with a spirit of

wisdom"). This "wisdom" referred to technical skill, which was, however, a fruit of the Lord's Spirit. Although many parallels to e.g., the
breastpiece and the ephod are thought to have been found in Syria, As-
syria, Greece, and Egypt (cf. Thiersch, *Ependytes und Epod*), we are
faced here with something that is of unique significance, made by spe-
cially bestowed skills.

Verse 4 lists the garments that were to be made for Aaron. Breastpiece
and ephod were already mentioned, in reverse order, in 25:7; we can
therefore not say whether the one was more excellent than the other on the
basis of verse 4, although the sequel seems to support the statement that the
ephod was made primarily for the sake of the breastpiece. Concerning the
tunic, see commentary on verse 39. Although I discuss each of the garments separately below, it might be helpful to note here that the breastpiece
was a square on which twelve relatively small precious stones were placed
in four horizontal rows of three stones each. The breastpiece was closely
attached to the ephod, a tight-fitting garment without sleeves, which probably reached below the hips. The ephod was worn over the robe or outer
garment, which was also sleeveless, and perhaps reached down to the feet;
around the hem of the robe alternating pomegranates and golden bells were
sown. The tunic, with sleeves, reached down to the feet, and was worn
under the robe.

This is the most likely concept; the details, as well as the turban and the
sash, will be discussed later. Verse 5, see commentary on 25:3–4.

28:6–14 *"Make the ephod of gold, and of blue, purple and scarlet yarn, and of
finely twisted linen—the work of a skilled craftsman. It is to have two shoulder
pieces attached to two of its corners, so it can be fastened. Its skillfully woven
waistband is to be like it—of one piece with the ephod and made with gold, and
with blue, purple and scarlet yarn, and with finely twisted linen.*

*"Take two onyx stones and engrave on them the names of the sons of Israel in the
order of their birth—six names on one stone and the remaining six on the other.
Engrave the names of the sons of Israel on the two stones the way a gem cutter
engraves a seal. Then mount the stones in gold filigree settings and fasten them on
the shoulder pieces of the ephod as memorial stones for the sons of Israel. Aaron is
to bear the names on his shoulders as a memorial before the LORD. Make gold
filigree settings and two braided chains of pure gold, like a rope, and attach the
chains to the settings."*

These verses describe the ephod (cf. 39:2–7). The root of the word
"ephod" probably means "to put on" (cf. 29:5; Lev. 8:7). "Ephod" is
used as the name of both a priestly garment and an idol. When "ephod" is
used of a priestly garment it can refer to the specific garment of the high

priest as in these verses, or it is used with *bad* (''linen'') to indicate the linen ephod worn by the ordinary priest (cf. Noordtzij on 1 Chron. 15:27 in this series). ''Ephod is also used in Judges 8:26f.; 17:5; 18:14, 17f.; Hosea 3:4, where some interpreters think of an idol, but where most likely it also refers to a garment (cf. Noordtzij, *Gods Woord*, pp. 366–367). We can translate ''ephod'' as ''covering,'' ''that which is put on.'' The LXX uses one word (*epōmis*, lit. ''the upper part of the shoulder'') for both ''ephod'' and ''shoulder pieces,'' Thiersch has established parallels between the ephod and the *ependytēs* of antiquity. He describes it as a sheath-like garment. Before the Greek period a type of idol was found in the eastern part of the Mediterranean, usually small and depicting a very rigid attitude, which was dressed in a sheath-like garment, giving the statue a stiff and solemn air. Thiersch has traced the history and occurrence of this type of garment as fully as possible, and has reached interesting conclusions (pp. 108–110), of which I only mention that the *ependytēs* was worn over the long undergarment; it was a tight-fitting garment without sleeves, usually reaching down to the knees, which enclosed the entire body like a sheath. When it was long enough to cover the chest as well it could be attached with small shoulder straps or by means of clasps, placed on the shoulders; it could also be worn with a belt around the waist, in which case the garment was open at the back. It was decorated with a design of squares, filled with symbolic elements. The breast especially was heavily decorated. The *ependytēs* was worn primarily by statues of gods and by high priests, kings, emperors, and prophets (?), who were viewed as more or less superhuman beings. Statues that wore an *ependytēs* were usually associated with divining the future by means of casting dice. The origin of this kind of statue lies in Syria. Thiersch identifies this *ependytēs* with the ephod of the Old Testament. The similarities are indeed striking, showing once again that the Lord made use of objects similar to those that were used by other nations of that time, and gave them a unique significance. We should note that, according to Thiersch, the *ependytēs* was not found in either Egypt or Mesopotamia. Thiersch's study is important in that it helps us form a concept of the shape of the ephod.

Verses 5–6 list the materials from which the ''skilled men'' (v. 3) were to make the ephod (see commentary on 25:3–4). ''The work of a skilled craftsman'' and ''finely twisted linen,'' see commentary on 26:1. Thiersch and Friedrich Beck assume that the ephod was decorated with a pattern of squares; they speak of a chessboard pattern and believe that the white linen served as background, while the four colors (including the gold threads, cf. 39:3), were used for the variegated decoration. This would then be in agreement with the possible interpretation of verse 39, referring to a pattern woven into the tunic (see below), and also be most likely in view of the simple looms that were available. I merely mention this view, which cannot however be proven on the basis of the text.

"Shoulder pieces," see commentary on 27:14–15. "Fastened," cf. 26:3; here the participle of the verb "to be joined" is used. The two "corners" (KJV "edges") refer to the two upper edges. Verse 8 refers to the waistband of the ephod, which was to be "of one piece with the ephod" (cf. 25:19, 31; 27:2). Two onyx stones were to serve as rosettes on the shoulders ("onyx," Heb. *shoham* stones, see commentary on 25:7). "Birth" (v. 10), cf. Aalders on Genesis 2:4. According to Bolman the Egyptian goldsmiths and gem cutters had achieved a high level of skill during that period; the delicate compositions, the beautiful color combinations, as well as the tasteful shapes and the application of appropriate techniques are still surprising (p. 24). "Memorial" (v. 12), cf. 12:14. The people, who could not enter the tabernacle themselves, were thus represented before the Lord, which is the meaning of the two shoulder pieces. In the New Testament Jesus is the High Priest, who entered heaven itself to appear before God on our behalf (Heb. 9:24). Verse 12 speaks of God in anthropomorphic terms, as happens frequently in the Scriptures; in a sense the entire Bible speaks anthropomorphically. The Lord is omniscient, and thus did not need these memorial stones to be reminded of Israel, but it was a consolation for the Israelites, who could see the high priest as a permanent mediator. According to Flavious Josephus the names of the six eldest sons were engraved on the stone on the right shoulder, the names of the six younger sons on the left shoulder piece. These stones were encased in "gold filigree settings" (v. 11); "gold filigree settings" (vv. 13–14) with chains also had to be made; the latter served to attach the breastplate to the ephod (cf. vv. 22–25). "Pure gold," see commentary on 25:11. "Braided chains," see van Gelderen on 1 Kings 7:20.

28:15–30 *"Fashion a breastpiece for making decisions—the work of a skilled craftsman. Make it like the ephod: of gold, and of blue, purple and scarlet yarn, and of finely twisted linen. It is to be square—a span long and a span wide—and folded double. Then mount four rows of precious stones on it. In the first row there shall be a ruby, a topaz and a beryl; in the second row a turquoise, a sapphire and an emerald; in the third row a jacinth, an agate and an amethyst; in the fourth row a chrysolite, an onyx and a jasper. Mount them in gold filigree settings. There are to be twelve stones, one for each of the names of the sons of Israel, each engraved like a seal with the name of one of the twelve tribes.*

"For the breastpiece make braided chains of pure gold, like a rope. Make two gold rings for it and fasten them to two corners of the breastpiece. Fasten the two

gold chains to the rings at the corners of the breastpiece, and the other ends of the chains to the two settings, attaching them to the shoulder pieces of the ephod at the front. Make two gold rings and attach them to the other two corners of the breastpiece on the inside edge next to the ephod. Make two more gold rings and attach them to the bottom of the shoulder pieces on the front of the ephod, close to the seam just above the waistband of the ephod. The rings of the breastpiece are to be tied to the rings of the ephod with blue cord, connecting it to the waistband, so that the breastpiece will not swing out from the ephod.

"Whenever Aaron enters the Holy Place, he will bear the names of the sons of Israel over his heart on the breastpiece of decision as a continuing memorial before the LORD. *Also put the Urim and the Thummim in the breastpiece, so they may be over Aaron's heart whenever he enters the presence of the* LORD. *Thus Aaron will always bear the means of making decisions for the Israelites over his heart before the* LORD."

These verses describe the breastpiece (cf. 39:8–21). Verse 15, see commentary on verse 6. The Hebrew word translated "breastpiece" is *choshen;* its derivation and meaning are uncertain, so that the translation of the word is based on the description of this high-priestly garment. "Breastpiece for making decisions," i.e., divine decisions, judicial decisions, judgment. Verse 15 indicates that the breastpiece was to be made from the same materials as the ephod; it is thus a misconception to think of the breastpiece as made only of gold. It is best to conceive of the ephod as leaving the breast uncovered, while the breastpiece fits exactly in the area left uncovered by the ephod. The breastpiece then was a piece of cloth with golden settings for the precious stones.

The question is how we are to envision the use of this breastpiece in the making of "divine decisions." Verse 16 states that the breastpiece was to be square, a span (one half cubit) long and wide, and folded double (cf. 27:1; 26:9). The usual conception is that the breastpiece formed a sack in which the Urim and Thummim were placed (cf. v. 30). We do not know what the Urim and Thummim were; perhaps they were two stones that represented "yes" and "no." Thiersch rejects the idea of a sack in verse 16, and considers it a fundamental exegetical error. He believes that the breastpiece contained two layers of material because the gold settings and the precious stones would otherwise cause the breastpiece to wear out too rapidly. He does not believe that the Urim and Thummim were separate objects, since no separate instructions were given as to how they were to be made. They were in his view not distinct from the twelve stones, but rather refer to the spiritual meaning of the latter. He finds support for this view in Jewish tradition which, although it developed in a wrong direction, since it spoke of a "lighting up" or "remaining dull" of the stones, shows that it

267

was originally held that the Lord showed His presence in the twelve stones of the breastpiece and in the two memorial stones (v. 12). According to Thiersch, the Urim and Thummim were something divine that dwelled in the human apparatus as long as the people remained faithful to God. Hempel pointed out that verse 30 and Leviticus 8:8 can only refer to the putting in of material objects; but Thiersch believes that this only seems to be the case, and he speaks of the dual nature of the breastpiece, which had some kind of sacramental character.

I have presented this view in some detail because it is very appealing. Although I cannot accept it in view of verse 30 and Leviticus 8:8, I feel that it is of great importance because of the close connection it establishes between the Urim and the Thummim and the precious stones. I also reject the idea that verse 16 refers to a sack or bag, since the word that is used can mean either "folded double" or "double" (RSV); other arguments can be brought against this view as well.

The breastpiece was square, with four horizontal rows of three precious stones placed one below the other. Everywhere else breast decorations assumed the shape of a horizontal rectangle: "But this is precisely the distinguishing characteristic of the highpriestly ornament which has been given by special revelation (which is binding), through highly specific instructions and down to the smallest detail. This distinguished this ephod and its *choshen* in fact from all other sacral garments and emblems of other nations and times. It was and remained, like the completely lightless Most Holy Place of the temple, something unique, a stranger in this world" (Thiersch, p. 136). Similar breastpieces, albeit different in form, have also been found on Egyptian mummies and on the portraits of Assyrian kings.

The twelve stones that were to be mounted on the breastpiece are listed in verses 17–20.[24]

Driver observes that "the identity of several of the stones mentioned is very uncertain; for philology throws little or no light upon the meaning of the names, and the ancient versions in several cases give inconsistent renderings, or renderings which are themselves of uncertain interpretation" (pp. 302–303). This uncertainty is clearly illustrated when the lists of the twelve stones as given in various versions and commentaries are placed side by side:

---

[24]The author identifies and describes each of the twelve stones (based on Bolman, *De edelstenen uit den Bijbel gezien in het licht der hedendaagsche edelsteenkunde.* Amsterdam, 1938). This section has been omitted and the following paragraph and chart have been inserted, since (as the chart shows), Gispen's list agrees in only three instances with the NIV (nephrite is a variety of jasper) (tr.).

	NIV	KJV	RSV	GISPEN	LANGE
Row 1	ruby	sardius	sardius	jasper	sardius
	topaz	topaz	topaz	chrysolite	topaz
	beryl	carbuncle	carbuncle	malachite	emerald
Row 2	turquoise	emerald	emerald	haematite	carbuncle
	sapphire	sapphire	sapphire	lapis lazuli	sapphire
	emerald	diamond	diamond	green jasper	diamond
Row 3	jacinth	ligure	jacinth	amber	ligure
	agate	agate	agate	agate	agate
	amethyst	amethyst	amethyst	amethyst	amethyst
Row 4	chrysolite	beryl	beryl	turquoise	chrysolite
	onyx	onyx	onyx	chrysophrase	onyx
	jasper	jasper	jasper	nephrite	jasper

The only stones on which there is full agreement are the agate and the amethyst. It is beyond the scope of the present work to attempt to clarify the problems involved in the identification of the twelve stones (The reader is therefore referred to ZPEB, "Jewels and Precious Stones," 3:586–589).

The stones were probably smaller than is usually assumed, most likely no more than 1½ - 2 cm. (Thiersch, p. 177). The name of one of the twelve tribes of Israel was engraved on each of the twelve stones, probably in the order of birth (v. 21). "Engraved like a seal," cf. verse 11. Verse 22, cf. commentary on verse 14. Verses 22–28 indicate how the breastpiece was to be attached to the ephod (cf. vv. 13–14; v. 22 is a restatement of v. 14). The chains were attached to the two rings at the corners of the breastpiece, while the other end of the chains was attached to the two settings. Another possible interpretation (cf. RSV) is that the chains were pulled through the rings and that both ends of each chain were attached to the gold filigree settings. Two gold rings were also attached to the lower corners of the breastpiece on the inside, i.e., the side that was turned toward the ephod (v. 26). Two further gold rings were to be attached to the bottom of the shoulder pieces on the front of the ephod, close to the seam just above the waistband of the ephod, cf. verses 7–8 (v. 27). A blue cord then was pulled through the rings and the breastpiece was attached to the ephod in such a way that it could not move from its place. Thus Aaron would bear the names of the sons of Israel over his heart whenever he entered the sanctuary "as a continuing memorial before the Lord" (v. 29). "Blue," see commentary on 25:4. "Breastpiece of decision," see commentary on verse 14. "Memorial," see commentary on verse 12. Josephus mentions that later two larger rings were attached to the top of the breastpiece, which were connected with two rings on the back of the ephod by means of a cord.

"Urim and Thummim," see above. The literal meaning of Urim and Thummim is "lights" and "perfections." As stated above, we do not know what they were. Böhl's translation "holy dice" represents the most common view. Verse 29 supports in my opinion the view that they could not refer to the stones of the breastpiece (since Aaron already bore the names over his heart), unless we see verse 30 as parallel to verse 29. Thiersch's view is attractive, but it hinges on the (possible) translation "on the breastpiece" rather than "in the breastpiece" in verse 30 (see my commentary on Lev. 8:8). The Samaritan Pentateuch adds, "and you shall make the Urim and the Thummim," indicating that they were considered separate objects at a very early date. The LXX renders Urim and Thummim "manifestation and truth." The NIV translation "decisions *for* the Israelites" is better than "judgment (i.e., decision) *of* the Israelites" (KJV, RSV). The text does not help us much to arrive at a clear conception of what is meant by the Urim and Thummim. A final note: Aaron carried the names of the tribes on his shoulders (since v. 29 states "sons of Israel" we must perhaps assume that Joseph's name was engraved, rather than the names of Ephraim and Manasseh) and over his heart (vv. 12, 29). The emblem of one's official position was carried on the shoulder (cf. Isa. 9:6; 22:22), while an object that one wished to guard, like a seal on a chain or rope, was carried over the heart (cf. Song of Songs 8:6). The names of the tribes of Israel carried on Aaron's shoulder and over his heart thus expressed official care and responsibility, as well as love.

28:31–35 *"Make the robe of the ephod entirely of blue cloth, with an opening for the head in its center. There shall be a woven edge like a collar around this opening, so that it will not tear. Make pomegranates of blue, purple and scarlet yarn around the hem of the robe, with gold bells between them. The gold bells and the pomegranates are to alternate around the hem of the robe. Aaron must wear it when he ministers. The sound of the bells will be heard when he enters the Holy Place before the LORD and when he comes out, so that he will not die."*

Verses 31–35 give instructions concerning the robe (cf. 39:22–26). For a general description of the robe, see commentary on verse 4. The Hebrew *me'il* is perhaps derived from a root meaning "to cover"; it refers to "an exterior tunic, wide and long, reaching to the ankles, but without sleeves" (Gesenius-Tregelles), hence the translation "robe" (cf. Noordtzij on 1 Kings 15:27). This is somewhat confusing, since the "robe" was worn over the "tunic" (v. 39), but under the ephod (cf. Lev. 8:7). Thiersch thinks that the robe was basically another ephod. Josephus described the robe as resembling a tube or cylinder. The robe had to be made entirely of blue cloth (see commentary on 25:4). It was apparently put on over the head (v. 32). "Woven," cf. commentary on 26:1. The word translated "collar" (v. 32) is of uncertain meaning; it has been variously translated "collar," "coat of mail," "corselet." The Hebrew word may be related to an Egyptian word for "leather," although the Egyptians were very adept in making mail shirts of linen. The "collar" was apparently woven (v. 31: 39:22); its function was to reinforce the opening so that it would not tear.

Verse 33, see commentary on 25:4. The pomegranates were made from colored yarn and finely twisted linen. The pomegranate *(Punica granatum)* is still one of the more important products of Palestine; its fruit is dark red, about the size of an orange. The word used for "bell" (v. 34–35) probably indicates that the bells were open. The purpose of the bells was not (according to v. 35) to remind the people waiting outside of the service of the high priest in the sanctuary, so that they could assist him in prayer. Keil seeks the reason for the fact that the high priest would not die in the meaning of the sound of the bells. He believes that the pomegranates symbolized the Word as precious food, while the sound of the bells symbolized the sound of that Word. The high priest then did not die because only he, as the representative of the people, dressed in the robe of God's Word, the bearer of the divine witness, could approach the Lord. But the references cited by Keil (Pss. 19:8–11; 119:25, 43, 50; Deut. 8:3; Prov. 9:8; and Eccl. 15:3—but cf. 45:9) do not in my opinion support his view. In his *Archaeologie* he also points out that the rabbis compare the commandments to pomegranates, and he quotes Proverbs 25:11 as a general statement. But it is better to keep in mind verse 43; the bells were to remind the high priest as to whether he was dressed as required. The implied thought is then that the high priest could approach the Lord without danger to his life, not as an individual, but in his official capacity. The robe was then the garment that reminded both the high priest and (humanly speaking) the Lord of the glory, the exaltedness, and the sacredness of the office. Only in this way could Aaron "minister" and "live" (v. 35). The only exception was the Day of Atonement (Lev. 16). The bells continuously drew attention to his sacred garments; the pomegranates reminded the high priest of the commandments (cf. also Num. 15:37–41), which he was to keep as well.

As to the fulfillment of the high priestly office, we must note that as our High Priest Christ pleased the Lord *both* in His person and in His office (cf. Ps. 40:8; Heb. 5:5). The Scriptures do not support the idea that the sound of the gold bells served to scare off the evil spirits, as some have taught.

28:36–38 *"Make a plate of pure gold and engrave on it as on a seal:* HOLY TO THE LORD. *Fasten a blue cord to it to attach it to the turban; it is to be on the front of the turban. It will be on Aaron's forehead, and he will bear the guilt involved in the sacred gifts the Israelites consecrate, whatever their gifts may be. It will be on Aaron's forehead continually so that they will be acceptable to the* LORD.*"*

Next is the sacred "plate" or "diadem" (39:30), which was to be made of "pure gold" (see commentary on 25:11; 28:14). "Engrave," see commentary on verse 9. "As on a seal," see commentary on verse 11. Cf. 39:30–31. "Blue cord," see commentary on verse 28. "Turban," cf. verse 4. "On the front of": the same expression is used in verse 27. Verse 38 indicates that we must understand the expression "HOLY TO THE LORD" (v. 36) in the sense that the diadem *was* something holy to the Lord, and thus served as indemnity for those holy things that Israel sinfully withheld from the Lord, through trespasses committed out of ignorance ("sacred gifts" [v. 38] is the plural of the word "holy" in v. 36). Cf. 1 Kings 7:51 and the Mishna tract Pesachim VII, 7. Humanly speaking the diadem reminded the Lord of the fact that the Israelites had voluntarily given Him their most precious possessions to make the tabernacle and all its objects. But above all, the diadem characterized its wearer, the high priest, as the Lord's possession, consecrated to Him. The diadem clearly expressed the mediating aspect of the high priestly office, as well as its substitutionary character (cf. 19:6; Ps. 106:16). "Sacred gifts" (lit. "holy things"), cf. 30:37; 31:15; Leviticus 27:23, 30; Zechariah 14:20. "Bear the guilt," cf. Leviticus 22:16. Thus the presence of the diadem resulted in their being acceptable before the Lord (cf. Lev. 1:3; 19:5; 22:19–21; 23:11). The forehead is the most conspicuous place to wear something. Concerning the fulfillment in Christ, cf. Isaiah 53:11; John 1:29; Hebrews 9:28; 1 Peter 2:24; and now, in His exaltation, Hebrews 2:9; Revelation 1:16. Christ bore the mark of the curse in order to atone for the guilt attached to the "sacred things," and now bears the emblems of glory in His appearance as our Head (cf. Rev. 1:13–16). Concerning the diadem, cf. 29:6; 39:30; Leviticus 8:9. Calvin points out that these "sacred things" themselves were unclean and in need of forgiveness (cf. Heidelberg Catechism, Question and Answer 62).

28:39 *"Weave the tunic of fine linen and make the turban of fine linen. The sash is to be the work of an embroiderer."*

Finally Moses received instructions concerning the tunic. "Weave": the verb implies weaving in a pattern, specifically a checkered pattern (cf. RSV;

see commentary on vv. 6–14). The tunic was worn as an undergarment next to the skin. It probably reached down to the feet and had sleeves, according to Josephus. "Fine linen," see commentary on 25:4. The turban (lit. "something wound round") was already mentioned in verse 4 and verses 36–38; it was also to be made of fine linen. "The work of an embroiderer," cf. 26:36. According to tradition the "sash" was very long. Verses 39–43, cf. 39:27–29.

28:40–43 *"Make tunics, sashes and headbands for Aaron's sons, to give them dignity and honor. After you put these clothes on your brother Aaron and his sons, anoint and ordain them. Consecrate them so they may serve me as priests.*

"Make linen undergarments as a covering for the body, reaching from the waist to the thigh. Aaron and his sons must wear them whenever they enter the Tent of Meeting or approach the altar to minister in the Holy Place, so that they will not incur guilt and die.

"This is to be a lasting ordinance for Aaron and his descendants."

In verse 40 Moses was instructed to provide clothing for the ordinary priests (cf. 39:27). "Dignity and honor," lit. "glory and beauty" (cf. KJV). After all these things had been made the priests were to be anointed and ordained; verse 41 thus forms a transition to chapter 29, which deals with the consecration of the priests. Moses himself had to consecrate them (cf. Lev. 8). "Ordain" (lit. "fill their hand"): Moses was to provide the necessary offerings for Aaron and his sons (cf. Lev. 7:37). The expression "to fill one's hand" is also a technical Babylonian-Assyrian term for "installing someone in an office" (cf. van Gelderen on 1 Kings 13:33). "Serve me as priests," cf. verse 1. Verse 42, cf. 39:28. Verses 42–43, see commentary on 20:26. Verse 43, cf. verse 35. "Tent of Meeting" and "a lasting ordinance," see commentary on 27:21.

J. The consecration of the priests (29:1–37)

The instructions given to Moses in these verses elaborate on 28:41; their implementation is recorded in Leviticus 8.

29:1–3 *"This is what you are to do to consecrate them, so they may serve me as priests: Take a young bull and two rams without defect. And from fine wheat flour, without yeast, make bread, and cakes mixed with oil, and wafers spread with oil. Put them in a basket and present them in it—along with the bull and the two rams."*

First Moses is told what he will need for the consecration of the priests ("them" refers to Aaron and his sons; cf. 28:43). "Serve me as priests," see commentary on 28:1. "Consecrate," see commentary on 19:10, 14; cf.

28:2. "Without defect," see commentary on 12:5. "Without yeast" (KJV: "unleavened"), see commentary on 12:8. "Oil" is again olive oil, which was commonly used in food preparation. "Basket," see Aalders on Genesis 40:15.

29:4–9 *"Then bring Aaron and his sons to the entrance to the Tent of Meeting and wash them with water. Take the garments and dress Aaron with the tunic, the robe of the ephod, the ephod itself and the breastpiece. Fasten the ephod on him by its skillfully woven waistband. Put the turban on his head and attach the sacred diadem to the turban. Take the anointing oil and anoint him by pouring it on his head. Bring his sons and dress them in tunics and put headbands on them. Then tie sashes on Aaron and his sons. The priesthood is theirs by a lasting ordinance. In this way you shall ordain Aaron and his sons."*

Aaron and his sons had to be washed and dressed. "The entrance to the Tent of Meeting," cf. 26:36; 27:21. Washing with water here symbolized the removal of uncleanness that was the result of sin; this was carried out in 40:12–13 and Leviticus 8:6–9 (cf. Heb. 10:22 for its significance). The text does not indicate whether this washing involved merely the hands and feet, or immersion; the latter is more probable. Note that Moses, the mediator, was appointed by the Lord to perform the ceremony. Aaron and his sons would represent the permanent mediatorship of the priesthood, and assume a significant portion of Moses' task.

Verse 5, cf. chapter 28. "Tunic," cf. 28:39. "Robe of the ephod," cf. 28:31–35. "Ephod," cf. 28:6–14. "Breastpiece," cf. 28:15–30. "Fasten," cf. 28:6. "Waistband," cf. 28:8. "Turban," cf. 28:4, 39. "Sacred diadem": the "plate of pure gold" in 28:36–38. Concerning the anointing, cf. Van Gelderen on 1 Kings 1:34; cf. also 30:30; Leviticus 8:12; Psalm 133:2. Aaron's sons were also to be anointed (cf. 28:41; 30:30; 40:15; Lev. 7:35–36; 10:7; Num. 3:3); but these verses and Leviticus 8:12 mention only the anointing of Aaron himself. Leviticus 21:10 indicates that the manner in which Aaron was anointed was different from the anointing of his sons. The anointing oil was poured only over the head of the high priest; the rabbis, among others, have correctly concluded that the priests were anointed differently, e.g., by applying oil to the forehead. It is probable that later any priest was anointed before taking office; this was definitely the case with the high priest. The composition of the anointing oil is given in 30:22–33. The anointing followed after Aaron was dressed; it symbolized ordination and enablement, the oil being symbolic of the Holy Spirit. Verse 8, cf. verse 3 and 28:40. "Sashes," cf. 28:4, 39. "Headbands," cf. 28:40. "A lasting ordinance," see commentary on 28:43. "Ordain," see commentary on 28:41.

29:10-14 *"Bring the bull to the front of the Tent of Meeting, and Aaron and his sons shall lay their hands on its head. Slaughter it in the LORD's presence at the entrance to the Tent of Meeting. Take some of the bull's blood and put it on the horns of the altar with your finger, and pour out the rest of it at the base of the altar. Then take all the fat around the inner parts, the covering of the liver, and both kidneys with the fat around them, and burn them on the altar. But burn the bull's flesh and its hide and its offal outside the camp. It is a sin offering."*

Verses 10-14, cf. Leviticus 8:14-17. According to verse 14 the bull was a sin offering (concerning the sin offering, cf. Lev. 4:1-5:13 and my commentary on Leviticus). Here the bull was a sin offering to atone for the sins committed by Aaron and his sons in the past. After Moses had brought Aaron and his sons to the entrance of the Tent of Meeting (v. 4), they had to lay their hands on the head of the bull (the verb is singular, indicating that Aaron was considered to be prominent). With this symbolic gesture they transferred the sins, or the desire for atonement for their sins, to the bull; the sacrificial animal became *their* sacrifice, their substitute. This ceremony presents a clear parallel with the substitutionary sacrifice of Christ (cf. Heidelberg Catechism, Lord's Day 16, Ans. 19). Even the sins that would make a person unworthy to assume spiritual leadership are placed on Him and borne by Him. After this meaningful act Moses was to slaughter the bull at the entrance to the Tent of Meeting in the presence of Israel's God (v. 11). He then was to apply some of the bull's blood to the horns of the altar of burnt offering (cf. 27:1-8). The rest of the blood was poured at its base, so that it touched the altar, and was thereby consecrated to the Lord, albeit not in such a special way as the part that was applied to the horns of the altar. The blood was too precious to be discarded in any other way (cf. also Rev. 6:9). The most select parts of the bull were to be burned on the altar as a gift to the Lord (v. 13); the same was to be done in the case of the fellowship offering (Lev. 3:4-5, 16; 7:23-25). This gift was to propitiate the Lord. "Inner parts," cf. 12:9. "The covering of the liver" was the so-called *lobus caudatus*, which played an important role in divination among pagan nations (cf. my commentary on Lev. 3:4). "Hide" (v. 14) is the same word as "skin" in 25:5. Verse 14, cf. Leviticus 4:11-12; Numbers 19:5. The bull's flesh, hide, and offal were entirely permeated by the transferred sin, and was therefore to be burned outside the camp (cf. Heb. 13:11-13: Christ has become our sin offering in the fullest sense of the word). The bull was treated as a sin offering of which the blood was brought into the sanctuary; otherwise the priest would be allowed to eat of it (cf. Lev. 6:25-30).

29:15–18 *"Take one of the rams, and Aaron and his sons shall lay their hands on its head. Slaughter it and take the blood and sprinkle it against the altar on all sides. Cut the ram into pieces and wash the inner parts and the legs, putting them with the head and the other pieces. Then burn the entire ram on the altar. It is a burnt offering to the LORD, a pleasing aroma, an offering made to the LORD by fire."*

Cf. Leviticus 8:18–21. One of the two rams was used for a burnt offering (v. 18; see commentary on 20:24). By laying their hands on the animal's head Aaron and his sons transferred to it the consecration of themselves, body and soul, to the Lord. This was possible when the burnt offering for atonement had been brought, and also in those cases where the burnt offering had not been brought first: the animal was slaughtered, its blood was sprinkled against the altar on all sides, and the entire animal was burned after it was cut into pieces (cf. Lev. 1). The ram, like the bull, represented Aaron and his sons. "Legs," cf. 12:9; Leviticus 1:9. "A pleasing aroma," cf. Genesis 8:21; Leviticus 1:9. The aroma was pleasing to the Lord because of what it represented. "Offering made . . . by fire" (v. 18) may be derived from a root meaning "to unite, to join"; it would then refer to the means by which friendship with God could be effected. Here "offering made by fire" refers to a part of the burnt offering. The entire ram was for the Lord and went up in smoke on the altar.

29:19–28 *"Take the other ram, and Aaron and his sons shall lay their hands on its head. Slaughter it, take some of its blood and put it on the lobes of the right ears of Aaron and his sons, on the thumbs of their right hands, and on the big toes of their right feet. Then sprinkle blood against the altar on all sides. And take some of the blood on the altar and some of the anointing oil and sprinkle it on Aaron and his garments and on his sons and their garments. Then he and his sons and their garments will be consecrated.*

"Take from this ram the fat, the fat tail, the fat around the inner parts, the covering of the liver, both kidneys with the fat around them, and the right thigh (This is the ram for the ordination.) From the basket of bread made without yeast, which is before the LORD, take a loaf, and a cake made with oil, and a wafer. Put all these in the hands of Aaron and his sons and wave them before the LORD as a wave offering. Then take them from their hands and burn them on the altar along with the burnt offering for a pleasing aroma to the LORD, an offering made to the LORD by fire. After you take the breast of the ram for Aaron's ordination, wave it before the LORD as a wave offering, and it will be your share.

"Consecrate those parts of the ordination ram that belong to Aaron and his sons: the breast that was waved and the thigh that was presented. This is always to be the regular share from the Israelites for Aaron and his sons. It is the contribution the Israelites are to make to the LORD from their fellowship offerings."

The second ram was called the "ram for the ordination" in verse 22, lit. "ram of filling" (see commentary on v. 9; 28:41). After Aaron and his sons had laid their hands on the animal's head and it was slaughtered its blood was used for various purposes (vv. 20–21). The actual consecration and ordination of Aaron and his sons took place with this offering. The application of the blood to the parts of the body listed in verse 20 consecrated the hearing, actions, and walk of Aaron and his sons to the Lord and to His service (cf. my commentary on Lev. 8:23; cf. Lev. 8:22–24; 14:14–18, 25–29; 21:6). The blood of this ram, like that of the ram that served as the burnt offering (v. 16), was sprinkled against the altar on all sides (see commentary on 24:6–8). Then Aaron and his sons and their garments were sprinkled with some of the blood from the altar and some anointing oil; thus they were consecrated to the Lord and His service (v. 21; cf. v. 37). This act complements, and is a response to, what was expressed in the sin and burnt offerings: Moses, on God's behalf, accepted Aaron and his sons in their official garments as the Lord's priests.

Verses 22–24 prescribe the wave offering that Aaron and his sons had to bring. Moses first was to fill their hands on God's behalf with the fat of the ram, its fat tail (which is still considered a delicacy in Palestine and Syria), and other parts of the ram (v. 22, cf. v. 13), including its right thigh (cf. 1 Sam. 9:24). It is not without reason that this ram was called the "ram of filling": its choices parts filled the hands of Aaron and his sons, so that they did not appear empty-handed before the Lord at their ordination (cf. 23:15). A loaf, a cake made with oil, and a wafer were added, so that both the bloody and the bloodless sacrifices were represented (cf. vv. 2–3). Moses then was to wave them before the Lord, an act that was later performed by the priests. This waving expressed the fact that these things were offered to the Lord, who then returned them to the priest. Moses could therefore treat them again as a sacrifice (v. 25) and burn them on the altar along with the burnt offering (see also commentary on v. 18). The breast of the ram for the ordination (see commentary on v. 22) was treated entirely as a wave offering; since Moses functioned here as priest it became his share (v. 26).

In verses 27–28 Moses was instructed to consecrate the "breast that was waved and the thigh that was presented"[25] in the manner prescribed in verses 22–26. Verse 28 applies this to all the fellowship offerings of the

---

[25] "The thigh that was presented" or, "the thigh of the (heave) offering" (see commentary on 25:3), or, "the thigh of contribution," i.e., the contribution of the Israelites to the Lord. Verses 22 and 24 give the impression that the entire wave offering was to be burnt. Verse 26 gives the first exception (the breast), to which is added a second exception (the thigh) in verse 27 (tr.).

Israelites; it was to be done "always" (lit. "a lasting ordinance," cf. v. 9). The priest was thus entitled to the breast and the right thigh of every animal that was brought as a fellowship offering. (Cf. Lev. 7:31, 34; 10:14; Num. 18:8, 11, 10.)

29:29–37 *"Aaron's sacred garments will belong to his descendants so that they can be anointed and ordained in them. The son who succeeds him as priest and comes to the Tent of Meeting to minister in the Holy Place is to wear them seven days.*

"Take the ram for the ordination and cook the meat in a sacred place. At the entrance to the Tent of Meeting, Aaron and his sons are to eat the meat of the ram and the bread that is in the basket. They are to eat these offerings by which atonement was made for their ordination and consecration. But no one else may eat them, because they are sacred. And if any of the meat of the ordination ram or any bread is left over till morning, burn it up. It must not be eaten, because it is sacred.

"Do for Aaron and his sons everything I have commanded you, taking seven days to ordain them. Sacrifice a bull each day as a sin offering to make atonement. Purify the altar by making atonement for it, and anoint it to consecrate it. For seven days make atonement for the altar and consecrate it. Then the altar will be most holy, and whatever touches it will be holy."

"Sacred garments" see commentary on 28:2; cf. Numbers 20:26, 28. "Ordained," see commentary on verse 9. Verse 30 indicates that the ordination ceremony of Aaron's successors took seven days, but this also applied to the ordination of Aaron himself (cf. v. 35; Lev. 8:33–36). It is best to assume that the ceremony described above, including the anointing, was repeated every day for seven days.

Moses was also instructed to cook the ram for the ordination (i.e., the breast and the thigh, v. 27) "in a sacred place," i.e., in the courtyard. Aaron and his sons could eat it and the bread in the basket (vv. 31–32). "Tent of Meeting," cf. 27:21. Verse 31, cf. Leviticus 8:31. "Basket," see commentary on verses 3, 23. "At the entrance to the Tent of Meeting," cf. 26:36; 27:21. "No one else may eat them" (v. 33), lit. "a stranger shall not eat (of it)"; "stranger" here is not *gēr* (see commentary on 22:21) but refers rather to an unauthorized individual, in this case someone who is not a priest. The meat and bread were sacred, set apart for the Lord's service and His servants. That is also why, if any meat or bread was left over, it was to be burned the next morning, in part to keep it from falling into unauthorized hands. This is another indication of the limited fellowship Israel enjoyed with its God. (Cf. Lev. 10:14; Matt. 12:4.) Verse 35, cf. verse 30. The bull for the sin offering is mentioned separately in verse 36. The altar also was to be purified, anointed, and consecrated, at least on the occasion of the first ordination of the priests. This also had to be done for seven days (v. 37; cf. Lev. 8:15; Ezek. 43:18–27). After this the altar would be most holy (cf. 26:45 and Aalders on Dan. 9:24). Whatever (or, whosoever) touched the altar would partake of the holiness of the altar and be holy (cf. v. 21). Thus, anyone who sought refuge by taking hold of the horns of the altar was safe, protected from the danger that threatened (cf. also Hag. 2:11f.; Matt. 23:19; and my commentary on Lev. 6:11). ''Holy'' here can also mean ''belonging to the Lord.'' The first use of the altar on the occasion of the first ordination of the priests was followed by instructions concerning the regular use of the altar.

K. *The daily morning and evening offerings* (29:38–46)

29:38–42 *''This is what you are to offer on the altar regularly each day: two lambs a year old. Offer one in the morning and the other at twilight. With the first lamb offer a tenth of an ephah of fine flour mixed with a fourth of a hin or oil from pressed olives, and a fourth of a hin of wine as a drink offering. Sacrifice the other lamb at twilight with the same grain offering and its drink offering as in the morning—a pleasing aroma, an offering made to the LORD by fire.*

''For the generations to come this burnt offering is to be made regularly at the entrance to the Tent of Meeting before the LORD. There I will meet you and speak to you.''

The Lord gave Moses precise instructions as to what was to be offered on the altar of burnt offering each day in the morning and at twilight. Cf. Numbers 28:1–8. ''A year old,'' see commentary on 12:5. ''At twilight,'' see commentary on 12:6. ''A tenth of an ephah'' (lit. ''a tenth''), cf. Numbers 28:5, 9; this is thus equal to one omer (cf. 16:36). Verse 39b, cf. Psalm 141:2. ''Fine flour mixed with . . . oil,'' see commentary on 29:2; cf. Leviticus 2:1f. ''Oil from pressed olives,'' see commentary on 27:20. The ''hin'' was a liquid measure, equal to approximately 3⅔ liters. ''A pleasing aroma, an offering made to the Lord by fire,'' see commentary on 29:18. ''This burnt offering is to be made regularly'' (KJV: ''continual burnt offering), cf. 27:20; Daniel 8:12f.; 11:31; 12:11; ''burnt offering,'' see commentary on 20:24. ''Tent of Meeting'' and ''meet,'' see commentary on 25:22; 27:21. In verse 42 ''you'' is plural, ''to you'' singular. Cf. also 1 Kings 18:29, 36; 2 Kings 16:15; Ezekiel 46:13–15; Ezra 9:4; Nehemiah 10:33.

29:43–46 *''There also I will meet with the Israelites, and the place will be consecrated by my glory.*

''So I will consecrate the Tent of Meeting and the altar and will consecrate Aaron and his sons to serve me as priests. Then I will dwell among the Israelites

*and be their God. They will know that I am the L*ORD *their God, who brought them
out of Egypt so that I might dwell among them. I am the L*ORD *their God.''*

The promise, which is renewed in verse 42 (cf. 25:22), is further elaborated in verses 43–46. The Lord would meet with the Israelites at the
entrance to the Tent of Meeting, that is, at the altar of burnt offering
(40:29). This was possible when regular daily offerings were made; here
also fellowship was based on atonement (see 40:34). The LXX, Syriac, and
Targums read the first person singular in verse 43b: "and I shall consecrate
Myself by my glory"; but there is no compelling reason to make this
change in the text. The Hebrew reads "*it* shall be sanctified (RSV), which
may refer to "the place" where the Lord and the Israelites would meet
(NIV, KJV), but it is better to assume that *Israel* would be consecrated by the
Lord's glory (thus e.g., Keil). Verse 44b, see commentary on 29:1. Verse
45, cf. 24:16; 25:8; and 6:7; 19:6; Genesis 17:7. Verse 46, cf. 20:2; and
commentary on 6:6; 16:6, 12; and p. 3.

L. *The altar of incense* (30:1–10)

In verses 1–6 the Lord instructs Moses to make an altar of incense, and
how to make it; verses 7–10 describe how Aaron was to use this altar.
Many interpreters have expressed surprise at the fact that the altar of
incense was not mentioned until now, and they consider it to be a later
addition. But then all other references to the altar of incense in the Pentateuch must also be deleted in order to maintain the view that the tabernacle, as originally described by P, did not have an altar of incense. The
argument is thus circular. The Samaritan Pentateuch places verses 1–10
after 26:35; but this is not necessary, although we cannot discern a particular reason why these verses are found here. Dillmann's explanation that
the statements concerning the purpose and use of the altar of incense
presuppose the Aaronic priesthood (cf. 29) may well be correct. But I do
not believe that Dillmann can prove his thesis that the altar of incense is
less important than the table, the lampstand and the altar of burnt offering.

30:1–6 *"Make an altar of acacia wood for burning incense. It is to be square, a
cubit long and a cubit wide, and two cubits high—its horns of one piece with it.
Overlay the top and all the sides and the horns with pure gold, and make a gold
molding around it. Make two gold rings for the altar below the molding—two on
opposite sides—to hold the poles used to carry it. Make the poles of acacia wood
and overlay them with gold. Put the altar in front of the curtain that is before the
ark of the Testimony—before the atonement cover that is over the Testimony—
where I will meet with you.''*

The Lord still spoke to Moses (see 25:1). Moses was probably also shown the plan of the altar of incense (cf. 25:9 etc.). "Incense," see commentary on 25:6. "Acacia wood," see commentary on 25:5. Cf. also 37:25–28. Verse 2, see commentary on 25:10. "Square," cf. 27:1; 28:16. "Of one piece with it," see commentary on 27:2. "Horns," see commentary on 27:2. "Overlay . . . with pure gold," see commentary on 25:11; 27:2. The altar of incense was much smaller than the altar of burnt offering (cf. 27:1), and also smaller than the ark (cf. 25:10) and the table (cf. 25:23). Excavations in Palestine have brought to light small stone altars with horns, which were used to offer incense. The dimensions of such an altar found at Gezer are 40 by 22 by 25 cm. (approx. 16 by 9 by 10 inches), while at Taanach an altar has been found of approximately the same size as the one described in these verses. These small altars were used in the home to offer incense to the gods, something that the Israelites were strictly forbidden to do. The horns of the altars found in Palestine were also of one piece with the altar. The altar that the Lord instructed Moses to make was much more costly. "Gold molding," see commentary on 25:11, 24f. "Rings" (v. 4), cf. 25:12, 14f., 26f.; 26:24, 29; 27:4, 7. "On opposite sides," lit. "upon the two sides of it upon its two sides"; this seems tautologous, hence the translation "upon the two corners thereof upon its two sides," meaning (probably) "on opposite sides" (25:12, 14; 26:20, 26–27, 35; 27:7). "To hold the poles," cf. 25:27. The altar of incense was thus also to be constructed in such a way that it could be transported. "To carry it," cf. 25:14, 27; 27:7. "Acacia wood," see verse 1. Verse 5, cf. 25:13, 28. In verse 6 the Lord indicates where Moses was to place the altar of incense: in the Holy Place, in front of the curtain (see commentary on 26:31, 33, 35 and 40:5), which was before the ark of the Testimony (see commentary on 25:16, 21–22 and 27:21), before the atonement cover (see commentary on 25:17–22) which was over the Testimony, where "I will meet with you" (see commentary on 25:22; 29:42). The Lord indicated through this description that there was peace between Him and Israel, a peace in which He wanted to enjoy their incense. The altar of incense stood before His throne among Israel (cf. Rev. 5:8; 8:3–4; Ps. 141:2). Hebrews 9:4, as it relates to this subject, has created a problem for some. See Grosheide on Hebrews in this commentary series. The expression "before the atonement cover" points to the close connection between the ark and this altar.

30:7–10 *"Aaron must burn fragrant incense on the altar every morning when he tends the lamps. He must burn incense again when he lights the lamps at twilight so incense will burn regularly before the LORD for the generations to come. Do not* *offer on this altar any other incense or any burnt offering or grain offering, and do not pour a drink offering on it. Once a year Aaron shall make atonement on its horns. This annual atonement must be made with the blood of the atoning sin offering for the generations to come. It is most holy to the Lord."*

The Lord now states what Aaron was to do with the altar of incense. "Fragrant incense," see commentary on 25:6. "Burn," cf. 29:13, 18. "Tends the lamps," see commentary on 25:37. Not only the high priest, but also the ordinary priests could offer the incense (cf. Luke 1:9). "Lights the lamps," see commentary on 25:37. "At twilight," see commentary on 29:41. The incense offering and the evening burnt offering were thus brought at the same time. The offering was to be made "regularly" (see commentary on 29:42), "for the generations to come" (see commentary on 27:21). The incense offering symbolized the prayers of the saints (see above), but also atonement for that which was sinful in those prayers. In the New Testament this is fulfilled in Christ, who intercedes for us in heaven (cf. also Greijdanus on Rev. 8:3 in this commentary series). The incense offering undoubtedly has more appeal for us than the blood sacrifice, but we must not forget that without the shedding of blood there is no forgiveness.

The altar of incense could also be desecrated (v. 9). "Other incense," lit. "strange incense," see commentary on 29:33; 30:34–38; Leviticus 10:1. The verb forms in verse 9 are plural. "Burnt offering," see commentary on 29:42. "Grain offering," cf. 29:41. "Drink offering," cf. 29:40. The altar of incense was thus to be used exclusively for the burning of incense; only once a year, on the Day of Atonement, was Aaron to apply blood to the horns of the altar (cf. 30:10; Lev. 4:7; Lev. 16:18 refers to the altar of burnt offering, but cf. Lev. 16:19). This indicates a cleansing of the altar of incense (cf. 29:37; Heb. 9:22–23), as is stated in verse 10; Aaron was to make atonement, and this was to be done "for the generations to come." "Atone," cf. 29:36. "Most holy," cf. 29:37.

M. *The atonement money* (30:11–16)

30:11–16 *Then the Lord said to Moses, "When you take a census of the Israelites to count them, each one must pay the Lord a ransom for his life at the time he is counted. Then no plague will come on them when you number them. Each one who crosses over to those already counted is to give a half shekel, according to the sanctuary shekel, which weighs twenty gerahs. This half shekel is an offering to the Lord. All who cross over, those twenty years old or more, are to give an offering to the Lord. The rich are not to give more than a half shekel and the poor are not to give less when you make the offering to the Lord to atone for your lives. Receive the* *atonement money from the Israelites and use it for the service of the Tent of Meeting. It will be a memorial for the Israelites before the LORD, making atonement for your lives."*

In these verses the Lord made provisions for the expenses of the service of the tabernacle (cf. esp. v. 16). The Lord was still speaking to Moses on the mountain (24:18; 25:1). "For his life," lit. "for his soul" KJV; RSV: "for himself"). "Ransom," cf. 21:30. "Plague," see commentary on 12:13. Verse 12b, cf. 2 Samuel 24. The Lord is a jealous God. Hertz points out that the word for "ransom" is used three times in the Law, referring in all three cases to money paid by someone who was guilty of taking a human life under circumstances that made it less than murder (e.g., 21:30). The soldier, ready to go into battle, was in the eyes of heaven a potential taker of human life, albeit not a premeditated murderer. That is why he had to pay a "ransom for his life" (cf. Num. 31:50). But it is perhaps better to think here of the Lord's jealousy in connection with the fact that this census could lead to pride, since Hertz' view has a distinctly "western" flavor. Or the two views can be combined, while we should also think of the sins of those who are counted. Those already counted belong to the Lord; they do not constitute an independent army, but when they enter into the ranks of those who are fit for battle they must think of Him, and He will remember them favorably ("memorial," v. 16). Cf. Numbers 1:2. "Cross over" (v. 14), i.e., from those who have not yet been counted to those who have been counted. This is a clear indication of the fact that the Lord was Israel's King (cf. e.g., 19:5–6).

"Shekel," see commentary on 21:32. A "gerah" equals .8185 grams, ten gerahs equal one beqa' or 8.185 grams, while a shekel equals 2 beqa' or 20 gerahs: 16.37 grams (cf. Lev. 27:25; Num. 3:47; Ezek. 45:12). "Offering," see commentary on 25:2. No one was exempted from this offering, but since each individual was equally valuable in the Lord's eyes, no one could give more or less than a half shekel. This principle does not apply to us in determining how much we voluntarily contribute to the church, since verse 15 specifically states that this offering was "to atone for your lives." Besides, each of those who were counted gave the half shekel only once; it did not become an annual temple tax until much later (cf. Matt. 17:24; 2 Chron. 24:6, 9). Verse 15, cf. 29:36–37. In verse 16 Moses was instructed to use the money thus collected for the "service of the Tent of Meeting" (see commentary on 25:22; 27:21; cf. 28:43). "Memorial," cf. 28:12, 29; Numbers 31:54. Hertz paraphrases: "That the Lord may remember the Israelites in grace and forgiveness, and grant them atonement for the blood shed in battle; cf. Num. 31:54." The total amount of money collected is given in 38:25: 100 talents and 1,775 shekels (about 3.4 metric tons).

N. *The basin for washing* (30:17–21)

30:17–21 *Then the L*ORD *said to Moses, "Make a bronze basin, with its bronze stand, for washing. Place it between the Tent of Meeting and the altar, and put water in it. Aaron and his sons are to wash their hands and feet with water from it. Whenever they enter the Tent of Meeting, they shall wash with water so that they will not die. Also, when they approach the altar to minister by presenting an offering made to the L*ORD *by fire, they shall wash their hands and feet so that they will not die. This is to be a lasting ordinance for Aaron and his descendants for the generations to come."*

The bronze basin for washing was shown to Moses (25:9, 40), but we have no description of it; only its purpose is stated. It goes without saying that such a basin had to be made; the Lord did not tolerate uncleanness; dust on hands or feet was reminiscent of the uncleanness of sin (cf. Isa. 52:11; John 13:1–10). "Basin" indicates a round object (cf. "pan" in 1 Sam. 2:14; and 2 Chron. 6:13, where the same word is translated "platform"). The stand is always mentioned separately (cf. 31:9; 35:16; 39:39; 40:11; Lev. 8:11), from which Keil draws the (in my opinion correct) conclusion that basin and stand were separable. "Bronze" (see commentary on 25:3) is used because the basin was placed in the courtyard between the Tent of Meeting (see commentary on 29:42) and "the altar," i.e., the altar of burnt offering (cf. also 38:8; 40:30). The priests had to wash their hands and feet with water "from it" (the basin may have had faucets, and the water was thus transferred to smaller containers, or the priests may have dipped whatever needed from the basin). Their hands touched consecrated objects, and they had to be clean whenever they entered the tabernacle or went up the altar (see commentary on 27:1–8). Verse 20 indicates that failure to wash their hands and feet would result in death (cf. 28:35), which is in line with 19:22 and chapter 29. "An offering made . . . by fire": cf. 29:13, 18; 30:7. Verse 21b, see commentary on 12:14; 27:21; 28:43; 29:9, 28 (KJV); 30:8. For the believer, in his position as priest, the requirement of cleanness remains, even though Christ has also fulfilled this ordinance. The basin symbolizes the need for purity in thought and deed, a purity that can be found and realized only in Christ, according to the sacrament of baptism. The basin for washing was thus part of the ministry of reconciliation! Cf. also 1 Kings 7:23; Revelation 15:2. The Jews later made this ordinance the basis for frequent washings of the hands (cf. Mark 7:3f.).

O. *The sacred anointing oil* (30:22–30)

The Lord gave Moses detailed instructions for the preparation of the sacred anointing oil (vv. 22–25), as well as for its use (vv. 26–30), while Moses also had to warn the Israelites against the unauthorized preparation and use of this oil (vv. 31–33).

30:22–25 *Then the LORD said to Moses, "Take the following fine spices: 500 shekels of liquid myrrh, half as much (that is, 250 shekels) of fragrant cinnamon, 250 shekels of fragrant cane, 500 shekels of cassia—all according to the sanctuary shekel—and a hin of olive oil. Make these into a sacred anointing oil, a fragrant blend, the work of a perfumer. It will be the sacred anointing oil."*

"Spices," see commentary on 25:6. These spices had to be of the finest quality, since they were to be used for a sacred purpose. "Liquid myrrh," a resin that dripped spontaneously from the myrrh tree *(balsomodendron myrrha)* without the need for making an incision in the tree (cf. Matt. 2:1; Mark 15:23; John 19:39). The myrrh plant "is of medium size, and has long, flexible branches, small leaves, and round brown nuts. During the summer months its bark exudes a yellowish, pungent fluid" (de Visser, Vol. I, p. 105); it was found especially in southern Arabia. This myrrh, which flows spontaneously, was the best kind (cf. Song of Songs 5:5, 13). The caravans from Arabia traded myrrh, and it is quite possible that the Israelites purchased it from these caravans. Myrrh was also used by itself as an ointment or perfume (cf. Ps. 45:8; Prov. 7:17; Song of Songs 1:13; 5:5). The Hebrew implies "shekels" in verses 23–24a ("500 of liquid myrrh," etc.); verse 24b indicates that the quantities were measured "according to the sanctuary shekel" (see commentary on 30:13). "Fragrant cinnamon": the word for "fragrant" is the same word used for "spices." Genuine cinnamon was very rare; the Phoenicians brought it from Ceylon (cf. Prov. 7:17; Song of Songs 4:14; Rev. 18:13). The "fragrant cane" (KJV "calamus") was imported from India, but also grew in Arabia and Syria (cf. Song of Songs 4:14; Isa. 43:24; Jer. 6:20; Ezek. 27:19). "Cassia" is probably the dried bark of a species of cinnamon tree (cf. Ezek. 27:19; in Ps. 45:8 a different word with the same meaning is used). "Olive oil," see commentary on 25:6; 27:20. "Hin," see commentary on 29:40. "Sacred anointing oil," see commentary on 29:7; 37:29. These ingredients were mixed by Bezalel to make the anointing oil (cf. 31:2, 6, 11). Verses 25, cf. 30:35.

30:26–30 *"Then use it to anoint the Tent of Meeting, the ark of the Testimony, the table and all its articles, the lampstand and its accessories, the altar of incense, the* *altar of burnt offering and all its utensils, and the basin with its stand. You shall consecrate them so they will be most holy, and whatever touches them will be holy.*

"Anoint Aaron and his sons and consecrate them so they may serve me as priests."

Verses 26–30 list the objects and persons whom Moses had to anoint with this oil (cf. 40:9–11; Lev. 8:10f.; concerning the significance of the anointing, see commentary on 29:7). "Tent of Meeting," see commentary on 25:22. "Ark of the Testimony," see commentary on 25:21. "The table and all its articles," see commentary on 25:23–30. "The lampstand and its accessories," see commentary on 25:31–40. "The altar of incense," see commentary on 30:1–10. "The altar of burnt offering and all its utensils," see commentary on 27:1–8. "The basin with its stand," see commentary on 30:17–21. "Consecrate" (v. 29) means "to set apart for the Lord's service." "Most holy," cf. 30:10. Verse 29b, see commentary on 29:37. Verse 30, see commentary on 29:1, 7, 21.

30:31–33 *"Say to the Israelites, 'This is to be my sacred anointing oil for the generations to come. Do not pour it on men's bodies and do not make any oil with the same formula. It is sacred, and you are to consider it sacred. Whoever makes perfume like it and whoever puts it on anyone other than a priest must be cut off from his people.'"*

Moses finally received a command for the Israelites, a strict prohibition against making oil according to the same formula, or to use it on men's bodies ("men" in the sense of "ordinary men," cf. Ps. 82:7; Isa. 8:1. The application of oil to the body was a common practice in the East, cf. Luke 7:46). "For the generations to come" (v. 31), see commentary on 30:8, 21. "Formula" is related to the word for "quota" used in 5:18, and refers to the composition (KJV) or correct proportions of the ingredients. "You" (v. 32) is plural. Verse 33 reads literally "Whoever shall make like unto it, to smell of it, he shall be cut off from his people"; the RSV translates, "Whoever makes any like it to use as perfume." The penalty was severe: the offender was to be cut off from his people (see commentary on 12:15; Gen. 17:14). The line between sacred and non-sacred had to be drawn very clearly in the Old Testament.

P. *The sacred incense* (30:34–38)

This section is structured along the same lines as the preceding section. First the composition of the incense is given (vv. 34–35), then instructions for its use (v. 36), and finally a warning against private use of the formula and of the incense (vv. 37–38).

30:34, 35 *Then the* L*ord* *said to Moses, "Take fragrant spices—gum resin, onycha and galbanum—and pure frankincense, all in equal amounts, and make a fragrant blend of incense, the work of a perfumer. It is to be salted and pure and sacred."*

The Lord still addressed Moses. "Fragrant spices," see commentary on 25:6; 30:7. "Gum resin": the Hebrew word is from a root "to drip"; this word is used in the plural in Job 36:27 ("drops of water"). The lxx translates "stacte" (cf. kjv, rsv), which refers to the spontaneously dripping myrrh juice (cf. commentary on 30:23). The word can also refer to other types of resin, hence the translation "gum resin." "Onycha" refers to the shells of molluscs that are found in India and also in the Red Sea. These shells do not have a pleasant aroma as such, but they intensify and prolong the fragrance of the spices with which they are mixed. On the basis of the words "fragrant spices," however, Bähr, Schouten, and others think it probable that we should think here of an ingredient that itself has a pleasant aroma. Then it may be a type of treesap or resin. But because of the versions, the first interpretation seems, in my opinion, stronger. Driver also takes "onycha" to refer to a mollusc shell, "which, when burnt, emits a strong aromatic odor. Onycha is still gathered along the coasts of the Red Sea; and is largely used as an ingredient in the perfumery of Arab women; it is also said to be the principal component of incense in India and elsewhere." "Galbanum" is a pungent resin that was imported from Syria. It strikes us as curious that this ingredient, like the onycha, does not have a pleasant smell of itself; but tests have shown that the incense made according to the formula given here does indeed have a very pleasant aroma. "Pure frankincense": frankincense was a resin from southern Arabia. The Hebrew name ("whiteness") refers to its color. The Israelites could have purchased this, as well as the other ingredients, from caravans in the desert. Frankincense was "pure" when it did not contain any foreign matter (cf. commentary on 27:20), and when it had been collected in the fall, when the resin dripped from the plant spontaneously. Moses was to mix these four ingredients in equal proportions and thus make "incense" (see commentary on 25:6; cf. also 37:29). "The work of a perfumer," see commentary on 30:25. "Pure," see commentary on 25:11; 31:8; 39:37. Here it means "without any admixture." "Salted": a necessary ingredient of every offering was salt (cf. Lev. 2:13). Salt prevents spoilage, but here it was to be included to make the mixture burn and smoke more readily. This incense was "sacred," and was thus to be used only for the Lord (cf. vv. 37–38).

30:36 *"Grind some of it to powder and place it in front of the Testimony in the Tent of Meeting, where I will meet with you. It shall be most holy to you."*

Incense offerings were very common, as the many small altars of incense that have been found by excavations in Palestine show (cf. commentary on 30:1–6). Moses (and later the priests) had to take charge of the service of the altar of incense. He was to break pieces off the hard lump of incense and grind it into a powder ready for use. This verse may indicate that Moses was to place this powder inside the Holy Place, so that there was always a supply ready for use, but this is not certain. "The Testimony," see commentary on 25:16. "The Tent of Meeting," see commentary on 25:22. "Where I will meet with you (singular)," see commentary on 27:21; 29:42; 30:6. "To you" is plural. "Most Holy," see commentary on 29:37; 30:10, 29.

30:37, 38 *"Do not make any incense with this formula for yourselves; consider it holy to the Lord. Whoever makes any like it to enjoy its fragrance must be cut off from his people."*

"Incense," see above on verse 35. "With this formula," see commentary on 30:32. Verse 38, see commentary on verse 33. The temptation to make this incense for personal use was great, since the people of the East had a great liking for incense (cf. Prov. 27:9). Special guests or visitors were honored by lighting incense (cf. Dan. 2:46). The burning of incense in the tabernacle and temple was a form of rendering homage to the Lord, who wanted to dwell in Israel's midst (cf. 25:8), and making this incense for private use infringed therefore on the Lord's rights (cf. Acts 12:22–23). Offering incense to other gods, i.e., honoring other gods, was thus also strictly prohibited by Israel's God. Incense can be symbolic of prayer (see commentary on 30:7–10).

Q. *Bezalel and Oholiab appointed* (31:1–11)

The appointment of Bezalel and Oholiab shows that the Lord works "organically" and that He uses people with special skills and abilities in His service. Moses was not suited to make those things that the Lord wanted to be made. But these craftsmen had received their skills, which they were to use in the work on the tabernacle, from the Lord (cf. vv. 3, 6). Cf. 35:30–35.

31:1–11 *Then the Lord said to Moses, "See, I have chosen Bezalel son of Uri, the son of Hur, of the tribe of Judah, and I have filled him with the Spirit of God, with* *skill, ability and knowledge in all kinds of crafts—to make artistic designs for work in gold, silver and bronze, to cut and set stones, to work in wood, and to engage in all kinds of craftsmanship. Moreover, I have appointed Oholiab son of Ahisamach, of the tribe of Dan, to help him. Also I have given skill to all the craftsmen to make everything I have commanded you: the Tent of Meeting, the ark of the Testimony with the atonement cover on it, and all the other furnishings of the tent—the table and its articles, the pure gold lampstand and all its accessories, the altar of incense, the altar of burnt offering and all its utensils, the basin with its stand— and also the woven garments, both the sacred garments for Aaron the priest and the garments for his sons when they serve as priests, and the anointing oil and fragrant incense for the Holy Place. They are to make them just as I commanded you."*

Verse 1, cf. 30:17, 22, 34. "See" is stronger than "behold" in verse 6 (cf. KJV; NIV: "moreover"). "I have chosen," lit. "I have called by name"; no one but Bezalel could be the foreman of this project. Bezalel means "In the shadow of God's protection." "Hur," see commentary on 17:10; 24:14; this is probably not the same Hur. According to this verse and 1 Chronicles 2:20 Bezalel was thus the grandson of Hur (cf. Noordtzij on 1 Chron. 2:20). The Spirit of God, with which Bezalel was filled, was undoubtedly the Holy Spirit, who is the source of the gifts enumerated in verse 3 (see also commentary on 28:3). But at the same time I believe that the fact that Bezalel, rather than Moses, or Aaron, or someone else was chosen, points to a natural aptitude on Bezalel's part (cf. also van Gelderen on 1 Kings 7:14). "In all kinds of crafts" is the same expression as "in all kinds of craftsmanship" in verse 5. "To make" (v. 4), lit. "to devise, to design." "Artistic designs" is from the same root as the preceding verb. Verse 4b, see commentary on 25:3.

Oholiab means "Tent of the father," or rather, "the father (God) is my tent," a meaning similar to that of the name "Bezalel." Other craftsmen were also appointed to help Bezalel and Oholiab (cf. 35:10). But Bezalel remained the one in charge, and Oholiab was his righthand man (cf. 36:1–2; 37:1; 38:22f.). The Lord's instructions to Moses contained the specifications, but verse 4a seems to warrant the conclusion that Bezalel could contribute his own ideas. Not everything was spelled out in detail in chapters 25–30, so that there was room for Bezalel's creativity.

For the items listed in verses 7–11, see commentary on 27:21; 25:21, 17, 23, 31; 30:1f.; 27:1–8; 30:17–21; chapter 28; 30:22f.; 25:6; 30:34f. "Woven garments" (v. 10) is a word of uncertain meaning, probably meaning "finely wrought garments" (some ancient versions read "garments of service," cf. KJV). Verse 10, see commentary on 28:1. Verse 11 (cf. v. 6b) states again that everything was to be done in accordance with the Lord's instructions to Moses (cf. 25:9, 40).

R. *The Sabbath* (31:12–17)

31:12–17 *Then the L*ORD *said to Moses, "Say to the Israelites, 'You must observe my Sabbaths. This will be a sign between me and you for the generations to come, so you may know that I am the L*ORD*, who makes you holy.*

*"'Observe the Sabbath, because it is holy to you. Anyone who desecrates it must be put to death; whoever does any work on that day must be cut off from his people. For six days work is to be done, but the seventh day is a Sabbath of rest, holy to the L*ORD*. Whoever does any work on the Sabbath day must be put to death. The Israelites are to observe the Sabbath, celebrating it for the generations to come as a lasting covenant. It will be a sign between me and the Israelites forever, for in six days the L*ORD *made the heavens and the earth, and on the seventh day he abstained from work and rested.'"*

It may strike us as curious that the Lord would conclude the instructions concerning the tabernacle by impressing on the Israelites the Sabbath commandment. The statement in verse 13, "You must observe my Sabbaths," is emphatic: "Surely you shall keep my Sabbaths"; the Dutch Authorized Version margin says: "It is as if God said: although the work on the tabernacle must be finished as soon as possible, you shall nevertheless not work on it during the Sabbath." Before Moses began to implement the instructions received on the mountain, he first reminded Israel of the Sabbath commandment (35:1–3); see commentary on 16:22–30; 20:8–11. The work on the sanctuary was not to interfere with the observance of the Sabbath. Moses was to convey to the Israelites this emphatic restatement of the Sabbath law; hence the use of the plural "you" in verse 13. "Observe," cf. 23:15. "My Sabbaths," (cf. Lev. 19:3, 30; 26:2; Isa. 56:4; Ezek. 20:12–13; 16:20–21, 24; 22:8, 26; 23:38; 44:24): the Sabbath was instituted by the Lord when He finished creating the world; but at Sinai the Sabbath was made a sign of the covenant between Him and Israel, a sign that served to keep the knowledge before Israel that God was the Lord, who had set them apart for His service, for Himself (see commentary on 19:5–6; cf. Deut. 5:15; Ezek. 20:12). In verse 14 the Sabbath is called "holy to you" (cf. 30:32) and the death penalty was imposed for violating the Sabbath. "Cut off from his people," see commentary on 30:33, 38; cf. Numbers 15:32–36. "A Sabbath of rest" (v. 15), cf. 16:23 ("a day of rest").

Verse 15a is similar to 20:9; this whole section is reminiscent of the fourth commandment, which it seeks to inculcate. It is possible that this emphatic restatement was necessary because Israel was not faithful in observing the Sabbath; in any case, the observance of the Sabbath, both as a day of rest on which no "work" (cf. 12:16; 30:9) was to be done, and as a sign of the covenant, was demanded, under penalty of death. It was holy, for both the Israelites (v. 14) and the Lord (v. 15). "For the generations to come," see above, verse 13. Verse 17, like 20:11, looks back to Genesis 1:31; 2:2–3. "Abstained from work and rested" (v. 17), lit. "rested and was refreshed" (KJV, RSV; cf. 23:12): a highly anthropomorphic statement. The verb translated "abstained from work" is not the same verb used in 20:11 ("rested"), but is also found in Genesis 2:2–3 (see Aalders on those verses).

12. *Moses Receives the Two Tablets* (31:18)

31:18 *When the LORD finished speaking to Moses on Mount Sinai, he gave him the two tablets of the Testimony, the tablets of stone inscribed by the finger of God.*

This verse provides the transition to what follows: the sin with the golden calf. The period of forty days (24:18), during which Moses received the instructions recorded in 24:1–31:17, had come to an end. "Mount Sinai," see commentary on 24:16. "The two tablets of the testimony," see commentary on 25:16, 21. These two tablets contained the ten words or commandments (cf. 32:15–16; 34:28; Deut. 4:13; 5:22; 9:9–10; 10:4); they were relatively small (cf. 32:15–16). This gift from the Lord was a beautiful ending to Moses' stay on Mount Sinai. The sanctuary was yet to be built, but the "Testimony," Israel's constitution, had already been given. But how Moses had misjudged Israel! "The finger of God," see commentary on 8:19. Moses had gone up the mountain to receive these two tablets (cf. 24:12). Many nations of antiquity inscribed their laws on tablets of wood, stone, or metal. On the basis of the so-called vassal treaties Kline believes that there were two tablets, each containing all ten commandments (see also commentary on 20:1–17).

13. *Israel Breaks, and the Lord Renews the Covenant* (32:1–34:35)

A. *The golden calf* (32:1–33:11)

Chapter 32 continues the narrative that was interrupted after 24:18. The contrast between what took place on the mountain and what happened in the desert is beautifully worked out in this chapter. See e.g., Deuteronomy 9:8–21; Psalm 106:19–23; Nehemiah 9:18. Chapters 32–34 form an ignominious and terrible interlude between the laws concerning Israel's worship and their implementation. They constitute an unforgettable incident that provides an insight into the depraved nature of even the members of the covenant people.

291

32:1–6 *When the people saw that Moses was so long in coming down from the mountain, they gathered around Aaron and said, "Come, make us gods who will go before us. As for this fellow Moses who brought us up out of Egypt, we don't know what has happened to him."*

Aaron answered them, "Take off the gold earrings that your wives, your sons and your daughters are wearing, and bring them to me." So all the people took off their earrings and brought them to Aaron. He took what they handed him and made it into an idol cast in the shape of a calf, fashioning it with a tool. Then they said, "These are your gods, O Israel, who brought you up out of Egypt."

When Aaron saw this, he built an altar in front of the calf and announced, "Tomorrow there will be a festival to the Lord.*" So the next day the people rose early and sacrificed burnt offerings and presented fellowship offerings. Afterward they sat down to eat and drink and got up to indulge in revelry.*

These first six verses describe the sin with the golden calf. The length of Moses' stay on the mountain was a test for the people, and they failed. Aaron was the leader; not a different Aaron, as has been suggested on the basis of Numbers 12, but the same Aaron who was to be high priest. Hur (cf. 24:14) is not mentioned. The people came to Aaron with the politely phrased request to make them gods who could lead them through the wilderness. The plural "gods" may indicate a direct violation of the first commandment, or it may refer to a substitute of the true God; Nehemiah 9:18 would support the latter, Acts 7:40 the former. I believe that the text of verse 1 indicates that the people wanted another god than the God who had revealed Himself anew to Moses (chs. 3–4). Their ingratitude is revealed in the indifferent language they used in speaking about Moses: they were apparently not very concerned about what might have happened to him on the mountain (cf. 2 Kings 2:16–18).

The request of the people showed their need for a god. They believed that with Moses they had also lost the possibility of fellowship with the Lord (cf. 20:19; 19:9). Their fellowship depended too much on one person. And now an image (perhaps an image of the true God, albeit in pagan form) was to take over the function of Moses, who represented the invisible God in their midst. Their request also showed their need for a leader, since they turned to Aaron. But note that they were ready with the radical solution. Aaron was placed in a difficult position, and he showed himself to be a leader who gave in to the godless pressure of the whole nation (v. 3); the leader was led, he was weak. But it would have been extremely difficult for him to lead the people away from their desire.

"Take off" (v. 2), lit. "tear off": Aaron used a rough expression (a different verb is used in 35:5, 21–22), as if he were angry with himself for giving in. Or perhaps he thought that they would not be willing to sacrifice their possessions. Idolatry carries a heavy price tag. The Arabs and Bedouins were fond of gold jewelry (cf. Judg. 9:24–26), and in Egypt both men and women wore it. The whole nation was willing to give up their gold rings for the realization of their wish (which, incidentally, shows that the golden calf was not worshiped because it was made of gold. Cf. 3:22). Aaron now felt that he had no choice but to go on. He melted the gold down and made it into the form of a calf, "fashioning it with a tool." The "tool" was probably similar to a stylus (the same word is translated "pen" in Isa. 8:1). Luther thought that Aaron first made a drawing of the golden calf, which he submitted to the people for their approval; but the verb translated "fashion" here also is used in 1 Kings 7:15 (NIV: "cast") and in Jeremiah 1:5 (NIV: "formed"), which argues against Luther's view. Others interpret "tool" in the sense of "mold" for casting the calf. Keil thinks that the idol was made of wood, overlaid with gold.

The idol represented a calf, i.e., a young bull; bulls were worshiped in Egypt (Apis), and elsewhere in the East (cf. van Gelderen on 1 Kings 12:28). Aaron probably wanted to express the Lord's power in this idol. Israel unanimously proclaimed that these were their gods who brought them up out of Egypt. The plural expresses the fact that there were more gods than this one; more of these idols could be made, even though each one could represent the true God (cf. 1 Kings 12:28). It is also possible that the plural must be understood as a singular (see commentary on v. 1).

Some assume that the calf, rather than being a representation of the deity, was merely the visible pedestal on which the invisible deity stood. "Among Canaanites, Aramaeans, and Hittites we find the gods nearly always represented as standing on the back of an animal or as seated on a throne borne by animals—but never as themselves in animal form."[26]

It is also possible that Aaron wanted to prevent more serious developments and attempted to shift from a sin against the first commandment to a sin against the second commandment by building an altar in front of the idol, and especially by announcing a festival to the Lord. Having lost control of the people, he tried to make the best of a bad situation. The Peshitta expresses this by reading (with a change in the vocalization): "Then Aaron became afraid," which fits in well with the context. The altar was added so that the feast could serve as a sop to the people; and the feast was then to honor the Lord, the true God!

"Burnt offerings," "Fellowship offerings" (v. 6), see commentary on

---

[26]W. F. Albright, *From the Stone Age to Christianity* (Garden City: Doubleday and Company, 1957), p. 299.

20:24; cf. also 18:12 and 1 Corinthians 10:7. "To indulge in revelry" (lit. "to play"): this included dancing (vv. 18–19; see Aalders on Gen. 21:9). The festivities bore little resemblance to a "festival to the Lord"!

32:7–14 *Then the LORD said to Moses, "Go down, because your people, whom you brought up out of Egypt, have become corrupt. They have been quick to turn away from what I commanded them and have made themselves an idol cast in the shape of a calf. They have bowed down to it and sacrificed to it and have said, 'These are your gods, O Israel, who brought you up out of Egypt.'*

"I have seen these people," the LORD said to Moses, "and they are a stiff-necked people. Now leave me alone so that my anger may burn against them and that I may destroy them. Then I will make you into a great nation."

But Moses sought the favor of the LORD his God. "O LORD," he said, "why should your anger burn against your people, whom you brought out of Egypt with great power and a mighty hand? Why should the Egyptians say, 'It was with evil intent that he brought them out, to kill them in the mountains and to wipe them off the face of the earth'? Turn from your fierce anger; relent and do not bring disaster on your people. Remember your servants Abraham, Isaac and Israel, to whom you swore by your own self: 'I will make your descendants as numerous as the stars in the sky and I will give your descendants all this land I promised them, and it will be their inheritance forever.'" Then the LORD relented and did not bring on his people the disaster he had threatened.

The narrative now shifts to what happened on the mountain while these things took place. The Lord spoke to Moses about what He saw happening down below. He told Moses to go down because the people had "become corrupt." The Lord spoke of "*your* people, whom *you* brought up"; He addressed Moses as their deliverer, and it is as if the Lord no longer wanted to have anything to do with them. It sounds as if the Lord reproached Moses, the leader and representative of the people, the mediator (cf. also commentary on vv. 1, 4). "God no longer thinks Israel worthy to be called His people, since it had made a calf its god" (Dutch Authorized Version, margin). "Brought up," see commentary on verse 1, where the people also referred to Moses as the one who brought them up out of Egypt. The Lord informed Moses about the sin with the golden calf. Moses had to go down, because the people were sinning. The Lord was long-suffering; Moses was to go down and straighten things out, so to speak.

Verse 8 describes how the people had "become corrupt" (cf. Deut. 9:12; 32:5; Hos. 9:9; the LXX uses a form of the verb "to act lawlessly"). They did indeed turn "quickly" after the making of the covenant (chs. 19–24; cf. Gal. 1:6). Note that the Lord says "what *I* commanded them": Moses brought them up out of Egypt, but the Lord had told them how to live and act (the LXX and Vulgate read "what you commanded them," which would make Moses also the one who gave Israel its laws and who made the covenant). Verse 8, see commentary on verse 4. Aaron was no more than a tool of the people. In spite of what Aaron said in verse 5, the offerings were brought to the calf, not to the Lord. The LXX omits verse 9; it has been assumed that it was inserted in the Hebrew text on the basis of Deuteronomy 9:13, but the text can be retained as it stands, although the translators of the LXX may have known a manuscript that did not include this verse. Note the anthropomorphic nature of verses 9–14. "I have seen" (v. 9) can be understood in the sense of "I have had experience with," "I have come to know well." "Stiff-necked": they were unwilling to bow their neck under the Lord's yoke (cf. 33:3, 5; 34:9; Deut. 9:6, 13; 31:27; Acts 7:51).

Verse 10 is even more anthropomorphic than verse 9; but it shows the special relationship that existed between the Lord and Moses. The Lord asked that Moses leave Him alone, to allow Him a free hand, to allow His anger to burn against the Israelites. The Lord's anger rose when He remembered how His people had repeatedly shown themselves to be stiff-necked (in their grumblings!). Moses could stay if he wanted to, and let the Lord's anger burn against the Israelites and destroy them. The Lord concluded with the flattering offer to make Moses into a great nation; a highly anthropomorphic statement in the light of Genesis 49:10 and Exodus 2:1–21. The Lord *could not* do what He suggested here to Moses, unless Jacob turned out to be a false prophet. But Moses' moving intercession that followed was pleasing to Him; it was what He wanted. "God puts the fate of the nation into the hand of Moses, that he may remember his mediatorial office, and show himself worthy of his calling" (Keil). Moses passed the test (also with respect to any possible ambition on his part) and, according to verses 11–13, refused the Lord's request without hesitation. He deeply loved his people in spite of their behavior, in contrast to their attitude toward him (cf. Ps. 106:23). Moses, a true mediator between the Lord and his people, tried to change the Lord's mind (cf. Aalders on Jer. 26:19). First he asked the Lord (cf. 3:14) why His anger would burn against *His* people, whom *He* brought up out of Egypt (see commentary on v. 7) "with great power and a mighty hand" (cf. 3:19; 6:5). The recent display of the Lord's power and might would have been wasted. Moses thus pointed first to the fact that Israel was the Lord's people, then to His deeds in the recent past (v. 11), and to the fact that the Lord's honor was at stake: if the Lord destroyed Israel, the Egyptians would say that the Lord led them out of Egypt to kill them in the mountains and to wipe them off the face of the earth (cf. Deut. 9:28). The Egyptians would then win after all (cf. ch. 1). That is why the Lord had to turn from His anger and relent (cf. Gen. 6:6;

Num. 14:13f.; etc.). And Moses concluded with his strongest argument: at stake were not only His people, His deeds, and His name among the Egyptians, but His very essence, His trustworthiness, the truth of His oath (Gen. 22:16; Heb. 6:13, 17), the promise of His covenant, His name (3:15). He was to remember Abraham, Isaac, and Israel (Sam. Pent., LXX: ''Jacob'') who served Him, and to whom He swore by Himself the promise that Moses repeated (cf. Gen. 12:7; 13:15; 15:5, 7, 18; 22:17; 26:4; 28:13; Deut. 34:4; see commentary on Exod. 2:24; 6:8).

In the face of this earnest request, the Lord relented (v. 14; KJV, RSV: ''repent.'' Cf. Pss. 99:6; 106:45; Jer. 18:8; 26:3, 13, 19; Amos 7:3, 6; Jonah 3:10; James 5:16). ''Of course, forgiveness for the people's apostasy has not yet been secured by this (cf. v. 30), nor is v. 14 prophetic; only the actual destruction of the people, or the Lord's first burst of anger, has been averted, while at the same time Moses has shown himself here to be the mediator, far removed from all personal ambition, faithful and successful'' (Dillmann-Ryssel).

32:15–20 *Moses turned and went down the mountain with the two tablets of the Testimony in his hands. They were inscribed on both sides, front and back. The tablets were the work of God; the writing was the writing of God, engraved on the tablets.*

When Joshua heard the noise of the people shouting, he said to Moses, ''There is the sound of war in the camp.''

Moses replied:

> *''It is not the sound of victory,*
> *it is not the sound of defeat;*
> *it is the sound of singing that I hear.''*

When Moses approached the camp and saw the calf and the dancing, his anger burned and he threw the tablets out of his hands, breaking them to pieces at the foot of the mountain. And he took the calf they had made and burned it in the fire; then he ground it to powder, scattered it on the water and made the Israelites drink it.

After his intercession on the mountain, Moses appeared in the camp as an angry avenger. He made the people feel God's wrath, but not without allowing himself to be carried away in his anger, especially when he broke the two tablets. It appears that the Lord, after relenting, did not say anything further to Moses, and Moses descended (v. 15). He now carried out the Lord's instructions of verse 7. ''The two tablets of the Testimony,'' see commentary on 31:18; cf. also 24:12; 25:16; 34:29. Here is added that they were inscribed on both sides; if the tablets contained only the Ten Commandments (which was very likely the case, cf. 24:12; 34:1, 28; Deut. 4:13), they were probably relatively small. Babylonian and Assyrian clay tablets were frequently inscribed on both sides; it has been suggested that the two tablets were inscribed in cuneiform, but this cannot be proven and is improbable. Böhl thinks that the tablets were made of dressed limestone rather than baked clay (but cf. 20:25). Verses 15b–16 are parenthetical and draw attention to the great value of the two tablets: they were completely covered with writing, inscribed by God Himself (cf. 24:12; 31:18), and given by Him to Moses in their final form. This parenthetical statement indicates that Moses' subsequent breaking of the tablets was wrong: even he, the interceding mediator (cf. vv. 7–14), fell into sin. Verse 16, cf. Deuteronomy 9:10. It would have been much more impressive and would have placed the focus much more on God if Moses had presented the two tablets to the people side by side with the golden calf; that would have been a lesson in comparative religion! Moses had violated "the work of God," where He only had a right to destroy the work of sinful people!

Joshua waited for Moses on the mountain while all this took place (cf. 24:13). It is possible that he was with Moses when God spoke to him, but Joshua was unaware of what had happened, so that it is probable that Moses left Joshua behind, half-way up the mountain, and went on alone (cf. 24:16–18). Moses then did not say anything to Joshua about what the Lord had told him. Joshua heard the noise of the people shouting and mistook it for the sound of war. Moses, prepared by the Lord, soon perceived that it was neither the sound of victory, nor of defeat (cf. 17:11), but the sound of singing.

Verse 18 has a poetic character and contains a play on words.[27] The feast was in full swing when Moses approached the camp. When he saw with his own eyes what was happening, he fully realized the wickedness of the people. The calf and the dancing kindled his anger (cf. v. 10), and he threw down and broke the tablets at the foot of the mountain. In Moses' case, it was temper (cf. v. 10), albeit mixed with a holy zeal (cf. 2:11–13). This outburst of temper is so understandable that he was not punished for it (but cf. Num. 20:11–12). The tablets of the Testimony, on which the Lord expressed His will, and which were also the tablets of the covenant, were shattered. The people had broken the covenant and Moses, in a symbolic act, broke those tablets before their eyes (Deut. 9:17). The golden calf was utterly destroyed (cf. 2 Kings 23:4). Moses then forced the Israelites to drink the remains of the "god," "so that thereby they would learn to

---

[27]Lit. " 'It is not the sound of the answering of might, neither is it the sound of the answering of weakness; the sound of answering-in-song do I hear;' i.e., not the answering cries of victors and vanquished, but the answering voices of singers, are what Moses hears. . . . There is a play on the double sense of the word "answer.' " (Driver); cf. also 15:31 (tr.).

understand the insignificance of such gods, which they could drink'' (Dutch Authorized Version, margin). Cf. Deuteronomy 9:21; Numbers 5:18; the people were made to drink their own sin. Some think here of the drinking of some kind of cursed water, which resulted in an outbreak of the plague (v. 35). Aaron made the calf (v. 20 indicates that ''they,'' the Israelites, made it), Moses ground it to powder in great anger (cf. Ps. 69:9; John 2:17). ''Ground it to powder'' can mean two things: if the calf was made of solid gold, then Moses melted it down into clumps, which he then ground to powder with rocks; if, on the other hand, the calf was made of wood, overlaid with gold (see commentary on v. 4), then Moses burned the wooden parts and pulverized the overlay. Cf. Deuteronomy 9:21.

32:21–24 *He said to Aaron, ''What did these people do to you, that you led them into such great sin?''*

''Do not be angry, my lord,'' Aaron answered. ''You know how prone these people are to evil. They said to me, 'Make us gods who will go before us. As for this fellow Moses who brought us up out of Egypt, we don't know what has happened to him.' So I told them, 'Whoever has any gold jewelry, take it off.' Then they gave me the gold, and I threw it into the fire, and out came this calf!''

Moses now turned to Aaron and called him to account as the one who was responsible (see commentary on v. 1). The question in verse 21 implies love for Israel. The word for ''sin'' refers to a ''missing of the mark.'' What a difference between the two brothers! Aaron shifted the blame (cf. Gen. 3:12–13) entirely onto the people. Note the respect with which he addressed Moses (cf. Num. 11:28; 12:11). Aaron's love for the people was not as great as that of Moses; he considered them thoroughly bad (cf. the Lord's appraisal in v. 9). He was afraid of Moses' anger being directed against him. Verse 23, cf. verse 1; Aaron omitted ''come'' (lit. ''get up''). Perhaps he wanted to prejudice Moses against the people by telling him what the people had said about him. Verse 24, cf. verses 2–3. ''Out came this calf'': he glossed over his own activity and tried to excuse his own role in the matter. ''He speaks of the calf as if it came about more by accident than through his will or ability'' (Dutch Authorized Version, margin). Concerning the Lord's anger against Aaron, cf. Deuteronomy 9:20.

32:25–29 *Moses saw that the people were running wild and that Aaron had let them get out of control and so become a laughingstock to their enemies. So he stood at the entrance to the cave and said, ''Whoever is for the LORD, come to me.'' And all the Levites rallied to him.*

Then he said to them, ''This is what the LORD, the God of Israel, says: 'Each man strap a sword to his side. Go back and forth through the camp from one end to the other, each killing his brother and friend and neighbor.'" The Levites did as Moses commanded, and that day about three thousand of the people died. Then Moses said, "You have been set apart to the LORD today, for you were against your own sons and brothers, and he has blessed you this day."

We are not told what Moses' response to Aaron's "defense" was. His attention was probably diverted to the behavior of the people. When he looked at the people again, he became angry (cf. v. 19). The golden calf had been disposed of, but this did not put an end to the debauchery of the people. We might interpret "running wild" (lit. "unloosed") in the sense of "nakedness" (cf. KJV), since the appearance of Moses had probably settled them down, unless we are to assume an orgy of such dimensions that the masses in the camp continued to run around as if crazed. I am inclined to accept the latter interpretation, in which case only those who were near Moses had seen him destroy the golden calf. It is also possible that the destruction of the calf did not take place until afterward; or Moses may have destroyed the calf and forced the Israelites to drink the water and powder later (cf. Deut. 9:21). "Were running wild" and "had let them get out of control" (v. 25) are both forms of a verb that means "to loose"; the same verb was also used in 5:4. Aaron, in spite of the fact that he denied his part in it, was responsible for letting the people get out of control by organizing a festival. The "enemies" in verse 25 are most likely those enemies who would later hear about this incident. The word translated "laughingstock" is found only here; it literally means "(derisive) whisper" (cf. also v. 12; Deut. 28:37). Moses went and stood at the entrance to the camp (probably the main entrance), and invited all those who were for the Lord (KJV: "who are on the LORD's side") to come to him. The Levites, the tribe to which Moses and Aaron belonged, responded; it is thus probable that the Levites had not participated in the wild festivities.

For the sake of interest, I mention here the view that this was the beginning of the tribe of Levi, which then consisted of those who were faithful to the Lord. It is also possible that the Levites participated in the feast, but were the first to obey Moses again. Moses' command in verse 27, to go back and forth through the camp killing even those who were closest to them, seems cruel; but we must keep in mind that as a prophet, he based his command on a direct inspiration from the Lord. A verse like this raises the question as to what the Lord's purpose was in giving such a command. And then we come to Matthew 10:37 and Luke 14:26, and the demand for absolute holiness (cf. what was already stated in 19:6). One cannot trifle with the Lord. Israel's *existence* was at stake; otherwise, it would be spiritually conquered as soon as it reached Canaan, and swept into paganism. The ultimate issue was that the Messiah was to come from Israel. This measure was in keeping with the times and the dispensation in which Israel lived. The sons of Levi were given a very difficult task: they were to kill their brothers, their friends, and their neighbors. They carried out Moses' command, and the toll was heavy: about 3,000. Still, as Calvin pointed out, this number was relatively small when we remember that in the case of a mutiny, a military leader would decimate the guilty, while here no more than 3,000 were killed out of a total of 600,000.

Verse 29 presents a problem. The NIV follows the LXX, Vulgate, and Targum: the Levites were "set apart" or consecrated to the Lord because they carried out Moses' command. I prefer to translate verse 29 as follows: "For Moses had said" (cf. KJV) when he issued the order to kill brother, friend, and neighbor, "offer today to the LORD, each one his brother, his friend, and his neighbor, in order that the LORD may bless you today"; this rendering agrees with that of Buber-Rosenzweig, and the KJV. Cf. Deuteronomy 33:9. The Lord wanted them to kill even those who were closest to them, should they find them in sin; this was pleasing to the Lord.

Moses did not yet specify the nature of the blessing that the Levites had earned. The thought of an ordination or consecration offering suggests itself (cf. 28:41; 29:1ff.); according to some the Levites made themselves worthy of the priestly office by bringing such a consecration offering here; or, if we accept the NIV rendering, Moses stated with grim sarcasm that today they had brought their ordination offering. "You have been set apart" is literally "you have filled your hand" (the same phrase is translated "ordain" in 28:41); although the ordination offering was mentioned only in relation to Aaron and his sons, it is not improbable that this thought was implied in Moses' choice of words here. The phrase was usually used in the specific sense of "ordination" (cf. Judg. 17:5, 12; 1 Kings 13:33), although it could also be used of offering in general (cf. e.g., 1 Chron. 29:5; 2 Chron. 29:31). Here it then means "you have filled your own hand," i.e., you have ordained yourselves as priests, and thus consecrated yourselves to the special service of the Lord. The sin of the people had ruined much; but the Levites had turned the curse (Gen. 49:7) into a blessing (cf. Num. 3). Concerning the zeal of the Levites, cf. Genesis 34 and Exodus 2 (see commentary on 2:1). In contrast to Genesis 34, they now had placed their relationship with the Lord above blood ties.

32:30 *The next day Moses said to the people, "You have committed a great sin. But now I will go up to the LORD; perhaps I can make atonement for your sin."*

The following day Moses encouraged the people, who were undoubtedly greatly affected and repentant. He impressed on them the magnitude of their sin (see commentary on v. 21), but also announced his intention to go up to the Lord on the mountain and to try to make "atonement" (from a root "to cover," "to blot out") for their sin. Moses, the mediator between the Lord and his people, wanted to go back up the mountain as the representative of people. But he dared not assure them that his attempt to propitiate the Lord would be successful. "You" (v. 30a) is plural and emphatic.

32:31, 32 *So Moses went back to the* LORD *and said, "Oh, what a great sin these people have committed! They have made themselves gods of gold. But now, please forgive their sin—but if not, then blot me out of the book you have written."*

Moses returned to the Lord and honestly confessed the great sin. "They have made themselves gods of gold," cf. v. 1ff.; 20:23. Nevertheless, he asked the Lord to forgive their sin. "Please forgive their sin" reads literally "If you will forgive their sin" (the LXX reads "forgive their sin"); the statement is incomplete, but the thought is clear. Moses was moved; he stood in the gap for his people with deep emotion. In verse 32b, he made a magnificent offer (cf. Paul in Rom. 9:3). Anyone who has this great a love for the sinful people is rightfully a type of the Mediator Christ Jesus. This offer transcended Moses' intercession in verses 11–13. The people did not deserve Moses' love (v. 1), as Moses well knew (v. 23). "Blot out," cf. 17:14. "The book you have written" is not mentioned before in the Scriptures. Moses knew of the existence of such a book, and the Lord did not deny it. Moses probably had heard of this book in the teaching he received from his mother. It is not yet clear what this book was. But Moses knew that his name was written in it. The Lord may have revealed this to him. Or, he may have deduced this from what he had been told about the book (cf. Heb. 11:26b). The context indicates that he, whose name was blotted out of the book (cf. the Egyptian custom mentioned below) would perish, as Israel would perish if it would not receive forgiveness for its sin. We may conclude from this that they, whose names are written in the book by the Lord, do not need to fear His anger, but may share in His love and receive His blessings. It is thus the book that contains the names of those who have found favor with the Lord, His friends. Later the Bible reveals more about this book (cf. Ps. 69:28; Mal. 3:16; Phil. 4:3; Rev. 3:5; 20:12, 15; 21:27; cf. also Isa. 4:3; Ezek. 13:9; Dan. 12:1, and Aalders on this verse; Luke 20:20). If this interpretation is correct, Moses' offer meant more than merely "let me die" (Num. 11:15). As Driver says, "the 'book' which God has written is the 'book of life' or 'of the living' (Ps. 69:28; cf. Isa. 4:3), i.e., the book in which the names of the living are said metaphorically to be inscribed."

In Moses' time, books were not unknown in Babylonia and Egypt, although they were, of course, different from our books in terms of shape and material. The Egyptians had a black, non-fading ink, and smooth paper made from the marrow of the papyrus plant. Books were made by glueing sheets of papyrus together. Beautiful manuscripts have been found, 20 m. and 40 m. in length. Usually only one side was used. Sometimes an old book was reused after its contents had been erased. Poor people wrote on potsherds. It is curious that Moses spoke of the Lord Himself writing, since kings had scribes who did their writing for them; but "the book you have written" does not necessarily preclude the idea of "the book you had had written." In any case, the Lord was in charge of the names and of this book. It goes without saying that "book" is a symbolic representation of that which the Lord has fixed and determined with regard to the rewarding of His friends. Moses' love for Israel was so great that their perdition would overshadow any blessing he would receive (cf. his choice in Exod. 2; Heb. 11:24–26). This love is seen most gloriously in Christ Jesus (cf. Phil. 2:5–8; Heb. 2:10–15; etc.). An entirely different question was whether or not Moses' offer constituted a possible option.

32:33, 34 *The LORD replied to Moses, "Whoever has sinned against me I will blot out of my book. Now go, lead the people to the place I spoke of, and my angel will go before you. However, when the time comes for me to punish, I will punish them for their sin."*

In verse 33, the Lord says that it was impossible for Him to accept the offer Moses made in verse 32. Being blotted out of His book does not depend on anyone's will, but solely on Him. And He punishes only those who have sinned against Him, without respect of persons. "Sin," see commentary on verse 31. Verse 33, cf. Ezekiel 18:4. The Lord did not say that He *always* did this; He merely cut off Moses in his attempt to move the Lord to blot him out of the book. Moses also sinned against the Lord, and the Lord did not destroy him (cf. e.g., Num. 20). We must see this verse in the context of the whole Bible, which later reveals more about this book and about the Lord's elective decree. Yet Moses' offer did have an effect, as verse 34 shows. He was told to go and lead the people (cf. 13:17; 15:13) to Canaan (cf. 3:8). But there was a major difference now: in the past (3:8; 12:42, 51; 13:17; 15:13; 20:2; etc.), it was the Lord who led; Moses led (see pp. 1–2) only as the Lord's servant (cf. 14:31). Now it was Moses and an angel (a servant and messenger, albeit a heavenly messenger) who were to lead. Moses and the people were deeply aware of the fact that this was a retrogression. This was what the people had accomplished with their sinful desire for gods who were to go before them instead of the Moses who had "disappeared." And in addition, the Lord gave them the prospect of a day of judgment; He reserved for Himself the option of bringing punishment in the future. "You" in verse 34 is singular. "Punish," lit. "visit," here used in a negative sense (cf. 20:5 kjv) rather than in a positive sense (cf. 3:16; 4:31; 13:19; kjv). Verse 34, cf. Deut. 32:35; Romans 12:19. Israel had turned itself into a pagan nation, and was treated as such. This is what the author finally points out in verse 35.

32:35 *And the Lord struck the people with a plague because of what they did with the calf Aaron had made.*

"Struck," cf. 7:25; 8:2; 12:23, 29. The Lord punished the people because of their guilt; they were as responsible as Aaron for the golden calf (cf. vv. 1–6). We cannot yet speak of propitiation, although Israel would not be destroyed and would reach Canaan. Moses had not fully accomplished his purpose (cf. v. 30). This is how serious this sin was in the eyes of the Lord.

33:1–3 *Then the Lord said to Moses, "Leave this place, you and the people you brought up out of Egypt, and go up to the land I promised on oath to Abraham, Isaac and Jacob, saying, 'I will give it to your descendants.' I will send an angel before you and drive out the Canaanites, Amorites, Hittites, Perizzites, Hivites and Jebusites. Go up to the land flowing with milk and honey. But I will not go with you, because you are a stiffnecked people and I might destroy you on the way."*

These verses are a continuation of 32:34; the Lord still spoke to Moses (v. 1a). The Lord sent him away with the command to leave Sinai with the people which he, Moses, had brought up out of Egypt (see commentary on 32:7). Verse 1 and 32:34 imply that Moses did not have to take the tabernacle and its accessories (cf. ch. 25–31 and vv. 7–11). This sign of the Lord's dwelling among Israel was no longer necessary, since the Lord withdrew that which it represented, His presence. The pillar of cloud and fire would also disappear (cf. 13:21). Only the land that He promised on oath to Abraham, Isaac, and Jacob (cf. 32:13) remained the purpose of the journey. An angel would take the Lord's place (v. 2). But this was not the angel of the Lord (cf. e.g., 23:20f.). "Drive out," cf. 2:17; 5:24. See commentary on 3:8 concerning the various nations mentioned here and concerning the "land flowing with milk and honey." From a material standpoint, Israel would not suffer from the fact that the Lord was no longer among them (cf. 17:7). An angel could drive out these nations as well. As a matter of fact, the Lord's presence could be dangerous for Israel because of their obstinacy (see commentary on 32:9). The Lord was not sure of Himself if He had to go with such people (anthropomorphic!). Israel was put to shame. A mediator was constantly needed.

33:4–6 *When the people heard these distressing words, they began to mourn and no one put on any ornaments. For the LORD had said to Moses, "Tell the Israelites, 'You are a stiff-necked people. If I were to go with you even for a moment, I might destroy you. Now take off your ornaments and I will decide what to do with you.'" So the Israelites stripped off their ornaments at Mount Horeb.*

Yet, in spite of the fact that the Lord had told them how dangerous His presence could be to them (cf. also v. 5), the people mourned when they heard the distressing words (cf. Ezek. 24:17; 26:16); they humbled themselves before the Lord (cf. Gen. 37:34). They would rather have the Lord than His angel, even though the angel could also bring them to the Promised Land. They expressed their sorrow by not putting on any ornaments (see commentary on 32:2–3). The LXX omits this, perhaps to harmonize verse 4 with verses 5–6. The usual interpretation of these verses is that the people took off their ornaments at Mount Horeb (see commentary on 3:1) in response to an explicit command of the Lord, which Moses was to pass on to the Israelites. Nevertheless, I believe that verses 5–6 are a continuation of the narrative, and that we must not translate it as a pluperfect ("For the LORD had said to Moses"); I base this on the expression "and I will decide what to do with you." The people's sorrow had caused the Lord to reconsider the question of His presence in their midst. At His command, they were now to take off their ornaments. And the Israelites "stripped off" (lit. "robbed themselves"; the same verb is used in 3:22) their ornaments. There is thus a ray of light (cf. Nineveh's repentance in the Book of Jonah). Nothing suggests that the purpose of this taking off of the ornaments was to supply the materials needed for the making of the ark and of the tabernacle; it would be better to assume that it was done to outfit the "tent of meeting," that is mentioned in verse 7. They were to be prepared to offer their ornaments to the Lord, and they did this (in contrast to 32:2–3). The Lord tested them without specifying the purpose. But it is best not to make too much of the expression "stripped off," since it is parallel to "no one put on" in verse 4. "At Mount Horeb" can also mean "from Mount Horeb onward"; Keil interprets this to mean that they took off the ornaments that they had worn up to this time, thus signifying a spirit of continual penance. This seems to be the most natural interpretation. We are not told how long the people persevered in this; perhaps it ended when the tabernacle was completed. In connection with these verses, cf. the garments of the high priest on the Day of Atonement (Lev. 16) and Psalm 22:1.

33:7–11 *Now Moses used to take a tent and pitch it outside the camp some distance away, calling it the "tent of meeting." Anyone inquiring of the LORD would go to the tent of meeting outside the camp. And whenever Moses went out to the tent, all the people rose and stood at the entrances to their tents, watching Moses until he entered the tent. As Moses went into the tent, the pillar of cloud would come down and stay at the entrance, while the LORD spoke with Moses. Whenever the people saw the pillar of cloud standing at the entrance to the tent, they all stood and worshiped, each at the entrance to his tent. The LORD would speak to Moses face to face, as a man speaks with his friend. Then Moses would return to the camp, but his young aide Joshua son of Nun did not leave the tent.*

The question relating to verse 7 is whether the verbs refer to something Moses did repeatedly (NIV), or to what Moses did after the events described in verses 1–6. If the former is correct, then verses 7–11 are parenthetical, indicating what Moses did each time Israel set up camp (cf. Gesenius-Kautzsch, 2nd ed., 112e. Verse 11b excludes the possibility that Moses did this whenever he wanted to inquire of the Lord). But this interpretation has serious problems. This is the first time we hear of the "tent of meeting," although the Lord had referred to the tabernacle, which was yet to be built, as the "Tent of Meeting" (27:21; 28:43; 20:42–44; etc. Cf. 25:22). Some maintain that Moses erected this tent to house the ark, which was brought from Egypt, but this cannot be supported in view of 25:10–22. A second problem is that verse 12 does not state that Moses went to the tent of meeting, which is an indication that verses 7–11 continue the narrative. And how can we explain the fact that Moses pitched the tent of meeting *outside* the camp, except on the basis of the estrangement that existed between the Lord and Israel after their sin with the golden calf? The name that Moses gave this tent is probably based on the name the Lord gave to the future tabernacle (see above). "Meeting" here also refers to a meeting between the Lord and Moses (see commentary on 27:21).

If the narrative continues in verse 7, then Moses pitched the tent after the people had stripped off their ornaments. "A tent," lit. "the tent" (but see commentary on 20:24; such a tent had not yet been mentioned). The LXX and Peshitta read "his tent," which indicates that the translators also considered this verse a continuation of the preceding, since it is unlikely that Moses' tent would always have been pitched outside the camp. It cannot refer to the tabernacle ("His"—i.e., the Lord's—"tent"), since it had not yet been built (ch. 35–39). "Pitched it," lit. "for him" for "for himself"; the literal rendering is problematic. I already mentioned the view that this tent served to house the ark; a variant on this is that Moses pitched a tent for the ark which was made from the ornaments that had been stripped off. The simplest solution is "pitched it for himself," since at this point Moses was the only one with whom the Lord had fellowship. By means of this tent, Moses wanted to attempt to get the Lord to go back on His resolve, and to continue to meet with him and through him with His people. This is an initiative worthy of a mediator! And thus this tent, while acknowledging the separation between the Lord and His people ("outside the camp some distance away"), is a visible prayer, based on the mourning of the people (vv. 4, 6). Pitching this tent only for himself and outside the camp are two proofs of Moses' acknowledgment of what the Lord had said (vv. 1–3, 5): the matter between the Lord and Israel had not yet been settled in Israel's favor. Anyone who wanted to inquire of the Lord had to go outside the camp. "Inquire," lit. "seek," which here is almost true in a literal sense: it requires a mediator and a going to the tent. Apparently this situation lasted for some time (several days?), verse 7b. The margin of the Dutch Authorized Version states that Moses lived temporarily in the tent outside the camp, while the people came to him for advice until the time came when they would be reconciled with God; but in view of verse 11, I do not believe this to be correct.

Verse 8 indicates that whenever Moses went to the tent in his role as mediator, the people anxiously watched him. Verse 9 then tells what happened when Moses entered the tent. "Pillar of cloud," see commentary on 13:21; cf. Numbers 11:25; 12:5; Deuteronomy 31:15. The Lord still had fellowship with Moses and spoke with him. The presence of the pillar of cloud shows that the Lord had not yet carried out His threat of verses 1–3. The people showed respect from a distance by worshiping. Verse 10 gives the impression that the pillar of cloud descended only occasionally. Note the contrast in verse 10 between "at the entrance to *the* tent" and "at the entrance to *his* tent." The statement in verse 11a has made a deep impression (cf. Num. 13:6–8; Deut. 5:4; 34:10); the Lord never again spoke in this manner to any of the prophets. To the other prophets, God spoke in visions or dreams, but with Moses He spoke in an audible voice. Joshua, Moses' "young aide" (cf. 24:13), stayed in the tent, perhaps because of the possibility that the Lord might summon Moses. Note that Joshua had accompanied Moses up the mountain, so that he had not participated in the sin with the golden calf (cf. also 17:9).

Proponents of the source hypothesis see in verses 7–11 an older tradition, which is attributed to E. The later priestly tradition (P) then would have replaced this simple sanctuary with its idea of a luxurious tabernacle. In E, Joshua, an Ephraimite, was then the original keeper of the tabernacle, replaced by Aaron and the Levites in P (Cf. also Introduction, pp. 13–15.)

B. *The Lord's response to Moses' intercession* (33:12–23)

33:12, 13 *Moses said to the* Lord, *"You have been telling me, 'Lead these people,' but you have not let me know whom you will send with me. You have said, 'I know you by name and you have found favor with me.' If I have found favor in your eyes, teach me your ways so I may know you and continue to find favor with you. Remember that this nation is your people."*

The situation described in verses 7–11 lasted several days (cf. v. 7). Moses, to whom the Lord spoke face to face (v. 11), then made another attempt to atone for the sin of his people. The mourning of the people, the stripping off of their ornaments, the pitching of the tent of meeting outside the camp, and their reverence for the pillar of cloud were now awarded with this renewed intercession. The connection with the preceding section can be expressed in the words of Lange: "As before he would not hear to a destruction of the people in which he should not be involved, so now he cannot conceive that he has found grace in Jehovah's eyes for himself alone; rather, in this personal favor he finds a reference to his people—a hopeful prospect which he must become acquainted with."[28]

Verse 12, cf. 32:34; 33:1–3, where we read that the Lord would send an angel before Israel, but that He Himself would no longer go with them. But Moses, used to the Lord's presence, apparently did not set much store by the angel; at the same time, he did not feel capable of leading Israel himself. Others interpret this verse to mean that Moses complained to the Lord that He had not shown him the confidence he was led to expect. "Lead," cf. 3:8, 17. "I know you by name," cf. commentary on 31:2; the meaning is "to know well or intimately," as in the case of a king who knew only his closest servants, and also "to know on the basis of election." The Lord had called Moses to be the leader of Israel, the mediator between the Lord and His people (chs. 3–4), cf. 3:4, 10, and Genesis 18:19; Isa. 43:1; 45:3–4. "Found favor," cf. commentary on 20:4–6; 3:21; Genesis 6:8. "Favor" is derived from a verb that indicates the showing of unmerited kindness; the word thus indicates condescending, free, and gracious kindness, goodness not based on obligation. We do not have a direct statement of the Lord to Moses that expresses this, but cf.

---

[28]Lange, *Exodus*, p. 140.

verse 17 below, and 32:10, 32, 33; 33:11. Moses based his plea on the Lord's own words to him, which is what made him so strong. He appealed to the Lord's favor toward him, in order to achieve something in the interest of his people (cf. 32:32; for the form of v. 13, cf. Gen. 18:3; 30:27).

Moses asked the Lord to teach him His ways, to show him His plans, so that he could know the Lord and find proof of His favor toward him. But the Lord was to remember that this nation was His people, that He was the God who made His covenant with them. In other words, any favor toward Moses was to be accompanied by a demonstration of the Lord's love for Israel. The Lord had to have plans, since the situation could not continue as it was. Moses was insistent, cf. Genesis 32:26. He considered it an impossibility that he would lead the people without the Lord's presence. The margin of the Dutch Authorized Version adds: "show me the means by which you intend to guide and protect this nation; or, what your plans are for this nation." Others interpret verse 13 more broadly. Thus, Driver, referring to Deuteronomy 32:4 and Exodus 34:6f., interprets "ways" to mean "the Lord's ways of dealing with men," and "so I may know you and continue to find favor with you" to mean "to understand what your nature and character is, and shape my petitions accordingly, that so I may find favor with you, and my future prayers may be answered." Although Driver's view has merit, I believe that it is better to relate these words primarily to the Lord's present plans for Israel; Moses was concerned with getting his present, rather than his future, prayers answered. Driver's view concludes that verses 14–16 are in the wrong place, since he feels that verse 14 does not contain an appropriate answer to verse 13. However, the answer in verse 14 is appropriate if Moses inquired after the Lord's present plans for Israel. The revelation of those plans would be proof that Moses had found favor in the Lord's eyes. After these tension-filled days (vv. 7–11) Moses wanted to know the Lord's decision (see commentary on vv. 5–6).

33:14–17 *The Lord replied, "My Presence will go with you, and I will give you rest."*

Then Moses said to him, "If your Presence does not go with us, do not send us up from here. How will anyone know that you are pleased with me and with your people unless you go with us? What else will distinguish me and your people from all the other people on the face of the earth?"

And the Lord said to Moses, "I will do the very thing you have asked, because I am pleased with you and I know you by name."

Most versions, including the LXX, KJV, and NIV, read verse 14 as a statement: "My Presence will go with you." This means that verse 17 essentially repeats what the Lord said in verse 14. I believe that it is better to read verse 14 as a question (as does the Dutch NBG translation, as well as the margin of the Dutch Authorized Version: "Shall my presence go with you and shall I give you rest?" Moses did not state his request directly; rather, the Lord asked Moses a question in order to elicit a clear petition on his part. The "you" is singular, but refers to Israel as a whole, represented by Moses (cf. 34:11f.). Matthew 11:28 has been pointed to as a parallel, but the "rest" referred to here is the rest in Canaan (cf. Deut. 3:20; 12:10; Josh. 22:4). "Presence," cf. verse 11; 20:3; Deuteronomy 4:37; Isaiah 63:9; see also Aalders on Genesis 32:20 in this commentary series. The Lord could also be represented by e.g., an angel (cf. v. 2); but the Lord's question indicates that He was almost ready to grant Moses' request. Moses realized this, and now stated his petition in the decided form of verse 15: "If your Presence does not go with us, do not send us up from here." Moses did not dare take another step without the Lord. The wilderness with the mountain of God was better than a peaceful life in Canaan if the Lord Himself did not accompany them. And in verse 16 Moses once again used the argument that he had used in 32:12: What would the other nations say if the Lord did not go with them? The only way Moses and the Lord's people (note the close connection: "pleased with me and with your people") could know that the Lord was pleased with them was when the Lord went with them. Moses asked the Lord whether this was not true. And he also said that this would be the basis for his own and Israel's unique position in the future (cf. 19:5–6; Deut. 4:7; 7:6).

On the basis of this argument, which is supported by Moses' and the people's attitude during the previous days, the Lord granted Moses' petition. But note that the ultimate reason for the Lord's response was His goodness and His love toward Moses: He was pleased with Moses and He knew Moses by name; that is why the Lord Himself would once again go with Israel. This exemplifies Moses' role as mediator (see Introduction, VIII). "I will do the very thing," lit.: "I will do this thing also" (KJV), referring to 32:14, 34; first the Lord relented and did not bring the threatened disaster on His people (32:14), then the people could continue their journey, led by Moses and an angel (32:34; 33:1–2), and now the Lord Himself would accompany them, rather than the angel, and the construction of the tabernacle could begin. From a human standpoint all this was due to Moses, the mediator, but from God's standpoint it was the result of His being pleased with Moses, His knowing Moses by name, and His election of Moses as an individual and as mediator. Thus the principle remains: "soli deo gloria," to God alone be the glory (cf. Ps. 99:6). It has been pointed out correctly that Moses' prayers penetrated ever more deeply.

33:18–23 *Then Moses said, "Now show me your glory."*

And the LORD said, "I will cause all my goodness to pass in front of you, and I will proclaim my name, the LORD, in your presence. I will have mercy on whom I will have mercy, and I will have compassion on whom I will have compassion. But," he said, "you cannot see my face, for no one may see me and live."

Then the LORD said, "There is a place near me where you may stand on a rock. When my glory passes by, I will put you in a cleft in the rock and cover you with my hand until I have passed by. Then I will remove my hand and you will see my back; but my face must not be seen."

On the basis of what the Lord told him in verse 17b Moses now dared to take the liberty to make another major request of the Lord, namely, that the Lord would show him His glory. We must understand that "glory" as His radiant splendor (cf. Ezekiel's visions, e.g., Ezek. 1, and the vision of John on Patmos, Rev. 4) although Moses probably thought of a seeing of God Himself as He was, a seeing of the Lord's face (or presence, cf. v. 20). We might consider this request something that Moses wanted for himself, a deep desire that he dared to voice after the encouragement of verse 17b, and, if it was granted, he expected to strengthen his faith in the promise of verse 17 (cf. v. 13). The Lord was willing to do much, He was even willing to give to Moses the revelation of Himself as Jahweh (cf. Rom. 9:15f.; we can think here of both Moses and the people: Moses received a sign of the Lord's favor, the people received forgiveness). But Moses' petition could not be granted, not because the Lord was unwilling, but because man could not bear the full vision of that radiance. In verse 20 the Lord seemed to deliberate, as it were, whether there might be a way to at least partially grant Moses' request; and thus, in verses 21–23, the Lord made Moses an offer that would allow him to see at least something of His glory. Of course, the Lord spoke here in anthropomorphic terms. He had a "face" and a "back" only in the sense that there were degrees in His revelation of Himself. His "face" was then, so to speak, the focus of the radiance of His appearance on the mountain (cf. 34:5), while His "back" was, as it were, the "fringe" of that radiance as it passed by (cf. Job 26:14). It was like the glow of the sun immediately after it has set. Another possible conclusion is that the Lord revealed Himself to Moses in human form, and that this vision was a prophecy of the incarnation of the Word; in this case "face" and "back" can be understood literally. Verse 20, see commentary on 24:10–11.

The Old Testament believers were deeply aware of the fact that "no one may see me and live" (cf. Isa. 6:5; Judg. 6:22; 13:22), probably in part as a result of this statement (cf. 1 Tim. 6:16; Exod. 19:21). The "rock" in verse 21 was on Mount Sinai (cf. 34:5f.; 1 Kings 19:9f.). "Cover" (v. 22) see commentary on 25:20: the Lord protected Moses from seeing His full radiance because Moses was not only a creature, but also a sinful creature. "Back" is the same word translated "rear" in 26:12. The Lord granted Moses' request, insofar as this was possible, and thus proved to him that what He had promised in verse 17 was true.

C. *The new stone tablets* (34:1–35)

This chapter tells us of the renewal of the covenant after the sin with the golden calf. Many exegetes see in verses 10–27 a second Decalogue, the so-called cultic Decalogue, attributed to J, while 20:1–17 is attributed to E. But this chapter must be explained on the basis of its context, rather than on the assumption that part of the chapter is a later addition. Although it does indeed contain a repetition of earlier legal provisions, there is no reason to see this chapter as anything but a description of what happened after the events of chapter 33. After Israel broke the covenant, the Lord renewed it, and the regulations that were given with the renewal fully emphasized the ceremonial aspect; this showed that after the sin with the golden calf, which broke the second commandment, the ceremonial aspect was impressed on Israel and henceforth Israel's covenant relationship with the Lord was in the foreground. Nevertheless, the Lord Himself wrote the Ten Commandments (20:1–17) on the new stone tablets (v. 28); they remained the basis of the covenant. Later Christ forcefully emphasized their spiritual-moral requirement, in order to fulfill it forever.

34:1–3 *The Lord said to Moses, "Chisel out two stone tablets like the first ones, and I will write on them the words that were on the first tablets, which you broke. Be ready in the morning and then come up on Mount Sinai. Present yourself to me there on top of the mountain. No one is to come with you or be seen anywhere on the mountain; not even the flocks and herds may graze in front of the mountain."*

The command of verse 1 was probably given shortly after 33:23. "Stone tablets", see commentary on 31:18. The "first ones" were inscribed by the Lord Himself, and given to Moses (cf. 31:18; 32:16; Deut. 9:9). "The words" are the same as the Ten Commandments given in 20:1–17 (see commentary on 20:1). Verse 1, see commentary on 32:19; cf. Deuteronomy 10:1. "Broke" is the same verb used in 23:24, where it was translated "break to pieces." Verse 2, see commentary on 19:11, 15. "Present yourself," lit. "place yourself" (cf. 17:9; 33:8, 21). "In the morning," cf. 7:15. "Come up," cf. 24:18. Verse 3, cf. 19:12–13. It was clear that a renewal of the covenant and a new theophany were imminent (cf. v. 5).

311

34:4–7 *So Moses chiseled out two stone tablets like the first ones and went up Mount Sinai early in the morning, as the LORD had commanded him; and he carried the two stone tablets in his hands. Then the LORD came down in the cloud and stood there with him and proclaimed his name, the LORD. And he passed in front of Moses, proclaiming, "The LORD, the LORD, the compassionate and gracious God, slow to anger, abounding in love and faithfulness, maintaining love to thousands, and forgiving wickedness, rebellion and sin. Yet he does not leave the guilty unpunished; he punishes the children and their children for the sin of the fathers to the third and fourth generation."*

Moses obeyed the Lord's command (v. 4) and went up on Mount Sinai alone (in contrast to 24:13; 32:17). Verses 5–7 describe Moses' experience on the mountain in fulfillment of the promise in 33:21–23. The Lord descended (cf. e.g., Gen. 11:5) in a cloud (see commentary on 24:16) and "stood there with him" (cf. 2:4; 14:13). The Lord proclaimed His own name (cf. 33:19). And then the Lord in His glory passed in front of Moses; but the most important aspect of this experience was that the Lord proclaimed His name, Jahweh, before Moses (cf. ch. 3), and thus revealed Himself to Moses in those attributes that constitute His Being. Each word in this mighty "proclamation" of the Lord is of paramount importance. "The LORD, the LORD," see commentary on chapter 3. The immutability and reality of His Being came first and were emphasized (the Name is proclaimed twice). To His people He would always be the same. The renewal of the covenant was necessary not because the Lord changed, but because His people were fickle and changing. "God" *(El)* emphasized especially God's power: His compassion and grace were not based on weakness (cf. 15:2). "Compassion," cf. 33:19: the powerful God had compassion on His elected people. "Gracious": God bestowed His favor freely, His people had no claim on it. "Slow to anger," unlike the desert demon to which Jahweh is demoted in some circles. "Love," see commentary on 20:6; this is the counterpart of His "grace." "Faithfulness" is found in 18:21 in the sense of "reliability, trustworthiness," the attribute of someone one can depend on (the Hebrew *emet* is from the same root as our "amen," "it is certain"). The phrase "love and faithfulness" is found elsewhere in the Scriptures, referring to both God (cf. Gen. 32:10) and people (cf. Gen. 24:49). The love to which the Lord obligated Himself in the making and renewing of His covenant never disappointed. The Lord never broke His covenant; on the contrary, He maintained "love to thousands" (v. 7). See commentary on 20:6. "Wickedness," see commentary on 20:5. "Rebellion" (KJV: "transgression"), see commentary on 22:9. "Sin": missing the mark, the transgression of a commandment. "He does not leave the guilty unpunished," see commentary on 20:7. The Decalogue already contained much of this proclamation. "He punishes the children . . . fourth generation," see commentary on 20:5. This was a covenant *renewal,* and thus restated much of what had been revealed previously. Verses 6–7, cf. Numbers 14:18; Deuteronomy 5:10; 2 Chronicles 30:9; Nehemiah 9:17, 31; Psalms 86:15; 103:8; 111:4; 112:4; 116:5; 145:8; Jeremiah 32:18; Joel 2:13; Jonah 4:2; Nahum 1:3; Ephesians 4:32; 1 John 4:9, 15; 1 Kings 19.

34:8, 9 *Moses bowed to the ground at once and worshiped. "O Lord, if I have found favor in your eyes," he said, "then let the Lord go with us. Although this is a stiff-necked people, forgive our wickedness and our sin, and take us as your inheritance."*

When the Lord descended and passed in front of Moses, Moses immediately (v. 8) showed his reverence by his posture and by worshiping (cf. 4:31; 12:27). He then "officially" restated his request that the Lord go with Israel (cf. 33:15). "Lord" (not covenant name): because of this appearance Moses now saw the Lord in the first place in His greatness and majesty, as Sovereign. "If I have found favor in your eyes," cf. 3:21; 11:3; 12:36. "Stiff-necked," see commentary on 32:9; 33:3, 5. Moses agreed with the Lord's assessment of Israel, but included himself in the wickedness and sin of the people ("our"). He also acknowledged that he was not capable of leading this people without the Lord's personal presence, and prayed for forgiveness for himself and the people. He concluded with a prayer that Israel once again be accepted by the Lord as His inheritance (see commentary on 19:5; "take us," see commentary on 23:30; 32:13). Cf. Leviticus 25:38; Psalms 28:8; 33:12; Zechariah 2:12.

34:10–26 *Then the LORD said: "I am making a covenant with you. Before all your people I will do wonders never before done in any nation in all the world. The people you live among will see how awesome is the work that I, the LORD, will do for you. Obey what I command you today. I will drive out before you the Amorites, Canaanites, Hittites, Perizzites, Hivites and Jebusites. Be careful not to make a treaty with those who live in the land where you are going, or they will be a snare among you. Break down their altars, smash their sacred stones and cut down their Asherah poles. Do not worship any other god, for the LORD whose name is Jealous, is a jealous God.*

"Be careful not to make a treaty with those who live in the land; for when they prostitute themselves to their gods and sacrifice to them, they will invite you and you will eat their sacrifices. And when you choose some of their daughters as wives for your sons and those daughters prostitute themselves to their gods, they will lead your sons to do the same.

"Do not make cast idols.

"Celebrate the Feast of Unleavened Bread. For seven days eat bread made without yeast, as I commanded you. Do this at the appointed time in the month of Abib, for in that month you came out of Egypt.

"The first offspring of every womb belongs to me, including all the firstborn males of your livestock, whether from herd or flock. Redeem the firstborn donkey with a lamb, but if you do not redeem it, break its neck. Redeem all your firstborn sons.

"No one is to appear before me empty-handed.

"Six days you shall labor, but on the seventh day you shall rest; even during the plowing season and harvest you must rest.

*"Celebrate the Feast of Weeks with the firstfruits of the wheat harvest, and the Feast of Ingathering at the turn of the year. Three times a year all your men are to appear before the Sovereign L*ORD*, the God of Israel. I will drive out nations before you and enlarge your territory, and no one will covet your land when you go up three times each year to appear before the L*ORD *your God.*

"Do not offer the blood of a sacrifice to me along with anything containing yeast, and do not let any of the sacrifice from the Passover Feast remain until morning.

*"Bring the best of the firstfruits of your soil to the house of the L*ORD *your God.*

"Do not cook a young goat in its mother's milk."

We already discussed the fact that many consider this to be a second, so-called cultic Decalogue (see also Introduction, IV). In response to Moses' prayer the Lord made a covenant (v. 10). In view of the fact that a covenant had already been made (ch. 19–24, esp. ch. 24), and book of the Covenant had been given, this covenant was to be a renewal of the first covenant, which had been broken by the sin of the golden calf. In view of this sin a number of legal provisions that had been given earlier were restated: the warning against any mixing with the inhabitants of Canaan was repeated, the celebration of Israel's own feasts was underlined, the Lord's claim on all of Israel was restated in terms of the claim on every firstborn (vv. 19–20), and Israel was reminded of the Sabbath and other feasts, as well as of other provisions of a ceremonial nature. In other words, Israel was to know and remember what the Lord instituted, since in the sin with the golden calf it had transgressed, not against its neighbor, but against its *God*. If this seemed to be a burden, then Israel was to remember the Lord's blessings: Canaan (v. 11), the Lord's jealousy (v. 14), the Exodus from Egypt (v. 18). The dividing wall between Israel and the nations was reinforced (cf. Eph. 2:14), in order to make the answer to Moses' prayer possible (vv. 8–9). All these things were part of the covenant. The making (lit. "cutting," since the making of a covenant involved the cutting of animals, cf. Gen. 15:9–21) of the covenant took place on the

Lord's initiative, it was His doing, although Moses prayed for the renewal. "Behold" (v. 10, KJV; omitted in NIV) indicates that what followed was important. First came the promise of miracles (cf. 3:20), which the Lord would perform before Moses' people ("your people" not spoken in anger as in 32:7). "You live among": "you" is emphatic. "Will do for you": "you" is singular, i.e., Moses, but also Moses as the representative of all of Israel. Verse 10, cf. Deuteronomy 5:2; Joshua 10:12–13; as well as other miracles on the wilderness journey. "Never before done": lit. "created," cf. Numbers 16:30; Isaiah 45:7; 48:7; Jeremiah 31:22; see also Aalders on Genesis 1 in this commentary series. Verse 10 indicates that the purpose of the renewal of the covenant was the Lord's own glory: all the people would see His work, and they would acknowledge Him.

Then follows in verse 11 the general exhortation to obey what the Lord commanded that day (the KJV and ASV place a colon after "today," which relates the first phrase of verse 11 more specifically to the command concerning the mixing with strangers, rather than to all that follows in vv. 11–26.) "Obey": singular, indicating that Moses was addressed as the representative of Israel as a whole and of each individual Israelite. What follows looks ahead to the time when Israel was settled in Canaan, and was directed against the "Canaanization" of the Lord's people (cf. 1 Cor. 6:15).

Verse 12, see commentary on 23:32–33; cf. also Numbers 33:50; Deuteronomy 7:2ff. "Snare," see commentary on 23:33. "Smash their sacred stones," see commentary on 23:24. "Asherah poles," see Noordtzij on 2 Chronicles 14:3. Israel was to be completely hostile to the sensual religions of Canaan, without compromise (cf. v. 14; see also commentary on 20:3, 5, 23). The Lord's "jealousy" was doubly emphasized; "God" *(El),* see commentary on verse 6. The Lord was able to make His jealousy felt, and this knowledge was to keep Israel from making a treaty with the inhabitants of Canaan. Verse 15 is a restatement of verse 12; the "snare" is further explained and the consequences of mixing, especially through intermarriage (v. 16), are described. Cf. also Numbers 25; Deuteronomy 7:3; Judges 3:6; 1 Kings 11:2. In the New Testament marriage with an unbeliever is still forbidden (cf. 2 Cor. 6:14–18).

"Cast idols" (v. 17), see commentary on 32:4; cf. also 20:23. In verse 18 the Israelites were urged to "celebrate" (see commentary on 23:15, 31:14) the Feast of Unleavened Bread (see commentary on 12:15–20). "At the appointed time," see commentary on 13:10. "In the month of Abib," see commentary on 13:4. Verse 19, cf. 13:2, 12; 22:29; Ezekiel 44:30; Luke 2:23. "Herd" (lit. "ox"), cf. 20:17; 21:32–33; 21:1, 4, 9–10, 30;

23:4, 12. "Flock" (lit. "sheep"), cf. 22:1, 4, 9–10. Verse 20 is very similar to 13:13; for verse 20b, see commentary on 23:15. "No one is to appear before me emptyhanded": the Israelites were to appear before the Lord in the sanctuary like the subject of an earthly kingdom appears before his king. Verse 21, see commentary on 20:9; labor is a duty, but also a following of God's example (cf. John 5:17). "Rest," cf. 16:30; 23:12; 31:17. Even during the busiest times of the year, the plowing season and the harvest, the Israelites were to rest on the Sabbath. "The Feast of Weeks" is the Feast of Pentecost, as it was later called, or the feast of the "firstfruit of the wheat harvest" (see commentary on 23:16). "Wheat," see commentary on 9:32; 29:2. "The Feast of Ingathering," see commentary on 23:16. "The turn of the year" is, where the religious year is concerned, in the spring (see commentary on 12:2; cf. Noordtzij on 2 Chron. 24:23). Verse 23 is virtually the same as 23:17. Israel was to trust God to take care of the land when the men of Israel appeared before the Lord three times a year on the occasion of the three feasts mentioned here (v. 24). "Covet," see commentary on 20:17. "Go up" and "appear" indicates that the Lord thought of the sanctuary in which He dwelled visibly. Verse 25, see commentary on 23:18. Verse 25b, see commentary on 12:10. Verse 26 is the same as 23:19.

34:27, 28 *Then the LORD said to Moses, "Write down these words, for in accordance with these words I have made a covenant with you and with Israel." Moses was there with the LORD forty days and forty nights without eating bread or drinking water. And he wrote on the tablets the words of the covenant—the Ten Commandments.*

In verse 27 Moses was told to "write down these words," referring to what the Lord said in verses 10–26. This was the foundation on which the renewal of the covenant rested (cf. 24:4). According to the direct statement of the Scriptures Moses himself thus recorded both 34:10–26 and the "Book of the Covenant." The new covenant was made in the first place with Moses ("with *you* and with Israel"). Verse 28, see commentary on 24:18. According to verse 1 the Lord was the subject of "wrote" in verse 28: Moses wrote down the Lord's words in verses 10–26, but the Lord Himself wrote the Ten Commandments on the new stone tablets, which underlines their greater importance. "Tablets," see commentary on verse 1. "The words of the covenant—the Ten Commandments" is the Decalogue, see commentary on 20:1–17. The fact that Moses survived without food or water for forty days and forty nights was a miracle: the Lord Himself sustained him (cf. Deut. 9:9, 18; Matt. 4:2).

34:29–35 *When Moses came down from Mount Sinai with the two tablets of the Testimony in his hands, he was not aware that his face was radiant because he had spoken with the L*ORD*. When Aaron and all the Israelites saw Moses, his face was radiant, and they were afraid to come near him. But Moses called to them; so Aaron and all the leaders of the community came back to him, and he spoke to them. Afterward all the Israelites came near him, and he gave them all the commands the L*ORD *had given him on Mount Sinai.*

*When Moses finished speaking to them, he put a veil over his face. But whenever he entered the L*ORD'*s presence to speak with him, he removed the veil until he came out. And when he came out and told the Israelites what he had been commanded, they saw that his face was radiant. Then Moses would put the veil back over his face until he went in to speak with the L*ORD.

When Moses came down from Mount Sinai (see commentary on v. 2), his face was radiant. "The two tablets of the Testimony," see commentary on 31:18. The verb translated "was radiant" (KJV: "shone") is related to the Hebrew word for "horn"; consequently Moses is sometimes shown in artistic representations with horns coming out of his head. The connection between "horn" and "ray" is readily apparent. The radiance of Moses' face was the effect of his speaking with the Lord; but Moses himself "was not aware that his face was radiant." This is another indication that Joshua did not accompany Moses this time. The fear of Aaron and the Israelites to approach Moses is understandable (v. 30). Moses called Aaron and the leaders of Israel, as well as all the Israelites (vv. 31–32), and when they approached Moses (first Aaron and the leaders, and then finally also the rest of Israel) he conveyed to them the commands the Lord had given him on Mount Sinai (34:10–26). The reflection of the Lord's radiance (see commentary on 33:21–23) lends additional force to these commands. Afterward Moses put a veil over his face (v. 33), which he removed only when he entered the Lord's presence (see commentary on 33:8–9; what is meant is probably Moses' entering the Lord's presence in the Tent of Meeting, although he may also have returned to the mountain). The text gives the impression that the radiance gradually faded; it served to enhance Moses' authority, and was a concession to the weakness of Israel, a people that wanted to *see* (cf. 32:1).

14. *The Implementation of the Instructions Concerning the Tabernacle* (35:1–39:43)

A. *Sabbath regulations* (35:1–3)

After the covenant, which had been broken by the sin with the golden calf, had been renewed and God and Israel had been reconciled, Moses could implement the instructions given in chapters 25–31. Chapters 35:1–39:43 give a detailed description of the construction of the tabernacle, which is an indication of the importance the Word of God places on the building of this sanctuary. Since these chapters contain largely the same terminology as chapters 25–31, frequent reference will be made to the commentary on those chapters.

35:1–3 *Moses assembled the whole Israelite community and said to them, "These are the things the LORD has commanded you to do: For six days, work is to be done, but the seventh day shall be your holy day, a Sabbath of rest to the LORD. Whoever does any work on it must be put to death. Do not light a fire in any of your dwellings on the Sabbath day."*

The first three verses of chapter 35 contain Moses' inculcation of the Sabbath regulations of 31:12–17; verse 2, cf. 31:15. Verse 3 is an addition, although in a sense it contains nothing new, since the same thought is expressed in 16:23. The rabbis consider this applicable only to the lighting of fires for the purpose of cooking or baking, although some Jewish sects believe that any use of fire on the Sabbath is forbidden. "Your dwellings": the house of the Lord is exempted. Cf. also 12:20. It is understandable that Moses began with the restatement of the Sabbath regulations (which concluded chs. 25–31), since they applied to the period during which the tabernacle was built. Verse 1 also states that Moses called together the entire Israelite community (cf. 12:3). The sequel shows that "these are the things the LORD has commanded you to do" refers back to the Lord's instructions in chapters 25–31, rather than to 34:10–26, which Moses had conveyed earlier (cf. 34:31–32). "You" in verse 2 is plural.

B. *Moses calls for an offering and for the construction of all that the Lord had commanded* (35:4–19)

Moses then mentioned the offering that the Lord had ordered and encouraged all those who were skilled to make everything the Lord had commanded.

35:4–9 *Moses said to the whole Israelite community, "This is what the LORD has commanded: From what you have, take an offering for the LORD. Everyone who is willing is to bring to the LORD an offering of gold, silver and bronze; blue, purple and scarlet yarn and fine linen; goat hair; ram skins dyed red and hides of sea cows; acacia wood; olive oil for the light; spices for the anointing oil and for the fragrant incense; and onyx stones and other gems to be mounted on the ephod and breastpiece.*

Verse 4, cf. 16:16. "The whole Israelite community," cf. 35:1. "This is what the LORD has commanded," cf. commentary on 35:1. Verses 5–9, cf. 25:2–7.

35:10–19 *"All who are skilled among you are to come and make everything the LORD has commanded: the tabernacle with its tent and its covering, clasps, frames, crossbars, posts and bases; the ark with its poles and the atonement cover and the curtain that shields it; the table with its poles and all its articles and the bread of the Presence; the lampstand that is for light with its accessories, lamps and oil for the light, the altar of incense with its poles, the anointing oil and the fragrant incense; the curtain for the doorway at the entrance to the tabernacle; the altar of burnt offering with its bronze grating, its poles and all its utensils; the bronze basin with its stand; the curtains of the courtyard with its posts and bases, and the curtain for the entrance to the courtyard; the tent pegs for the tabernacle and for the courtyard, and their ropes; the woven garments worn for ministering in the sanctuary—both the sacred garments for Aaron the priest and the garments for his sons when they serve as priests."*

"Skilled" (lit.: "wisehearted," cf. KJV): Moses' appeal was based on the instructions given to him in 28:3 (cf. 31:6). The appeal was made to all, before Bezalel and Oholiab were appointed specifically (35:30–35). Verse 11, cf. 26:1–14. "The tabernacle," cf. 26:1. "Covering," cf. 26:14. "Clasps," cf. 26:6. "Frames," cf. 26:15–25. "Crossbars," cf. 26:26–29. "Posts," cf. 26:32, 37. "Bases," cf. 26:19–21. Verse 12, cf. 25:10–22. "The ark," cf. 25:10–22. "Poles," cf. 25:13–15. "The atonement cover," cf. 25:17–21. "The curtain that shields it," lit.: "the veil of the covering," cf. KJV; "veil," cf. 26:31–35; "covering," cf. 26:36; 27:16. The NIV translates both words as "curtain." Verse 13, cf. 25:23–30; 30:27. Verse 14, cf. commentary on 25:31–40; 30:27. "Oil for the light," cf. commentary on 25:6; 35:8. "The altar of incense," cf. 30:1–10, 27. "The anointing oil," cf. 30:22–30. "Fragrant incense," cf. 30:34–38; 35:8. "The curtain for the doorway at the entrance to the tabernacle," cf. 26:36. Verse 16, cf. 27:1–8; 30:28. "Bronze grating," cf. 27:4. "The bronze basin with its stand," cf. 30:17–21, 28. "The curtains of the courtyard," cf. 27:9–18. "Posts," cf. 27:10. "Bases," cf. 27:10 (the bases for the posts; the Hebrew has a feminine singular here). "The curtain for the entrance to the courtyard," cf. 27:16.

"Pegs," cf. 27:19. "Ropes" were not mentioned before, but the "pins" implied the use of ropes; cf. Numbers 3:26.

Verse 19, cf. 31:10; chapter 28. "For ministering in the sanctuary," cf. 28:43; 29:30. Cf. also 28:35; 30:20. "The sacred garments," cf. 28:2. "Garments for his sons," cf. 28:40–43. "When they serve as priests," cf. 28:1.

C. *The offering* (35:20–29)

Israel responded willingly to Moses' call, as these verses, which describe the offering, indicate.

35:20–29 *Then the whole Israelite community withdrew from Moses' presence, and everyone who was willing and whose heart moved him came and brought an offering to the LORD for the work on the Tent of Meeting, for all its service, and for the sacred garments. All who were willing, men and women alike, came and brought gold jewelry of all kinds: brooches, earrings, rings and ornaments. They all presented their gold as a wave offering to the LORD. Everyone who had blue, purple or scarlet yarn or fine linen, or goat hair, ram skins dyed red or hides of sea cows brought them. Those presenting an offering of silver or bronze brought it as an offering to the LORD, and everyone who had acacia wood for any part of the work brought it. Every skilled woman spun with her hands and brought what she had spun—blue, purple or scarlet yarn or fine linen. And all the women who were willing and had the skill spun the goat hair. The leaders brought onyx stones and other gems to be mounted on the ephod and breastpiece. They also brought spices and olive oil for the light and for the anointing oil and for the fragrant incense. All the Israelite men and women who were willing brought to the LORD freewill offerings for all the work the LORD through Moses had commanded them to do.*

Verse 25 indicates that it took several days to raise the offering. "The whole Israelite community," cf. 35:1, 4. Verse 21, cf. 36:3; 1 Chronicles 29:5, 9,; 2 Corinthians 9:7. "Everyone whose heart moved him," lit. "whose spirit moved him" (cf. KJV), cf. 25:2, where the Hebrew uses "heart" rather than "spirit." Cf. also 35:5; the emphasis is on Israel's willingness. "An offering to the LORD," cf. 35:5; 25:2–7. "Work," cf. commentary on 35:2. "The Tent of Meeting," cf. commentary on 27:21. "Service," cf. commentary on 30:16. See also 27:19 (KJV); 1:14; 2:23. "Sacred garments," cf. 28:2; 35:19.

Verse 22 indicates that the women were also involved; the people expressed their joy at the restored covenant relationship with Jahweh. Note the contrast between verse 22 and 32:2–3 and 33:6. "All who were willing," cf. 35:5. "Brooches": the word is translated "hook" (for the nose or jaw) in 2 Kings 19:28; Isaiah 37:29; Ezekiel 19:4; 29:4; 38:4. "Earrings," cf. commentary on 32:2; Israel now showed that it was willing to give anything for the prescribed service of the Lord. "Rings" may refer to jewelry worn by either men or women; the same word was used for the rings of the various objects in the tabernacle (ark, table, etc.); cf. also 28:23ff. "Ornaments" (KJV: "necklaces") probably refers to necklaces made of golden beads. "A wave offering," cf. commentary on 28:24–26. The gold offered to the Lord was undoubtedly the gold the Israelites had received from the Egyptians during the night of the Exodus (cf. 12:35–36).

Verses 23–24, cf. commentary on 25:2–7. "Acacia wood," cf. 35:7. "For any part of the work": the expression is similar to "for all its service" in 35:21 and "whatever their function" in 27:19. The women offered their skills, verses 25–26, cf. 35:10 and Proverbs 31:19–24. "Willing," cf. commentary on 35:21.

"Leaders," cf. commentary on 16:22; 22:28. Everyone worked together: men, women, and leaders. Verse 28, cf. commentary on 25:6. The leaders contributed precious stones and spices. Cf. Acts 2:44–45. "Who were willing," lit.: "whose hearts impelled them," cf. 25:2. "Freewill offering" is derived from the verb "to impel." "All the work," cf. 25:24. And thus a willing nation gathered the materials necessary for the building of the tabernacle.

D. *The appointment of Bezalel and Oholiab (35:30–36:7)*

35:30–36:1 *Then Moses said to the Israelites, "See, the L*ORD *has chosen Bezalel son of Uri, the son of Hur, of the tribe of Judah, and he has filled him with the Spirit of God, with skill, ability and knowledge in all kinds of crafts—to make artistic designs for work in gold, silver and bronze, to cut and set stones, to work in wood and to engage in all kinds of artistic craftsmanship. And he has given both him and Oholiab son of Ahisamach, of the tribe of Dan, the ability to teach others. He has filled them with skill to do all kinds of work as craftsmen, designers, embroiderers in blue, purple and scarlet yarn and fine linen, and weavers—and all of them master craftsmen and designers.*

*So Bezalel, Oholiab and every skilled person to whom the L*ORD *has given skill and ability to know how to carry out all the work of constructing the sanctuary are to do the work just as the L*ORD *has commanded."*

Cf. 31:1–11. Verse 31 corresponds almost verbatim to 31:3. Verse 32 is almost the same as 31:4, and verse 33 parallels 31:5. Verse 34, cf. 31:6. "Craftsmen," cf. 26:1, 31; 28:6, 15. "Embroiderers," cf. commentary on 26:1; cf. 26:36; 27:16; 28:39. "Blue, purple, and scarlet yarn," cf. commentary on 25:4. "Weavers," cf. 28:32 and commentary on 26:1. "Designers," cf. 35:32; 31:4. "Skilled," cf. 35:10; 28:3; 35:25. "Skill and ability," cf. 35:31.

36:2–7 *Then Moses summoned Bezalel and Oholiab and every skilled person to whom the L*ORD *had given ability and who was willing to come and do the work. They received from Moses all the offerings the Israelites had brought to carry out the work of constructing the sanctuary. And the people continued to bring freewill offerings morning after morning. So all the skilled craftsmen who were doing all the work on the sanctuary left their work and said to Moses, "The people are* *bringing more than enough for doing the work the L*ORD *commanded to be done.''*

Then Moses gave an order and they sent this word throughout the camp: "No man or woman is to make anything else as an offering for the sanctuary." And so the people were restrained from bringing more, because what they already had was more than enough to do all the work.

"Willing," cf. commentary on 35:21. "Offerings," cf. 35:5. "Freewill offerings," cf. commentary on 35:29. Verse 5, cf. 2 Corinthians 8:1–5. Verses 4–5 indicate that the willingness of the people exceeded the need for materials, so that in verse 6 Moses had to ask the people not to bring any more. This is a still valid example of generosity toward the Lord's service.

E. *The construction of the tabernacle* (36:8–38)

36:8–38 *All the skilled men among the workmen made the tabernacle with ten curtains of finely twisted linen and blue, purple and scarlet yarn, with cherubim worked into them by a skilled craftsman. All the curtains were the same size—twenty-eight cubits long and four cubits wide. They joined five of the curtains together and did the same with the other five. Then they made loops of blue material along the edge of the end curtain in one set, and the same was done with the end curtain in the other set. They also made fifty loops on one curtain and fifty loops on the end curtain of the other set, with the loops opposite each other. Then they made fifty gold clasps and used them to fasten the two sets of curtains together so that the tabernacle was a unit.*

They made curtains of goat hair for the tent over the tabernacle—eleven all together. All eleven curtains were the same size—thirty cubits long and four cubits wide. They joined five of the curtains into one set and the other six into another set. Then they made fifty loops along the edge of the end curtain in one set and also along the edge of the end curtain in the other set. They made fifty bronze clasps to fasten the tent together as a unit. Then they made for the tent a covering of ram skins dyed red, and over that a covering of hides of sea cows.

They made upright frames of acacia wood for the tabernacle. Each frame was ten cubits long and a cubit and a half wide, with two projections set parallel to each other. They made all the frames of the tabernacle in this way. They made twenty frames for the south side of the tabernacle and made forty silver bases to go under them—two bases for each frame, one under each projection. For the other side, the north side of the tabernacle, they made twenty frames and forty silver bases—two under each frame. They made six frames for the far end, that is, the west end of the tabernacle, and two frames were made for the corners of the tabernacle at the far end. At these two corners the frames were double from the bottom all the way to the top and fitted into a single ring; both were made alike. So there were eight frames and sixteen silver bases—two under each frame.

They also made crossbars of acacia wood: five for the frames on one side of the tabernacle, five for those on the other side, and five for the frames on the west, at the far end of the tabernacle. They made the center crossbar so that it extended from end to end at the middle of the frames. They overlaid the frames with gold and made gold rings to hold the crossbars. They also overlaid the crossbars with gold.

They made the curtain of blue, purple and scarlet yarn and finely twisted linen, with cherubim worked into it by a skilled craftsman. They made four posts of acacia wood for it and overlaid them with gold. They made gold hooks for them and cast their four silver bases. For the entrance to the tent they made a curtain of blue, purple and scarlet yarn and finely twisted linen—the work of an embroiderer; and they made five posts with hooks for them. They overlaid the tops of the posts and their bands with gold and made their five bases of bronze.

Cf. commentary on 26:1–37. Verses 9–18, cf. commentary on 26:2–11. Verse 16 omits 26:9b. Part of 26:11 is omitted in verse 18. Verses 19–34, cf. commentary on 26:14–29. There are some differences between verse 29 and 26:24, verse 30 and 26:25, verse 32 and 26:27, verse 33 and 26:28. Verses 35–36, cf. commentary on 26:31–32. "Cast" (v. 36), cf. e.g., 25:12. Verses 37–38, cf. 26:36–37. "Bands" (v. 38), cf. 27:10. Verse 38 provides a clarification of 26:37. Note that the instructions concerning the setting up of the tabernacle are omitted, since that took place later, cf. 40:18–33. This indicates that the author was careful in his description of the events.

F. *The construction of the ark* (37:1–9)

37:1–5 *Bezalel made the ark of acacia wood—two and a half cubits long, a cubit and a half wide, and a cubit and a half high. He overlaid it with pure gold, both inside and out, and made a gold molding around it. He cast four gold rings for it and fastened them to its four feet, with two rings on one side and two rings on the other. Then he made poles of acacia wood and overlaid them with gold. And he inserted the poles into the rings on the sides of the ark to carry it.*

Cf. 25:10–14. There are minor differences between verse 2 and 25:11, and verse 5 and 25:14. Since the setting up of the tabernacle took place later, 25:15–16, 21–22 are omitted here. See commentary on 36:8–38.

37:6–9 *He made the atonement cover of pure gold—two and a half cubits long and a cubit and a half wide. Then he made two cherubim out of hammered gold at the ends of the cover. He made one cherub on one end and the second cherub on the other; at the two ends he made them of one piece with the cover. The cherubim had their wings spread upward, overshadowing the cover with them. The cherubim faced each other, looking toward the cover.*

Cf. 25:17–20. Verse 8 differs slightly from 25:19.

G. *The construction of the table* (37:10–16)

37:10–16 *They made the table of acacia wood—two cubits long, a cubit wide, and a cubit and a half high. Then they overlaid it with pure gold and made a gold molding around it. They also made around it a rim a handbreadth wide and put a gold molding on the rim. They cast four gold rings for the table and fastened them to the four corners, where the four legs were. The rings were put close to the rim to hold the poles used in carrying the table. The poles for carrying the table were made of acacia wood and were overlaid with gold. And they made from pure gold the articles for the table—its plates and ladles and bowls and its pitchers for the pouring out of drink offerings.*

Cf. 25:23–29. There is a slight difference between 25:26–27 and 37:13–14, and there are several differences between 25:29 and 37:16. The implementation of 25:30 had to wait, of course, until after the tabernacle was set up.

H. *The construction of the lampstand* (37:17–24)

37:17–24 *They made the lampstand of pure gold and hammered it out, base and shaft; its flowerlike cups, buds and blossoms were of one piece with it. Six branches extended from the sides of the lampstand—three on one side and three on the other. Three cups shaped like almond flowers with buds and blossoms were on one branch, three on the next branch and the same for all six branches extending from the lampstand. And on the lampstand were four cups shaped like almond flowers with buds and blossoms. One bud was under the first pair of branches extending from the lampstand, a second bud under the second pair, and a third bud under the third pair—six branches in all. The buds and the branches were all of one piece with the lampstand, hammered out of pure gold.*

They made its seven lamps, as well as its wick trimmers and trays, of pure gold. They made the lampstand and all its accessories from one talent of pure gold.

Cf. 25:31–39. There is a minor difference between 25:35, 39 and 37:21, 24. Verse 23 omits 25:37b, since its implementation came later; cf. commentary on preceding sections.

I. *The construction of the altar of incense* (37:25–28)

37:25–28 *They made the altar of incense out of acacia wood. It was square, a cubit long and a cubit wide, and two cubits high—its horns of one piece with it. They overlaid the top and all the sides and the horns with pure gold, and made a gold molding around it. They made two gold rings below the molding—two on opposite sides—to hold the poles used to carry it. They made the poles of acacia wood and overlaid them with gold.*

Cf. 30:1–5. There is some difference between 30:1–2 and 37:25, and between 30:4 and 37:27. Again, it is understandable that the author did not repeat 30:6–10 here.

J. *The preparation of the sacred anointing oil and the incense* (37:29)

37:29 *They also made the sacred anointing oil and the pure, fragrant incense— the work of a perfumer.*

Cf. 30:22–33 and 30:34–38, especially 30:25, 35, and 35:15.

K. *The construction of the altar of burnt offering* (38:1–7)

38:1–7 *They built the altar of burnt offering of acacia wood, three cubits high; it was square, five cubits long and five cubits wide. They made a horn at each of the four corners, so that the horns and the altar were of one piece, and they overlaid the altar with bronze. They made all its utensils of bronze—its pots, shovels, sprinkling bowls, meat forks and firepans. They made a grating for the altar, a bronze network, to be under its ledge, halfway up the altar. They cast bronze rings to hold the poles for the four corners of the bronze grating. They made the poles of acacia wood and overlaid them with bronze. They inserted the poles into the rings so they would be on the sides of the altar for carrying it. They made it hollow, out of boards.*

Cf. 27:1–8. Verse 1, cf. 27:1. Note the differences. The altar is here called the "altar of burnt offering." Verse 2, cf. 27:2. Verse 3 and 27:3 differ slightly. The order and choice of words in verses 4–5 differ somewhat from 27:4–5. Verse 6, cf. 27:6. There is some difference between verse 7 and 27:7–8.

L. *The construction of the basin* (38:8)

38:8 *They made the bronze basin and its bronze stand from the mirrors of the women who served at the entrance to the Tent of Meeting.*

Cf. 30:17–21, 28. Again, 30:19–21 has been omitted. A new element is introduced: the basin and its stand were made from the mirrors of the women who served at the entrance to the Tent of Meeting. "Tent of Meeting," cf. 25:22; 27:21. The tent referred to here is the tent of 33:7. Apparently there were women who served at the entrance to this tent. The verb for "serve" is also used to refer to going to war, as well as of the service of the Levites (cf. Num. 4:23; 8:24). 1 Samuel 2:22 also mentions women who served at the entrance of the Tent of Meeting. There is no indication as to the nature of this service. It has been suggested that a row of women stood at the entrance to the tent, but this is unlikely, considering the verb used here, although this view is found in Jewish tradition. The margin of the Dutch Authorized Version mentions a service consisting of fasting and praying (cf. Luke 2:37). Another possibility is that this service entailed cleaning of the tent, although it is not clear why so many women would be needed for this.

M. *The construction of the courtyard* (38:9–20)

38:9–20 *Next they made the courtyard. The south side was a hundred cubits long and had curtains of finely twisted linen, with twenty posts and twenty bronze bases, and with silver hooks and bands on the posts. The north side was also a hundred cubits long and had twenty posts and twenty bronze bases, with silver hooks and bands on the posts.*

The west end was fifty cubits wide and had curtains, with ten posts and ten bases, with silver hooks and bands on the posts. The east end, toward the sunrise, was also fifty cubits wide. Curtains fifteen cubits long were on one side of the entrance, with three posts and three bases, and curtains fifteen cubits long were on the other side of the entrance to the courtyard, with three posts and three bases. All the curtains around the courtyard were of finely twisted linen. The bases for the posts were bronze. The hooks and bands on the posts were silver, and their tops were overlaid with silver; so all the posts of the courtyard had silver bands.

The curtain for the entrance to the courtyard was of blue, purple and scarlet yarn and finely twisted linen—the work of an embroiderer. It was twenty cubits long and, like the curtains of the courtyard, five cubits high, with four posts and four bronze bases. Their hooks and bands were silver, and their tops were overlaid with silver. All the tent pegs of the tabernacle and of the surrounding courtyard were bronze.

Cf. 27:9–19. There are some differences between verses 9, 11–15 and 27:9, 11–16. Verse 16, cf. 27:6, but also 38:18. Verse 17 adds the silver overlay on the tops of the posts to what is stated in 27:17 (cf. 36:38). Verse 18, cf. 27:16, 18; "five cubits high": lit.: "five cubits high in width," indicating perhaps that the material from which these curtains were made consisted of squares measuring five cubits by five cubits. Verse 19 is an expansion of 27:16b. Verse 20, cf. 27:19; there are major differences between these verses.

N. *The cost of the tabernacle* (38:21–31)

38:21–31 *These are the amounts of the materials used for the tabernacle, the tabernacle of the Testimony, which were recorded at Moses' command by the Levites under the direction of Ithamar son of Aaron, the priest. (Bezalel son of Uri, the son of Hur, of the tribe of Judah, made everything the LORD commanded Moses;*

with him was Oholiab son of Ahisamach, of the tribe of Dan—a craftsman and designer, and an embroiderer in blue, purple and scarlet yarn and fine linen.) The total amount of the gold from the wave offering used for all the work on the sanctuary was 29 talents and 730 shekels, according to the sanctuary shekel.

The silver obtained from those of the community who were counted in the census was 100 talents and 1,775 shekels, according to the sanctuary shekel—one beka per person, that is, half a shekel, according to the sanctuary shekel, from everyone who had crossed over to those counted, twenty years old or more, a total of 603,550 men. The 100 talents of silver were used to cast the bases for the sanctuary and for the curtain—100 bases from the 100 talents, one talent for each base. They used the 1,775 shekels to make the hooks for the posts, to overlay the tops of the posts, and to make their bands.

The bronze from the wave offering was 70 talents and 2,400 shekels. They used it to make the bases for the entrance to the Tent of Meeting, the bronze altar with its bronze grating and all its utensils, the bases for the surrounding courtyard and those for its entrance and all the tent pegs for the tabernacle and those for the surrounding courtyard.

These verses list the quantities of gold, silver, and bronze that were used for the construction of the tabernacle. I believe that these verses constitute an elaboration on 35:22, 24. Furthermore, verses 25–28 and the choice of words in verse 21 form a counterpart to 30:11–16. Verse 21 is problematic, in terms of both translation and interpretation. "The amounts of the materials used for the tabernacle," lit. "the enumerated things of the tabernacle"; I prefer to translate "the costs of the tabernacle," since the Hebrew word that is used would have to be understood only here in the sense of "counting," which is not *necessary* in Numbers 4:49 and 7:2. As for the interpretation, the mention of the service of the Levites and of Ithamar seems to anticipate the appointment of the Levites, which came later. Some exegetes are therefore of the opinion that 38:21–31 does not belong here, or that these verses refer to something that took place later. But this is not necessarily the case; it is entirely possible that Moses appointed Ithamar and the Levites to determine the value of the gold, silver, and bronze used in the tabernacle, even though no mention is made of this elsewhere. It is hardly surprising that the author seems pleased to present the large amount donated by the Israelites toward the building of the sanctuary; such a grand total is indeed impressive.

"Tabernacle," cf. 25:8, 9; 26:1. The expression "tabernacle of the Testimony" shows that the "Testimony," the Ten Commandments (cf. 25:16, 21–22), give a profound significance to the Lord's dwelling place in Isarel. The Lord's covenant with His people had a moral character, and the law was of such paramount importance that it dominated the sacrificial service. We would say: the sacrifice of Christ was the price with which God purchased us to serve Him out of gratitude in a life lived in accordance with God's law (cf. Rev. 5:9–10). Everything that was part of the tabernacle was counted (cf. 30:12). "Ithamar," cf. 6:23; Numbers 4:28.

Verse 22, cf. 31:2; 35:30. Verse 23, cf. 31:6; 35:34–35. Verse 24 reports the total amount of gold. "Talent, shekel, and sanctuary shekel," see commentary on 21:32; 30:13. "Wave offering," cf. 35:22. Verses 25–26 indicate that the census, which was commanded in 30:11–16, had already been taken when the construction of the tabernacle began. Cf. Numbers 1:46. It is also possible that the "atonement money," which was to be collected during the census, was contributed voluntarily, while the total number of those counted nevertheless agreed with the results of the "official" census of Numbers 1. "Beka," cf. 30:13. "Crossed over to those counted," cf. 30:14. Verses 27–31, cf. 38:9–20; 27:1–8; 38:1–7; and commentary on 27:9–19. The bronze, unlike the silver, was again brought as a wave offering. "Entrance to the Tent of Meeting," cf. 38:8.

O. *The making of the priestly garments* (39:1–31)

39:1–31 *From the blue, purple and scarlet yarn they made woven garments for ministering in the sanctuary. They also made sacred garments for Aaron, as the* Lord *commanded Moses.*

They made the ephod of gold, and of blue, purple and sacrlet yarn, and of finely twisted linen. They hammered out thin sheets of gold and cut strands to be worked into the blue, purple and scarlet yarn and fine linen—the work of a skilled craftsman. They made shoulder pieces for the ephod, which were attached to two of its corners, so it could be fastened. Its skillfully woven waistband was like it—of one piece with the ephod and made with gold, and with blue, purple and scarlet yarn, and with finely twisted linen, as the Lord *commanded Moses.*

They mounted the onyx stones in gold filigree settings and engraved them like a seal with the names of the sons of Israel. Then they fastened them on the shoulder pieces of the ephod as memorial stones for the sons of Israel, as the Lord *commanded Moses.*

They fashioned the breastpiece—the work of a skilled craftsman. They made it like the ephod: of gold, and of blue, purple and scarlet yarn, and of finely twisted linen. It was square—a span long and a span wide—and folded double. Then they mounted four rows of precious stones on it. In the first row there was a ruby, a topaz and a beryl; in the second row a turquoise, a sapphire and an emerald; in the third row a jacinth, an agate and an amethyst; in the fourth row a chrysolite, an onyx and a jasper. They were mounted in gold filigree settings. There were twelve stones, one for each of the names of the sons of Israel, each engraved like a seal with the name of one of the twelve tribes.

For the breastpiece they made braided chains of pure gold, like a rope. They made two gold filigree settings and two gold rings, and fastened the rings to two of the corners of the breastpiece. They fastened the two gold chains to the rings at the corners of the breastpiece, and the other ends of the chains to the two settings, attaching them to the shoulder pieces of the ephod at the front. They made two gold rings and attached them to the other two corners of the breastpiece on the inside edge next to the ephod. Then they made two more gold rings and attached them to the bottom of the shoulder pieces on the front of the ephod, close to the seam just above the waistband of the ephod. They tied the rings of the breastpiece to the rings of the ephod with blue cord, connecting it to the waistband so that the breastpiece would not swing out from the ephod—as the LORD commanded Moses.

They made the robe of the ephod entirely of blue cloth—the work of a weaver—with an opening in the center of the robe like the opening of a collar, and a band around this opening, so that it would not tear. They made pomegranates of blue, purple and scarlet yarn and finely twisted linen around the hem of the robe. And they made bells of pure gold and attached them around the hem between the pomegranates. The bells and pomegranates alternated around the hem of the robe to be worn for ministering, as the LORD commanded Moses.

For Aaron and his sons, they made tunics of fine linen—the work of a weaver—and the turban of fine linen, the linen headbands and the undergarments of finely twisted linen. The sash was of finely twisted linen and blue, purple and scarlet yarn—the work of an embroiderer—as the LORD commanded Moses.

They made the plate, the sacred diadem, out of pure gold and engraved on it, like an inscription on a seal: HOLY TO THE LORD. *Then they fastened a blue cord to it to attach it to the turban, as the LORD commanded Moses.*

Cf. 28:1–43. Verse 1, cf. 31:10; 35:19; 28:2. "They made" refers to Bezalel and Oholiab and their apprentices. There is some difference between 28:6 and 39:2. "They" (v. 2): the Hebrew has a singular here and in verses 7, 8, 22, referring perhaps to Bezalel as the one ultimately in charge.

Verse 3 is an elaboration on 28:6, especially on "the work of a skilled craftsman." "Hammered out," cf. Numbers 16:39. "Strands" is the same word as "cords" in 28:28, 37. There is some difference between 39:4 and 28:7, and a slight difference between 39:5 and 28:8. In 39:5 is added "as the LORD commanded Moses," indicating the importance of the work (cf. vv. 1, 7, 21, 26, 29, 31, and 32). The instructions for the making of the priestly garments are rather detailed, since their manufacture presented special problems. There is considerable difference, especially in the word order, between 39:6 and 28:9–11. There is some difference between 39:7 and 28:12. The reminder that Aaron was to carry the names of his shoulder pieces was not necessary here. The difference between 39:8 and 28:15 is minimal, while verse 9 has a few more words than 28:16. The difference between 28:17 and 39:10 is insignificant. For 39:11–15, cf. 28:18–22. The conclusion of 39:13 differs slightly from 28:20. Verse 16, cf. 28:23.

The two gold filigree settings are not mentioned in 28:23, but cf. 28:25. Verses 17–20, cf. 28:24–27. There is an insignificant difference between 39:17 and 28:24. Verse 21, cf. 28:28; 28:29–30 have been omitted, since they do not belong here. Verses 22–23, cf. 28:31–32. The word order has been changed slightly. Verses 24–25, cf. 28:33; there is some difference. Verse 26, cf. 28:34–35. Since this chapter deals with the making of the garments, part of 28:34–35 has been omitted here. Verse 27, cf. 28:39; there is some difference. The verse refers to "the work of a weaver," rather than "the work of an embroiderer," but cf. 39:29. Verse 28, cf. 28:39, 40, 42. The choice of words is somewhat different. Verse 29 contains a further elaboration on 28:39. Verse 30, cf. 28:36; 29:6. Verse 31, cf. 28:37.

P. *Moses inspects the tabernacle* (39:32–43)

39:32–43 *So all the work on the tabernacle, the Tent of Meeting, was completed. The Israelites did everything just as the LORD commanded Moses. Then they brought the tabernacle to Moses: the tent and all its furnishings, its clasps, frames, crossbars, posts and bases; the covering of ram skins dyed red, the covering of hides of sea cows and the shielding curtain; the ark of the Testimony with its poles and the atonement cover; the table with all its articles and the bread of the Presence; the pure gold lampstand with its row of lamps and all its accessories, and the oil for the light; the gold altar, the anointing oil, the fragrant incense, and the curtain for the entrance to the tent; the bronze altar with its bronze grating, its poles and all its utensils; the basin with its stand; the curtains of the courtyard with its posts and bases, and the curtain for the entrance to the courtyard; the ropes and tent pegs for the courtyard; all the furnishings for the tabernacle, the Tent of Meeting; and the woven garments worn for ministering in the sanctuary, both the sacred garments for Aaron the priest and the garments for his sons when serving as priests.*

The Israelites had done all the work just as the LORD had commanded Moses. Moses inspected the work and saw that they had done it just as the LORD had commanded. So Moses blessed them.

This section emphasizes the fact that the Israelites made everything "just as the LORD commanded Moses" (vv. 32, 42, 43). Verse 43 is reminiscent of Genesis 1:31. Moses inspected and approved the work; to express his gratitude he rewarded the people by blessing them. This was a great moment in Israel's history. All that was left now was the setting up of the tabernacle, and then the Lord could come and dwell among Israel in His sanctuary (cf. 25:8).

"The tabernacle," cf. 25:1ff. "Tent of Meeting," cf. 27:21. Verse 33, cf. 35:11. Verse 34, cf. 35:7, 11. Verse 35, cf. 35:12; 25:16, 21. Verse 36, cf. 35:13. The bread of the Presence was also made, perhaps from manna (see commentary 16:32). Verse 37, cf. 35:14. "The row of lamps," lit.: "the lamps of arrangement," cf. 25:37, which indicates that the lamps were to be placed on the lampstand (cf. also 27:21). Verse 38, cf. 35:15. This section thus parallels in many respects 35:10–19 where the general instructions were given that had now been carried out accurately. Verse 39, cf. 35:16. Verse 40, cf. 35:17. "Ropes," cf. 35:18. Verse 41, cf. 35:19. Verse 42, cf. 39:32.

Now that the instructions had been carried out, the initiative was once again the Lord's, who commanded Moses to set up the tabernacle. The making of all that was necessary for the tabernacle is one of the most illustrious pages in Israel's history, and was the happiest period of the wilderness journey.

15. *Moses Sets Up the Tabernacle* (40:1–38)

Chapter 40 contains three sections: the Lord commanded Moses to set up the tabernacle (vv. 1–15); Moses carried out this command (vv. 16–33); the glory of the Lord filled the tabernacle (vv. 34–38).

40:1–15 *Then the LORD said to Moses: "Set up the tabernacle, the Tent of Meeting, on the first day of the first month. Place the ark of the Testimony in it and shield the ark with the curtain. Bring in the table and set out what belongs on it. Then bring in the lampstand and set up its lamps. Place the gold altar of incense in front of the ark of the Testimony and put the curtain at the entrance to the tabernacle.*

"Place the altar of burnt offering in front of the entrance to the tabernacle, the Tent of Meeting; place the basin between the Tent of Meeting and the altar and put water in it. Set up the courtyard around it and put the curtain at the entrance to the courtyard.

"Take the anointing oil and anoint the tabernacle and everything in it; consecrate it and all its furnishings, and it will be holy. Then anoint the altar of burnt offering and all its utensils; consecrate the altar, and it will be most holy. Anoint the basin and its stand and consecrate them.

"Bring Aaron and his sons to the entrance to the Tent of Meeting and wash them with water. Then dress Aaron in the sacred garments, anoint him and consecrate him so he may serve me as priest. Bring his sons and dress them in tunics. Anoint them just as you anointed their father, so they may serve me as priests. Their anointing will be to a priesthood that will continue for all generations to come."

Both verse 1 and verse 17 give us the impression that the tabernacle was to be set up in one day, by Moses. Since 39:32–43 indicates that everything needed for the tabernacle was ready, it is entirely possible that the tabernacle was indeed set up in one day, especially if we assume that the location had been chosen beforehand, probably the same place where the

Tent of Meeting had been (33:7 indicates that Moses had moved the Tent of Meeting temporarily outside the camp). Verse 17 further specifies the date: "the first day of the first month in the second year" after the Exodus, in the spring. The Israelites entered the Sinai desert in the third month after the Exodus (19:1), so that the tabernacle was set up less than nine months later. Keil came to the conclusion that the construction of the tabernacle took less than six months by subtracting from the nine months the two forty-day periods that Moses spent on Mount Sinai (24:18; 34:28), as well as the periods covered by the events of 19:1–24:11 and chapters 32–33. The importance of the tabernacle and all that was connected with it for Israel was once again underlined by these instructions that the Lord gave to Moses, and by the exact carrying out of these instructions. Furthermore, we must remember that we are dealing here with the facts on which Israel's ceremonial worship was based, which, especially with regard to the offerings, was then further regulated in Leviticus. "The tabernacle, the Tent of Meeting" (v. 2), cf. 39:32. Verses 3–8 give specific instructions for each of the objects that had a place in the tabernacle. First of all, of course, the "ark of the Testimony," cf. 25:16, 21–22; 39:35. How the ark was to be shielded with the curtain (i.e., the curtain that separated the Holy Place from the Most Holy Place) is further described in verse 21 (cf. also 26:33, and 33:22). The Lord mentioned the ark, His throne among Israel, first. Then the table was to be brought in (v. 4), and Moses had to "set out what belongs on it," lit. "set in order its arrangements," i.e., the bread of the Presence. For the exact location of the table cf. 26:35; 40:22, and for the location of the lampstand 27:21; 26:35. The location of the gold altar of incense is given in 30:6. The "curtain at the entrance to the tabernacle," cf. 26:36; 36:37. We are not certain as to the exact location of the altar of burnt offering and the basin (vv. 6–7); the altar of burnt offering probably did not stand directly in front of the tabernacle, while the basin was probably placed between the altar of burnt offering and the entrance to the tabernacle, but in such a way that there was sufficient room between the basin and the entrance. Moses was to put water in the basin immediately. Concerning the "curtain at the entrance to the courtyard" (v. 8), cf. 27:16; 38:18.

Verses 9–15 deal with the anointing of the tabernacle and its furnishings, and of Aaron and his sons (cf. 29:7, 36; 30:26–30). These instructions were carried out, although this is mentioned in Leviticus 8:10–12 rather than in these verses. "Anointing oil" (v. 9), cf. 30:22–25. "Consecrate" (lit.: "sanctify") is to be understood in the sense of "to set apart for the LORD's service." "Most holy," cf. 29:37; 30:10, 29, 36. The Israelites would consider touching the altar of burnt offering even less than touching the outside of the tabernacle itself. Verse 12, cf. 29:4. Verse 13, cf. 29:5, 7. "So he may serve me as priest," see commentary on 28:1. Verse 14, cf. 29:8. Verse 15 explicitly requires the anointing of the sons of Aaron. "For all generations to come," see commentary on 27:21. The priestly office is hereditary and was to pass to the descendants of Aaron's sons. Later high priests were anointed, but we do not know with certainty whether later priests were also anointed (see commentary on 29:4–9).

40:16–33 *Moses did everything just as the LORD commanded him.*

So the tabernacle was set up on the first day of the first month in the second year. When Moses set up the tabernacle, he put the bases in place, erected the frames, inserted the crossbars and set up the posts. Then he spread the tent over the tabernacle and put the covering over the tent, as the LORD commanded him.

He took the Testimony and placed it in the ark, attached the poles to the ark and put the atonement cover over it. Then he brought the ark into the tabernacle and hung the shielding curtain and shielded the ark of the Testimony, as the LORD commanded him.

Moses placed the table in the Tent of Meeting on the north side of the tabernacle outside the curtain and set out the bread on it before the LORD, as the LORD commanded him.

He placed the lampstand in the Tent of Meeting opposite the table on the south side of the tabernacle and set up the lamps before the LORD, as the LORD commanded him.

Moses placed the gold altar in the Tent of Meeting in front of the curtain and burned fragrant incense on it, as the LORD commanded him. Then he put up the curtain at the entrance to the tabernacle.

He set the altar of burnt offering near the entrance to the tabernacle, the Tent of Meeting, and offered on it burnt offerings and grain offerings, as the LORD commanded him.

He placed the basin between the Tent of Meeting and the altar and put water in it for washing, and Moses and Aaron and his sons used it to wash their hands and feet. They washed whenever they entered the Tent of Meeting or approached the altar, as the LORD commanded Moses.

Then Moses set up the courtyard around the tabernacle and altar and put up the curtain at the entrance to the courtyard. And so Moses finished the work.

Moses again carried out the Lord's instructions to the letter. Note here again the repeated statement: "as the LORD commanded him" (vv. 19, 21, 23, 25, 27, 29, 32). To us this kind of repetition sounds monotonous, but the Israelite appreciated such a regularly recurring expression. And the author (perhaps Moses, although he is referred to in the third person) understood that the reader was impressed with the care with which the instructions concerning the building and setting up of the tabernacle were carried out. The sanctuary was of such central importance that the reader had to suffer some minor inconvenience.

These last chapters of Exodus (chs. 25–40) radiate the joy Israel felt in establishing the dwelling of God among them; this may well indicate that these chapters were written fairly shortly after the tabernacle was built. Verse 17, see commentary on verse 2; Numbers 7:1. Verse 19, cf. 36:18. We do not need to assume that Moses singlehandedly set up the tabernacle. Verse 20, cf. 25:12, 14. "The shielding curtain" (v. 21), cf. 35:12; 39:34. Verse 23, cf. 25:30. Verse 24, cf. 26:35. "Fragrant incense" (v. 27), see commentary on 25:6. "Burned," cf. 29:18; 30:20. Verse 29 states that Moses himself placed offerings on the gold altar and on the altar of burnt offering on the day that they were installed, apparently before the anointing of Aaron and his sons (cf. Lev. 8:10–11). "Burnt offering," see commentary on 20:24. "Grain offering" (KJV: "meat offering," RSV: "cereal offering," ASV: "meal offering"), see ZPEB, "Sacrifice and Offerings, 5:205–206. It is curious that the sacred objects were used before they were consecrated with the anointing oil; verses 31–32 refer to acts that were performed on a regular basis after the anointing in Leviticus 8. But verse 29 does not mention a regularly repeated act since later Aaron and his sons, rather than Moses, brought the offerings. It is possible that Moses carried out the instructions given in 29:38–42 on an interim basis. "Used it to wash their hands and feet" (v. 31), lit.: "washed their hands and feet from it," which may indicate that faucets were installed on the basin.

40:34–38 *Then the cloud covered the Tent of Meeting, and the glory of the Lord filled the tabernacle. Moses could not enter the Tent of Meeting because the cloud had settled upon it, and the glory of the Lord filled the tabernacle.*

In all the travels of the Israelites, whenever the cloud lifted from above the tabernacle, they would set out; but if the cloud did not lift, they did not set out—until the day it lifted. So the cloud of the Lord was over the tabernacle by day, and fire was in the cloud by night, in the sight of all the house of Israel during all their travels.

Thus the tabernacle stood in the wilderness, in Israel's midst, but it was merely a beautiful structure (cf. Ezek. 37:8). On the same day, however, the cloud (cf. 24:15–16; 33:9) covered the Tent of Meeting (cf. 27:21) and the Lord came to dwell among His people (cf. 25:8; 25:43, 45). After descending from heaven on Mount Sinai, He now descended from Mount Sinai on the Tabernacle, to occupy His throne among Israel, between the two cherubim. His "glory" (cf. 16:7, 10; 24:16–17; 33:18, 22) filled the tabernacle, so that not even Moses could enter (cf. Num. 9:15–23); cf. also 1 Kings 8:10–11; 2 Chronicles 5:14; Ezekiel 43:4–5. The cloud "dwells" over the tabernacle (cf. 24:16). Henceforth the cloud gave Israel the sign to continue its journey. "Set out," cf. 13:20; 25:22; 17:1. The Lord now dwelled in their midst as their Leader, their King, and until they reached Canaan the Lord, by means of the cloud, determined whether Israel stayed or moved on. Verse 38, cf. 13:21; Numbers 14:14; Deuteronomy 1:33; Nehemiah 9:19; Psalms 78:14; 105:39; 1 Corinthians 10:1. "All the house of Israel," cf. 1:1; 16:31. This house, the *true* Israel, would one day be the true dwelling place of the Lord (cf. Acts 2:1–4; Rev. 21:3). Thus the Book of Exodus ends with the symbolic promise of the Lord's eternal dwelling among us, whom He has brought out from the slavery of sin (cf. 29:46).